Pork Chops and Apples, page 172

Spiced Mixed Nuts, page 20

Apricot Salsa Salmon, page 223

Granola in the Slow Cooker, page 31

Fix-It and Forget-It®

Slow Cooker Magic

Fix-It and Forget-It®

Slow Cooker Magic

550
Amazing Everyday Recipes

Phyllis Good

FIX-IT AND FORGET-IT® SLOW COOKER MAGIC

Good Books books may be purchased in bulk at special discounts for sales promotion, corporate gifts, fund-raising, or educational purposes. Special editions can also be created to specifications. For details, contact the Special Sales Department, Good Books, 307 West 36th Street, 11th Floor, New York, NY 10018 or info@skyhorsepublishing.com.

Good Books in an imprint of Skyhorse Publishing, Inc.®, a Delaware corporation.

Visit our website at www.goodbooks.com.

10 9 8 7 6 5 4 3 2 1

Library of Congress Cataloging-in-Publication Data is available on file.

Cover design by Cliff Snyder
Cover illustrations by Cheryl Benner
Insert photographs by Tim Lawrence and Abigail Gehring
Photographs in text by Jeremy Hess

Paperback ISBN: 978-1-68099-049-2
Comb binding ISBN: 978-1-68099-050-8
Ebook ISBN: 978-1-68099-089-8

Printed in the United States of America

Table of Contents

Welcome to *Fix-It and Forget-It Slow Cooker Magic!*

We all hope for magic when we cook. This book is filled with solid help from lots of good home cooks!

Here are family-favorite recipes, gathered from cooks who regularly hear, "Make it again!" as their slow cookers are emptied and every bite is eaten.

When I started cooking, I needed every step spelled out, so I'm committed to helping you cook successfully with a slow cooker. With more and more experience, I keep on learning about how to get a slow cooker to do its best work. For example—

- Finding out which kinds and cuts of meat respond best to its slow, moist heat.
- Discovering that some ingredients should be added near the end of the cooking time.
- Learning that there are advantages to browning ground beef before putting it into the slow cooker, but the recipe won't fail if you don't.

The recipes in *Fix-It and Forget-It Slow Cooker Magic* include this kind of useful information. And if you're already at home in the kitchen, you'll also find mighty good recipes here, along with tricks for making them work well in your slow cooker.

Here's to lots of magic as you cook these recipes and then bring the food to your table!

Phyllis Good

Hints for Cooking with a Slow Cooker

What kind of slow cooker should I buy?

• *Size?* If you're part of a 4-person household (2 adults and 2 kids under 12), you'll probably be happy with a 4-quart size. You'll be able to fit in 4 chicken legs or thighs or a 3-lb. beef or pork roast. Or make a full portion of lasagna.

On the other hand, a 6-quart cooker works well because it will comfortably hold a whole turkey breast or a whole butternut squash. And with that size you'll be able to put a 1½- or 2-quart baking dish on the floor of your cooker—or several individual little bakers—and make bread or muffins.

I like having several different sizes. A 1-quart for dips, a 5-quart for a main dish or vegetables, and a 6- or 7-quart for barbecued pulled pork for a neighborhood gathering or to take to a potluck.

• *Shape?* Ovals accommodate most shapes and cuts of meat. They also have more floor space, so they work well for "baking" layered bars. Or you can suspend a loaf pan filled with bread or cake batter on the edges of the crock itself and "bake" it.

• *Programmable, probe, or manual?* Programmable cookers allow you a lot of control, especially if you're going to be away for most of the day. You set the exact cooking time you want and choose High or Low. The cooker switches to Warm when the cooking time is up.

I really dislike dry, over-cooked meat. That's why I'm also drawn to slow cookers with a probe, which allows you to read the actual temperature of food as it cooks. The temperature shows up on the slow cooker's control panel.

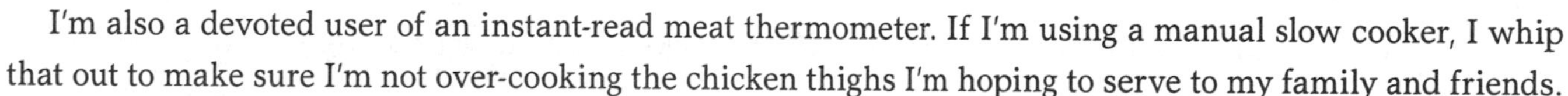

I'm also a devoted user of an instant-read meat thermometer. If I'm using a manual slow cooker, I whip that out to make sure I'm not over-cooking the chicken thighs I'm hoping to serve to my family and friends.

• *Other handy features?* If you're planning to carry a slow cooker full of food in the car, you'll be happier if you have a lid that locks.

Getting acquainted with your slow cooker (Don't skip this step!)

Slow cookers have personalities. Just like your car. Just like your microwave and stove. So learn to know your slow cooker. Plan a little get-acquainted time.

None of us knows what kind of temperament our slow cooker has until we try it out—especially how hot it cooks—so don't assume anything.

Save yourself a disappointment and make the first recipe in your new slow cooker on a day when you're at home. Cook it for the shortest amount of time the recipe calls for. Then check the food to see if it's done. Or if you start smelling food that seems to be finished, turn off the cooker and rescue your food.

Then write in your cookbook, next to the recipe you've made, exactly how long it took to cook it. Next time you won't need to try to remember.

Apply what you've learned to the next recipes you make in your cooker. If you've got a fast and furious model, cut the cooking time. You can always cook the dish longer, or finish it in the microwave.

Maximizing what a slow cooker does best

- Slow cookers tend to work best when they're ⅔ full. You may need to increase the cooking time if you've exceeded that amount, or reduce it if you've put in less than that.

- Cut the hard veggies going into your cooker into chunks of about equal size. In other words, make your potato and carrot pieces about the same size. Then they'll be done cooking at nearly the same time.

- There are consequences to lifting the lid on your slow cooker while it's cooking. To compensate for the lost heat, you should plan to add 15-20 minutes of cooking time for each time the lid was lifted off.

  On the other hand, moisture gathers in a slow cooker as it works. To allow that to cook off, or to thicken the cooking juices, take the lid off during the last half hour of cooking time.

Internal cooking temperatures for meat

Here's what you should know when you use your instant-read meat thermometer or your slow cooker's probe:

- Beef: 125-130°F (rare); 140-145°F (medium); 160°F (well done)
- Pork: 140-145°F (rare); 145-150°F (medium); 160°F (well done)
- Turkey and Chicken: 165°F

Other tips worth knowing

1. Add fresh herbs 10 minutes before the end of the cooking time to get the biggest boost from their flavors.
2. If your recipe calls for sour cream or cream, stir it in 5 minutes before the end of the cooking time. You want it to heat, but not boil or simmer.
3. One hour of cooking on High is equal to about 2½ hours of cooking on Low.
4. A working slow cooker gets hot on the outside—and I mean the electrical unit, as well as the inner crock and lid. Make sure that curious and unsuspecting children or adults don't grab hold of any of those parts. Use oven mitts when lifting any part of a hot cooker.

Hints for Using *Fix-It and Forget-It Slow Cooker Magic!*

Two kinds of recipes in this book

- *Quick and Easy*

Some days I need to cook without thinking. I need a recipe that makes itself. We've marked those kinds of recipes throughout the book, "Quick and Easy." And we included an index of "Quick and Easy" recipes on pages 273–275. Flip there for the list, drop your finger on any of those recipes, and you've got dinner. Well, almost.

These are good beginner recipes, too.

- *A Little More Challenging*

Sometimes I'm looking for a little more challenge in the kitchen. I'm ready to do some browning, a little more involved prepping, adding ingredients to the slow cooker in stages. Those kinds of recipes are here, too.

Find the recipes that match your mood—or the time you have available to prep. Note that Prep Time is listed at the top of each recipe.

Make this book your own

Write in it. On a recipe, note the cooking time that worked for you. Star the recipes you—and the people at your table—like.

Flip to the Index and put a big dot next to a recipe that was a hit. Then you can spot it at a glance when you're looking for cooking inspiration.

If you added or subtracted ingredients, write them in the margins next to the ingredient list.

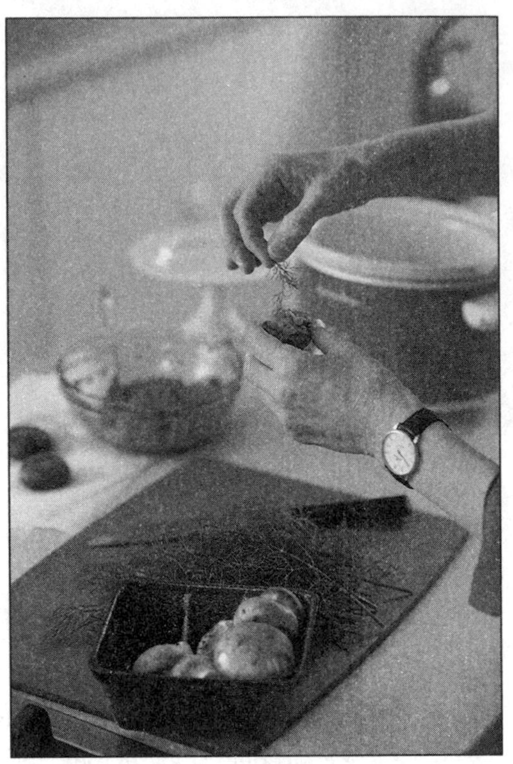

This is a community

When you cook from this book, you're in the company of cooks from all across North America who do their best to bring delicious, satisfying food to their families and friends.

The Tips spread among the recipes give you the kind of advice and encouragement your mother or good-cook-neighbor or favorite aunt might offer if she or he were cooking with you.

May the recipes in ***Fix-It and Forget-It Slow Cooker Magic*** help make your meal prep less pressured and your mealtimes more satisfying!

Appetizers, Snacks, Spreads, and Beverages

Bacon Spinach Dip

Amy Bauer
New Ulm, MN

Makes 8-10 servings

Prep. Time: 15 minutes
Cooking Time: 1-2 hours
Ideal slow-cooker size: 3 qt.

½ lb. bacon, diced
1 lb. cheddar cheese, shredded
8-oz. pkg. cream cheese, room temperature
10-oz. pkg. frozen chopped spinach, thawed and drained
14½-oz. can Rotel tomatoes and green chilies, undrained

1. Fry bacon in skillet until crisp. Remove bacon and set aside on a paper towel. Transfer bacon drippings to slow cooker.
2. Add rest of ingredients (except bacon pieces) and stir.
3. Cover and cook on Low 2 hours, or until cheese is melted.
4. Just before serving, stir in the bacon pieces.

Good go-alongs with this recipe:

Serve with carrot and celery sticks, or with thin slices of sourdough bread.

Reuben Dip

Leona Miller
Millersburg, OH

Makes 12-14 servings

Prep. Time: 15 minutes
Cooking Time: 3-4 hours
Ideal slow-cooker size: 3 qt.

8-oz. pkg. cream cheese, room temperature
1 cup Greek yogurt, room temperature
1½ cups shredded Swiss cheese
½ lb. deli corned beef, chopped finely
2 cups sauerkraut, drained
3 green onions, chopped finely
¼ cup ketchup
2 Tbsp. sweet pickle relish
1 Tbsp. cider vinegar
pepper, to taste
¼ tsp. caraway seeds, optional

1. In mixing bowl, stir together cream cheese and yogurt until smooth. Add rest of ingredients, stirring until combined.
2. Transfer mixture to lightly greased slow cooker.
3. Cover and cook on Low for 3-4 hours.
4. Serve with rye bread cubes or pumpernickel melba toast for dipping.

Variations:

Use as a sandwich filling in hearty buns.

If you love bacon, buy bacon ends and pieces—it's much cheaper but just as flavorful. Chop it into small pieces in a food processor, or with a good old-fashioned knife, and sauté until crisp. Drain, then freeze in ¼-cup amounts. You've got it handy for seasoning many dishes—salads, baked potatoes, omelets.

Mushroom Dip

Monica Wagner
Quarryville, PA

Makes 12-15 servings

Prep. Time: 20 minutes
Cooking Time: 4 hours
Ideal slow-cooker size: 3 qt.

2 cups white wine
2 oz. dried mushrooms, such as shiitake
2 cups chopped fresh mushrooms
2 8-oz. pkgs. cream cheese, room temperature, cubed
1 cup feta cheese
1 cup mild white cheese, such as mozzarella or muenster
1 tsp. dried thyme
1 tsp. salt
½ tsp. black pepper
½ cup flour
½ cup plain yogurt, room temperature

1. Place wine and dry mushrooms in slow cooker. Cook on High 1½ hours until wine is steaming and mushrooms are hydrated.
2. Use immersion blender to puree mushrooms and wine in cooker, or remove to a stand blender and puree with lid slightly ajar.
3. Add fresh mushrooms, cream cheese, feta, white cheese, thyme, salt, and pepper to mushroom puree.
4. Cook 2 hours on High.
5. Whisk together flour and plain yogurt. Stir into Dip and cook on High until thickened, 20-30 minutes.

Tips:

Serve with toasted baguette slices or crackers.

Spinach Dip Mexican-Style

Laura Peachey
Goshen, IN

Makes 12-15 servings

Prep. Time: 15 minutes
Cooking Time: 2-3 hours
Ideal slow-cooker size: 3 qt.

10-oz. box frozen spinach, thawed and chopped
16-oz. jar salsa (I use medium)
2 cups shredded sharp cheese
8-oz. pkg. cream cheese, room temperature
1 cup Greek yogurt, room temperature
½ cup chopped black olives
2 Tbsp. lime juice
1 tsp. chili powder

1. Combine all ingredients in slow cooker.
2. Heat on Low 2-3 hours. Stir twice.
3. Serve as a dip for tortilla chips, bread cubes, or carrot and celery sticks.

I had just begun to date my future husband. As he is an army reservist, his unit had to do their Annual Training, which lasted 2 weeks. Well, the night before he came home, I baked banana nut bread, browned a roast, and cut up vegetables. I took my slow cooker to work that morning and proceeded to cook his roast in the break room at the clinic where I worked. The smell drove everyone, including the patients, crazy. Needless to say he asked me to marry him 4 months after that and 17 years later, he still brags on my cooking. —Sally Skupien, Spring, TX

Buffalo Chicken Dip

Beverly Hummel
Fleetwood, PA

Makes 8 servings

Prep. Time: 10 minutes
Cooking Time: 2 hours on High, 4 hours on Low
Ideal slow-cooker size: 3 qt.

2 8-oz. pkgs. cream cheese, room temperature
3 cups sour cream
2 cups cooked, finely shredded chicken
6 Tbsp. hot sauce, or to taste
2 cups shredded cheddar cheese
tortilla chips, for serving

1. In mixing bowl, beat together cream cheese and sour cream until smooth.
2. Stir in chicken and hot sauce.
3. Place mixture in greased slow cooker and sprinkle with cheese.
4. Cover and cook on High for 2 hours or Low for 4 hours.
5. Serve hot with tortilla chips.

Tips:

Keep cooked shredded chicken in freezer in 1-cup packages for ease of preparation.

Variations:

Use blue cheese dressing instead of sour cream.

—Donna Suter

Use 1 cup ranch dressing instead of sour cream.

—Kelly Bailey

Creamy Taco Dip

Sylvia High
Ephrata, PA

Makes 20 servings

Prep. Time: 30 minutes
Cooking Time: 2 hours
Ideal slow-cooker size: 4 qt.

1 lb. ground beef
2 cups cooked rice
2 cups salsa
16-oz. can refried beans
10.5-oz. can cream of chicken soup
10.5-oz. can cream of mushroom soup
1.25-oz. pkg. taco seasoning
1 lb. Velveeta cheese, cubed
tortilla chips, for serving

1. Fry beef in skillet. Drain.
2. Place beef in slow cooker. Add rest of ingredients.
3. Cover and cook on Low for 2 hours. Stir before serving, to distribute cheese.
4. Serve as a dip with tortilla chips.

Variations:

Add 1 extra pound of meat and 2 more cups of rice to turn this into a main dish. I serve it with a salad and tortilla chips.

Taco Dip

Carol Eveleth
Hillsdale, WY

Makes 8 servings

Prep. Time: 15 minutes
Cooking Time: 1 hour
Ideal slow-cooker size: 3 qt.

1 lb. ground beef, browned
1 lb. Velveeta cheese, cubed
8 oz. mild taco sauce
1 tsp. chili powder
1 tsp. Worcestershire sauce
½ tsp. garlic salt

1. Mix ingredients together in lightly greased slow cooker.
2. Cook on High for 1-2 hours, stirring once or twice, until cheese is melted and Dip is thoroughly hot.
3. Serve hot with chips or tortilla chips.

Mexican Bean Dip

Jenny Unternahrer
Wayland, IA

Makes 15 servings

Prep. Time: 20 minutes
Cooking Time: 1-2 hours
Ideal slow-cooker size: 3 qt.

2 lbs. ground beef
1 small onion, chopped
16-oz. jar salsa
1½ tsp. taco seasoning
2 cups Mexican blend shredded cheese
16-oz. can refried beans

1. Fry ground beef in skillet. Drain. Transfer beef to slow cooker.
2. Add rest of ingredients.
3. Cover and cook on Low until cheese is melted, 1-2 hours. Stir to combine.

Tips:

This can be made the day ahead and then heated back up in the slow cooker.

Variations:

Omit onion. Add 2 8-oz. pkgs. cream cheese.

—Lorna Rodes

Good go-alongs with this recipe:

Serve with tortilla chips.

Hot Beef Dip

Sarah Miller
Harrisonburg, VA

Makes 8-10 servings

Prep Time: 15 minutes
Cooking Time: 3-4 hours
Ideal slow-cooker size: 3 qt.

2 8-oz. pkgs. cream cheese, softened
8 oz. grated sharp cheese
½ cup finely chopped green bell pepper
¼ cup very finely chopped onion
¼ lb. dried chipped beef, rinsed and squeezed dry

1. Mix cream cheese and cheese. Fold in rest of ingredients.
2. Place mixture in lightly greased slow cooker.
3. Cook 3-4 hours on Low.
4. Serve hot with crackers.

Super Bowl Super Dip

Colleen Heatwole
Burton, MI

Makes 12 servings

Prep. Time: 20 minutes
Cooking Time: 1-2 hours
Ideal slow-cooker size: 2.5-3 qt.

1 lb. ground beef
1 lb. Velveeta cheese, Mexican preferred, cubed
8 oz. salsa of choice (mild, medium, or hot)
½ tsp. chili powder
¼ tsp. ground cumin
tortilla chips, for serving

1. In a skillet, brown ground beef and drain off grease. Crumble it into fine pieces and place in slow cooker.
2. Place cubed cheese on top.
3. Cover. Cook on High 45 minutes or until cheese melts, stirring occasionally.
4. Add salsa, chili powder, and cumin. Reduce heat to Low and cook until heated through, checking frequently and stirring once.

Tips:

This recipe takes a little more watching than most slow-cooker recipes. You can burn the dip if the cooker gets too hot.

Variations:

My son prefers hot salsa, so he just adds a little hot sauce to his serving since I use mild salsa for the rest of the family.

My tips for converting oven and stove-top recipes into good slow-cooker recipes:

Don't remove lid unless instructed to do so.

New Year's Dip

Janie Steele
Moore, OK

Makes 6-8 servings

Prep. Time: 15 minutes
Cooking Time: 1-2 hours
Ideal slow-cooker size: 3 qt.

14-oz. can black-eyed peas, drained, partially mashed
¼ cup chopped onion
¼ cup sour cream
8 jalapeños, chopped finely
1 cup grated sharp cheddar cheese
hot sauce, to taste

1. Combine ingredients in lightly greased slow cooker.
2. Cook on Low 1-2 hours until hot and just bubbling at edges.
3. Serve with tortilla chips or cornbread crackers.

When you're browning meat, use tongs or a metal spatula to flip it over or take it out of a pan. Resist using a fork. Tasty juices escape if you jag the meat.

Colorful Fruit Salsa

Joyce Shackelford
Green Bay, WI

Makes 8-10 servings

Prep. Time: 25 minutes
Cooking Time: 2 hours
Ideal slow-cooker size: 3 qt.

11-oz. can mandarin oranges
8½-oz. can sliced peaches in juice, undrained
8-oz. can pineapple tidbits in juice, undrained
1 medium onion, chopped finely
½ cup finely chopped green bell pepper
½ cup finely chopped red bell pepper
1 jalapeño, chopped finely
3 garlic cloves, minced
3 Tbsp. cornstarch
1 tsp. salt
juice of 1 lime
zest of 1 lime, cut in fine strips (not finely grated)
¼ cup chopped cilantro
tortilla chips, for serving

1. Combine fruits, onion, peppers, garlic, cornstarch, and salt in slow cooker.
2. Cover and cook on High for 2 hours, stirring once each hour. Salsa should be thick and steaming, the peppers softened.
3. Add lime juice and zest. Add cilantro. Remove Salsa from slow cooker to serving dish. Allow to cool for about 15 minutes before serving with tortilla chips.

Tips:

I use my vegetable peeler to take off the skin of the lime, then I chop it into narrow strips with a knife. There are also some zesters that make ribbons of zest instead of finely grated zest. The strips of lime zest look pretty in the Salsa.

Good go-alongs with this recipe:

Also delicious on top of a cheese omelet at breakfast.

Pizza Fondue

Virginia Graybill
Hershey, PA

Makes 8-10 servings

Prep. Time: 10 minutes
Cooking Time: 2-3 hours
Ideal slow-cooker size: 3 qt.

24-oz. jar spaghetti sauce
2 cups shredded mozzarella cheese
¼ cup grated Parmesan cheese
2 tsp. dried oregano
½ tsp. dried basil
4 garlic cloves, minced
1-lb. loaf Italian bread, cubed

1. Combine all ingredients except Italian bread in slow cooker.
2. Cover and cook on Low for 2-3 hours, until cheese is melted.
3. Serve hot with bread cubes for dunking.

Tips:

Add finely minced favorite pizza toppings: pepperoni, mushrooms, green bell pepper, onions, hot peppers, black olives, etc.

Variations:

Serve any leftover Fondue over steamed veggies as a side dish.

Make notes in your cookbooks, right next to the recipe that you just made. I'll write, "Great. We loved it." Or, "Don't make again." I often write in adjustments I made, too—like cooking it for less time, or adding more of a particular seasoning. I also write a letter grade in the Index next to the recipes I've made. Then when I'm trying to remind myself of recipes we like, I can easily spot the A's!

Pesto Tomato Spread

Nanci Keatley
Salem, OR

Makes 12 servings

Prep. Time: 20 minutes
Cooking Time: 2-3 hours
Ideal slow-cooker size: 2 qt.

2 8-oz. pkgs. cream cheese, room temperature
⅔ cup prepared pesto
3 medium tomatoes, chopped
½ cup sliced black olives
½ cup chopped fresh basil
1 cup shredded mozzarella
½ cup grated Parmesan

1. Place cream cheese in bottom of lightly greased slow cooker. Push gently to make an even layer.
2. Layer rest of ingredients on top in order given.
3. Cover and cook on Low for 2-3 hours until cheese is melted and Spread is hot through.
4. Serve as a spread on crackers or thin slices of Italian bread or toast.

Herbed Cheese Terrine

Nancy J. Reppert
Mechanicsburg, PA

Makes 20 servings

Prep. Time: 20 minutes
Cooking Time: 3-5 hours
Chilling Time: 9 hours
Ideal slow-cooker size: 6 qt.

2 8-oz. pkgs. cream cheese, room temperature
½ cup crumbled feta cheese
½ tsp. garlic powder
⅛ tsp. black pepper
½ cup plain Greek yogurt
2 eggs
2 tsp. finely grated lemon peel
½ cup chopped fresh herbs, any combination of parsley, basil, cilantro, or dill
2 green onions, thinly sliced
¼ cup minced sun-dried tomatoes, drained if oil packed
¼ cup chopped Greek black olives
red and green lettuce leaves, for serving
crackers or baguette slices, for serving

1. In a mixing bowl, beat cream cheese. Add feta, garlic powder, and black pepper and beat again.
2. Mix in yogurt, eggs, and lemon peel until just smooth again.
3. Stir in herbs, onions, tomatoes, and olives.
4. Pour water in slow cooker to depth of 1-2".
5. Prepare an 8" loaf pan by greasing it well and placing a rectangle of parchment paper on its bottom. Pour cheese mixture in prepared pan.
6. Lower pan into water in cooker—the water should come up about halfway on the pan.
7. Cover and cook on High for 3-5 hours, until center of loaf is softly set.
8. Wearing oven mitts to protect your knuckles, remove hot pan from cooker and allow to cool for 1 hour. Cover and chill for at least 8 hours.
9. Gently unmold terrine on bed of lettuce leaves on platter. Serve with crackers or baguette slices.

Don't measure ingredients over the bowl in which you're mixing or baking the recipe, in case more comes out than you want.

Slow-Cooker "Baked" Brie

Sharon Timpe
Jackson, WI

Makes 12 servings

Prep. Time: 10 minutes
Cooking Time: 1-3 hours
Ideal slow-cooker size: 2 qt.

½ cup dried cherries, cut in half
¼ cup cherry preserves
1 Tbsp. brandy
2 8-oz. brie cheese rounds

1. Combine dried cherries, preserves, and brandy.
2. Place unwrapped brie rounds in slow cooker.
3. Spoon the cherry mixture over the top of brie. Cover slow cooker and cook on Low for 2-3 hours or High 1 hour, until brie is softened but not melted.
4. Gently lift brie out of cooker with large spatulas and arrange on serving platter, spooning preserves and cherries again on top. Serve with crackers or toasted bread.

Variations:

Instead of cherries, cherry preserves, and brandy, use ½ cup dried cranberries, ½ tsp. finely grated orange rind, ¼ cup orange marmalade, and 2 tsp. brown sugar.

Kielbasa Bites

Shelia Heil
Lancaster, PA

Makes 6 servings

Prep. Time: 5 minutes
Cooking Time: 2-3 hours
Ideal slow-cooker size: 4 or 5 qt.

12-oz. kielbasa ring, sliced on the bias in ¼" slices
12-oz. can dark cola
⅓ cup brown sugar

1. Combine kielbasa slices, cola, and brown sugar in slow cooker.
2. Cover and cook on Low for 2-3 hours, stirring several times. Cook until thickened.
3. Serve with toothpicks.

Tips:

May also be used as a sauce over rice or pasta.

Maryland Crab Dip

Betty Gray
Ellicott City, MD

Makes 12 servings

Prep. Time: 15 minutes
Cooking Time: 2-3 hours
Ideal slow-cooker size: 3 qt.

2 8-oz. pkgs. cream cheese, room temperature
1 cup Greek yogurt or sour cream
2 Tbsp. mayonnaise
1 Tbsp. lemon juice
1 tsp. Worcestershire sauce
1 tsp. Old Bay seasoning
1 lb. crab meat
14 oz. can petite diced tomatoes, well drained
¾ cup shredded sharp cheddar

1. In mixing bowl, combine cream cheese, Greek yogurt, mayonnaise, lemon juice, Worcestershire sauce, and Old Bay. Stir until smooth.
2. Fold in crab meat.
3. Spread mixture in bottom of lightly greased crock.
4. Sprinkle with diced tomatoes and cheddar.
5. Cover and cook on Low for 2-3 hours until hot and bubbling at sides.

Tips:

Serve warm with toasted baguette slices or crackers. Garnish with small parsley sprigs.

Tangy Sweet Meatballs

Lavina Hochstedler
Grand Blanc, MI

Makes 10 servings

Prep. Time: 10 minutes
Cooking Time: 3-5 hours
Ideal slow-cooker size: 5-6 qt.

80 small frozen meatballs
2 cups honey barbecue sauce
¼ cup sweet and sour sauce
⅓ cup apple cider vinegar
¼ cup brown sugar
½ tsp. garlic powder
¼ tsp. black pepper

1. Place meatballs in slow cooker.
2. In a bowl, stir together rest of ingredients until smooth.
3. Pour over meatballs.
4. Cover and cook on Low for 3-5 hours or High 2-3 hours.

Tips:

Serve as an appetizer, or serve with mashed potatoes and a green salad for a meal.

My tricks for getting my slow cooker to do its best work:

Heat it up before adding the ingredients (or partially)—it will cook faster.

The condensation that forms on the inside of the slow-cooker lid bastes what you're cooking, helping to keep it moist.

Cocktail Meatballs

Kelly Bailey
Dillsburg, PA

Makes 10-12 servings

Prep. Time: 10 minutes
Cooking Time: 1½-6 hours
Ideal slow-cooker size: 4-6 qt.

1½ cups sugar
4 Tbsp. cornstarch
1 cup pineapple juice
1 cup white vinegar
½ cup soy sauce
32-oz. bag frozen meatballs

1. In a saucepan, blend sugar and cornstarch. Add juice, vinegar, and soy sauce. Cook and whisk over low heat until thickened.
2. Combine sauce with meatballs in slow cooker.
3. Cover and cook 1½-3 hours on High or 5-6 hours on Low.

Tips:

I'll make up the sauce a day or two before needed and refrigerate. On the day of the party, all I need to do is pour everything in my slow cooker, and I'm ready to go.

Variations:

Use 2 16-oz. packages of Little Wieners instead of meatballs. Add some pineapple chunks.

Bourbon Dogs

Lois Ostrander
Lebanon, PA

Makes 20 servings

Prep. Time: 10 minutes
Cooking Time: 4 hours
Ideal slow-cooker size: 3 qt.

4 cups ketchup
1½ cups brown sugar
1½ cups bourbon whiskey
2 Tbsp. chopped onion
½ cup water
3-lb. pkg. Little Smokies

1. Combine ketchup, brown sugar, bourbon, onion, and water in slow cooker. Cook on High for 2 hours.
2. Gently stir in Little Smokies and cook on Low for an additional 4 hours.

Tips:

This makes a great appetizer for any meal, but it is a real success at a buffet or Superbowl Party.

We all like to check on what we're cooking. But remember that every time you lift the lid of a working slow cooker, heat escapes. You should add 15 minutes or so to the cooking time for each time you do that!

Jalapeño Poppers

Amanda Gross
Souderton, PA

Makes 10 servings

Prep. Time: 10 minutes
Cooking Time: 2-3 hours
Ideal slow-cooker size: 5.5 qt.

10 medium jalapeños
4 oz. cream cheese, room temperature
¼ cup sour cream, room temperature
9 slices bacon, cooked and crumbled
¼ tsp. garlic salt
⅓ cup water

1. Cut off the tops and remove seeds and membranes to hollow out jalapeños.
2. In a bowl, mix together cream cheese, sour cream, bacon, and garlic salt.
3. Gently stuff cheese mixture into peppers.
4. Put water in the bottom of the slow cooker. Place peppers on top.
5. Cover and cook on High 2-3 hours, until peppers look slightly wrinkly and wilted.

Tips:

Wear gloves to prepare the jalapeños if you are sensitive to the burning oils in hot peppers.

Southern Boiled Peanuts

Mary June Hershberger
Lynchburg, VA

Makes 32 servings

Prep. Time: 5 minutes
Cooking Time: 7-8 hours
Standing Time: 8 hours or overnight
Ideal slow-cooker size: 5 qt.

2 lbs. raw peanuts in the shell
7 Tbsp. salt
water to cover peanuts

1. Wash unshelled peanuts in water until the water is clear.
2. Soak peanuts overnight in water to cover with 7 Tbsp. salt.
3. In the morning, turn cooker to Low and cook for 7-10 hours until peanuts are desired tenderness. Boiled peanuts should be tender, not crunchy hard, and the shells will be quite soft.
4. Drain peanuts and allow to cool 10 minutes before serving. Peel shells off peanuts and eat.
5. Store leftover boiled peanuts in refrigerator, or freeze. Reheat before eating.

Tips:

If you have access to freshly picked, green peanuts in the shell, they make the tastiest Boiled Peanuts. Green peanuts also do not need to cook as long as raw peanuts. Do not boil roasted (cooked) peanuts.

Variations:

Add Cajun spice mix to the water if you like spicy peanuts.

Savory Snack Mix

Ruthie Schiefer
Vassar, MI

Makes 16 servings

Prep. Time: 10 minutes
Cooking Time: 2 hours
Ideal slow-cooker size: 6 qt.

4 cups Corn Chex cereal
2 cups Wheat Chex cereal
2 cups mini pretzels
1½ cups square cheese crackers
1 cup roasted cashews
2 Tbsp. butter, melted
1 Tbsp. (⅔ of a 1-oz. envelope) powdered ranch dressing
1 tsp. Worcestershire sauce
1 tsp. paprika
½ tsp. chili powder, optional

1. Place Corn Chex, Wheat Chex, pretzels, crackers, and cashews into slow cooker.
2. Gently stir in melted butter.
3. Whisk together remaining ingredients and sprinkle over mixture in cooker, stirring once or twice as you sprinkle so all the pieces get some seasoning.
4. Cook on Low for 1 hour, covered.
5. Stir. Cook uncovered 1 more hour.
6. Spread Snack Mix on sheet pan and let cool at least 15 minutes before serving. When totally cool, store in airtight container.

Tips:

Rice Chex will get soggy in this mix! May use other kinds of nuts instead of cashews.

Spiced Mixed Nuts

Sharon Wantland
Menomonee Falls, WI

Makes 12-16 servings

Prep. Time: 15 minutes
Cooking Time: 2 hours
Ideal slow-cooker size: 3 qt.

1 egg white
2 tsp. vanilla extract
1 cup almonds
1 cup pecan halves
1 cup walnuts
1 cup unsalted cashews
1 cup sugar
1 cup packed brown sugar
4 tsp. ground cinnamon
2 tsp. ground ginger
1 tsp. ground nutmeg
½ tsp. ground cloves
⅛ tsp. salt
2 Tbsp. water

1. In a large bowl, whisk egg white and vanilla together until blended.
2. Stir in nuts until well-coated.
3. In a small bowl, mix sugars, spices, and salt together.
4. Add to nut mixture and toss to coat.
5. Transfer mixture to slow cooker. Cover and cook nuts on High for 1½ hours, stirring every 15 minutes.
6. Sprinkle in water, stirring gently.
7. Cook covered on Low 20-30 more minutes.
8. Spread onto wax paper and let cool. Store in airtight container up to 1 week.

A glass lid for a slow cooker seems like a good idea because you can look without lifting the lid—supposedly. But the lid usually steams up so it's a little hard to tell what's going on inside!

Almond Hot Chocolate

Jessalyn Wantland
Paris, TX

Makes 10-15 servings

Prep. Time: 5 minutes
Cooking Time: 3-4 hours
Ideal slow-cooker size: 4-5 qt.

5 cups nonfat dry milk
¾ cups unsweetened cocoa powder
¾ cups sugar
11 cups water
2 tsp. almond extract

1. Combine all ingredients in slow cooker.
2. Cover and cook on Low for 3-4 hours. Stir occasionally.

Tips:

Top each cup with whipped cream and a dash of cinnamon.

Feels-So-Good Hot Cocoa

Shirley Unternahrer
Wayland, IA

Makes 12 servings

Prep. Time: 10 minutes
Cooking Time: 2-3 hours
Ideal slow-cooker size: 4 qt.

14-oz. can sweetened condensed milk
7 cups whole milk
1 cup heavy cream
2 cups semisweet chocolate chips
2 tsp. pure vanilla extract
⅛ tsp. ground cinnamon, plus more for sprinkling
whipped cream, for serving
chocolate syrup, for serving

1. Combine both milks, cream, vanilla, chocolate chips, and ⅛ tsp. cinnamon in slow cooker.
2. Cover and cook on Low 2-3 hours, stirring 2-3 times.
3. Serve hot in mugs, garnished with a dollop of whipped cream, a drizzle of chocolate syrup, and a sprinkle of cinnamon.

Tips:

Great for cold, wintry gatherings of friends . . . or take a portion in a thermos to games with a bag of marshmallows instead of whipped cream.

Crockery Hot Chocolate

Emily Fox
Bethel, PA

Makes 8 servings

Prep. Time: 10 minutes
Cooking Time: 2-4 hours
Ideal slow-cooker size: 3 qt.

14-oz. can sweetened condensed milk
8½ cups water
1½ tsp. vanilla extract
½ cup unsweetened cocoa powder
⅛ tsp. salt
marshmallows, for serving

1. Combine milk, water, and vanilla in slow cooker. Whisk in cocoa powder and salt.
2. Cook on High 2 hours or Low for 4 hours.
3. Serve hot in mugs topped with marshmallows.

Tips:

Can also add whipped cream and a sprinkle of cinnamon instead of marshmallows. This is not a very sweet recipe, so it is ideal for sweet stir-ins and dark chocolate lovers!

Variations:

Use coffee instead of water for a flavor change.

Hot Grape Cider

Evelyn Page
Gillette, WY

Makes 14-16 servings

Prep. Time: 30 minutes
Cooking Time: 6 hours
Ideal slow-cooker size: 5-6 qt.

5 lbs. Concord grapes, off the stems
8 cups water, divided
¾ cup sugar
4 whole cloves
2 4" cinnamon sticks
dash nutmeg, optional

1. Combine grapes and 2 cups water in cooker. Cook on High until steaming, 2-3 hours.
2. Press grapes and liquid through strainer (may line strainer with cheesecloth if you wish—I don't bother). Discard skins and seeds.
3. Pour grape juice back into slow cooker. Add remaining 6 cups water and rest of ingredients.
4. Cover and cook on Low for 3 hours. Discard cloves and cinnamon sticks. Serve hot.

Tips:

I store leftover Cider in the fridge and reheat it cup by cup in the microwave. Lovely as a breakfast drink in chilly weather instead of cold juice.

Good go-alongs with this recipe:

We love this with popcorn on an autumn Sunday evening.

Hot Spiced Cherry Cider

Jessalyn Wantland
Paris, TX

Makes 10 servings

Prep. Time: 5 minutes
Cooking Time: 4 hours
Ideal slow-cooker size: 4-6 qt.

3½ quarts apple cider
2 cinnamon sticks
3-oz. pkg. cherry-flavored gelatin

1. In slow cooker, add cinnamon sticks to apple cider and stir.
2. Cover and heat on High 3 hours.
3. Stir in gelatin. Cover and leave on High for 1 hour, until gelatin dissolves, stirring once or twice.
4. Turn on Low to keep warm. Remove cinnamon sticks before serving.

Tips:

For a more intense cherry flavor, add an additional package of gelatin.

Hot Mulled Cider

Karen Ceneviva
Seymour, CT

Makes 8 servings

Prep. Time: 5 minutes
Cooking Time: 2-8 hours
Ideal slow-cooker size: 3-4 qt.

2 quarts apple cider
½ cup brown sugar
1 tsp. whole allspice
1½ tsp. whole cloves
orange slices

1. Put ingredients in cooker. If desired, tie whole spices in cheesecloth or put in tea strainer for easier removal. Otherwise, strain before serving.
2. Cook on Low 2-8 hours. Serve hot.

Tips:

Use clear mugs and make sure to put an orange slice in each mug. Can add a cinnamon stick, too.

Variations:

Replace ¼ cup of the sugar with ¼ cup cinnamon red-hot candies.

—Joyce Cox

Good go-alongs with this recipe:

Vanilla ice cream with cinnamon sprinkled on it.

My tricks for getting my slow cooker to do its best work:

Vegetables should be sliced or chopped—they take longer than meat. Parboil or sauté eggplant first due to its strong flavor.

My tips for converting oven and stove-top recipes into good slow-cooker recipes:

Trim fats from meats and wipe them well to keep them dry. Use whole leaf herbs and spices for all-day cooking. If you must use ground spices and herbs, stir them in only in the last hour of cooking.

Winter Cider

Marcia S. Myer
Manheim, PA

Makes 12 servings

Prep. Time: 5 minutes
Cooking Time: 3 hours
Ideal slow-cooker size: 5 qt.

3 quarts apple cider
½ cup brown sugar
¼ cup sugar
½ cup orange juice
2 6-oz. cans pineapple juice
juice of 1 lemon
1 Tbsp. mulling spice

1. Combine all ingredients in slow cooker.
2. Heat on High for 3 hours until steaming hot.

The great thing about using a slow cooker in hot weather is that it doesn't heat up your kitchen like an oven does.

Cranberry Tea

Anita Troyer
Fairview, MI

Makes 12-14 servings

Prep. Time: 10 minutes
Cooking Time: 3 hours
Ideal slow-cooker size: 6 qt.

3 quarts water
1 quart cranberry juice
1 cup orange juice
½ cup lemon juice
1½ cups sugar
1 tsp. ground cinnamon
1 lemon or 1 orange, optional

1. Heat all together on Low for 3 hours.
2. Slice lemon or orange in thin rings and float on top of tea if you wish.

Tips:

Serve in cups garnished with a cinnamon stick.

Basil Mint Tea

Nancy T. Dickman
Marblemount, WA

Makes 10 servings

Prep. Time: 10 minutes
Cooking Time: 2 hours
Ideal slow-cooker size: 3 qt.

20 fresh basil leaves, or 3 Tbsp. dried
20 fresh spearmint or peppermint leaves, or 3 Tbsp. dried
10 cups water
¼ cup sugar

1. Place herbs in slow cooker. If using fresh herbs, mash gently with a spoon. If using dried herbs, put in tea-ball infusers or cheesecloth bag.
2. Add water and sugar.
3. Cover and cook on Low for 2 hours, until fragrant and steaming. Serve hot, or chill completely and serve cold.

Tips:

May mix some lemonade and lemon slices in the chilled tea.

Hot Orange Lemonade

Sharon Timpe
Jackson, WI

Makes 10-12 servings

Prep. Time: 10 minutes
Cooking Time: 2-3 hours
Ideal slow-cooker size: 3½ qt.

12-oz. can lemonade concentrate, thawed
5 cups orange-pineapple juice or orange-mango juice
4 cups water
½ cup sugar, or to taste
2 4" cinnamon sticks
1 lemon, sliced in ¼" slices
1 orange, sliced in ¼" slices

1. Combine all ingredients in slow cooker and mix well.
2. Cover and cook on Low 2-3 hours. Serve hot.

Tips:

Garnish each mug with a fresh wedge of lemon or orange.

Breakfasts and Breads

French-Toast Casserole

Michele Ruvola
Vestal, NY

Makes 9 servings

Prep. Time: 30 minutes
Cooking Time: 2-4 hours
Ideal slow-cooker size: 5-6½ qt.

2 eggs
2 egg whites
1½ cups milk, preferably 2%
5 Tbsp. honey, divided
1 tsp. vanilla extract
1 tsp. ground cinnamon, divided
9 slices bread of your choice
3 cups finely diced apple
1 tsp. lemon juice
⅓ cup chopped, toasted pecans

1. In a mixing bowl, whisk together eggs, egg whites, milk, 2 Tbsp. honey, vanilla, and 1 tsp. cinnamon.

2. Separately, combine apple, remaining 3 Tbsp. honey, pecans, remaining 1 tsp. cinnamon, and lemon juice. Set aside.

3. In greased slow cooker, place one layer of bread, cutting to fit (triangles are good).

4. Layer in ¼ of the apple filling. Repeat layers, making 3 layers of bread and 4 of filling, ending with filling on top.

5. Pour egg mixture gently over all.

6. Cover and cook on High 2-2½ hours or Low 4 hours, or until bread has soaked up the liquid and apples are soft.

Tips:

Serve with maple syrup.

Variations:

Can use 3 diced bananas instead of apples. May use soy milk or almond milk instead of cow's milk.

Slow-Cooker French-Toast Casserole

Donna Suter
Pandora, OH

Makes 6 servings

Prep. Time: 20 minutes
Cooking Time: 3-5 hours
Ideal slow-cooker size: 6 qt.

1 loaf white bread, cut into 1" cubes
8 eggs
1½ cups milk
½ cup heavy cream
¼ cup maple syrup
zest of 1 orange
½ cup chopped, toasted pecans
3 Tbsp. butter, cut into cubes
maple syrup, for serving
whipped cream, for serving
sliced bananas, for serving

1. Place bread cubes on a baking sheet and toast in 400° oven for 8-10 minutes or until golden brown. Remove from oven and cool.
2. In large bowl, whisk together eggs, milk, cream, maple syrup, and orange zest. Add in the toasted bread cubes and toss to coat with the egg mixture. Add pecans.
3. Grease slow cooker well. Pour bread and egg mixture into cooker. Dot top with cubed butter.
4. Cook on High for 3 hours or Low for 5 hours, until set.
5. Serve hot, topped with maple syrup, whipped cream, and bananas.

Overnight French Toast

Rebekah Zehr
Lowville, NY

Makes 8 servings

Prep. Time: 20 minutes
Cooking Time: 7 hours
Ideal slow-cooker size: 5 qt.

1 cup brown sugar
½ cup (1 stick) butter, room temperature
2 Tbsp. corn syrup
16-oz. loaf multi-grain French bread in 1" slices
4 eggs
1 cup milk
1 tsp. vanilla extract
¼ cup orange juice
¼ tsp. ground cinnamon
⅛ tsp. ground allspice

1. Turn slow cooker on High.
2. Place brown sugar, butter, and corn syrup in crock. Heat until melted, about 1 hour. Stir to combine.
3. Lay bread slices on the top of the syrup mixture, fitting tightly together.
4. Whisk together remaining ingredients and pour over top of bread.
5. Cover and cook on Low for 6 hours.
6. Remove crock from cooker and invert French Toast onto serving platter.

Variations:

After cooking syrup, mix in pecans in Step 2 and continue with directions. May melt syrup ingredients in microwave or saucepan if you don't want to wait for the slow cooker to melt them.

Pumpkin Breakfast Custard

Audrey Hess
Gettysburg, PA

Makes 4-6 servings

Prep. Time: 20 minutes
Cooking Time: 1½-2 hours
Ideal slow-cooker size: 2.5-3 qt.

2½ cups cooked pumpkin or winter squash
2 Tbsp. blackstrap molasses
3 Tbsp. sugar
¼ cup half-and-half
3 eggs
1 tsp. cinnamon
½ tsp. ground ginger
½ tsp. ground nutmeg
¼ tsp. ground cloves
¼ tsp. salt

1. Puree ingredients in blender until smooth.
2. Pour into greased slow cooker.
3. Cook on High for 1½-2 hours, until set in the middle and just browning at edges.
4. Serve warm in scoops over hot cereal, baked oatmeal, or as a breakfast side dish with toast or muffins.

Tips:

Toasted walnuts are a nice topping if you're serving this as a side dish. Leftover custard will weep a little in the fridge, but it's still fine to use. May serve chilled, too.

Custard Cinnamon Rolls

Sue Hamilton
Benson, AZ

Makes 8 servings

Prep. Time: 5 minutes
Cooking Time: 2 hours
Ideal slow-cooker size: 4 qt.

1 pkg. 8 refrigerator cinnamon rolls with icing
3½ cups full-fat vanilla ice cream (half a 1¾-quart box)

1. Turn slow cooker on High to preheat.
2. Place ice cream in crock, flattening it out as the ice cream softens.
3. Press cinnamon rolls into ice cream.
4. Cover and cook on High for 2 hours, when the ice cream is a thick custard and the rolls are baked through.
5. Serve a roll with custard, and top with icing.

Variations:

You can use orange rolls in place of the cinnamon.

Make an alphabetical list of all the spices in your cupboard, and tape it inside your cupboard door for easy reference. Arrange your spices in alphabetical order so you can easily find them.

Chunky Applesauce

Colleen Heatwole
Burton, MI

Makes 8 servings

Prep. Time: 20 minutes
Cooking Time: 8-10 hours
Ideal slow-cooker size: 5 qt.

10 large cooking apples such as Granny Smith, Fuji, Braeburn, Jonagold, or Cameo
½ cup water
1 tsp. ground cinnamon
¼-¾ cup sugar, to taste

1. Peel, core, and chop apples.
2. Combine apples with rest of ingredients in slow cooker. Start with the lesser amount of sugar and taste again at the end.
3. Cover and cook on Low for 8-10 hours. Serve warm.

Variations:

My brother-in-law likes to add cashews to his uncooked apples.

My tricks for getting my slow cooker to do its best work:

I know the temperatures of my slow cookers.

My tips for converting oven and stove-top recipes into good slow-cooker recipes:

Vegetables usually go into the slow cooker first. They generally take longer to cook than meat.

Apple Butter

Janet Batdorf
Harrisburg, PA

Makes 2.5 quarts

Prep. Time: 15 minutes
Cooking Time: 7-12 hours
Ideal slow-cooker size: 5 qt.

3 quarts unsweetened applesauce
2½ cups sugar
3 Tbsp. vinegar
dash ground allspice
dash cinnamon, optional
dash cloves, optional

1. Cook applesauce in slow cooker for 1-2 hours until hot.
2. Add remaining ingredients and cook on High, uncovered, stirring occasionally, until darkened and reduced to desired thickness, about 5-10 hours.
3. Place Apple Butter in sterilized jars and keep in fridge.

Good go-alongs with this recipe:

Spread on toast or biscuits, or eat as a sauce on cottage cheese or Pennsylvania Dutch scrapple.

After a party at my house one night, several friends spent the night. So before I went to bed, I threw some fruits and oats into the slow cooker to make a breakfast cobbler. I made a sign and stood it in front of the cooker that said, "Good Morning! Help yourself." My friends got a delicious breakfast, and I didn't have to wake up early to cook.
— Deanna Wright, Leechburg, PA

Overnight Oat Groats

Rebekah Zehr
Lowville, NY

Makes 6 servings

Prep. Time: 5 minutes
Cooking Time: 8-10 hours
Ideal slow-cooker size: 3 qt.

1½ cups oat groats
4 cups water
2 cups almond milk or milk
1-2 cinnamon sticks
½ cup brown sugar
½-1 cup dried apples
2 scoops vanilla-flavored protein powder, optional

1. Combine all ingredients in slow cooker.
2. Cook on Low for 8-10 hours.

Tips:

Serve with a variety of toppings including coconut, nuts, granola, chia seeds, and yogurt. Oat groats are the most whole form of oats; steel-cut oats are simply oat groats that have been cut into several pieces to shorten cooking time.

Overnight Steel-Cut Oatmeal

Lavina Hochstedler
Grand Blanc, MI

Makes 10 servings

Prep. Time: 5 minutes
Cooking Time: 6-7 hours
Ideal slow-cooker size: 3 qt.

1 cup steel-cut oats, uncooked
1 cup dried cranberries
1 cup dried, chopped apricots
3 cups water
1½ cups milk
pinch salt, optional

1. Combine all ingredients in slow cooker.
2. Cover and cook on Low for 6-8 hours. Stir again. Serve hot.

Tips:

I love to mix this up before bed and have it hot for breakfast in the morning. If you have a newer slow cooker, it may cook hot, so reduce the time and use a timer or the programmable feature on the cooker. Do not use instant steel-cut oats!

Good go-alongs with this recipe:

Top with vanilla or plain yogurt. Great with a half grapefruit and a cup of coffee.

Apple Cider Cinnamon Steel-Cut Oatmeal

Jenny Unternahrer
Wayland, IA

Makes 4-6 servings

Prep. Time: 15 minutes
Cooking Time: 6 hours
Ideal slow-cooker size: 5-6 qt.

3 medium Granny Smith apples, peeled and chopped
2 cups apple cider
1½ cups water
1 cup steel-cut oats
¼ tsp. ground cinnamon
⅛ tsp. salt
1 Tbsp. sugar
chopped pecans or walnuts, optional
maple syrup, optional

1. Pour a little water in crock. Place a heat-safe baking dish in the crock.
2. Combine apples, cider, water, oats, cinnamon, salt, and sugar in baking dish.
3. Cover and cook on Low for 6 hours or until oats are tender. Stir gently.
4. Serve with a drizzle of maple syrup and a sprinkle of nuts.

Tips:

You can put all of the ingredients into the slow cooker before bed, set a timer (in the electric section of the store that will turn your cooker on and off for you based on how you set it), or program your slow cooker. The oatmeal cooks without effort while you sleep, and in the morning, you will have an aroma that smells like baked apple pie filling your kitchen.

Variations:

May use 3½ cups apple cider and omit water.

Slow-Cooker Oatmeal

Barbara Hoover
Landisville, PA

Makes 6-8 servings

Prep. Time: 10 minutes
Cooking Time: 8-9 hours
Ideal slow-cooker size: 4 qt.

2 sliced apples
¼ cup brown sugar
1 tsp. ground cinnamon
2 cups rolled oats
2 cups milk
2 cups water

1. Layer in order listed in lightly greased slow cooker. Do not stir.
2. Cook on Low 8-9 hours. Stir before serving.

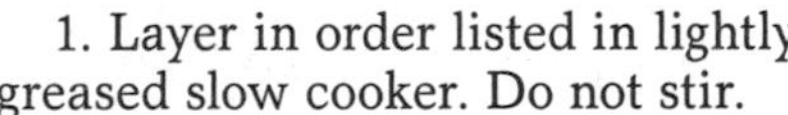

Tips:

I like to cook this overnight so the house smells good when I get up the next morning.

Variations:

Could add raisins. Sprinkle individual servings with toasted nuts.

Granola in the Slow Cooker

Earnie Zimmerman
Mechanicsburg, PA

Makes 10-12 servings

Prep. Time: 10 minutes
Cooking Time: 3-8 hours
Ideal slow-cooker size: 6 qt.

5 cups rolled oats
1 Tbsp. flax seeds
¼ cup slivered almonds
¼ cup chopped pecans or walnuts
¼ cup unsweetened shredded coconut
½ cup dried fruit
¼ cup maple syrup or honey
¼ cup melted butter or oil of your choice

1. In slow cooker, mix together oats, flax seeds, almonds, pecans, and coconut.
2. Separately, combine maple syrup and butter. Pour over dry ingredients in cooker and toss well.
3. Place lid on slow cooker with a wooden spoon handle or chopstick venting one end of the lid.
4. Cook on High for 3-4 hours, stirring every 30 minutes, or cook on Low for 8 hours, stirring every hour. You may need to stir more often or cook for less time, depending on how hot your cooker cooks.
5. When Granola smells good and toasty, pour it out onto a baking sheet to cool.
6. Add dried fruit to cooled Granola and store in airtight container.

Tips:

Tired of burning granola in the oven? Give your slow cooker a try.

Variations:

Add whatever fruit or nuts you like. I've used dried cranberries, apples, and apricots. Pecans, walnuts, almonds, and sunflower seeds all taste delicious. Wonderful with milk or yogurt for breakfast.

Cheese Grits

Janie Steele
Moore, OK

Makes 6 servings

Prep. Time: 20 minutes
Cooking Time: 2-3 hours
Ideal slow-cooker size: 3-4 qt.

4 cups water
1 tsp. salt
1 cup regular (not instant) grits, uncooked
3 eggs
¼ cup (½ stick) butter, cut in chunks
1¾ cups grated sharp cheese
¼ tsp. pepper, optional

1. In saucepan, bring water and salt to boil. Slowly add grits, stirring.
2. Cook until grits are thick and creamy, 5-10 minutes.
3. Beat eggs in small bowl. Add spoonful of hot grits to eggs, stirring. This tempers the eggs.
4. Slowly stir egg mixture into rest of hot grits, stirring.
5. Add butter, cheese, and optional pepper. Stir.
6. Pour grits into lightly greased slow cooker. Cook on High 2-3 hours until set in middle and lightly browned around edges.

Tips:

Serve with eggs for breakfast or brunch, or serve with cooked greens and black-eyed peas for supper. Excellent topped with a juicy barbecue beef.

Variations:

Use pepper-jack cheese for a kick.

Spray a little cooking spray on your cheese grater before grating cheese. It keeps the grater free of gummed-up cheese, and cleanup is a breeze.

Breakfast Polenta with Bacon

Margaret W. High
Lancaster, PA

Makes 8-10 servings

Prep. Time: 20 minutes
Cooking Time: 2½ hours
Ideal slow-cooker size: 5-6 qt.

4 eggs, room temperature
2 cups whole milk, room temperature
2 cups stone-ground (coarse) cornmeal
⅔ cup shredded Parmesan cheese, divided
½ cup cooked, diced bacon
2 Tbsp. finely diced onion
2 cups chopped fresh spinach
1 tsp. salt
pepper, to taste
4 cups boiling water

1. In a large mixing bowl, beat eggs. Whisk in milk, cornmeal, and ⅓ cup Parmesan.
2. Whisk in boiling water.
3. Gently stir in bacon, onion, spinach, salt, and pepper.
4. Pour mixture into well-greased slow cooker.
5. Cover and cook on High for 2 hours, stirring once to be sure cornmeal is evenly distributed as it cooks.
6. When polenta is thick, sprinkle with remaining ⅓ cup Parmesan. Remove lid and allow to cook on High for an additional 30 minutes as cheese melts and any extra liquid evaporates. Polenta will be softer when hot, but will firm up as it cools. Serve hot, warm, or chilled.

Kelly's Company Omelette

Kelly Bailey
Dillsburg, PA

Makes 12 servings

Prep. Time: 15 minutes
Cooking Time: 7-9 hours
Ideal slow-cooker size: 6 qt.

32-oz. bag frozen hash brown potatoes, or 5 cups cooked, shredded potatoes
1 lb. ham, bacon, or sausage, cooked and chopped
1 onion, chopped
1 green bell pepper, chopped
1 cup sliced fresh mushrooms
2 cups shredded cheddar cheese
12 eggs
1 cup whole milk
1 Tbsp. thyme, basil, rosemary, or tarragon, depending on what you like
½ tsp. cayenne pepper

1. In lightly greased slow cooker, place ⅓ of potatoes, ⅓ of ham, ⅓ of onion, ⅓ of green pepper, ⅓ of mushrooms, and ⅓ of cheese.
2. Repeat layers twice, ending with cheese.
3. In mixing bowl, whisk together eggs, milk, the herb you chose, and cayenne.
4. Pour gently over the layers in the slow cooker.
5. Cover and cook on Low 7-9 hours, until Omelette is set in the middle and lightly browned at edges.

Tips:

I made this in our hotel room for my daughter's first alumni tailgating brunch. The hotel staff said they wanted to come along because it smelled so delicious!

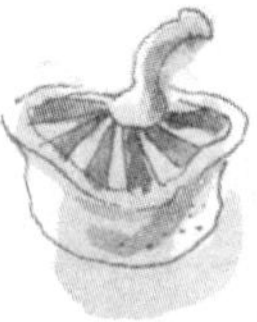

Spinach Frittata

Shirley Unternahrer
Wayland, IA

Makes 4-6 servings

Prep. Time: 15 minutes
Cooking Time: 1½-2 hours
Ideal slow-cooker size: 5 qt.

4 eggs
½ tsp. salt
½ tsp. dried basil
fresh ground pepper, to taste
3 cups chopped fresh spinach, stems removed
½ cup chopped tomato, liquid drained off
⅓ cup freshly grated Parmesan cheese

1. Whisk eggs well in mixing bowl. Whisk in salt, basil, and pepper.
2. Gently stir in spinach, tomato, and Parmesan.
3. Pour into lightly greased slow cooker.
4. Cover and cook on High for 1½-2 hours, until middle is set. Serve hot.

Variations:

May add 1 cup browned, crumbled sausage. May add ½ tsp. minced garlic.

Good go-alongs with this recipe:

Biscuits or hash brown potatoes.

Huevos Rancheros in the Crock

Pat Bishop
Bedminster, PA

Makes 6 servings

Prep. Time: 25 minutes
Cooking Time: 2 hours
Ideal slow-cooker size: 6 qt.

3 cups salsa, room temperature
2 cups cooked beans, drained, room temperature
6 eggs, room temperature
salt and pepper to taste
⅓ cup grated Mexican-blend cheese, optional
6 tortillas, for serving

1. Mix salsa and beans in slow cooker.
2. Cook on High for 1 hour or until steaming.
3. With a spoon, make 6 evenly spaced dents in the salsa mixture; try not to expose the bottom of the crock. Break an egg into each dent.
4. Salt and pepper eggs. Sprinkle with cheese if you wish.
5. Cover and continue to cook on High until egg whites are set and yolks are as firm as you like them, approximately 20-40 minutes.
6. To serve, scoop out an egg with some beans and salsa. Serve with warm tortillas.

Tips:

May sprinkle with chopped cilantro or chopped spring onions after cooking.

Variations:

Serve with hot cooked rice instead of tortillas.

Overnight Mexican Breakfast Casserole

Carrie Fritz
Meridian, ID

Makes 6-8 servings

Prep. Time: 20 minutes
Cooking Time: 6-8 hours
Ideal slow-cooker size: 6 qt.

30-oz. bag frozen shredded hash brown potatoes
1 lb. spicy sausage, cooked and crumbled
2 cups shredded sharp or cheddar cheese
1 green or red bell pepper, chopped
¾ cup sliced green onions
4-oz. can chopped green chiles
12 eggs
1 cup milk
½ tsp. salt
¼ tsp. pepper

1. Grease slow cooker.
2. Layer in half the hash browns, half the sausage, half the cheese, half the green onions, half the peppers, and half the chiles.
3. Repeat layers.
4. In a mixing bowl, whisk eggs, milk, salt, and pepper.
5. Pour egg mixture gently over layers in slow cooker.
6. Cover and cook on Low for 6-8 hours.

Tips:

Add ½ tsp. chili powder and ½ tsp. dried oregano. Use Mexican-blend cheese in place of cheddar.

Variations:

Cooked ham or bacon works in place of the sausage.

Good go-alongs with this recipe:

Fruit and yogurt.

Sausage Breakfast Casserole

Shelia Heil
Lancaster, PA

Makes 8-10 servings

Prep. Time: 20 minutes
Cooking Time: 4-8 hours
Ideal slow-cooker size: 6 qt.

32-oz. pkg. frozen shredded hash brown potatoes
1 lb. bulk sausage, cooked and drained
2 cups shredded cheese of your choice
14-oz. can diced tomatoes, drained
6 green onions, sliced
¼ cup diced red bell pepper
12 eggs
½ cup milk
½ tsp. salt
¼ tsp. ground black pepper

1. Place half of potatoes in lightly greased slow cooker.
2. Top with half the sausage, half the cheese, half the tomatoes, half the onion, and half the bell pepper.
3. Repeat layers.
4. Beat eggs, milk, salt, and pepper in mixing bowl until well combined.
5. Pour evenly over potato-sausage mixture.
6. Cover and cook on Low for 6-8 hours or on High for 4 hours, until Casserole is firm in the middle because eggs have set.

Tips:

May add up to 1 tsp. dried herbs or 1 tsp. hot sauce to egg mixture in Step 4.

Variations:

I sometimes use red onion rather than green onions for a stronger taste.

My tricks for getting my slow cooker to do its best work:

Fill crockpot ½-⅔ full for best cooking. An emptier or fuller crockpot does not work as well.

My tips for converting oven and stove-top recipes into good slow-cooker recipes:

Don't be afraid to experiment using the crockpot. Most recipes can be converted.

Slow cookers come in a variety of sizes—from 1-8 quarts. The best size for a household of four or five is a 5-6-quart one.

Shirred Eggs

Margaret W. High
Lancaster, PA

Makes 4 servings

Prep. Time: 20 minutes
Cooking Time: 2 hours
Ideal slow-cooker size: 4-5 qt.

4 eggs, room temperature
1 Tbsp. butter
salt and pepper to taste

1. Have ready a shallow baking dish that fits into your slow cooker without touching the sides. Butter it.
2. Break eggs into buttered dish, being careful not to break the yolks. Salt and pepper.
3. Place dish on jar lid or ring or trivet in slow cooker.
4. Cover and cook on High until whites are set and yolks are as firm as you like them, about 2 hours.
5. Wearing oven gloves to protect your knuckles, remove hot dish from cooker. Gently cut eggs apart into 4 servings, and serve immediately.

Tips:

Serve like a poached egg on buttered toast.

Variations:

Sprinkle with grated cheese in Step 2. Place a few fresh spinach leaves on top in Step 2. The spinach will wilt by the end of cooking.

Dilly Cornbread

Paula Winchester
Kansas City, MO

Makes 10 servings

Prep. Time: 30 minutes
Cooking Time: 3-4 hours
Standing Time: 20 minutes
Ideal slow-cooker size: 6 qt.

1 cup all-purpose flour
1 cup stone-ground cornmeal
3 tsp. baking powder
3 Tbsp. sugar
1 tsp. salt
2 Tbsp. dried dill
1 cup corn kernels, thawed if frozen, drained
2 eggs
⅔ cup milk
⅓ cup oil

1. In a mixing bowl, stir together flour, cornmeal, baking powder, sugar, salt, dill, and corn.
2. Separately, whisk together eggs, milk, and oil.
3. Make a well in dry ingredients and pour egg mixture into well. Mix just until combined; streaks of flour are fine.
4. Make sure your loaf pan fits in your oval 6-quart slow cooker. Grease and flour loaf pan. Set it on a jar ring or other heat-resistant thing to keep it off the floor of the cooker.
5. Pour batter into prepared loaf pan.
6. Put lid on cooker, propping it open at one end with a chopstick or wooden spoon handle.
7. Cook on High for 3-4 hours, until tester inserted in middle comes out clean.
8. Wearing oven mitts (to protect your knuckles!), remove hot pan from hot cooker and allow it to cool for 10 minutes. Run a knife around the edge and turn loaf out on cooling rack to cool for an additional 10 minutes before slicing.

Good go-alongs with this recipe:

Great served with whipped butter, cream of tomato soup, and a green salad for a nice ladies' lunch.

Taste-test your slow-cooker dish just before serving and adjust the seasoning if necessary. Long, slow cooking can dilute the flavor of some herbs and spices.

Pineapple Cheddar Cornbread

Moreen and Christina Weaver
Bath, NY

Makes 10-12 servings

***Prep. Time:* 25 minutes**
***Cooking Time:* 3-4 hours**
***Ideal slow-cooker size:* 6 qt.**

1 cup whole wheat flour
1 cup yellow cornmeal
2 Tbsp. sugar
2 tsp. baking powder
1 tsp. salt
½ cup (1 stick) butter
3 eggs, beaten
14-oz. can cream-style corn
8-oz. can crushed pineapple, drained
1 cup shredded cheddar cheese

1. In mixing bowl, combine flour, cornmeal, sugar, baking powder, and salt.
2. Separately, beat butter well. Add eggs and beat again.
3. Stir corn, pineapple, and cheese into butter mixture.
4. Add flour mixture, stirring gently until just combined.
5. Prepare a loaf pan that fits in your slow cooker by greasing it and flouring it.
6. Pour batter into prepared pan. Set pan on a jar ring, jar lid, or trivet on the floor of the crock.
7. Cover. Raise lid at one end with a wooden chopstick or wooden spoon handle so lid is vented.
8. Cook on High for 3-4 hours, until tester inserted in middle of loaf comes out clean.
9. Wearing oven gloves to protect your knuckles, remove hot pan from cooker and allow to cool for 10 minutes. Run a knife around the edge and turn loaf out onto cooling rack. Serve warm.

Tips:

Leftover bread is great the next day toasted with butter for breakfast.

Good go-alongs with this recipe:

Spicy chili.

Greek Bread

Nancy Raleigh
Belcamp, MD

Makes 10 servings

***Prep. Time:* 30 minutes**
***Cooking Time:* 3-4 hours**
***Standing Time:* 40 minutes**
***Ideal slow-cooker size:* 6 qt.**

2 cups whole wheat flour
1 cup all-purpose flour
2 Tbsp. sugar
3 tsp. baking powder
1 tsp. salt
⅛ tsp. pepper
2 tsp. dried thyme
1 Tbsp. dried oregano
1 Tbsp. dried parsley
12-oz. beer, any kind, room temperature
2 Tbsp. olive oil

1. In a mixing bowl, combine flours, sugar, baking powder, salt, pepper, thyme, oregano, and parsley.
2. Add beer and mix.
3. Find a loaf pan to fit in your oval 6-quart cooker. Place a metal trivet or heat-proof jar lid under the pan so it's not sitting directly on the floor of the crock.
4. Grease and flour loaf pan.
5. Pour batter into prepared pan. Smooth top. Drizzle with olive oil.
6. Place pan of batter into crock on jar lid. Cover and place wooden chopstick or spoon handle under lid to vent at one end.
7. Cook on High for 3-4 hours, until tester inserted in middle of loaf comes out clean.
8. Wearing oven mitts to protect your knuckles, remove hot pan from cooker. Allow to cool 10 minutes. Run a knife around the edge, and turn loaf out onto cooling rack for 10 more minutes before slicing. Serve warm.

Variations:

Add ½ cup chopped olives. Substitute Italian herb seasoning for thyme and oregano, add ½ cup chopped sun-dried tomatoes, and sprinkle some grated cheese on top of the olive oil. Call it pizza bread!

You can use a loaf pan or a 2-quart baking dish for "baking" breads and cakes in your slow cooker. Leave the cooker lid slightly open to let extra moisture escape.

Hearty Irish Soda Bread

Margaret W. High
Lancaster, PA

Makes 8-10 servings

Prep. Time: 20 minutes
Cooking Time: 2-3 hours
Ideal slow-cooker size: 4 qt.

2 cups whole wheat flour
2 Tbsp. brown sugar
½ tsp. salt
1 tsp. baking soda
1 egg
½ cup plain yogurt

1. In mixing bowl, mix flour, sugar, salt, and baking soda.
2. Separately, mix egg and yogurt.
3. Stir together wet and dry mixtures until soft dough forms.
4. Cut a large square of parchment paper and grease the middle. Tuck it inside the slow cooker, greased side up, to line it.
5. Nudge the dough out of the mixing bowl into the center of the greased parchment in the cooker. Shape and smooth it as needed so it makes a low loaf.
6. Cover the cooker and tuck a chopstick or wooden spoon under one end of the lid to vent it.
7. Cook on High for 2-3 hours, until bread is firm on the top and lightly browned.
8. Carefully lift parchment and bread out of the cooker. Allow to rest for 10 minutes, then slice and serve warm.

Variations:

Add ½ tsp. ground cardamom OR ½ tsp. caraway seeds.

Good go-alongs with this recipe:

Lemon curd, jam, butter; wonderful next to corned beef and cabbage.

Dutch Apple Batter Bread

Margaret W. High
Lancaster, PA

Makes 10 servings

Prep. Time: 25 minutes
Cooking Time: 4 hours
Standing Time: 40 minutes
Ideal slow-cooker size: 6 qt.

½ cup (1 stick) butter
1 cup sugar
2 eggs
1 cup whole wheat flour
1 cup all-purpose flour
1 tsp. baking soda
½ tsp. salt
½ tsp. ground cinnamon
¼ tsp. ground nutmeg
1 cup chopped apples, peeled or not
½ cup chopped walnuts
⅓ cup buttermilk

1. Cream together butter, sugar, and eggs.
2. Separately, combine flours, baking soda, salt, cinnamon, nutmeg, apples, and walnuts.
3. Add flour mixture to creamed mixture alternately with buttermilk.
4. Make sure you have a loaf pan that fits in your 6-quart cooker. Place pan on jar ring or metal trivet to keep it off the floor of the slow cooker.
5. Grease and flour loaf pan.
6. Pour batter into pan and place pan in cooker. Prop lid open at one end with a wooden chopstick or spoon handle.
7. Cook on High for 3-4 hours, until tester inserted in middle comes out clean.
8. Wearing oven mitts to protect your knuckles, remove hot pan and set aside to cool for 10 minutes. Run knife around the edge and turn bread out of pan to cool an additional 30 minutes on rack before slicing.

Tips:

Great with butter or cream cheese, or toasted for breakfast.

Variations:

Add ⅓ cup chopped raw cranberries or raisins.

Raspberry Chocolate Chip Bread

Rosanna Martin
Morgantown, WV

Makes 10 servings

Prep. Time: 25 minutes
Cooking Time: 3-4 hours
Ideal slow-cooker size: 6 qt.

1 cup whole wheat flour
⅔ cup all-purpose flour
¾ cup rolled oats
⅔ cup sugar
2 tsp. baking powder
1 tsp. baking soda
½ tsp. salt
½ tsp. ground cinnamon
¾ cup fresh or unsweetened frozen raspberries (do not thaw)
⅔ cup chocolate chips
1 egg, lightly beaten
¾ cup buttermilk
⅓ cup canola oil
1 tsp. vanilla extract

1. In large bowl, mix flours, oats, sugar, baking powder, baking soda, salt, and cinnamon. Gently stir in raspberries and chocolate chips.
2. Separately, mix egg, buttermilk, oil, and vanilla.
3. Gently stir wet ingredients into dry until just barely mixed—streaks of flour are fine.
4. Make sure your loaf pan fits in your oval 6-quart slow cooker. Grease and flour loaf pan. Set it on a jar ring or other heat-resistant thing to keep it off the floor of the cooker.
5. Pour batter into prepared loaf pan.
6. Put lid on cooker, propping it open at one end with a chopstick or wooden spoon handle.
7. Cook on High for 3-4 hours, until tester inserted in middle comes out clean.
8. Wearing oven mitts (to protect your knuckles!), remove hot pan from hot cooker and allow it to cool for 10 minutes. Run a knife around the edge and turn loaf out on cooling rack to cool for an additional 30 minutes before slicing.

Tips:

Serve with butter or cream cheese, if you wish, but I love it by itself with a glass of milk.

Zucchini Bread

Esther J. Yoder
Hartville, OH

Makes 10 servings

Prep. Time: 25 minutes
Cooking Time: 4 hours
Ideal slow-cooker size: 6 qt.

2 eggs
2 cups shredded zucchini
1 cup brown sugar
⅔ cup oil
1 tsp. vanilla extract
1 cup chopped walnuts, optional
8-oz. pkg. cream cheese, softened
1½ cups whole wheat flour
½ cup rolled oats
1 tsp. baking powder
1 tsp. baking soda
1½ tsp. ground cinnamon
½ tsp. nutmeg
1 tsp. salt

1. Mix eggs, zucchini, sugar, oil, vanilla, and nuts. Mix in cream cheese until smooth.
2. Separately, mix flour, oats, baking powder, baking soda, cinnamon, nutmeg, and salt.
3. Combine wet and dry ingredients, mixing gently until just combined.
4. Make sure you have a loaf pan that fits in your oval 6-quart cooker. Set it on a jar lid or other heat-proof object so the pan is not sitting on the floor of the insert.
5. Grease and flour loaf pan. Pour batter into prepared pan and place in cooker.
6. Prop lid open at one end with a chopstick or wooden spoon handle. Cook on High for 3-4 hours, until tester inserted in middle comes out clean.
7. Wearing oven mitts to protect your knuckles, remove hot pan and allow to sit for 10 minutes. Run knife around edges and turn loaf out to cool for 30 more minutes before slicing.

Poppy Seed Tea Bread

Julie Hurst
Leola, PA

Makes 10 servings

Prep. Time: 30 minutes
Cooking Time: 3-4 hours
Standing Time: 30 minutes
Ideal slow-cooker size: 6 qt.

½ cup whole wheat flour
1½ cups all-purpose flour
¾ cup sugar
2 tsp. baking powder
¼ tsp. salt
¼ cup poppy seeds
2 eggs, room temperature
½ cup (1 stick) salted butter, melted
¾ cup whole milk, room temperature
½ tsp. almond extract
½ tsp. vanilla extract

1. In a mixing bowl, combine flours, sugar, baking powder, salt, and poppy seeds.
2. Separately, whisk together eggs, butter, milk, and extracts.
3. Pour wet ingredients into flour mixture, stirring until just combined.
4. Make sure your loaf pan fits in your oval 6-quart slow cooker. Grease and flour loaf pan. Set it on a jar ring or other heat-resistant thing to keep it off the floor of the cooker.
5. Pour batter into prepared loaf pan.
6. Put lid on cooker, propping it open at one end with a chopstick or wooden spoon handle.
7. Cook on High for 3-4 hours, until tester inserted in middle comes out clean.
8. Wearing oven mitts (to protect your knuckles!), remove hot pan from hot cooker and allow it to cool for 10 minutes. Run a knife around the edge and turn loaf out on cooling rack to cool for an additional 20 minutes before slicing.

Tips:

Serve with pineapple whipped cream cheese and tea.

Caramel Rolls

Jessalyn Wantland
Paris, TX

Makes 6-8 servings

Prep. Time: 20 minutes
Cooking Time: 2-3 hours
Ideal slow-cooker size: 5 qt.

½ cup brown sugar
½ tsp. ground cinnamon
¼ cup (½ stick) butter
2 8-oz. pkgs. refrigerator biscuits

1. Mix sugar and cinnamon together in small bowl.
2. Melt butter in another small bowl.
3. Dip individual biscuits into melted butter and then into cinnamon and sugar mixture.
4. Place each covered biscuit in greased slow cooker.
5. Cover and cook on High for 2-3 hours, or until rolls are done. Check rolls in center after 2 hours to see if they are done.

During the spring, we use the slow cooker a lot in our truck due to chasing 3 kids with 3 separate baseball schedules. It is fun to watch people ask my kids where that plate of hot food came from when my kids walk up to the bleachers. When people find out I have dinner cooking or just staying warm in my truck while at baseball practice, they are amazed. — Malinda Irvine, Thompson Falls, MT

At the school where I taught a kindergarten reading program, the staff wanted to do something fun for the students on "Go Western Day." With permission from parents and the principal, each of the teachers brought a slow cooker and chili ingredients to school. The ingredients were assembled, none of them too spicy, and the slow cooker was started first thing in the morning while the students observed the first stage of the chili cook-off. All day, the aroma filled the classrooms. Later that afternoon, each student got a spoon and the teachers took turns dishing up delicious chili into tiny cups for each student to sample a variety of chilis. It was a wonderful way to add a little flavor to a day of learning, and the students absolutely loved the grand finale to a special day. — Yen Parrott, Houston, TX

Soups, Stews, and Chilis

Favorite Vegetable Beef Soup

Judy Buller
Bluffton, OH

Makes 8 servings

***Prep. Time:* 30 minutes**
***Cooking Time:* 6-7 hours**
***Ideal slow-cooker size:* 5 qt.**

¾ lb. ground beef
1 small onion, chopped
salt and pepper, to taste
1 potato, cubed
2 carrots, sliced
2 ribs celery, sliced
½ cup peas
½ cup lima beans
1 cup sweet corn
8-oz. can tomato sauce
1 Tbsp. ketchup
4 cups tomato juice or V-8 juice
2 cups beef broth
1 tsp. sugar
¼ cup dry pearl barley
2 bay leaves
4 whole allspice

1. Brown ground beef in skillet with onion and season with salt and pepper. Drain off any grease. Transfer to slow cooker.
2. Add rest of ingredients to slow cooker.
3. Cover and cook on Low 6-7 hours, until vegetables are tender.
4. Remove allspice and bay leaves before serving.

Tips:

This soup freezes well.

Variations:

I use whatever vegetables I have in my garden, so any vegetables can be mixed or matched. You could even buy frozen mixed vegetables if you don't have time to cut up veggies.

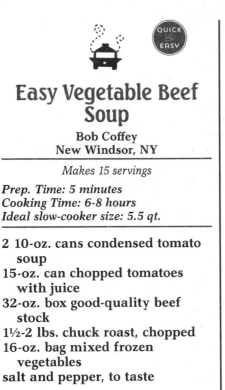

Easy Vegetable Beef Soup

Bob Coffey
New Windsor, NY

Makes 15 servings

Prep. Time: 5 minutes
Cooking Time: 6-8 hours
Ideal slow-cooker size: 5.5 qt.

2 10-oz. cans condensed tomato soup
15-oz. can chopped tomatoes with juice
32-oz. box good-quality beef stock
1½-2 lbs. chuck roast, chopped
16-oz. bag mixed frozen vegetables
salt and pepper, to taste

1. Combine all ingredients in slow cooker.
2. Cover and cook on Low for 6-8 hours, until beef is done.
3. Season to taste with salt and pepper.

Variations:

This is a very flexible recipe that can be adjusted to accommodate tastes or available ingredients. Pretty much any vegetables or cut of beef will work; I even used diced London broil once because it was on sale, and the recipe did not suffer at all.

My tricks for getting my slow cooker to do its best work:

I have two slow cookers: one with a traditional dial and the other with a digital touch screen. On rainy or windy days when I'm afraid the power might dip, I reach for the one with the dial. That way if we do lose power for a minute the cooker will just resume doing its thing when it comes back. The digital one would be flashing and waiting for me to turn it on when I get home.

Creamy Vegetable Beef Stew

Lorna Rodes
Port Republic, VA

Makes 6-8 servings

Prep. Time: 20 minutes
Cooking Time: 5-7 hours
Ideal slow-cooker size: 4 qt.

1 lb. ground beef
4 cups tomato juice
½ cup chopped onion
1 cup diced potatoes
1 cup diced carrots
¼ tsp. pepper
½ tsp. dried basil
2 tsp. salt
2 Tbsp. butter
2 Tbsp. flour
1⅓ cups milk

1. Place beef, tomato juice, onion, potatoes, carrots, pepper, basil, and salt in slow cooker.
2. Cover and cook on Low 4-6 hours, stirring once to break up beef. When beef is done and vegetables are tender, make white sauce.
3. In saucepan, melt butter. Whisk in flour and stir and cook until flour and butter are bubbly.
4. Pour in milk gradually, whisking, and whisk until smooth. Stir over low heat until sauce thickens.
5. Pour white sauce into soup, stirring. Cook an additional hour on Low.

Good go-alongs with this recipe:

Bread sticks.

Sturdy vegetables—potatoes, carrots, green beans—take a while to cook in a slow cooker. Put them in at the start of the cooking time. Other, more delicate vegetables—peas, mushrooms, spinach—take very little time. Stir them in 10-15 minutes before the end of the cooking time.

Aunt Thelma's Homemade Soup

Janice Muller
Derwood, MD

Makes 10 servings

Prep. Time: 20 minutes
Cooking Time: 4½-5½ hours
Ideal slow-cooker size: 6 qt.

1 lb. 12-oz. can whole tomatoes
1 cup diced raw potatoes
1 cup thinly sliced carrots
1 cup chopped onions
12-oz. bag frozen peas
12-oz. bag frozen corn
16-oz. bag frozen lima beans
4 vegetable bouillon cubes
1 Tbsp. salt
¼ tsp. pepper
½ tsp. dried basil
1 bay leaf
¼ tsp. dill seed
7 cups water, divided
2 Tbsp. cornstarch

1. Mix all the ingredients in slow cooker except ½ cup water and cornstarch.
2. Cover and cook on Low for 4-5 hours, until vegetables are tender.
3. Mix cornstarch and ½ cup water until smooth.
4. Whisk mixture into hot soup and cook for an additional 30 minutes until thickened. Stir before serving.

Good go-alongs with this recipe:

A loaf of warm Italian bread is welcomed for dunking in this hearty soup.

Hamburger Vegetable Soup

Judy Diller
Bluffton, OH

Makes 6-8 servings

Prep. Time: 20 minutes
Cooking Time: 4-8 hours
Ideal slow-cooker size: 4-5 qt.

1 lb. ground beef
1 cup chopped onion
1 cup chopped celery
1 cup chopped carrots
5 cups water
1 Tbsp. beef bouillon
1 bay leaf
⅓ cup barley
16-oz. can chopped tomatoes
½ cup ketchup
2 tsp. seasoned salt
salt and pepper to taste

1. Brown onion and beef together in skillet. Drain off grease.
2. Transfer beef and onion to slow cooker. Add rest of ingredients.
3. Cover and cook 4 hours on High or 6-8 hours on Low.

Good go-alongs with this recipe:

Great with homemade bread and salad.

Mom's Vegetable Soup

Sharon Miller
Holmesville, OH

Makes 6-8 servings

Prep. Time: 30 minutes
Cooking Time: 6-8 hours
Ideal slow-cooker size: 6 qt.

1 lb. lean ground beef
1 cup diced onion
⅓ cup barley
4 cups mixed vegetables (your choice of corn, green beans, carrots, potatoes, etc.)
½ cup chopped green or red bell pepper
2 15-oz. cans diced tomatoes
1 tsp. dried basil
1 tsp. chili powder
½ tsp. black pepper
1 tsp. minced garlic
2 tsp. Worcestershire sauce
1 beef bouillon cube
1 chicken bouillon cube
1 tsp. sugar
¼ cup ketchup
1 qt. V-8 tomato juice
2 cups water

1. Brown beef and onions in skillet. Drain off grease.
2. Transfer beef and onions to slow cooker. Add rest of ingredients and mix well.
3. Cover and cook 6-8 hours on Low.

Good go-alongs with this recipe:

Garlic bread.

Vegetarian Vegetable Soup

Jean Harris Robinson
Pemberton, NJ

Makes 8-10 servings

Prep. Time: 25 minutes
Cooking Time: 4-6 hours
Ideal slow-cooker size: 4 qt.

2 Tbsp. olive oil
1 large white onion, Vidalia preferred, diced
2 medium carrots, diced
2 cloves garlic, minced
20-oz. pkg. frozen cubed butternut squash, or 4 cups chopped fresh
2 cups finely chopped cabbage
1 cup chopped kale, packed
½ tsp. ground allspice
¼ tsp. ground ginger, or 1 Tbsp. finely grated fresh ginger
4 sprigs fresh thyme, or 1 tsp. dried thyme
1 tsp. salt, or to taste
14-oz. can diced tomatoes with juice
1 quart no-salt vegetable broth

1. Combine all ingredients in cooker.
2. Cook on Low 4-6 hours until veggies are soft.

Tips:

Refrigerate for several days or freeze for later. It is a family pleaser. I like to prep the vegetables the night before. I often use frozen vegetables and sometimes add leftover green beans or broccoli at the last minute before serving.

Good go-alongs with this recipe:

Add a dollop of Greek yogurt to the top of each bowl. Place some hot cooked grains, such as brown rice or quinoa, in soup bowls before ladling in soup.

Vegetable Barley Soup

Colleen Heatwole
Burton, MI

Makes 8 servings

Prep. Time: 20 minutes
Cooking Time: 6-8 hours
Ideal slow-cooker size: 5 qt.

½ lb. lean ground beef
½ cup chopped onion
1 clove garlic, minced
¾ cup pearl barley
9-oz. pkg. frozen mixed vegetables
½ cup sliced celery
½ cup diced carrots
5 cups water
14½-oz. can diced tomatoes, undrained
2 beef bouillon cubes
½ tsp. dried basil
1 bay leaf

1. Brown beef in skillet. Drain grease. Transfer to slow cooker.
2. Add rest of ingredients and cook on Low 6-8 hours.
3. Remove bay leaf before serving.

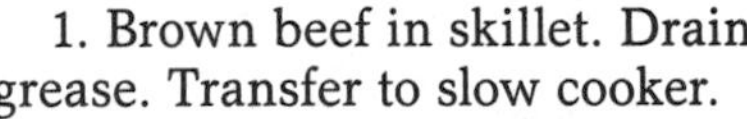

One Super Bowl Sunday my hubby invited all his friends over, but I was bushed from a long, hard, busy Saturday night at the restaurant I work at. I wondered what I could make for 20 people when I wasn't too happy to be cooking for a crowd again. I made chili in my slow cooker. Then I made cornbread, corn salad, and brownies with other stuff I had on hand. My husband was stoked. Needless to say I got the rest I needed, and now it is a tradition. — Gayle Hall, Harbor, OR

Bison Chili

Willard Roth
Elkhart, IN

Makes 12 servings

Prep. Time: 20 minutes
Cooking Time: 3-5 hours
Ideal slow-cooker size: 7 qt.

1½ lbs. ground bison
1 Tbsp. olive oil
1 tsp. ground cumin
1 Tbsp. chili powder
1 tsp. powdered garlic
1½ cups chopped onion
1 cup port, divided
4 15-oz. cans red kidney beans, divided
3 15-oz. cans diced tomatoes
⅓ cup dark brown sugar
4 1-oz. squares unsweetened baking chocolate (100% cacao)

1. In skillet, brown bison in oil with cumin, chili powder, garlic, onion, and ½ cup port for 15 minutes. Stir frequently, breaking up the meat into small chunks.
2. Spray slow cooker with cooking spray. Turn on High. Put in 3 cans of beans with juice. Add meat mixture.
3. Stir in tomatoes and brown sugar.
4. In same skillet, melt baking chocolate, watching carefully so it doesn't burn.
5. Stir in remaining can of beans and juice. Add to slow-cooker mixture.
6. Over medium heat, stir in remaining port, stirring up browned bits from skillet with a wooden spoon. When they're all loosened, add to slow cooker.
7. Cook on High for 3 hours, or Low for 5 hours.

Variations:

You can substitute ground beef (or venison) for the bison and have a wonderfully tasty dish!

Black Bean Chili

Joyce Cox
Port Angeles, WA

Makes 8 servings

Prep. Time: 20 minutes
Cooking Time: 8-12 hours
Ideal slow-cooker size: 6 qt.

1½ cups fresh-brewed coffee
1½ cups vegetable broth
2 15-oz. cans diced tomatoes with juice
15-oz. can tomato sauce
8 cups cooked black beans, drained
1 medium yellow onion, diced
4 garlic cloves, minced
2 Tbsp. brown sugar, packed
2 Tbsp. chili powder
1 Tbsp. ground cumin
salt to taste

1. Combine all ingredients except salt in slow cooker.
2. Cover and cook on Low for 6-8 hours. Add salt near end of cooking.

Tips:

Great served in bowls with cilantro, cubed avocados, Greek yogurt or sour cream, and grated cheese on top.

Variations:

Use 4 15-oz. cans of black beans, rinsed and drained. Mash some of the beans with a potato masher before adding to cooker. The chili will be thicker.

No-Beans Chili

Sharon Timpe
Jackson, WI

Makes 10-12 servings

Prep. Time: 35 minutes
Cooking Time: Low 9-10 hours; High 6-7 hours
Ideal slow-cooker size: 5-6 qt.

1 cup red wine
1½ tsp. dried oregano
2 tsp. dried parsley
2-3 Tbsp. oil
1½ lbs round steak, cubed
1½ lbs. chuck steak, cubed
1 medium onion, chopped
1 cup chopped celery
1 cup chopped carrots
28-oz. can stewed tomatoes
8-oz. can tomato sauce
1 cup beef broth
1 Tbsp. vinegar
1 Tbsp. brown sugar
2 Tbsp. chili powder
1 tsp. cumin
¼ tsp. pepper
1 tsp. salt

1. Place oregano and parsley in red wine and set aside, ideally for about 15 minutes.
2. Heat oil in a skillet and brown the beef cubes. You may have to do this in two batches.
3. Put browned beef in slow cooker.
4. Add wine mixture to skillet and stir, scraping up browned bits. Scrape mixture into slow cooker.
5. Add rest of ingredients to slow cooker.
6. Cook on Low 9-10 hours or High 6-7 hours, until meat is very tender.

Tips:

Serve in bowls garnished with toppings like grated cheese, sour cream, blue cheese crumbles, croutons, or (my favorite!) oyster crackers.

Pepperoni Pizza Chili

Melissa Cramer
Lancaster, PA

Makes 8 servings

Prep. Time: 15 minutes
Cooking Time: 4-6 hours
Ideal slow-cooker size: 4-5 qt.

1 lb. ground beef, cooked and drained
16-oz. can kidney beans, rinsed and drained
15-oz. can pizza sauce
14-oz. can Italian stewed tomatoes
8-oz. can tomato sauce
1 cup water
3.5-oz. pkg. sliced pepperoni
½ cup chopped green bell pepper
½ cup chopped onion
1 tsp. Italian herb seasoning
shredded part-skim mozzarella cheese, for topping

1. Place all ingredients in slow cooker except cheese.
2. Cook on Low 4-6 hours.
3. Serve in bowls with cheese on top.

Tips:

Add good crusty bread on the side or for dipping.

Favorite Chili

Carol Eveleth
Hillsdale, WY

Makes 10 servings

Prep. Time: *20 minutes*
Cooking Time: *3-10 hours*
Ideal slow-cooker size: *5 qt.*

2 16-oz. cans chili beans
2 14-oz. cans crushed tomatoes, or tomato sauce
2 lbs. ground beef, browned and drained
1 green bell pepper, diced
1 medium onion, diced
2 cloves garlic, crushed, or 1 tsp. garlic powder
3 Tbsp. chili powder
1 tsp. pepper
1 tsp. ground cumin
2 tsp. salt

1. Combine all ingredients in slow cooker.
2. Cook on Low for 8-10 hours or High 3-4 hours.

Tips:

Serve with sour cream, corn chips, and shredded cheese for a Nacho Chili version. Serve Chili over baked potatoes for a filling meal.

—Michele Ruvola

This is an easy recipe to double to feed a crowd. To keep costs down, don't double the meat.

—Beverly Hummel

Variations:

Use some bulk sausage in place of part of the ground beef.

—Pat Bishop

Use 1 Tbsp. Worcestershire sauce instead of salt.

—Beverly Hummel

To make Tex-Mex chili, add 1 ½ cups salsa and top with shredded Mexican cheese.

—Betty Moore

Ohio Chili

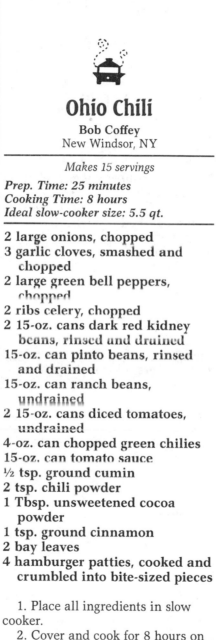

Bob Coffey
New Windsor, NY

Makes 15 servings

Prep. Time: *25 minutes*
Cooking Time: *8 hours*
Ideal slow-cooker size: *5.5 qt.*

2 large onions, chopped
3 garlic cloves, smashed and chopped
2 large green bell peppers, chopped
2 ribs celery, chopped
2 15-oz. cans dark red kidney beans, rinsed and drained
15-oz. can pinto beans, rinsed and drained
15-oz. can ranch beans, undrained
2 15-oz. cans diced tomatoes, undrained
4-oz. can chopped green chilies
15-oz. can tomato sauce
½ tsp. ground cumin
2 tsp. chili powder
1 Tbsp. unsweetened cocoa powder
1 tsp. ground cinnamon
2 bay leaves
4 hamburger patties, cooked and crumbled into bite-sized pieces

1. Place all ingredients in slow cooker.
2. Cover and cook for 8 hours on Low.

Tips:

Serve with grated cheddar or Mexican-blend cheese on top. We call it Ohio Chili because it's a great mix of Cincinnati chili and the chili you get at Wendy's, the burger chain from Columbus, Ohio. Makes a lot and the first night we usually just eat it plain in bowls. As a "planned over," the next night we add a little more tomato sauce when re-heating it and serve it over spaghetti with cheese and chopped onion, just like the famous 5-way chili in Cincinnati.

Variations:

Add some chopped jalepeños or a few shakes of your favorite hot sauce.

Chicken Chili

Sharon Miller
Holmesville, OH

Makes 6 servings

Prep. Time: 15 minutes
Cooking Time: 6 hours
Ideal slow-cooker size: 4 qt.

2 lbs. boneless, skinless chicken breasts, cubed
2 Tbsp. butter
15-oz. can red kidney beans, rinsed and drained
2 14-oz. cans diced tomatoes, undrained
1 cup diced onion
1 cup diced red bell pepper
1-2 Tbsp. chili powder, according to your taste preference
1 tsp. ground cumin
1 tsp. ground oregano
salt and pepper, to taste

1. In skillet on high heat, brown chicken cubes in butter until they have some browned edges. Place in greased slow cooker.
2. Pour one of the cans of tomatoes with its juice into skillet to get all the browned bits and butter. Scrape and pour into slow cooker.
3. Add rest of ingredients, including other can of tomatoes, to cooker.
4. Cook on Low for 5-6 hours.

Tips:

Can be served with shredded cheddar cheese and sour cream.

Chipotle Chili

Janie Steele
Moore, OK

Makes 6-8 servings

Prep. Time: 30 minutes
Cooking Time: 3-6 hours
Ideal slow-cooker size: 3-4 qt.

2 cloves garlic, chopped
1¼ lbs. boneless, skinless chicken thighs, cubed
1 lb. butternut squash, peeled and cubed
15-oz. can pinto beans, rinsed and drained
juice and zest of ½ an orange
2-3 chipotle peppers in adobo sauce, minced
2 Tbsp. tomato paste
2 green onions, sliced
chopped cilantro, optional

1. Combine garlic, chicken, squash, beans, orange juice, orange zest, peppers, and tomato paste in slow cooker.
2. Cook 3-4 hours on High or 5-6 hours on Low, until chicken is done.
3. Mash some of the stew with potato masher to make it thicker.
4. Stir in green onions and optional cilantro. Serve hot.

Variations:

Use zest and juice of 1 lime instead of the orange.

When chicken is on special—and you've got a bit of time—buy a whole one, or a bunch of legs and thighs, and cook them in your slow cooker. Cool and de-bone them. Then pack the cooked chicken in 1- or 2-cup containers, mark what's in them and the date, and put them in your freezer. There are so many good dishes that call for cooked chicken—and you've got it in the "bank"!

White Chicken Chili

Lucille Hollinger
Richland, PA

Makes 8 servings

Prep. Time: 10 minutes
Cooking Time: 5-6 hours
Ideal slow-cooker size: 3 qt.

4 cups cubed, cooked chicken
2 cups chicken broth
2 14.5-oz. cans cannellini beans
14.5-oz. can garbanzo beans
¼ cup chopped onion
¼ cup chopped bell pepper
2 tsp. ground cumin
½ tsp. dried oregano
¼ tsp. cayenne pepper
¼ tsp. salt

1. Combine all ingredients in slow cooker.
2. Cover and cook on Low for 5-6 hours.

Tips:

Serve with sour cream, shredded cheese, and tortilla chips.

Variations:

Omit garbanzo beans. Shred chicken instead of cubing it. Add 1 tsp. Italian herb seasoning.
—Beverly Hummel

Good go-alongs with this recipe:

Cornbread and salad.

Southwestern Chili

Colleen Heatwole
Burton, MI

Makes 12 servings

Prep. Time: 30 minutes
Cooking Time: 6-8 hours
Ideal slow-cooker size: 5-6 qt.

28-oz. or 32-oz. can tomatoes
15-16 oz. salsa
15-oz. can chicken broth
1 cup barley
3 cups water
1 tsp. chili powder
1 tsp. ground cumin
15-oz. can black beans
15-oz. can whole-kernel corn
3 cups cooked chicken, chopped, about 1½ lbs.
shredded cheddar cheese, optional
sour cream, optional

1. Combine all ingredients in slow cooker except for optional cheese and sour cream.
2. Cover and cook 6-8 hours on Low, until barley is tender.
3. Serve in bowls with optional cheese and sour cream on top.

Tips:

I always cook my own beans, using my slow cooker, and keep them packaged in the freezer for ready use. Use 2 cups cooked beans in place of the 15-oz. can. I also use home-canned tomatoes and salsa for this recipe. This is a good everyday dish, but special enough for company. Even my grandchildren like it.

Good go-alongs with this recipe:

I often add homemade artisan bread and applesauce for a complete meal.

My tricks for getting my slow cooker to do its best work:

Don't remove the cover unnecessarily when cooking.

My tips for converting oven and stove-top recipes into good slow cooker recipes:

Use less water and remember that most slow-cooker recipes are forgiving.

Chicken Tortilla Soup

Marla Folkerts
Batavia, IL

Makes 4 servings

Prep. Time: 20 minutes
Cooking Time: 3-4 hours
Ideal slow-cooker size: 4 qt.

2 lbs. boneless, skinless chicken
1 medium onion, chopped
2 cloves garlic, minced
14-oz. can diced tomatoes
15-oz. can Rotel tomatoes
14.5-oz. can beef broth
14.5-oz. can chicken broth
10-oz. can tomato soup
1½ cans of water (use soup can)
1 tsp. ground cumin
1 tsp. chili powder
1 tsp. salt
½ tsp. lemon-pepper seasoning
2 tsp. Worcestershire sauce
½ tsp. Tabasco sauce, or to taste

1. Place all ingredients in slow cooker. Stir.
2. Cover and cook on Low for 3-4 hours, until chicken is tender.
3. Remove chicken to bowl or platter. Shred chicken with 2 forks. Return chicken and any juices back to slow cooker. Cook a bit longer, 20-30 minutes, to be sure soup is hot.
4. Stir. Taste to adjust seasoning.

Tips:

Can assemble ahead of time, and freeze! Thaw, put in slow cooker, and cook.

Variations:

Add toppings to each bowl of soup, such as grated cheese, tortilla chips, avocado, sour cream, chopped fresh cilantro, and jalapeños.

Southwest Chicken Soup

Phyllis Good
Lancaster, PA

Makes 6-8 servings

Prep. Time: 15 minutes
Cooking Time: 3½-9 hours
Chilling Time: 30 minutes
Ideal slow-cooker size: 6 qt.

3-lb. whole chicken, or 3 chicken breasts
6 cups water
1 cup onion, chopped
1 cup celery, chopped
1½ Tbsp. olive oil
15.5-oz. can black beans, rinsed
10-oz. pkg. frozen corn
15.5-oz. can diced tomatoes
4-oz. can chopped green chilies
½ tsp. cumin
½ tsp. black pepper
2 tsp. chili powder
salt to taste
½ cup cilantro, chopped

1. Place whole chicken in slow cooker. Add 6 cups water. Or place chicken breasts in cooker. Add 6 cups water.
2. Cover cooker. If cooking a whole chicken, cook on Low 5-8 hours, or until meat thermometer stuck into thickest part of the thigh (without touching the bone) registers 165°. Start checking at 5 hours, and do not overcook.

   If cooking breasts, cook on Low 1½-3 hours, until chicken registers 165° on a meat thermometer. Start checking at 1½ hours and do not overcook.
3. Remove whole chicken or breasts from cooker and allow to cool until you can handle the meat without burning yourself. Chop meat into bite-sized chunks. Set aside.
4. While chicken is cooking, sauté chopped onion and celery in olive oil in a skillet just until softened.
5. Add softened vegetables to broth in cooker, along with all remaining ingredients, except the cilantro.
6. Cover. Cook on Low for 2 hours, or on High for 1 hour, or until everything is heated through.
7. Ten minutes before serving, stir in chicken pieces. Heat.
8. Top individual servings with chopped fresh cilantro.

Tips:

This is super easy and quick to make. It's probably the soup recipe I make the most because it's the soup that gets the most compliments!

Beef Taco Soup

Kayla Snyder
Saegertown, PA

Makes 6 servings

Prep. Time: 20 minutes
Cooking Time: 4-6 hours
Ideal slow-cooker size: 3 qt.

1 lb. ground beef
1 small onion, chopped finely
4 cups tomato juice
2 cups tomato sauce
2 cups corn
1 pkg. taco seasoning
15-oz. can hot chili beans
corn chips, sour cream, and shredded cheddar, for serving

1. In a skillet, fry together beef and onion until browned. Drain off grease.
2. Transfer beef/onion to slow cooker.
3. Add tomato juice, tomato sauce, corn, seasoning, and beans. Stir.
4. Cover and cook on High for 4 hours or Low for 6 hours.
5. Serve in bowls with corn chips, sour cream, and cheddar.

Variations:

This is a very versatile recipe. You can use what you have on hand. If you don't have tomato sauce, use all-tomato juice instead. You can also stretch your meat by making double the recipe with just 1 pound of ground beef. It's still delicious. Use 2 cans of beans and add a 16-oz. jar of salsa.

—Earnie Zimmerman

Good go-alongs with this recipe:

I like to serve this soup with toppings like sour cream, shredded cheese, diced jalapeños, and/or corn chips or tortilla chips. My kids love this because they can add whatever toppings they like.

—Earnie Zimmerman

Tex-Mex Soup with Crunchy Tortillas

Deb Kepiro
Strasburg, PA

Makes 6 servings

Prep. Time: 10 minutes
Cooking Time: 5-7 hours
Ideal slow-cooker size: 3 qt.

2 boneless, skinless chicken breasts, cubed
1 onion, chopped
1 clove garlic, crushed
14.5-oz. can chopped tomatoes
4 cups chicken broth
¼ tsp. salt
⅛ tsp. pepper
1 mild green chile, seeded and chopped
2 Tbsp. vegetable oil
4 corn tortillas, cut in half and then in ¼" strips
shredded Monterey Jack cheese, for serving
chopped fresh cilantro, for serving

1. Combine chicken, onion, garlic, tomatoes, broth, salt, pepper, and green chile in slow cooker.
2. Cover and cook on Low 5-7 hours.
3. Heat oil in large skillet and add tortilla strips. Cook, stirring, over medium heat until crisp. Drain strips on paper towels.
4. If desired, put 1 tablespoon or 2 of shredded Monterey Jack cheese in each serving bowl.
5. Ladle soup into bowls and top with tortilla strips. Sprinkle with chopped cilantro.

Good go-alongs with this recipe:

Tossed salad.

Have one or two special meals that you can make when friends show up unexpectedly. Keep the ingredients on hand so you're ready. You'll be relaxed and so will they.

Cider Beef Stew

Jean Turner
Williams Lake, British Columbia

Makes 8 servings

Prep. Time: 30 minutes
Cooking Time: 8 hours
Ideal slow-cooker size: 3 qt.

2 lbs. stewing beef, cut into 1" cubes
6 Tbsp. flour, divided
2 tsp. salt
¼ tsp. pepper
¼ tsp. dried thyme
3 Tbsp. cooking oil
4 potatoes, peeled and quartered
4 carrots, quartered
2 onions, sliced
1 rib celery, sliced
1 apple, chopped
2 cups apple cider or apple juice
1-2 Tbsp. vinegar
½ cup cold water

1. Stir together beef, 3 Tbsp. flour, salt, pepper, and thyme. Brown coated in oil in skillet. Do in two batches if necessary to avoid crowding the meat.
2. Place vegetables and apple in slow cooker. Place browned meat cubes on top.
3. Pour over apple cider and vinegar.
4. Cover and cook on Low for 8-10 hours.
5. Turn slow cooker to High. Blend cold water with remaining 3 Tbsp. flour. Stir into hot stew.
6. Cover and cook on High for 15 minutes or until thickened.

Tips:

Great served with garlic bread or cheese bread.

Good go-alongs with this recipe:

A side salad is all that is needed for a complete meal.

Beef and Barley Stew

Jenny Unternahrer
Wayland, IA

Makes 6-8 servings

Prep. Time: 20 minutes
Cooking Time: 8-9 hours
Ideal slow-cooker size: 5 qt.

2-lb. beef roast, trimmed and cubed
olive oil
6 cups beef broth
1 cup water
1¼ cups sliced carrots
½ cup chopped celery
⅓ cup chopped onion
1 tsp. salt
¼ tsp. pepper
½ cup quick barley (more or less as you change the dish's consistency)
1 cup frozen peas

1. Heat oil in skillet. Brown beef pieces on high heat, searing on all sides.
2. Transfer meat to slow cooker.
3. Pour some broth into skillet to get all the drippings and browned bits.
4. Add rest of the broth, water, carrots, celery, onion, salt, and pepper to slow cooker.
5. Cover and cook on Low 7-8 hours.
6. Add barley. Cook for another hour, until barley and beef are both tender.
7. Add frozen peas. Stir gently. The hot stew will thaw the peas, but they will still be nice and green.

Tips:

After about 30 minutes after adding barley check the thickness of the stew. If it is too thin, add a little bit more barley. May skip searing the beef if you don't have time.

My tips for converting oven and stove-top recipes into good slow cooker recipes:

I have made this dish on the stove top as well. When I converted it to the slow cooker I used less liquid.

Beef Stew

Carol Eveleth
Hillsdale, WY

Makes 10 servings

Prep. Time: 20 minutes
Cooking Time: 5-7 hours
Ideal slow-cooker size: 5 qt.

2-lb. boneless beef chuck roast, cut into 1½" chunks
6 large carrots, sliced
4 medium potatoes, peeled or not, chopped
4 ribs celery, sliced
1 large onion, chopped
3 tsp. salt
¼ tsp. coarsely ground black pepper
3 Tbsp. minute tapioca
½ cup ketchup
1 cup tomato juice
1 cup water

1. Grease interior of slow cooker crock.
2. Place beef, carrots, potatoes, celery, and onion in crock.
3. Sprinkle seasonings and tapioca on top.
4. Pour ketchup, tomato juice, and water over all. Stir everything together well.
5. Cover. Cook for 5-7 hours on Low, or until instant-read meat thermometer registers 145° when stuck in center of beef chunks and vegetables are as tender as you like them.

Variations:

Omit ketchup. Reduce salt to 1½ tsp. and add 1 tsp. Worcestershire sauce. Add 1 Tbsp. brown sugar.
—Mary Ann Bowman

Add 1 green bell pepper, chopped.
—Carole Bolatto

Good go-alongs with this recipe:

Serve over noodles or rice.
—Carole Bolatto

Can't Beet Beef Stew!

Bob Coffey
New Windsor, NY

Makes 15 servings

Prep. Time: 30 minutes
Cooking Time: 6-8 hours
Ideal slow-cooker size: 5.5 qt.

4 large beets, roasted in the oven at 425° until tender, then cooled, peeled, and diced, or, if you don't have time for that much food prep, 2 15.5-oz. jars prepared beets, drained
2 large onions, diced
3 garlic cloves, diced
2 large carrots, peeled and diced
2 large parsnips, peeled and diced
2 ribs celery, diced
15.5-oz. can petite diced tomatoes, undrained
1 bay leaf
2 lbs. boneless beef chuck roast, cut into 1½" chunks
4 cups beef broth
¼ cup finely chopped fresh dill
coarse salt and pepper to taste

1. If roasting beets yourself, halve them. Place face down in greased baking pan, cover, and bake at 425° until tender, about 20 minutes. Uncover and allow to cool until you can handle them. Peel. Dice.
2. Place onion and garlic in crock. Stir in beets.
3. Add rest of ingredients, except dill, to crock.
4. Cover. Cook on High for 1 hour, then on Low for 5 hours, or until vegetables are tender.
5. Stir in dill. Season to taste with salt and pepper.
6. Find bay leaf and serve.

Tips:

1. When making recipes with bay leaves, I keep an index card next to my slow cooker and make a note on it, saying how many I used. Then I know how many to fish out later on.

2. The same beet pigment that will turn this Stew a beautiful deep ruby color will turn your fingertips pink for days when handling them. Plan ahead and have disposable gloves ready so you won't be caught red-handed!

3. From the tester: This is a great recipe. If you're wary about red beets, you barely taste them, if at all. But they help to make the stew a wonderful rich color.
—A. Catherine Boshart

Chet's Trucker Stew

Janice Muller
Derwood, MD

Makes 10 servings

Prep. Time: 20 minutes
Cooking Time: 3-4 hours
Ideal slow-cooker size: 4-6 qt.

1 lb. Jimmy Dean sausage, cooked and drained
1 lb. ground meat, cooked and drained
27-oz. can pork & beans with juice
14-oz. can wax beans, rinsed and drained
14-oz. can lima beans, rinsed and drained
15-oz. can red kidney beans with juice
15-oz. can white kidney beans (cannellini) with juice
1 cup brown sugar
1 cup ketchup
1 Tbsp. Gulden's Spicy Mustard

1. Combine all ingredients in slow cooker.
2. Cover and cook on High for 3-4 hours, until hot and bubbling.

Variations:

I've varied the beans depending on what I have in the house. Chickpeas are a great substitute if you can't find wax beans.

Good go-alongs with this recipe:

Add a fresh salad, and you have a fun and tasty meal that the kids will love!

Lamb Stew

Dottie Schmidt
Kansas City, MO

Makes 6-8 servings

Prep. Time: 40 minutes
Cooking Time: 6-8 hours
Ideal slow-cooker size: 6 qt.

2 lbs. boneless lamb shoulder roast, cut into 1" cubes (if you can find only a bigger roast, use it anyway, freezing whatever you don't need for this recipe for another time)
½ tsp. sugar
2 Tbsp. oil
1½ tsp. salt
¼ tsp. black pepper
¼ cup flour
2 cups water
15-oz. can chicken broth
2 tsp. Worcestershire sauce
6-8 carrots, sliced
3 small onions, cut into eighths
4 ribs celery, sliced
3 medium potatoes, peeled or not and diced
fresh chopped parsley, optional

1. Grease interior of slow cooker crock.
2. Sprinkle lamb cubes with sugar. Brown in oil in skillet for just a few minutes. Remove lamb cubes, leaving fat behind, and place in slow cooker.
3. Stir salt, pepper, and flour into skillet drippings, then stir in water, broth, and Worcestershire sauce until smooth.
4. Stir and cook over low heat until broth simmers and thickens.
5. Pour sauce into slow cooker over lamb.
6. Add carrots, onions, celery, and potatoes to cooker. Stir.
7. Cover and cook on Low for 6-8 hours, or until lamb and vegetables are tender.
8. Serve meat, vegetables, and broth together in a big bowl. Garnish with fresh parsley if you wish.

Moroccan Beef Stew

Joyce Cox
Port Angeles, WA

Makes 4-6 servings

Prep. Time: 30 minutes
Cooking Time: 8-10 hours
Ideal slow-cooker size: 4 qt.

3 Tbsp. olive oil, divided
5 garlic cloves, minced
2 cups thinly sliced onion
2-lb. beef chuck roast, cut into 2″ cubes, seasoned with salt and pepper
15-oz. can diced tomatoes with juice
1 cup beef broth
1 Tbsp. honey
2 tsp. ground cumin
2 tsp. ground coriander
1 tsp. ground ginger
1 tsp. ground turmeric
1 cinnamon stick
1 bay leaf
1 cup pitted, chopped prunes

1. Heat 1½ Tbsp. olive oil in large frying pan and sauté onions until golden brown. Add garlic and cook 1 more minute. Transfer to slow cooker.
2. Heat remaining 1½ Tbsp. oil in pan. Sear beef cubes on all sides. Transfer to slow cooker.
3. Add rest of ingredients to slow cooker. Stir well.
4. Cover and cook on Low for 8-10 hours. Remove cinnamon stick and bay leaf before serving.

Tips:

Serve over hot cooked couscous or brown rice.

Variations:

Sprinkle servings with chopped parsley and some grated lemon or orange zest.

Tuscan Beef Stew

Orpha Herr
Andover, NY

Makes 12 servings

Prep. Time: 20 minutes
Cooking Time: 8-9 hours
Ideal slow-cooker size: 6 qt.

2 lbs. stew beef, cut into 1″ pieces
10.75-oz. can tomato soup
10.5-oz. can beef broth
½ cup burgundy wine or other red wine
1 tsp. Italian herb seasoning
½ tsp. garlic powder
14.5-oz. can diced Italian-style tomatoes, undrained
½ cup diced onion
3 large carrots, cut in 1″ pieces
2 16-oz. cans cannellini beans, rinsed and drained

1. Stir soup, broth, wine, Italian seasoning, garlic powder, tomatoes, onion, carrots, and beef into slow cooker.
2. Cover and cook on Low 8-9 hours or until vegetables are tender crisp.
3. Stir in beans. Turn to High until heated through, 10-20 minutes more.

Sausage and Kale Stew with Mashed Potatoes

Margaret W. High
Lancaster, PA

Makes 6 servings

Prep. Time: 25 minutes
Cooking Time: 5-7 hours
Ideal slow-cooker size: 6 qt.

4 cups canned tomatoes and juice, roughly crushed
1 large onion, chopped
2-3 garlic cloves, roughly chopped
1 lb. sweet or hot Italian sausage
fresh ground pepper
2-3 large potatoes, scrubbed
7 cups chopped kale
½ cup olive oil
½ cup milk, room temperature
salt

1. Combine tomatoes, onion, garlic, sausage, and several grinds of pepper in bottom of slow cooker.
2. Nestle the whole, unpeeled potatoes down into the tomato mixture.
3. Put the chopped kale on top of everything—it should come up to the top of the slow cooker.
4. Cover. Cook on Low 5-7 hours, until potatoes are soft when pricked and kale is cooked down.
5. Fish the potatoes out of the stew and place in serving dish. Pour in olive oil and milk, and salt to taste. Mash with potato masher until well combined.
6. Cut sausage in serving pieces.
7. To serve, place dollop of mashed potatoes in soup bowl and add some Potato/Sausage/Kale Stew on top.

Tips:

Serve with good bread to mop up the delicious juices.

Variations:

Top with freshly grated Parmesan at the table. Brown sausages before adding to cooker.

Quick Sausage Stew

Beverly Hummel
Fleetwood, PA

Makes 10 servings

Prep. Time: 20 minutes
Cooking Time: 4-5 hours
Ideal slow-cooker size: 7 qt.

1 lb. fresh or Italian sausage, sliced thin
½ cup chopped onion
½ cup chopped bell pepper
1-lb. bag frozen carrots
1-lb. bag frozen green beans
4 medium potatoes, cubed
24-oz. can spaghetti sauce
2 cups water
2 Tbsp. beef bouillon
salt and pepper, to taste
1 Tbsp. Worcestershire sauce

1. Dissolve beef bouillon in the 2 cups water.
2. Brown sausage in skillet. Transfer to slow cooker.
3. Pour in bouillon/water and rest of ingredients.
4. Cover and cook on Low for 4-5 hours.

Tips:

This is a hearty soup, a great way to feed a large group.

Variations:

Substitute ground beef for sausage.

Sausage and Kale Chowder

Beverly Hummel
Fleetwood, PA

Makes 6 servings

Prep. Time: 20 minutes
Cooking Time: 5 hours
Ideal slow-cooker size: 4-5 qt.

1 lb. bulk sausage
1 cup chopped onion
6 small red potatoes, chopped
1 cup thinly sliced kale, ribs removed
6 cups chicken broth
1 cup milk, room temperature
salt and pepper to taste

1. Brown sausage. Drain off grease. Transfer sausage to slow cooker.
2. Add onion, potatoes, kale, and broth.
3. Cook on High for 4 hours, until potatoes and kale are soft.
4. Add milk and cook on Low for 1 hour. Season to taste with salt and pepper.

Tips:

If you prefer a thicker soup, add 2 Tbsp. cornstarch to milk in Step 4 before adding to cooker. Stir several times in the last hour as Chowder thickens.

Good go-alongs with this recipe:

Italian bread and salad.

Zuppa Toscana (Better Than Olive Garden!)

Shelia Heil
Lancaster, PA

Makes 8 servings

Prep. Time: 30 minutes
Cooking Time: 3-6 hours
Ideal slow-cooker size: 6 qt.

1 lb. Italian sausage, sliced
4-6 potatoes, chopped
1 onion, chopped
3-4 garlic cloves, minced
32-oz. carton chicken broth
1 cup chopped kale or Swiss chard
1 cup heavy whipping cream, room temperature
2 Tbsp. flour
salt and pepper, to taste

1. Brown sausage slices in skillet until edges are browned. Transfer to slow cooker.
2. Add potatoes, onion, garlic, and broth to cooker. Add just enough water to cover vegetables and sausage.
3. Cover and cook on High 3-4 hours or Low 5-6 hours, until potatoes are tender.
4. Separately, whisk together flour and cream until smooth.
5. Thirty minutes before serving, add cream/flour mixture to cooker. Stir. Add kale.
6. Cook on High for 30 minutes, until broth thickens slightly. Taste for salt and pepper, and adjust as needed.

Variations:

If you prefer to prepare without milk products, skip the cream and flour mixture. It is delicious either way.

Good go-alongs with this recipe:

Good served with crusty bread.

Kale and Friends Winter Soup

Bob Coffey
New Windsor, NY

Makes 12 servings

Prep. Time: 20 minutes
Cooking Time: 8 hours
Ideal slow-cooker size: 5.5 qt.

1 bunch of kale, torn into bite-sized pieces
1 butternut squash, peeled and cubed
2 15-oz. cans cannellini beans, drained and rinsed
1 cup diced, cooked chicken
4-6 cups chicken broth
1 tsp. dried basil
½ tsp. dried rosemary
½ tsp. dried thyme
salt and pepper, to taste

1. Combine all ingredients in slow cooker.
2. Cover and cook on Low 8 hours.
3. Taste to correct seasonings. Add more broth if too thick or you're trying to stretch the soup.

Tips:

If using frozen squash, wait until the final 20 minutes of cooking to add.

Variations:

Use any herbs you like (I'd avoid dill). Use fresh herbs if you have some on hand, but add in the last 20 minutes of cooking.

Good go-alongs with this recipe:

With some hot garlic bread or Texas toast and a fresh salad, this is a satisfying meal.

My tricks for getting my slow cooker to do its best work:

As with every broth-based soup, good-quality stock is the key. Find a brand you trust, or better yet, make your own and freeze until you need.

Kale Chowder

Colleen Heatwole
Burton, MI

Makes 8 servings

Prep. Time: 30 minutes
Cooking Time: 4 to 6 hours
Ideal slow-cooker size: 5 qt.
8 cups chicken broth

1 bunch kale, cleaned, stems removed, coarsely chopped
2 lbs. potatoes, peeled and diced
4 garlic cloves, minced
1 medium onion, diced
1 lb. cooked ham
½ tsp. pepper, or to taste

1. Combine all ingredients in slow cooker.
2. Cover and cook on Low 4-6 hours, until vegetables are tender.

Tips:

I made this often this summer and fall when we had kale in our garden. It was a hit with the entire family.

Variations:

Turkey ham can be used instead of regular ham.

Good go-alongs with this recipe:

I like to serve this Chowder with applesauce.

Kielbasa Soup

Janie Steele
Moore, OK

Makes 6-8 servings

Prep. Time: 20 minutes
Cooking Time: 5 hours
Ideal slow-cooker size: 4 qt.

1 lb. kielbasa, sliced thin
8 cups chicken broth
2 14-oz. cans cannellini beans with juice
1 onion, diced
1 bay leaf
1 tsp. dried thyme
¼ tsp. red pepper flakes
8 oz. rainbow rotini, uncooked
3 cloves garlic, minced
1 lb. chopped fresh spinach
salt and pepper, to taste

1. In skillet, brown kielbasa slices over high heat until some edges are brown.
2. Transfer kielbasa to slow cooker.
3. Add broth, beans, onion, bay leaf, thyme, and red pepper to slow cooker.
4. Cover and cook on Low for 4 hours.
5. Add rotini and garlic. Cook an additional hour on Low, or until pasta is as tender as you like it.
6. Stir in chopped spinach. Add salt and pepper to taste. Remove bay leaf.

Sausage and Cabbage Soup

Donna Suter
Pandora, OH

Makes 6-8 servings

Prep. Time: 20 minutes
Cooking Time: 6-8 hours
Ideal slow-cooker size: 4 qt.

1 lb. Bob Evans sausage
32-oz. carton vegetable broth
14-oz. can chicken broth
1 onion, chopped
½ head cabbage, chopped
4-6 ribs celery, sliced
6-8 carrots, peeled and chopped
4 cloves garlic, chopped
2 tsp. dried basil
1 tsp. salt
½ tsp. pepper

1. Brown sausage in skillet and drain off grease. Transfer sausage to slow cooker.
2. Add rest of ingredients to slow cooker.
3. Cover and cook on Low for 6-8 hours.

Cabbage and Beef Soup

Colleen Heatwole
Burton, MI

Makes 6-8 servings

Prep. Time: 20 minutes
Cooking Time: 6-8 hours
Ideal slow-cooker size: 5 qt.

1 lb. lean ground beef
½ tsp. garlic salt
¼ tsp. onion powder
¼ tsp. garlic powder
¼ tsp. pepper
16-oz. can kidney beans, undrained
2 ribs celery, chopped
½ medium head cabbage, chopped
1 can tomatoes, 28-32 oz., or 1 quart home-canned tomatoes
4 cups water
4 bouillon cubes
chopped fresh parsley, for garnish

1. Brown beef in large skillet. Add tomatoes and chop coarsely. Transfer to slow cooker.
2. Add remaining ingredients, except parsley.
3. Cover and cook 6-8 hours on Low.
4. Serve in bowls garnished with fresh parsley.

Variations:

Lean ground turkey can be used. Black beans or small red beans may be substituted for kidney beans. This soup freezes well.

My tricks for getting my slow cooker to do its best work:

If you plan to have this for dinner, you need to start early in the day. Starting on High and decreasing to Low can be helpful.

Stuffed Pepper Soup

Shelia Heil
Lancaster, PA

Makes 8-10 servings

Prep. Time: 45 minutes
Cooking Time: 3 hours
Ideal slow-cooker size: 6 qt.

1 lb. ground beef
1 small onion, diced
1 large green bell pepper, diced
26-oz. can diced tomatoes
10-oz. can condensed tomato soup
14-oz. can beef or chicken broth
2 cups cooked rice
1 Tbsp. sugar
1 tsp. garlic powder
salt and pepper, to taste

1. In a large skillet, brown beef, cutting into small pieces as it browns.
2. Add peppers and onions and fry briefly. Drain off drippings. Transfer mixture to slow cooker.
3. Add rest of ingredients. Stir.
4. Cover and cook on Low 3-4 hours, to meld flavors.

Variations:

May substitute frozen mixed vegetables for the green pepper. Still delicious, except that it becomes a stuffed vegetable soup.

Sausage Lentil Soup

Marcia S. Myer
Manheim, PA

Makes 8 servings

Prep. Time: 20 minutes
Cooking Time: 4½ hours
Ideal slow-cooker size: 5 qt.

1 lb. fresh chorizo sausage
1 onion, chopped
2 ribs celery, chopped
2 large carrots, chopped
2 cloves garlic, minced
4 cups chopped tomatoes with juice
2 quarts chicken broth
2 cups red lentils
juice from ½ lime
1 cup chopped spinach
salt and pepper, to taste

1. In skillet, brown chorizo. Transfer to slow cooker.
2. Add onion, celery, carrots, garlic, tomatoes, broth, and red lentils.
3. Cook on High for 4 hours.
4. Add lime juice, spinach, and salt and pepper to taste. Cook an additional 20 minutes.

Savory Lentil Soup

Margaret W. High
Lancaster, PA

Makes 6 servings

Prep. Time: 15 minutes
Cooking Time: 5 hours
Ideal slow-cooker size: 4 qt.

1½ cups dry lentils
4 cups beef stock
1½ cups water
½ cup red wine
1 onion, chopped
2 carrots, diced
2 Tbsp. olive oil
1 bay leaf
1 tsp. salt
¼ tsp. freshly ground pepper
1½ tsp. dried oregano
½ tsp. cumin
½ cup tomato sauce or 1 Tbsp. tomato paste
3 Tbsp. red wine vinegar
½ cup chopped fresh parsley
½ cup sliced black olives
2 garlic cloves, minced

1. Combine lentils, stock, water, wine, onion, carrots, olive oil, bay leaf, salt, pepper, oregano, and cumin in slow cooker.
2. Cook on Low 4 hours.
3. Add tomato sauce, vinegar, parsley, olives, and garlic. Cook on Low 1 more hour.

Tips:

I love to use homemade beef stock in this soup. Adjust salt in the soup as needed, depending on the saltiness of your stock/broth.

Variations:

Use chicken broth in place of beef. Use thyme instead of oregano and cumin. Use lemon juice instead of red wine vinegar. Omit parsley and black olives.

—Judy Buller

Red Lentil Soup

Carolyn Spohn
Shawnee, KS

Makes 4-6 servings

Prep. Time: 20 minutes
Cooking Time: 3-4 hours
Ideal slow-cooker size: 5 qt.

¾ cup red lentils
½ cup brown rice, uncooked
4 cups vegetable broth
1 small potato, diced
2 medium carrots, chopped
1 small onion, chopped
2 cloves garlic, chopped
½ tsp. turmeric
¼ tsp. ground cumin
¼ tsp. ground coriander
salt and pepper, to taste
plain yogurt, for serving

1. Combine all ingredients except plain yogurt in slow cooker.
2. Cover and cook on High for 3-4 hours, until vegetables are soft.
3. Puree with immersion blender until smooth.
4. Serve in bowls with a little plain yogurt dolloped on top.

Tips:

Other orange-colored vegetables can be used with or instead of carrots. Red or orange sweet peppers and/or butternut squash are good. This is a very flexible soup, as you can vary the vegetables according to what you have on hand.

Variations:

Sprinkle with chopped cilantro.

Good go-alongs with this recipe:

Pita bread and a green salad.

Scotch Broth

Jean Turner
Williams Lake, British Columbia

Makes 6-8 servings

Prep. Time: 15 minutes
Cooking Time: 4 hours
Ideal slow-cooker size: 4 qt.

2 lbs. lamb shoulder meat, chopped
6 cups water
1 large onion, chopped
1 cup chopped celery
1 cup diced carrots
⅓ cup pearl barley
½ cup yellow or green split peas, rinsed and picked over
1 tsp. salt
¼ tsp. ground black pepper
1 bay leaf
3 Tbsp. chopped fresh parsley

1. Combine all ingredients in slow cooker except parsley.
2. Cover and cook on High for 3-4 hours, until meat is tender and split peas are done.
3. Stir in parsley. Remove bay leaf before serving.

Tips:

Great with garlic bread for supper on a cold night.

Variations:

Beef can be used in place of lamb.

Vegetarian Split Pea Soup

Colleen Heatwole
Burton, MI

Makes 6 servings

Prep. Time: 30 minutes
Cooking Time: 5-6 hours
Ideal slow-cooker size: 5 qt.

1 lb. split peas, sorted and rinsed
2 quarts vegetable broth
2 cups water
1 large onion, minced
2 cloves garlic, minced
3 ribs celery, chopped
3 medium carrots, chopped finely
2 bay leaves
1 Tbsp. kosher salt
1 tsp. black pepper

1. Combine all ingredients and add to slow cooker.
2. Cook on Low 5-6 hours. If creamy texture is desired, blend with immersion blender.

Tips:

I like best served with artisan bread.

Variations:

This easily converts to non-vegetarian by adding 2-4 cups diced ham. Other broth such as chicken or beef can be substituted successfully if you are going non-vegetarian. Add 1-2 tsp. dried herbs such as thyme, marjoram, and rosemary.

My tricks for getting my slow cooker to do its best work:

My cookers vary in temperature and my 7-quart one runs very hot. So, I set High recipes to Low. It is important to know how your slow cooker functions.

Split Pea Soup

Phyllis Good
Lancaster, PA

Makes 8-10 servings

Prep. Time: 20 minutes
Cooking Time: 4-8 hours
Ideal slow-cooker size: 6 qt.

3 cups dried split peas (a little over 1 pound)
3 quarts water
½ tsp. garlic powder
½ tsp. dried oregano
1 cup of diced, or thinly sliced, carrots
1 cup chopped celery
1 tsp. salt
¼-½ tsp. pepper (coarsely ground is great)
1 ham shank or hock

1. Put all ingredients into slow cooker, except the ham. Stir well.
2. Settle ham into mixture.
3. Cover. Cook on Low 4-8 hours, or until ham is tender and falling off the bone, and the peas are very soft.
4. Use a slotted spoon to lift the ham bone out of the soup. Allow it to cook until you can handle it without burning yourself.
5. Cut the ham into bite-sized pieces. Stir it back into the soup.
6. Heat the soup for 10 minutes, and then serve.

Spring Pea Soup

Ary Bruno
Stevenson, MD

Makes 4-6 servings

Prep. Time: 15 minutes
Cooking Time: 4 hours
Ideal slow-cooker size: 4 qt.

2 cups fresh shelled peas
3 cups chicken stock
1 rib celery, minced
2 green onions, minced
1 Tbsp. fresh chopped mint, divided
pinch dried thyme
salt, to taste
1 cup milk, room temperature
2 Tbsp. flour

1. Place peas, stock, celery, onions, ½ Tbsp. mint, and thyme in slow cooker.
2. Cover and cook on Low for 3 hours, until peas are tender.
3. Add remaining ½ Tbsp. mint.
4. Use immersion blender to puree soup.
5. Whisk together milk and flour. Whisk into soup and cook on High for 30-40 minutes, until thickened.

Curried Chickpea Stew

Shari Jensen
Fountain, CO

Makes 6 servings

Prep. Time: 10 minutes
Cooking Time: 5 hours
Ideal slow-cooker size: 5 qt.

1½ lbs. chicken breast tenders, cubed, or 3-4 cups cubed leftover chicken or turkey
1 medium onion, diced
2 carrots, sliced thinly
2 cloves garlic, minced
14.5-oz. can petite diced tomatoes
15-oz. can garbanzo beans, drained and rinsed
15-oz. can black beans, drained and rinsed
15-oz. can pumpkin
1 cup frozen corn
2-3 chicken bouillon cubes
2 cups water
2 tsp. curry powder
¾ tsp. ground cumin
1 tsp. salt
1 tsp. coarsely ground pepper
14-oz. can evaporated milk
hot steamed rice, for serving
raisins, chopped cilantro, shredded coconut, finely chopped cashews or peanuts, optional

1. Place all ingredients, except the evaporated milk, rice, and toppings, in slow cooker. Stir gently until well mixed.
2. Cover and cook on Low 4 hours, or until chicken is white through the middle and tender.
3. Stir in evaporated milk 20 minutes before end of cooking time.
4. Serve Stew over steamed rice.
5. Pass the optional toppings at the table for diners to add on their own.

My tricks for getting my slow cooker to do its best work:

The hardest thing for me is keeping the children from lifting the lid during the cooking process. They love to sneak bites once the aroma begins to waft through the house. I set a little bowl of raisins and peanuts on the counter near the slow cooker so they can pick at those instead.

Pasta e Ceci

Margaret W. High
Lancaster, PA

Makes 4-6 servings

Prep. Time: 15 minutes
Cooking Time: 5-6 hours
Standing Time: 8-12 hours
Ideal slow-cooker size: 4 qt.

1½ cups dry garbanzo beans
1 tsp. dried rosemary
3 cloves garlic, chopped, divided
1 bay leaf
1 tsp. salt
fresh ground pepper, to taste
1 cup canned tomatoes with juice, roughly crushed
3 Tbsp. olive oil
1-2 cups small uncooked pasta, such as ditalini or orzo
Parmesan cheese, for serving

1. Soak garbanzos in slow cooker in water to cover by 2" overnight.
2. Add rosemary, half the garlic, and bay leaf. Cover and cook on Low until soft, 4-5 hours, depending on age of garbanzos.
3. Remove 1 cup garbanzos, leaving behind cooking liquid. Set aside. Remove bay leaf and discard.
4. Use an immersion blender to puree remaining garbanzos and liquid in crock.
5. Add whole chickpeas back to pureed chickpeas. Add remaining garlic, salt, pepper, tomatoes, and olive oil. Add more rosemary if you wish. Add more liquid (tomato juice, water, or white wine) if needed to achieve stew consistency.
6. Cook on Low 1-2 hours.
7. To serve, cook pasta according to package directions. Place some pasta in each soup bowl and ladle garbanzo mixture over top. Serve with Parmesan cheese at the table.

Variations:

Add chopped carrots or spinach to Step 5.

Good go-alongs with this recipe:

Good bread, dipped in olive oil; green salad.

Turkey and Garbanzo Soup

Michele Ruvola
Vestal, NY

Makes 7 servings

Prep. Time: 10 minutes
Cooking Time: 6-8 hours
Ideal slow-cooker size: 5-6½ qt.

1 lb. lean ground turkey
1 yellow onion, chopped
2 garlic cloves, chopped
3 Tbsp. chopped poblano pepper
1 cup diced carrots
1 cup diced celery
28-oz. can petite diced tomatoes
2 15-oz. cans garbanzo beans, drained
2 cups low-sodium, 99% fat-free chicken broth
2 tsp. turmeric
2 tsp. paprika
1 tsp. ground coriander
2 bay leaves
½ tsp. crushed red pepper flakes
2 tsp. coarse salt
2 Tbsp. chopped fresh Italian parsley or spearmint

1. Cook turkey in skillet for 10-12 minutes, until no longer pink. Transfer to slow cooker.
2. Add onion, garlic, pepper, carrots, celery, tomatoes, garbanzos, chicken broth, turmeric, paprika, coriander, bay leaves, red pepper flakes, and salt.
3. Cover and cook on Low for 6-8 hours. Remove bay leaves.
4. Stir in parsley or spearmint.

Tips:

Serve with warm crusty bread.

Vegetarian Peanut Stew

Willard Roth
Elkhart, IN

Makes 8 servings

Prep. Time: 15 minutes
Cooking Time: 4-10 hours
Ideal slow-cooker size: 5 qt.

3 cloves garlic
2 cups loosely filled chopped cilantro, leaves and stems
28-oz. can diced tomatoes
½ cup peanut butter (chunky is best)
2 tsp. ground cumin
½ tsp. ground cinnamon
¼ tsp. cayenne pepper, or to taste
¼ tsp. salt
1 cup water
4 medium sweet potatoes (about 3 lbs.), unpeeled or peeled, cut in 2″ chunks
15-oz. can garbanzo beans, drained
16-oz. pkg. frozen green beans

1. Combine garlic, cilantro, tomatoes, peanut butter, cumin, cinnamon, cayenne pepper, and salt in blender or food processor. Blend to puree, then pour into slow cooker.
2. Stir in water, sweet potatoes, and garbanzo beans.
3. Cook 8-10 hours on Low, or 4-5 hours on High.
4. Cook green beans separately until as soft as you like them. Add to Stew 5 minutes before serving.

Ham and Bean Stew

Sharon Wantland
Menomonee Falls, WI

Makes 4-6 servings

Prep. Time: 15 minutes
Cooking Time: 5-7 hours
Ideal slow-cooker size: 3 qt.

2 16-oz. cans baked beans
2 medium potatoes, peeled and cubed
2 cups cubed ham
2 ribs celery, chopped
1 onion, chopped
½ cup water
1 Tbsp. cider vinegar

1. In a slow cooker combine all ingredients. Mix well.
2. Cover and cook on Low for 5-7 hours, or until the potatoes are tender.

As a young married woman, I tried Irish stew first, but I overfilled the crock. The stew simmered over and down the sides and cooked the finish right off the metal surface! But the stew was delicious; I still make it regularly. —Amy Giannini, Zumbrota, MN

Black Bean Ham Soup

Colleen Heatwole
Burton, MI

Makes 8 servings

Prep. Time: 30 minutes
Cooking Time: 6-8 hours
Ideal slow-cooker size: 5 qt.

2 cups chopped carrots
1 cup chopped celery
2 garlic cloves, minced
1 medium onion, chopped
2 15.5-oz. cans black beans, undrained
2 14.5-oz. cans chicken or vegetable broth
15-oz. can crushed tomatoes
1½ tsp. dried basil
½ tsp. dried oregano
½ tsp. ground cumin
½ tsp. chili powder
¼ tsp. hot pepper sauce
1 cup diced cooked ham

1. Combine all ingredients in slow cooker.
2. Cover and cook on Low 6-8 hours or until vegetables are tender.

Tips:

Serve with hot cooked rice. Brown rice is more nutritious.

My tips for converting oven and stove-top recipes into good slow cooker recipes:

I don't bother sautéing onions and veggies in advance. In my experience it has not seemed to make a difference, especially when you are using a lot of ingredients.

Spicy Bean Soup

Becky Harder
Monument, CO

Makes 10 servings

Prep. Time: 30 minutes
Cooking Time: 6-8 hours
Ideal slow-cooker size: 6 qt.

16-oz. bag uncooked lentils, rinsed and picked over
2 15-oz. cans garbanzo beans, rinsed and drained
2 15-oz. cans kidney beans, rinsed and drained
2 15-oz. cans pinto beans, rinsed and drained
¼ cup bulgar wheat
6-oz. can tomato paste
2 vegetable bouillon cubes
8 cups water
½ cup chopped onions
½ cup chopped green or red bell pepper
1 jalapeño, minced
1 cup sliced carrots
3 cloves garlic, chopped
2 Tbsp. Italian herb seasoning
salt and pepper to taste

1. Combine all ingredients in slow cooker.
2. Cover and cook on Low for 6-8 hours, stirring once, until lentils and bulgar are tender.

Good go-alongs with this recipe:

Cornbread.

Slow-Cooker Bean Soup

Lois Ostrander
Lebanon, PA

Makes 8 servings

Prep. Time: 20 minutes
Cooking Time: 5-7 hours
Ideal slow-cooker size: 3 qt.

1 ham hock
40.5-oz. can Great Northern beans, rinsed and drained
1 medium onion, chopped
1 carrot, chopped
4-5 medium-sized potatoes, chopped
2 Tbsp. Mrs. Dash
32-oz. box chicken broth

1. Mix all ingredients in slow cooker, being sure ham hock is completely covered.
2. Cook on High for 3 hours, then turn down to Low for 2 hours.
3. Take out ham hock. Remove ham from bone, and chop ham into bite-sized pieces.
4. Return ham to slow cooker. Cook on Low an additional 30 minutes.

Tips:

It is better if it sits for a day. It will be watery at first and then it will thicken after setting.

Variations:

Cook 6-7 hours on Low. Add carrots halfway through cooking time so they keep their color.

Good go-alongs with this recipe:

Crusty bread.

Linguica and Navy Bean Soup

Bob Coffey
New Windsor, NY

Makes 8-10 servings

***Prep. Time:* 20 minutes**
***Cooking Time:* 8 hours**
***Standing Time:* 8 hours or overnight**
***Ideal slow-cooker size:* 5.5 qt.**

2 cups dry navy beans, picked over and well rinsed
1 Tbsp. olive oil
1 link linguica, chopped
3 large onions, diced
2 ribs celery, diced
5 garlic cloves, chopped
2 cups chicken broth
4-5 cups water
2 cups fresh baby spinach
coarse salt
freshly ground pepper

1. The night before cooking the soup, place beans in bowl and add water to cover them by at least 1". In the morning, drain off the soaking water. Rinse the beans.
2. In a small skillet, heat olive oil and brown linguica. Transfer to slow cooker.
3. In same skillet, cook onion for 3-5 minutes. Add garlic and cook for 1 minute more. Transfer to slow cooker.
4. Add celery, broth, 4 cups water, and rinsed beans to slow cooker.
5. Cover and cook on High for 1 hour, then Low for 7 hours or until beans are done but still firm.
6. Twenty minutes before serving, stir in baby spinach. Season soup to taste with coarse salt and freshly ground pepper.

Tips:

I first learned about linguica when my supermarket had links on clearance. The package sat in my freezer for a few months before I decided to see how it would be in a basic white bean soup. It worked well, but you could substitute chorizo or any slightly spicy sausage.

My tricks for getting my slow cooker to do its best work:

Nothing makes me feel more like a chef than turning a bag of dried beans into a satisfying meal; there are just a few tricks to being successful:

1. Always sort through beans for stones or anything that doesn't belong.
2. Rinse beans well before soaking overnight and make sure to cover them by at least 1" of water.
3. Rinse the beans again in the morning—the importance of this cannot be overstated!
4. When prepping the recipe the first thing I'll do is put my slow cooker on High with a bit of water in the bottom; this way it comes up to temperature quickly and will help in the proper cooking of the beans. Once you have a good feel for your cooker you'll know exactly how much time the beans will need to be tender and full of flavor.
5. If your beans come with a seasoning packet then throw it away! Those things are nothing more than pouches of salt and can't compare to fresh herbs and spices.
6. Don't add salt until the very end of the recipe—if you add it too early it will thicken the skins of the beans and no matter how long they cook they'll be mealy.

Italian Wedding Soup

Janie Steele
Moore, OK

Makes 6 servings

***Prep. Time:* 30 minutes**
***Cooking Time:* 3-7 hours**
***Ideal slow-cooker size:* 3-4 qt.**

2 eggs
½ cup bread crumbs
¼ cup chopped fresh parsley
2 Tbsp. grated Parmesan cheese
3 cloves garlic, minced
¼ tsp. red pepper flakes
½ lb. ground beef or turkey
½ lb. spicy pork sausage, casings removed
2 32-oz. cartons chicken broth
salt and pepper, to taste
⅔ cup uncooked pasta
1 cup chopped fresh spinach

1. Mix eggs, bread crumbs, parsley, garlic, red pepper flakes, ground meat, and sausage.
2. Form mixture into 1" meatballs. Brown in skillet or oven.
3. Transfer meatballs to slow cooker. Add chicken broth, salt, pepper, and pasta.
4. Cook on High for 3-4 hours or Low 6-7, adding spinach 30 minutes before end of cooking.

Herbed Spinach Borscht

Sharon Timpe
Jackson, WI

Makes 4-6 servings

Prep. Time: 30 minutes
Cooking Time: 3-5 hours
Ideal slow-cooker size: 4 qt.

3 small red-skinned potatoes, cut in ½" cubes
⅔ cup chopped carrots
⅓ cup chopped onion
5 cups chicken stock
½ tsp. dried tarragon
2 Tbsp. chopped fresh parsley
2 cups torn fresh spinach
1 tsp. lemon juice or cider vinegar
salt and pepper, to taste
2 hard-boiled eggs, sliced
finely chopped fresh chives, for garnish

1. In slow cooker, place potatoes, carrots, onion, chicken stock, tarragon, parsley, salt, and pepper.
2. Cover and cook on Low 5 hours or High 3 hours until vegetables are tender, but still hold their shape.
3. Fifteen minutes before serving, stir in spinach and lemon juice or cider vinegar. Correct seasonings if necessary.
4. Serve in soup bowls, garnished with sliced eggs and chives.

Tips:

This soup is good as a first course or a light lunch with sandwiches.

Good go-alongs with this recipe:

Bread sticks wrapped with half slices of bacon and baked in an oven until the bacon is crisp. I use partially cooked bacon for less grease.

Tortellini & Spinach Soup

Shari Jensen
Fountain, CO

Makes 6 servings

Prep. Time: 10 minutes
Cooking Time: 3-4 hours
Ideal slow-cooker size: 5 qt.

6 cups chicken broth
2 cups water
8 oz. fresh mushrooms, sliced
5-oz. can sliced water chestnuts, coarsely chopped
½ lb. fresh spinach, rinsed well, stems removed
2-3 cups imitation crab meat
1 tsp. dried basil
16-oz. pkg. cheese or artichoke tortellini
grated Parmesan cheese, for serving
5 green onions, sliced, for serving

1. In slow cooker, combine broth, water, mushrooms, water chestnuts, spinach, crab, basil, and tortellini.
2. Cover and cook on High for 3-4 hours, until tortellini is just tender. This depends on the brand and filling of tortellini.
3. Garnish each serving with Parmesan and chopped green onions.

Cooked pasta and rice should usually be added to the slow cooker during the last half hour of cooking time to keep them from turning to mush or completely disintegrating.

Creamy Zucchini Soup

Debbie Tissot
Albuquerque, NM

Makes 8 servings

Prep. Time: 20 minutes
Cooking Time: 4-5 hours
Ideal slow-cooker size: 4 qt.

4 cups diced fresh green zucchini, unpeeled
2 cups water
2 vegetable bouillon cubes
1 medium onion, chopped finely
2 cloves garlic, chopped finely
1 cup diced fresh mushrooms
1 Tbsp. dried basil
1 tsp. dried tarragon
¼ tsp. black pepper
salt, to taste
8 oz. cream cheese, room temperature, cubed
1 carrot, grated
3 Tbsp. fresh chopped parsley

1. In slow cooker, combine zucchini, water, bouillon, onion, garlic, mushrooms, basil, tarragon, pepper, and salt.
2. Cover and cook on Low for 4 hours.
3. Remove 2 cups of soup and puree in blender with lid ajar so steam can escape. Return puree to slow cooker.
4. Add cream cheese, carrot, and parsley. Stir. Cook an additional 30 minutes on Low, until cream cheese is melted and soup is heated through.

Tips:

Serve with croutons on top.

Potato Broccoli Soup

Janice Crist
Quinter, KS

Makes 8-10 servings

Prep. Time: 20 minutes
Cooking Time: 5½ hours
Ideal slow-cooker size: 6 qt.

2½ cups peeled, cubed potatoes
1 cup diced celery
1 cup diced carrots
1 small onion, diced
2 10-oz. cans cream of chicken soup
4 chicken bouillon cubes
4 cups water
3-4 cups chopped broccoli, fresh or frozen
1 cup cubed sharp cheese

1. In slow cooker, combine potatoes, celery, carrots, onion, chicken soup, bouillon, and water.
2. Cover and cook on Low for 5 hours.
3. Add broccoli and cheese. Cook additional 30 minutes on Low. Stir before serving.

My tricks for getting my slow cooker to do its best work:

I received a slow cooker with stirring paddles for Christmas. I think I will like using them for soups. So far I learned not to use the heavy-duty ones for tortellini soup. It tasted great, but looked like mush. It also has a Warm setting and I can use the timer so it will automatically go to that setting from High or Low. Think I am going to like that when I'm at work all day for recipes that cook for shorter times, like 6 hours. Still experimenting with it.

I have a soup party every year as a great way to break up winter up here in upstate New York. People bring their soup in their slow cookers; we've had as many as 14 different soups. It's an unusual party when you have to cook in order to come to it, but people actually ask if they can come! — Bonnie Sorensen, Laurens, NY

Simple Potato Soup

Joyce Cox
Port Angeles, WA

Makes 6 servings

Prep. Time: 10 minutes
Cooking Time: 6 hours
Ideal slow-cooker size: 4 qt.

6 potatoes, peeled and diced
5 cups low-sodium vegetable broth
2 cups diced onions
½ cup diced celery
½ cup diced carrots
¼ tsp. ground pepper
1½ cups evaporated milk
3 Tbsp. chopped fresh parsley

1. Combine potatoes, broth, onions, celery, carrots, and pepper in slow cooker.
2. Cover and cook on Low for 6 hours or until vegetables are tender.
3. Stir in evaporated milk and parsley. Taste to correct seasonings. Allow to heat on Low an additional 30 minutes.

Good go-alongs with this recipe:

Hot crusty bread with fresh butter.

Potato Soup

A. Catherine Boshart
Lebanon, PA

Makes 8 servings

Prep. Time: 20 minutes
Cooking Time: 6-7 hours
Ideal slow-cooker size: 6 qt.

5 lbs. potatoes, peeled and diced
1 medium onion, chopped
2 ribs celery, sliced
2 carrots, diced
½ lb. smoked turkey chunks
1 chicken bouillon cube
1 tsp. ground cumin
5 cups chicken or vegetable broth
1 Tbsp. salt
pepper, to taste
12-oz. can evaporated milk
2 Tbsp. fresh chopped parsley

1. Place all ingredients in slow cooker except milk and parsley.
2. Cook on Low 6-7 hours, until veggies are tender, adding milk and parsley in the last 30 minutes of cooking.

Variations:

Use your choice of meats: ham, bacon, or sausage.

Good go-alongs with this recipe:

Veggie trays and crackers with spreads are good with this soup.

Steak and Wild Rice Soup

Sally Holzem
Schofield, WI

Makes 6 servings

Prep. Time: 15 minutes
Cooking Time: 5 hours

4 cups beef stock
3 cups cubed, cooked roast beef
4 oz. sliced fresh mushrooms
½ cup chopped onion
¼ cup ketchup
2 tsp. cider vinegar
1 tsp. brown sugar
1 tsp. Worcestershire sauce
⅛ tsp. ground mustard
1½ cups cooked wild rice
1 cup frozen peas

1. Combine stock, beef, mushrooms, onion, ketchup, vinegar, sugar, Worcestershire sauce, and mustard in slow cooker.
2. Cook on Low 4 hours.
3. Add rice and peas. Cook an additional hour on Low.

Tips:

Great way to use up scraps of meat and broth left from a roast beef, and a nice way to transform leftover wild rice.

Good go-alongs with this recipe:

Crusty rolls and a green salad.

Hearty Green Bean Soup

Gladys Voth
Hesston, KS

Makes 6-8 servings

Prep. Time: 15-20 minutes
Cooking Time: 3-6 hours
Ideal slow-cooker size: 4 qt.

1 Tbsp. olive oil
1 cup diced onion
3 carrots, ½″ slices
3 cups 1″ pieces sweet and white potatoes
2-3 cups fresh or frozen cut green beans
1-1½ cups diced ham
¼ tsp. black pepper
salt, to taste
4 cups vegetable broth
2 cups water
1 Tbsp. dried parsley

1. Place all ingredients, except parsley, in slow cooker.
2. Cover and cook on Low 5-6 hours or on High 3-4 hours.
3. In the last 30 minutes of cooking time, crush parsley with fingers and add to soup.

My tips for converting oven and stove-top recipes into good slow-cooker recipes:

To speed the cooking process, cut vegetables into similar-sized pieces.

Some new slow cookers cook hotter and faster than older models. So get to know your slow cooker. I suggest a range of cooking times for many of the recipes since cookers vary. When you've found the right length of time for a recipe done in your cooker, write that in your cookbook. It will save you time and worry the next time you make the dish.

Three-Cheese Broccoli Soup

Deb Kepiro
Strasburg, PA

Makes 8 servings

Prep. Time: 15 Minutes
Cooking Time: 7-9 hours on Low or 4-6 hours on High
Ideal slow-cooker size: 4-5 qt.

4 cups chicken or vegetable broth
2 cups 2% milk
2 10-oz. bags frozen broccoli florets
½ cup very finely diced white onion
½ tsp. black pepper
½ tsp. kosher salt
½ tsp. ground nutmeg
3 cups three different grated cheeses, preferably Jarlsberg, Gruyère, and sharp cheddar

1. In slow cooker, combine broth, milk, broccoli, onion, pepper, salt, and nutmeg.
2. Cook on Low for 5-6 hours or High for 2-3, until onion is soft.
3. Add cheese 20 minutes before serving. Cheese may be stringy and stick to broccoli—that's fine.

Good go-alongs with this recipe:

Serve with your favorite rolls or drop biscuits.

Corn Chowder

Colleen Heatwole
Burton, MI

Makes 8 servings

Prep. Time: 20 minutes
Cooking Time: 5-6 hours on Low
Ideal slow-cooker size: 5 qt.

½ cup diced bacon
4 cups peeled, chopped potatoes, about 4 medium potatoes
1 medium onion, chopped
2 cups water
3 cups cream-style corn
2 tsp. salt
½ tsp. pepper
2 cups half-and-half

1. Fry bacon in skillet until crisp. Crumble and drain, reserving 2 Tbsp. of bacon drippings.
2. Add bacon and drippings to slow cooker.
3. Add potatoes, onion, water, corn, salt, and pepper.
4. Cover and cook on Low for 5-6 hours, until potatoes and onions are soft.
5. Warm half-and-half in saucepan or microwave until steaming hot. Do not boil. Add half-and-half to Chowder just before serving.

Tips:

Sprinkle with parsley before serving, either dried or fresh. Add some diced celery and shredded carrot to Step 3. Use diced ham in place of bacon.

Good go-alongs with this recipe:

I like to serve croutons with each bowl of Chowder and apple salad on the side. Apples add color to a yellow meal.

French Onion Soup

Linda Kosa-Postl
Granite Falls, WA

Makes 6 servings

Prep. Time: 30 minutes
Cooking Time: 8 hours
Ideal slow-cooker size: 4 qt.

3 Tbsp. butter
1 Tbsp. olive oil
6 cups thinly sliced onion
6 cups beef stock
1 cup red wine
1 bay leaf
1 tsp. salt
½ tsp. sugar
½ tsp. dried thyme
¼ tsp. fresh ground pepper
3 Tbsp. flour
1 cup water

1. Place butter, olive oil, and onions in slow cooker. Cover and cook on High for 4 hours. Onions should be soft and turning brown.
2. Add beef stock, wine, bay leaf, salt, sugar, thyme, and pepper.
3. Cover and cook on Low for 4 hours.
4. Whisk together flour and water. Stir into soup. Cook an additional 30-40 minutes on Low until thickened.

Tips:

Serve with bread and cheese on the side. Alternatively, place slices of bread under the broiler. When just turning toasty, place sliced cheese on bread. Broil. When browned and bubbly, cut into cubes and sprinkle on top of French Onion Soup in soup bowls.

Variations:

Sauté onions in ½ cup butter in skillet just until tender. Transfer to cooker and continue with Step 2, omitting thyme and adding 2 more bay leaves. Cook for 5-7 hours on Low.

—Frances Kruba

Butternut Soup

Gladys Voth
Hesston, KS

Makes 4-6 servings

Prep. Time: 15 minutes
Cooking Time: 2-4 hours
Ideal slow-cooker size: 4 qt.

2 Tbsp. coconut oil, or vegetable oil
½ cup chopped onion
¼ cup chopped green bell pepper
2 cups chopped butternut squash, peeled, seeds removed, cut into 1" pieces
1 large apple, peeled and chopped
1 clove garlic, minced
1 Tbsp. fresh ginger, finely diced
2 cups vegetable broth
13.5-oz. can coconut milk
parsley sprigs or toasted coconut, for garnish

1. Heat coconut oil in skillet. Sauté onion and green pepper until onion is slightly transparent. Place into slow cooker.
2. Add butternut squash, apple, minced garlic, and ginger.
3. Pour vegetable broth and coconut milk over ingredients.
4. Cook on High 2 hours or Low 3-4 hours.
5. Puree soup with an immersion blender, or carefully transfer to stand blender and puree with lid slightly ajar to allow steam to escape.
6. Serve in bowls, garnished with parsley sprigs and toasted coconut.

Tips:

Prepare this soup while autumn leaves fall; apples and butternut squash are plentiful and available at farmers' markets.

Creamy Pumpkin Soup

Janeen Troyer
Fairview, MI

Makes 6 servings

Prep. Time: 10 minutes
Cooking Time: 2½ hours
Ideal slow-cooker size: 4 qt.

29-oz. can pumpkin
2 15-oz. cans chicken broth
⅛ tsp. ground nutmeg
¼ tsp. ground allspice
½ tsp. curry powder
⅛ tsp. ground ginger
1 cup cream, at room temperature

1. In slow cooker, mix pumpkin, broth, and spices.
2. Cover and cook on High for 1½ hours and then turn to Low for 1 hour.
3. Add cream 20 minutes before serving.

Nutty Butternut Squash Soup

Phyllis Good
Lancaster, PA

Makes 6-8 servings

Prep. Time: 30-40 minutes
Cooking Time: 6¼-10¼ hours
Chilling Time: 15-20 minutes
Ideal slow-cooker size: oval 6 or 7 qt.

2-lb. butternut squash
2 Tbsp. water
1 large onion, chopped
1 cup roasted, unsalted cashews
1 garlic clove, minced
5 cups vegetable broth
2 Tbsp. fresh ginger, minced
2 tsp. ground cumin
2 tsp. ground coriander
1 tsp. curry powder
1 tsp. ground turmeric
½-¾ tsp. salt
⅓ tsp. coarsely ground black pepper
1 cup light coconut milk

1. Grease interior of slow cooker crock.
2. Poke whole squash all over with tines of sharp fork.
3. Place in microwave and cook on High 5 minutes.
4. Put on hot mitts and roll squash over in microwave. Cook on High 3 more minutes.
5. Let cool enough to handle. Then use a hefty, sharp knife to cut squash in half from top to bottom.
6. Lay halves, skin side down, in slow cooker.
7. Cover. Cook on Low 6-8 hours or on High 4-6 hours.
8. Use hot mitts, or 2 sturdy metal spatulas, to lift halves out of cooker.
9. Scoop out seeds and discard.
10. Let squash cool 15 minutes or so. Then either peel off skin or scoop out flesh.
11. Put flesh back into crock.
12. Stir in all other ingredients, except coconut milk, blending well.
13. Cover. Cook on Low 2-3 hours, or until all veggies are as tender as you like them.
14. Using an immersion blender, blend in crock until mixture is as smooth as you like.
15. Stir in coconut milk.
16. Cover. Cook on Low 15 minutes, or until Soup is heated through.

Thai Pumpkin Soup with Chicken

Bob Coffey
New Windsor, NY

Makes 6 servings

Prep. Time: 15 minutes
Cooking Time: 6-8 hours on Low
Ideal slow-cooker size: 5 qt.

1 large white onion, chopped
4 garlic cloves, chopped
1½ lbs. boneless, skinless chicken breasts, cut into bite-sized pieces
2 carrots, peeled and chopped
15-oz. can pumpkin
½ cup mango nectar
1 Tbsp. fresh minced ginger
1 tsp. red pepper flakes
½ cup creamy peanut butter
3 cups good-quality chicken stock
3 Tbsp. rice vinegar
juice and zest of 1 lime
fresh cilantro, chopped, for serving
green onions, chopped, for serving
roasted unsalted peanuts, roughly chopped, for serving
hot cooked white rice, for serving

1. Combine onion, garlic, chicken, carrots, pumpkin, mango nectar, ginger, red pepper flakes, peanut butter, and chicken stock.
2. Cover and cook on Low for 6-8 hours.
3. Stir in rice vinegar and lime juice and zest.
4. To serve, place a mound of cooked rice in a shallow soup plate for individual servings or large serving bowl for the whole table. Pour or ladle hot soup around the rice. Sprinkle both with cilantro, green onions, and peanuts.

Tips:

Rice from a Chinese take-out restaurant works great for this recipe and makes this an easy weeknight meal.

Orange Soup

Carolyn Spohn
Shawnee, KS

Makes 4-6 servings

Prep. Time: 15 minutes
Cooking Time: 3-4 hours
Ideal slow-cooker size: 4 qt.

4 cups chopped orange vegetables such as carrots, winter squash, red or orange sweet pepper, sweet potato, etc.
4 cups broth of choice
1 small onion, chopped
1 tart apple, cored and chopped
date syrup or brown sugar, to taste

1. Place all ingredients in slow cooker.
2. Cover and cook until vegetables are soft, 3-4 hours on High.
3. Puree with immersion blender, or transfer soup to stand blender and puree with lid slightly ajar for steam to escape.

Tips:

This soup is best with a variety of vegetables.

Good go-alongs with this recipe:

Whole grain bread and green salad.

Tomato Basil Soup

Janet Melvin
Cincinnati, OH

Makes 12 servings

Prep. Time: 15 minutes
Cooking Time: 3½ hours
Ideal slow-cooker size: 4 qt.

½ cup very finely diced onion
2 garlic cloves, minced
2 cups vegetable stock
2 28-oz. cans crushed tomatoes
¼ cup chopped fresh basil, plus more for garnish
1 Tbsp. salt
½ tsp. pepper
1 cup heavy cream, room temperature

1. Combine onion, garlic, stock, tomatoes, basil, salt, and pepper in slow cooker.
2. Cover and cook on High for 3 hours. May puree soup at this point if you wish for a totally smooth soup.
3. Stir in heavy cream and cook an additional 30 minutes on Low.
4. Garnish each serving with a few ribbons of fresh basil.

Tips:

Top with croutons or serve with bread.

San Francisco Fish Stew

Louise Stackhouse
Benton, PA

Makes 8 servings

Prep. Time: 20 minutes
Cooking Time: 5-6 hours
Ideal slow-cooker size: 4 qt.

1 large onion, chopped
2 carrots, diced
3 ribs celery, diced
3 medium potatoes, diced
½ cup chopped green bell pepper
28-oz. can whole tomatoes, roughly crushed, with juice
1 cup chicken stock
1 Tbsp. dried parsley
1 bay leaf
1½ tsp. dried thyme
1 tsp. sugar
1 tsp. salt, or to taste
¼ tsp. black pepper
1 lb. white fish, broken into pieces

1. Combine all ingredients in slow cooker except for fish.
2. Cover and cook on Low for 4-5 hours, until vegetables are tender.
3. Add fish. Stir gently. Cover and cook on Low an additional 20-30 minutes, until fish flakes easily and has turned opaque.

Good go-alongs with this recipe:

Serve over rice or thin spaghetti, or serve with crusty bread.

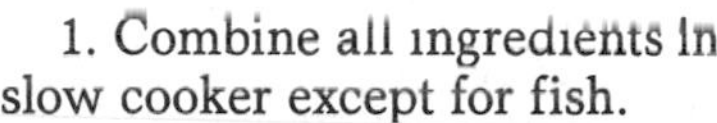

Aim to have your cut-up vegetables all about the same size so they cook uniformly in the slow cooker. The same for pieces of meat.

Spicy Red Clam Soup

Jean Harris Robinson
Pemberton, NJ

Makes 8 servings

Prep. Time: 30 minutes
Cooking Time: 3 hours on High
Ideal slow-cooker size: 3 qt.

24 littleneck clams, steamed and chopped
3 medium potatoes, peeled and diced in ½" cubes
2 carrots, sliced thinly
2 28-oz. cans crushed tomatoes
15-oz. can chicken broth
2-3 Tbsp. Old Bay seasoning, depending on how spicy you like things
2 bay leaves
3 Tbsp. chopped fresh parsley

1. Combine all ingredients except parsley in slow cooker.
2. Cover and cook on Low 8 hours.
3. Stir in parsley before serving. Remove bay leaves before serving.

Tips:

Good as a starter for any entrée. I developed this recipe after tasting this soup at an Italian restaurant; I think I came pretty close to their delicious soup.

Variations:

Use 3 6-oz. cans whole clams, chopped, in place of fresh clams.

Hot and Sour Soup

Marlene Fonken
Upland, CA

Makes 8 servings

Prep. Time: 20 minutes
Cooking Time: 5 hours
Ideal slow-cooker size: 6 qt.

½ lb. boneless, skinless chicken breasts, cut in thin strips
3 cups chicken broth
3 cups beef broth
2 cups shredded Chinese cabbage
1 cup shredded carrot
2 cups sliced fresh mushrooms
12-oz. box firm tofu, drained, cut in thin strips
¼ cup white vinegar
½ tsp. black pepper
3 Tbsp. cornstarch
¼ cup water
3-4 green onions, sliced
sesame oil, for serving

1. In slow cooker, combine chicken, both broths, cabbage, carrot, and mushrooms.
2. Cover and cook on Low for 4 hours, until chicken is tender.
3. Add tofu.
4. Separately, whisk together vinegar, pepper, cornstarch, and water. Stir into hot soup.
5. Cook additional 30-40 minutes on Low, until soup thickens and tofu is hot.
6. Serve in bowls garnished with some sliced green onion and a few drops of sesame oil.

Tips:

The "hot" is the black pepper and the "sour" is the vinegar. Increase or decrease these elements according to your taste.

Variations:

Use pork instead of chicken.

My siblings and I live in different states, and my mother always prepared vegetable soup on the stove top for us when we came home for a visit. Now, years later, we have all adapted that to the slow cooker and have it waiting when we visit each other. — Virginia Rose Hartman, Akron, PA

Gumbo

Dorothy Ealy
Los Angeles, CA

Makes 8 servings

Prep. Time: 30 minutes
Cooking Time: 5 hours
Ideal slow-cooker size: 5 qt.

2 onions, chopped
3 ribs celery, chopped
½ cup diced green bell pepper
2 cloves garlic, chopped
1 cup chopped fresh or frozen okra
½ cup diced andouille or chorizo sausage
2 15-oz. cans tomatoes, undrained
3 Tbsp. tomato paste
1 chicken bouillon cube
¼ tsp. freshly ground black pepper
¼ tsp. dried thyme
1½ lbs. raw shrimp, peeled and de-veined, chopped if large

1. In slow cooker, combine onions, celery, bell pepper, garlic, okra, sausage, tomatoes, tomato paste, bouillon cube, black pepper, and thyme.

2. Cover and cook on Low for 4-5 hours, until vegetables are soft.

3. Add shrimp. Cook for 15-20 more minutes on Low, until shrimp are just opaque and cooked through. Thin Gumbo if necessary with a little water, broth, or wine. Taste and adjust salt.

Tips:

Serve over rice, or serve with French bread. Pass the hot sauce so people can make it really authentically spicy! If you are peeling the shrimp yourself, save the shells. Place them in a saucepan with water or chicken broth just to cover and simmer for 30 minutes. Strain out shells and discard. This makes a tasty seafood-infused broth for making other soups or thinning the Gumbo.

I prep a lot of veggies for soups once a month and throw them in the freezer. Then I can pour them in the crock, stir, turn it on, and I am off to work. — Amy Freeman Marquez, Brevard, NC

I used my slow cooker on a hotel room dresser when I traveled to Disneyland with my husband and six kids. We were in California for a week. Before we got there, we planned out what we would cook each day, and made a grocery list of perishables we would need to buy when we arrived at our destination. We brought all other ingredients with us. We ate every meal in our hotel room while we were there, with the help of our slow cooker. With eight people, we saved hundreds of dollars! — Machen Stephenson, Bothell, WA

I gave my friends a slow cooker for a wedding gift. One Christmas, the oven on their stove went out so they cooked the turkey in the slow cooker. They loved it and told me about it, so I tried it. Now we like slow-cooked turkey because it doesn't dry out and it doesn't heat up the kitchen, which is warm enough here in central Florida at Christmas. — Nancy Kelley, Orlando, FL

Chicken and Turkey Main Dishes

Chicken Dijon Dinner

Barbara Stutzman
Crossville, TN

Makes 4-6 servings

Prep. Time: 20 minutes
Cooking Time: 4 hours
Ideal slow-cooker size: 6 qt.

2 lbs. boneless, skinless chicken thighs
2 garlic cloves, minced
1 Tbsp. olive oil
6 Tbsp. white wine vinegar
4 Tbsp. soy sauce
4 Tbsp. Dijon mustard
1 lb. sliced mushrooms

1. Grease interior of slow-cooker crock.
2. Place thighs in crock. If you need to add a second layer, stagger the pieces so they don't directly overlap each other.
3. Stir together garlic, oil, vinegar, soy sauce, and mustard until well mixed.
4. Gently stir in mushrooms.
5. Spoon sauce into crock, making sure to cover all thighs with some of the sauce.
6. Cover. Cook on Low for 4 hours, or until instant-read meat thermometer registers 160° when stuck in center of chicken.
7. Serve chicken topped with sauce.

Pot Roast Chicken

Carol Ebbighausen-Smith
Spokane, WA

Makes 6 servings

Prep. Time: 20 minutes
Cooking Time: 4-5 hours
Ideal slow-cooker size: 6 or 7 qt.

6 boneless, skinless chicken thighs
3 medium onions, quartered
8 ribs celery, cut in half lengthwise and then in thirds
8 medium carrots, cut in thirds
1½ tsp. dried rosemary
1½ tsp. dried thyme
1½ tsp. dried parsley
1½ tsp. dried sage
1½ tsp. dried oregano
2 tsp. coarsely ground black pepper
1 tsp. salt
1 lb. small red potatoes, halved
2 cups chicken broth
2 Tbsp. flour
¾ cup cold water

1. Grease interior of slow-cooker crock.
2. Place thighs in cooker. If you need to make a second layer, stagger the pieces so they don't directly overlap each other.
3. Mix onions, celery, carrots, herbs, pepper, salt, potatoes, and broth in good-sized bowl. Spoon into cooker beside and around the chicken.
4. Cover. Cook on Low 4-5 hours, or until vegetables are tender and instant-read meat thermometer registers 160°-165° when stuck into thighs.
5. While meal is cooking, place flour and cold water in a jar with a tight-fitting lid. Shake every now and then until no lumps remain. Set aside.
6. When everything is finished cooking, use a slotted spoon to lift chicken and vegetables to a large deep bowl or platter. Cover to keep warm.
7. Turn cooker to High so that broth remaining in cooker simmers. Shake jar with flour and water again. Then, stirring continuously, stream the water-flour mixture into the cooker. Continue stirring until broth thickens.
8. Ladle into bowl and serve with chicken and vegetables.

Whole Roast Chicken

Barbara Stutzman
Crossville, TN

Makes 4 servings

Prep. Time: 15-20 minutes
Cooking Time: 4-5 hours
Ideal slow-cooker size: oval 6 qt.

3-4-lb. chicken
2 tsp. dried thyme
1 tsp. dried rosemary
2 fresh garlic cloves, minced
1 tsp. salt
¾ tsp. coarsely ground black pepper
2 Tbsp. olive oil

Gravy:
2 cups chicken broth
½ cup cold water
¼ cup, plus 2 Tbsp., flour
salt and pepper to taste

1. Grease interior of slow-cooker crock.
2. Roll up 3-4 pieces of tin foil into 3″ balls and place evenly in bottom of crock.
3. In a small bowl, mix together thyme, rosemary, minced garlic, salt, pepper, and olive oil.
4. Using your hands, completely cover the chicken with herb mixture. Gently reach fingers under the skin and add it there, too.
5. Place chicken on top of foil balls.
6. Cover. Cook 4-5 hours on Low, or until instant-read meat thermometer registers 160°-165° when stuck in center of thigh, but not against bone.
7. Using sturdy tongs or 2 metal spatulas, remove chicken from crock and place in bowl or deep platter. Cover to keep warm.
8. In a jar with a tight-fitting lid, place ½ cup cold water. Add flour. Cover jar and shake until water and flour are mixed and no lumps remain.
9. Pour all juices from cooker into small saucepan. Add enough chicken stock to make approximately 2 cups total. Bring to boil.
10. Pour water-flour mixture into simmering broth, stirring constantly until it thickens into a smooth gravy.
11. Add salt and pepper if needed.
12. Carve chicken and serve with gravy. Or cut chicken off bones and refrigerate or freeze for future use.

Variations:

1. Use 6 Tbsp. A1 Garlic and Classic Herbs Dry Rub (instead of thyme, rosemary, minced garlic, salt, pepper, and olive oil as listed above) on outside of chicken and under its skin. 2. Place 1-2 Tbsp. minced garlic and ½ a large onion, cut into chunks, in chicken cavity before placing in crock to cook.

—Amanda Gross

Use 3 times as much of a fresh herb as you do of the same dried herb. In other words, if your recipe calls for 3 Tbsp. of fresh basil and you don't have it, you can use 1 tsp. dried basil.

Unforgettable Roast Chicken

Jeanne Allen
Los Alamos, NM

Makes 4 servings

Prep. Time: 15-20 minutes
Cooking Time: 4-5 hours
Ideal slow-cooker size: oval 6 qt.

1 medium onion, peeled
7 whole cloves
4-lb. stewing chicken
1 oz. brandy
salt to taste
1 lemon, peeled
1 orange, peeled
¼ stick (2 Tbsp.) butter

1. Grease interior of slow-cooker crock.
2. Stud onion with cloves.
3. Pat chicken dry with paper towels inside and out.
4. Rinse chicken cavity with brandy. Salt cavity.
5. Place lemon, orange, and onion in cavity. Tie shut using skewers and cooking thread.
6. Rub outside of chicken with butter.
7. Place in slow cooker.
8. Cover. Cook on Low 4-5 hours, or until instant-read meat thermometer registers 160° when stuck into breast (but not against any bones) and 170° when stuck into thighs (again, not against any bones).
9. When done cooking, lift chicken onto cutting board. Cover with foil. Let stand for 15 minutes.
10. Discard onion and fruit. Carve bird and serve.

Whole Roasted Chicken with Orange

Kaye Merrill
Olive Branch, MS

Makes 4-6 servings

Prep. Time: 20 minutes
Cooking Time: 4-5 hours
Ideal slow-cooker size: oval 7 qt.

5-lb. whole chicken
1 orange
1 medium onion
salt and pepper to taste
1 tsp. dried thyme
1 tsp. dried rosemary
½ cup white wine
3 Tbsp. butter, melted
3 Tbsp. Dijon mustard
3 Tbsp. honey
1 Tbsp. apricot marmalade
3 Tbsp. orange juice

1. Grease interior of slow-cooker crock.
2. Pat chicken dry. Place in crock.
3. Cut orange into quarters. Squeeze over chicken. Place orange quarters inside chicken.
4. Quarter onion and place inside chicken.
5. Sprinkle outside of chicken liberally with salt and pepper, thyme, and rosemary.
6. Pour wine along edge of cooker so you don't wash off the seasonings.
7. Cover. Cook on Low 3-4 hours.
8. Meanwhile, mix butter, mustard, honey, and marmalade in a small saucepan. Heat, stirring regularly, until all ingredients melt together. Stir in orange juice.
9. Pour glaze over chicken. Cover and continue cooking on Low 1 more hour, or until an instant-read meat thermometer registers 160° when stuck into the breast and 170° when stuck into thighs.
10. Lift chicken from cooker and place on cutting board. Cover with foil and allow to rest for 15 minutes.
11. Carve, spoon sauce and drippings over meat, and serve.

Chicken Marengo

Bernadette Veenstra
Rockford, MI

Makes 6 servings

Prep. Time: 20 minutes
Cooking Time: 4 hours
Ideal slow-cooker size: 5 qt.

6 boneless, skinless chicken thighs
1 Tbsp. flour
¾ tsp. dried basil
¼ tsp. garlic powder
¾-1 tsp. salt, according to taste
¼ tsp. black pepper
½ cup white wine or chicken broth
2 Tbsp. tomato paste
2 14.5-oz. cans stewed tomatoes
1 onion, cut into 8 wedges
½ coarsely chopped green bell pepper
½ cup olives, cut in half

1. Grease interior of slow-cooker crock.
2. Arrange thighs in cooker. If you need to make a second layer, stagger the pieces so they don't directly overlap each other.
3. In a medium-sized bowl, mix together flour, basil, garlic powder, salt, pepper, wine, tomato paste, tomatoes, and onions. Pour over chicken.
4. Cover. Cook on Low for 4 hours, or until instant-read meat thermometer registers 160°-165° when stuck into the thighs.
5. Thirty minutes before end of cooking time, stir chopped pepper and olives into sauce.
6. Serve meat and vegetables over butter noodles.

Cranberry Chili Chicken

Kelly Bailey
Mechanicsburg, PA

Makes 6 servings

Prep. Time: 10 minutes
Cooking Time: 4 hours
Ideal slow-cooker size: 5 qt.

6 boneless, skinless chicken thighs
½ cup chili sauce
2 Tbsp. orange marmalade
½ cup whole-berry cranberry sauce
¼ tsp. ground allspice

1. Grease interior of slow-cooker crock.
2. Place thighs in crock. If you need to make a second layer, stagger the pieces so they don't completely overlap each other.
3. In a bowl, mix together all other ingredients.
4. Spoon evenly over all the breasts, making sure to top the thighs on the bottom layer.
5. Cover. Cook on Low 4 hours, or until instant-read meat thermometer registers 160°-165° when stuck into thighs.
6. Serve thighs topped with the sauce.

Chili Chicken

Juanita Weaver
Johnsonville, IL

Makes 8 servings

Prep. Time: 10 minutes
Cooking Time: 3-4 hours
Ideal slow-cooker size: 5 qt.

8 good-sized boneless, skinless chicken thighs
1 cup soy sauce
1 cup ketchup
1 cup honey or brown sugar
1 Tbsp. chili powder
1 tsp. black pepper
2 cups diced onion

1. Grease interior of slow-cooker crock.
2. Cut each thigh into 4 strips. Place in crock.
3. Mix remaining ingredients together well.
4. Pour sauce over meat.
5. Cook on Low 3-4 hours, or until instant-read meat thermometer registers 160° when stuck into center of meat.

Good go-alongs with this recipe:

This is excellent served on top of a bed of fluffy, herb-seasoned rice, which can also be made in a slow cooker, using the same ratio as when you make it on a stove top

Szechuan-Style Chicken and Broccoli

Jane Meiser
Harrisonburg, VA

Makes 4 servings

Prep. Time: 30 minutes
Cooking Time: 1½-3 hours
Ideal slow cooker size: 4-qt.

2 whole boneless, skinless chicken breasts
1 Tbsp. canola oil
½ cup picante sauce
2 Tbsp. light soy sauce
½ tsp. sugar
2 tsp. quick-cooking tapioca
1 medium onion, chopped
2 garlic cloves, minced
½ tsp. ground ginger
2 cups broccoli florets
1 medium red bell pepper, sliced

1. Cut chicken into 1" cubes and brown lightly in oil in skillet. Place in slow cooker.
2. Stir in remaining ingredients.
3. Cover. Cook on high 1-1½ hours or on low 2-3 hours.

I had a washer repairman, who had to make several visits to our house, comment on how good my house always smelled at suppertime. My youngest son said the food always tastes that good, too, and invited the man to dinner.
— Julie Bazata

Fancy Baked Chicken

Denise Martin
Lancaster, PA

Makes 8 servings

***Prep. Time:** 20 minutes*
***Cooking Time:** 4-5 hours, or until meat thermometer registers 160°-165°*
***Ideal slow-cooker size:** 5 qt.*

1 stick (½ cup) butter, melted
¾ cup grated Parmesan cheese
1 tsp. garlic powder
½ tsp. salt
8 boneless, skinless chicken thighs
1½ cups soft bread crumbs

1. Grease interior of slow-cooker crock well.
2. Combine butter, cheese, garlic powder, and salt in a shallow bowl. Mix well.
3. Dip each piece of chicken in mixture. (Reserve remaining butter mixture.)
4. Coat each chicken thigh with bread crumbs.
5. As you finish with each piece, place into slow cooker. If you need to create a second layer, stagger the pieces so they don't completely overlap each other.
6. Spoon reserved butter mixture over top.
7. Cover. Cook on Low 4-5 hours, or until instant-read meat thermometer registers 160°-165° when inserted in chicken.
8. If you want to brown the chicken before serving, place on a rimmed baking sheet and run under the broiler for a few minutes. Watch carefully so it doesn't burn.

Garlic Mushroom Chicken Thighs

Elaine Vigoda
Rochester, NY

Makes 6 servings

***Prep. Time:** 15 minutes*
***Cooking Time:** 4 hours*
***Ideal slow-cooker size:** 5 qt.*

6 boneless, skinless chicken thighs
3 Tbsp. flour
8-10 garlic cloves, peeled and very lightly crushed
1 Tbsp. oil
¾ lb. fresh mushrooms, any combination of varieties, cut into bite-sized pieces or slices
⅓ cup balsamic vinegar
1¼ cups chicken broth
1-2 bay leaves
½ tsp. dried thyme or 4 sprigs fresh thyme
2 tsp. apricot jam

1. Grease interior of slow-cooker crock.
2. Place flour in strong plastic bag without any holes. One by one, put each thigh in bag, hold the bag shut and shake it to flour the thigh fully.
3. Place thighs in crock. If you need to make a second layer, stagger the pieces so they don't directly overlap.
4. If you have time, sauté garlic in oil in skillet just until it begins to brown.
5. Sprinkle garlic over thighs, including those on the bottom layer.
6. Scatter cut-up mushrooms over thighs, too, remembering those on the bottom layer.
7. Mix remaining ingredients together in a bowl, stirring to break up the jam.
8. When well mixed, pour into the cooker along the edges so you don't wash the vegetables off the chicken pieces.
9. Cover. Cook on Low for 4 hours, or until an instant-read meat thermometer registers 160°-165° when stuck into the thighs.
10. Serve meat, topped with vegetables, with sauce spooned over.

Sesame Baked Chicken

Sandra Haverstraw
Hummelstown, PA

Makes 6 servings

Prep. Time: 20 minutes
Cooking Time: 4 hours
Ideal slow-cooker size: 4 or 5 qt.

⅔ cup fine cracker crumbs (about 15 crackers, crushed)
¼ cup toasted sesame seeds
⅓ cup evaporated milk, or light cream
1 stick (½ cup butter)
6 boneless, skinless chicken thighs

1. Grease interior of slow-cooker crock.
2. Mix cracker crumbs and seeds in a shallow bowl.
3. Place milk in another shallow bowl.
4. Melt butter in still another shallow bowl.
5. Dip chicken in milk, one piece at a time.
6. Roll chicken in crumbs, one piece at a time.
7. Dip top of each thigh into melted butter, one piece at a time.
8. Place coated thighs in slow cooker, butter side up. If you need to make a second layer, stagger the pieces so they don't directly overlap each other.
9. Cover. Cook on Low for 4 hours, or until instant-read meat thermometer registers 160°-165° when inserted in thickest part of thighs.
10. If you wish, place chicken on rimmed baking sheet and run under the broiler to brown the meat. Watch carefully so it doesn't burn.

Slow-Cooker Honey-Mustard Chicken

Barbara Stutzman
Crossville, TN

Makes 6-8 servings

Prep. Time: 30 minutes
Cooking Time: 4-5 hours
Ideal slow-cooker size: 6 qt.

2-3 lbs. boneless, skinless chicken thighs
1 large onion, sliced, about ½ cup
3 garlic cloves, sliced
2 Tbsp. honey
¼ cup Dijon mustard
1 Tbsp. coarse-grain mustard
2 Tbsp. red wine vinegar
2 tsp. olive oil
1 tsp. coarsely ground black pepper
pinch cayenne pepper
½ cup water
2 green onions, sliced on an angle, for garnish, optional

1. Grease interior of slow-cooker crock.
2. Place chicken in crock. If you need to add a second layer, stagger the pieces so they don't directly overlap each other.
3. Mix onion and garlic slices, honey, mustards, vinegar, olive oil, peppers, and water together in a bowl.
4. Spoon sauce over chicken.
5. Cover. Cook on Low 4-5 hours, or until instant-read meat thermometer registers 165° when stuck into center of thighs.
6. Serve chicken topped with sauce, and garnished with green onions if you wish.

Sweet and Sour Chicken

Janette Fox
Honey Brook, PA

Makes 6-8 servings

Prep. Time: 15 minutes
Cooking Time: 4 hours
Ideal slow-cooker size: 5 qt.

3 lbs. boneless, skinless chicken thighs
½ cup chopped onions
½ green pepper, chopped
15-oz. can pineapple chunks, drained but juice reserved
¾-1 cup reserved pineapple juice
¾ cup ketchup
¼ cup brown sugar, packed
2 Tbsp. apple cider vinegar
2 tsp. soy sauce
½ tsp. garlic salt
½ tsp. salt
¼ tsp. black pepper
cooked rice

1. Grease interior of slow-cooker crock.
2. Put chicken in crock. If you need to add a second layer, stagger the pieces so they don't directly overlap each other.
3. Scatter onions and green peppers over top.
4. In a mixing bowl, combine pineapple chunks and juice, ketchup, brown sugar, vinegar, soy sauce, garlic salt, salt, and black pepper.
5. Spoon over chicken, onions, and green peppers.
6. Cover. Cook on Low 4 hours, or until instant-read meat thermometer registers 165° when stuck into center of thighs.
7. Serve over cooked rice.

Variations:

Not so many pineapples.

Tangy Chicken

Marilyn Kurtz
Willow Street, PA

Makes 6-8 servings

Prep. Time: 15 minutes
Cooking Time: 4-5 hours
Ideal slow-cooker size: 5 qt.

16-oz. jar chunky salsa, as hot or mild as you like
½ an envelope dry taco seasoning mix
½ cup peach or apricot preserves
4 lbs. boneless, skinless chicken thighs

1. Grease interior of slow-cooker crock.
2. Pour salsa into cooker, and then stir in taco seasoning and preserves, mixing well.
3. Place chicken down into sauce, making sure all pieces are covered as much as possible.
4. Cover. Cook on Low 4-5 hours, or until instant-read meat thermometer registers 160° when stuck in center of thighs.
5. Serve over cooked rice.

Good go-alongs with this recipe:

We like steamed broccoli.

Chicken Monterey

Sally Holzem
Schofield, WI

Makes 6 servings

Prep. Time: 20 minutes
Cooking Time: 4 hours
Ideal slow-cooker size: 5 qt.

6 slices bacon
6 boneless, skinless chicken thighs
¼ tsp. salt or a bit more, according to taste
¼ tsp. black pepper
¾ cup barbecue sauce, your favorite
1 cup shredded cheddar cheese
6 scallions, trimmed and sliced
1 medium tomato, chopped

1. Fry bacon in skillet until crisp. Remove from skillet and place on paper towels to drain.
2. Grease interior of slow-cooker crock while bacon is frying.
3. Place chicken in crock. If you need to make a second layer, stagger the pieces so they don't directly overlap.
4. Sprinkle each thigh with salt and pepper.
5. Spoon on the barbecue sauce, being careful not to wash off the seasonings.
6. Cover. Cook on Low for 4 hours, or until instant-read meat thermometer registers 160°-165° when stuck in thighs.
7. Just before serving, top each thigh with a bacon slice, along with chopped scallions and tomato pieces.

Tarragon Chicken

Cassius L. Chapman
Tucker, GA

Makes 6 servings

Prep. Time: 15-20 minutes
Cooking Time: 4 hours
Ideal slow-cooker size: 5 qt.

6 boneless, skinless chicken thighs
½ tsp. salt
½ tsp. black pepper, coarsely ground
1 tsp. dried tarragon
2 Tbsp. chopped onion
½ cup dry white wine
2 Tbsp. butter
2 Tbsp. flour
¼ tsp. salt
1 cup heavy cream
1 Tbsp. chopped fresh tarragon

1. Grease interior of slow-cooker crock.
2. Place thighs in cooker. If you need to create a second layer, stagger the pieces so they don't directly overlap each other.
3. In a small bowl, mix together salt, pepper, dried tarragon, chopped onion, and wine.
4. Spoon over thighs, making sure to top those on both levels with the sauce.
5. Cover. Cook on Low for 4 hours, or until instant-read meat thermometer registers 160°-165° when stuck in the thighs.
6. Close to end of cooking time, melt butter in skillet or small saucepan. Blend in flour and salt. Cook, stirring continuously over heat for 1-2 minutes to take the raw flour taste away.
7. Gradually pour in cream, stirring continuously over medium heat until sauce thickens.
8. To serve, place thighs on platter. Spoon sauce over. Sprinkle with chopped fresh tarragon leaves.

Taste-test your slow-cooker dish just before serving and adjust the seasoning if necessary. Long, slow cooking can dilute the flavor of some herbs and spices.

Parmesan Mustard Chicken

Janet Oberholtzer
Ephrata, PA

Makes 6 servings

Prep. Time: 15-20 minutes
Cooking Time: 4 hours
Ideal slow-cooker size: 4 or 5 qt.

5⅓ Tbsp. (⅓ cup) butter
1 cup grated Parmesan cheese
2 cups fine bread crumbs
⅓ cup prepared mustard
6 boneless, skinless chicken thighs

1. Grease interior of slow-cooker crock well.
2. Melt butter in a bowl. Stir in Parmesan cheese and bread crumbs until well mixed.
3. Coat thighs with thin layer of mustard.
4. Dip thighs into crumb mixture, pressing so it adheres.
5. Lay thighs into slow-cooker crock. If you need to make a second layer, stagger the thighs so they aren't completely on top of each other.
6. Cover. Cook on Low for 4 hours, or until instant-read meat thermometer registers 160°-165° when inserted in thighs.
7. If you wish, place the cooked chicken on a rimmed baking sheet and run it under the broiler for a few minutes to brown it. Watch it carefully so it doesn't burn.

Memories of Tucson Chicken

Joanna Harrison
Lafayette, CO

Makes 6 servings

Prep. Time: 20 minutes
Cooking Time: 4 hours
Ideal slow-cooker size: 6 qt.

1 medium onion, chopped coarsely
3 cloves garlic, minced
2-3 green chilies, chopped, or 4-oz. can chopped green chilies
1 cup chopped tomatoes
2 cups corn, fresh, frozen, or canned
2 tsp. dried oregano
1 tsp. ground cumin
1 tsp. dried basil
2 cups chicken broth
6 boneless, skinless chicken thighs
1 green bell pepper, chopped
1 or 2 zucchini, chopped
¼-½ cup cilantro leaves

1. Grease interior of slow-cooker crock.
2. Place onion, garlic, chilies, tomatoes, corn, oregano, cumin, basil, and broth in slow cooker. Stir until well mixed.
3. Place chicken in broth, submerging until covered, or nearly so.
4. Cover. Cook on Low 3 hours.
5. Lift out thighs and keep covered on platter.
6. Stir in bell pepper and zucchini.
7. Return chicken to cooker, again pushing the pieces down into the liquid.
8. Cover and continue cooking 1 more hour on Low, or until an instant-read meat thermometer registers 160°-165° when stuck in the thighs.
9. Place the chicken on a platter. Spoon vegetables and broth over top. Scatter cilantro leaves over all and serve.

Pizza Chicken

Mary June Hershberger
Lynchburg, VA

Makes 4 servings

Prep. Time: 15 minutes
Cooking Time: 4-5 hours
Ideal slow-cooker size: 4 or 5 qt.

2 cups chicken broth
1 cup uncooked brown rice
½ tsp. garlic powder
½ tsp. onion powder
1 tsp. salt
¼ tsp. black pepper
4 good-sized boneless, skinless chicken thighs
2 cups pizza sauce
2 cups shredded mozzerella cheese

1. Grease interior of slow-cooker crock.
2. Mix chicken broth, uncooked rice, garlic and onion powders, salt, and black pepper in crock until well blended.
3. Arrange chicken on top.
4. Cover with pizza sauce.
5. Top with shredded cheese.
6. Cover. Cook on Low 4-5 hours, or until rice is tender and instant-read meat thermometer registers 165° when stuck into center of meat.

Fiesta Chicken

Emily Fox
Bethel, PA

Makes 6 servings

Prep. Time: 5 minutes
Cooking Time: 3-4 hours
Ideal slow-cooker size: 4 qt.

1-1½ lbs. boneless, skinless chicken thighs
14-oz can diced tomatoes, undrained
10-oz can corn, drained
14-oz can black beans, rinsed and drained
1 envelope dry taco seasoning
cooked rice
grated cheese
sour cream
guacamole

1. Grease interior of slow-cooker crock.
2. Place thighs in crock.
3. In a bowl, stir together tomatoes, corn, black beans, and dry taco seasoning. Combine well.
4. Spoon veggies over chicken.
5. Cover. Cook on Low 4 hours, or until instant-read meat thermometer registers 160° when stuck into center of thigh.
6. Using a slotted spoon, lift chicken thighs out of sauce and into bowl.
7. Shred with 2 forks.
8. Stir shredded chicken back into sauce.
9. Serve over cooked rice. Top with grated cheese, sour cream, and guacamole.

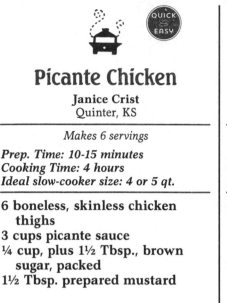

Picante Chicken

Janice Crist
Quinter, KS

Makes 6 servings

Prep. Time: 10-15 minutes
Cooking Time: 4 hours
Ideal slow-cooker size: 4 or 5 qt.

6 boneless, skinless chicken thighs
3 cups picante sauce
¼ cup, plus 1½ Tbsp., brown sugar, packed
1½ Tbsp. prepared mustard

1. Grease interior of slow-cooker crock.
2. Place thighs in cooker. If you need to make a second layer, stagger the pieces so they don't completely overlap each other.
3. In a small bowl, combine the picante sauce, brown sugar, and mustard. Pour over chicken.
4. Cover. Cook on Low 4 hours, or until an instant-read meat thermometer registers 160°-165° when stuck into the thighs.

Salsa Chicken

Barbara Smith
Bedford, PA

Makes 6 servings

Prep. Time: 15 minutes
Cooking Time: 4 hours
Ideal slow-cooker size: 4 or 5 qt.

6 boneless, skinless chicken thighs
1½ cups salsa, your choice of heat
2 Tbsp. dry taco seasoning mix
1½ cups shredded cheddar cheese
¼ cup sour cream, optional

1. Grease interior of slow-cooker crock.
2. Lay thighs in slow cooker. If you need to create a second layer, stagger the pieces so they don't completely overlap each other.
3. Spoon salsa over each thigh, making sure not to miss the ones on the first layer that are partly covered by pieces above.
4. Sprinkle taco seasoning mix over each thigh, again, making sure not to miss the ones on the first layer.
5. Cover. Cook on Low for 4 hours, or until instant-read meat thermometer registers 160°-165° when stuck into the meat.
6. Thirty minutes before the end of the cooking time, scatter shredded cheese over each thigh, including those on the first layer that are partly covered.
7. Top each thigh with sour cream as you serve the chicken, if you wish.

Spinach Frittata, page 33

Raspberry Chocolate Chip Bread, page 38

Asparagus Bake, page 242

Encore Dijon Chicken, page 99

Chicken Mole

Bernadette Veenstra
Grand Rapids, MI

Makes 8 servings

Prep. Time: 30 minutes
Cooking Time: 4-5 hours
Ideal slow-cooker size: 6 qt.

1 Tbsp. olive oil
8-10 chicken thighs, skinned and lightly salted and peppered
1 large onion
4 garlic cloves, minced, or more if you love garlic
4 tsp. chili powder
4 tsp. unsweetened cocoa powder
½ tsp. ground cinnamon
2½ cups chicken broth
2 Tbsp. creamy peanut butter
2 Tbsp. tomato paste
½ cup dark raisins
cooked rice
½ cup loosely packed cilantro leaves
lime wedges

1. Heat olive oil in a large skillet. In several batches, brown all sides of chicken (about 10 minutes total).
2. Place chicken in bottom of slow cooker lightly coated with cooking spray. Discard all but 1 Tbsp. of pan drippings.
3. Heat pan drippings or oil in same skillet. Add onion and cook, stirring until softened (about 5 minutes). Add garlic, chili powder, cocoa powder, and cinnamon to skillet and cook, stirring 1 minute.
4. Stir in broth, peanut butter, and tomato paste. Heat to boiling.
5. Pour sauce over chicken in slow cooker.
6. Cook on Low for 4-5 hours, or until chicken registers 165° on meat thermometer.
7. Add raisins for the last 15 minutes of cooking.
8. Serve over rice topped with cilantro and freshly squeezed lime juice.

Paradise Island Chicken

Rebecca Eldredge
Honolulu, HI

Makes 6 servings

Prep. Time: 15 minutes
Cooking Time: 4 hours
Marinating Time: 4-8 hours, or overnight
Ideal slow-cooker size: 5 qt.

½ cup soy sauce
2 Tbsp. brown sugar
1 tsp. cooking oil
1 tsp. sesame oil
½ cup orange juice
1 large clove garlic, minced
½ tsp. freshly grated ginger root
6 boneless, skinless chicken thighs

1. Mix all ingredients together in bowl except chicken thighs.
2. Pour into heavy plastic bag without holes, big enough to hold the chicken, too. Place thighs in bag. Tie it shut tightly. Swish the bag gently back and forth so all the chicken is covered with the sauce.
3. Place filled bag in large bowl and place in refrigerator for 4-8 hours, or overnight, to marinate meat.
4. Grease interior of slow-cooker crock.
5. Place thighs in cooker. If you need to create a second layer, stagger the pieces so they don't directly overlap each other.
6. Pour the marinade over the thighs, making sure that some of the sauce coats each thigh.
7. Cover. Cook on Low 4 hours, or until an instant-read meat thermometer registers 160°-165° when stuck in thighs.

Hawaiian Chicken

Sharon Miller
Holmesville, OH

Makes 6-8 servings

***Prep. Time:** 15 minutes*
***Cooking Time:** 4 hours*
***Ideal slow-cooker size:** 5 or 6 qt.*

2½-3 lbs. boneless, skinless chicken thighs
16-oz. can pineapple tidbits, drained
15-oz. can mandarin oranges, drained

Sauce:
¼ cup cornstarch
½ cup brown sugar
½ cup soy sauce
¼ cup lemon juice
1 tsp. ground ginger
salt and pepper to taste

1. Grease interior of slow-cooker crock.
2. Lay thighs in crock. If you need to make a second layer, stagger the pieces so they don't directly overlap each other.
3. In a bowl, mix sauce ingredients together well. Pour over the chicken.
4. Lay drained fruit over top of thighs.
5. Cover. Cook on Low for 4 hours, or until instant-read meat thermometer registers 165° when stuck into center of thighs.

Tips:

Serve over a bed of cooked brown rice.

Variations:

This has become my favorite recipe for guests. It is so easy and fast, and everyone has loved it. It is in my handwritten book of favorite keepers!

Good go-alongs with this recipe:

Salad, a cooked vegetable such as peas, and homemade dinner rolls.

Chicken with Fresh Fruit

Robin Schrock
Millersburg, OH

Makes 6 servings

***Prep. Time:** 20 minutes*
***Cooking Time:** 4 hours*
***Ideal slow-cooker size:** 5 qt.*

2 Tbsp. olive oil
¾ tsp. salt
¾ tsp. black pepper
½ tsp. garlic powder
6 large boneless, skinless chicken thighs
12 oz. canned pineapple tidbits, drained, or 1½ cups fresh pineapple chunks
1½ cups fresh strawberries, quartered
2 small kiwi, peeled, quartered, and sliced
⅓ cup chopped red onions
4-oz. can chopped green chilies
1½ tsp. cornstarch
½ cup orange juice

1. Grease interior of slow-cooker crock.
2. In a small bowl, combine oil, salt, pepper, and garlic powder.
3. Rub the mixture on all sides of each thigh.
4. Lay thighs into crock. If you need to make a second layer, stagger the pieces so they don't directly overlap each other.
5. Cover. Cook on Low 4 hours, or until instant-read meat thermometer inserted in thighs registers 160°-165°.
6. While chicken is cooking place pineapple pieces, strawberries, kiwi, onions, and chilies in bowl. Stir together gently.
7. In another small bowl, mix cornstarch and orange juice until smooth. Stir mixture into small saucepan. Cook, stirring continuously until mixture thickens, about 2 minutes.
8. Stir sauce into fruit.
9. Place cooked chicken on platter. Spoon fruit mixture over each thigh, making sure not to brush off the rub, and serve.

Polynesian Chicken

Sheila Plock
Boalsburg, PA

Makes 6 servings

Prep. Time: 15 minutes
Cooking Time: 4 hours
Ideal slow-cooker size: 5 qt.

6 boneless, skinless chicken thighs
1 medium onion, sliced in rings
16-oz. can sliced peaches, drained
16-oz. can dark sweet cherries, drained
1 cup sweet-and-sour salad dressing
1 cup barbecue sauce, your favorite flavor

1. Grease interior of slow-cooker crock.
2. Place thighs in crock. If you need to make a second layer, stagger the pieces so they don't completely overlap each other.
3. Scatter onion rings evenly over thighs.
4. Arrange peaches over onions.
5. Top with cherries.
6. In a small mixing bowl, combine sweet-and-sour sauce and barbecue sauce. Spoon evenly over all other ingredients.
7. Cover. Cook on Low 4 hours, or until instant-read meat thermometer registers 160°-165° when stuck in thighs.
8. Serve thighs topped with onions, fruit, and sauce.

Sweet Islands Chicken

Cynthia Morris
Grottoes, VA

Makes 6 servings

Prep. Time: 15-20 minutes
Cooking Time: 3-4 hours
Ideal slow-cooker size: 4 qt.

1 cup pineapple juice
½ cup brown sugar
⅓ cup soy sauce
2 lbs. boneless, skinless chicken thighs, cut in 1" chunks
1 Tbsp., plus 1 tsp., cornstarch

1. Grease interior of slow-cooker crock.
2. Mix pineapple juice, brown sugar, and soy sauce together in crock until well combined.
3. Stir in chicken chunks.
4. Cover. Cook on Low 3-4 hours, or until meat is cooked in center, but not dry.
5. When done cooking, spoon 1 Tbsp. and 1 tsp. sauce out of cooker and allow to cool in a small bowl.
6. Stir cornstarch into cooled sauce until smooth.
7. Stir cornstarch-sauce mix back into hot sauce remaining in crock. Continue stirring until sauce thickens.
8. Serve chicken and sauce over cooked rice or noodles.

Variations:

From the tester: Add ½ cup diced onion and ½ tsp. minced fresh ginger to Step 2.

—Anita Troyer

Kona Chicken

Jean Harris Robinson
Pemberton, NJ

Makes 6 servings

Prep. Time: 30 minutes
Cooking Time: 5 hours on Low
Ideal slow-cooker size: 5 qt.

6 good-sized boneless, skinless chicken thighs
2 Tbsp. olive oil
½ cup white wine
14.5-oz. can, or 1¾ cups homemade, chicken broth
20-oz. can pineapple chunks 2 Tbsp. packed dark brown sugar
1 Tbsp. soy sauce
1 minced clove garlic
1 medium green bell pepper, chopped
1 Tbsp. grated fresh ginger
3 Tbsp. cornstarch
3 Tbsp. cold water

1. Grease interior of slow-cooker crock.
2. Brown chicken briefly in large skillet in olive oil. Do it in batches over high heat so the pieces brown and don't just steam in each other's juices. Lay browned thighs in crock as they finish in skillet.
3. Deglaze pan with wine.
4. Combine wine and pan drippings, broth, pineapple chunks and their juice, brown sugar, soy sauce, garlic, green peppers, and fresh ginger in a bowl. Pour over chicken.
5. Cover. Cook on Low 4 hours, or until instant-read meat thermometer registers 160°-165° when stuck in center of thighs.
6. Lift cooked thighs onto platter, cover, and keep warm.
7. In a small bowl, stir together cornstarch and water until smooth.
8. Stir into sauce in crock until it's smooth.
9. Cover. Cook on High 10 minutes, or until thickened.
10. Serve chicken, on deep platter, covered with sauce.

Chicken with Lime Wedges

Marjorie Mills
Bethesda, MD

Makes 6 servings

Prep. Time: 10 minutes
Cooking Time: 4 hours
Ideal slow-cooker size: 5 qt.

6 boneless, skinless chicken thighs
1 medium onion, chopped
1 clove garlic, minced
⅛ tsp. red pepper flakes
½ tsp. ground cumin
½ tsp. crushed coriander seeds
¼ tsp. turmeric
2 Tbsp. soy sauce
3 limes

1. Grease interior of slow-cooker crock.
2. Place thighs in crock. If you need to create a second layer, stagger the pieces so they don't directly overlap each other.
3. In a bowl, mix together all other ingredients except limes.
4. Cover. Cook on Low 4 hours, or until an instant-read meat thermometer registers 160°-165° when stuck in the thighs.
5. Cut 2 limes in half. Squeeze fresh lime into bowl, remove any seeds, and pour juice into cooker. Cover. Allow to heat through, about 10 minutes.
6. To serve, place thighs on platter. Stir sauce in cooker so lime juice is distributed well. Spoon sauce over chicken.

Almond Lemon Chicken

Judi Janzen
Salem, OR

Makes 6 servings

Prep. Time: 15-20 minutes
Cooking Time: 4 hours
Marinating Time: 1 hour
Ideal slow-cooker size: 5 qt.

5 Tbsp. lemon juice
3 Tbsp. prepared mustard
2 cloves garlic, minced
6 Tbsp. olive oil, divided
6 boneless, skinless chicken thighs
1 cup sliced almonds
2 cups chicken broth
1 tsp. cornstarch dissolved in 1 Tbsp. water
2-4 Tbsp. orange marmalade (start with less and add more if you prefer a sweeter taste)
¼ tsp. red pepper flakes
2 Tbsp. chopped fresh parsley

1. In a large bowl, combine first 3 ingredients. Stir in 5 Tbsp. oil.
2. Add chicken to marinade, submerging the thighs in the liquid and turning them over so they have full contact with the liquid. Let stand for 1 hour at room temperature.
3. Meanwhile, grease the interior of the slow-cooker crock.
4. Add ½ Tbsp. oil to skillet. Sauté almonds until golden, stirring often so they don't burn.
5. Remove almonds and set aside. Keep pan drippings in skillet.
6. Drain chicken, reserving marinade. Place chicken in slow cooker. If you have to make a second layer, stagger the pieces so they don't directly overlap each other.
7. Add marinade to drippings in skillet, along with remaining ½ Tbsp. oil, chicken broth, dissolved cornstarch, marmalade, and red pepper flakes. Cook over high heat, stirring frequently, until mixture is reduced by half.
8. Taste sauce. If you prefer a sweeter taste, add more marmalade.
9. Pour sauce over chicken in cooker.
10. Cover. Cook on Low for 4 hours, or until instant-read meat thermometer shows 160°-165° when stuck in thighs.
11. To serve, place meat on platter, spoon sauce over top, and garnish with parsley and toasted almonds.

Fruity Mustard Chicken

Elaine Vigoda
Rochester, NY

Makes 6 servings

Prep. Time: 10 minutes
Cooking Time: 4 hours
Ideal slow-cooker size: 4 or 5 qt.

1 cup peach jam
¼ cup prepared mustard
1 Tbsp. lemon or lime juice
1 Tbsp. curry powder
6 boneless, skinless chicken thighs

1. Grease interior of slow-cooker crock.
2. In a small microwave-safe bowl, mix together jam, mustard, juice, and curry. Cover and microwave on High for 1 minute.
3. Stir. If jam hasn't melted, microwave another 30 seconds. Stir. Repeat until jam melts.
4. Pat chicken dry. Place in slow cooker. If you need to create a second layer, stagger the pieces so they don't completely overlap each other.
5. Pour sauce over chicken, making sure that the pieces on the bottom are also glazed.
6. Cover. Cook on Low for 4 hours, or until an instant-read meat thermometer registers 160°-165° when stuck into the thighs.

Brandied Peach Chicken

Phyllis Good
Lancaster, PA

Makes 6 servings

Prep. Time: 20 minutes
Cooking Time: 4-4½ hours
Ideal slow-cooker size: 5 qt.

6 boneless, skinless chicken thighs
1 tsp. salt
½ cup finely chopped onions
½ cup chopped pecans or cashews
½ tsp. ground ginger
5 canned peaches in heavy syrup, divided
5⅓ Tbsp. (⅓ cup) butter, melted
½ cup light brown sugar
2 tsp. prepared mustard
1 cup sour cream
1 Tbsp. brandy

1. Grease interior of slow-cooker crock.
2. Spread out thighs and flatten each one either with the heel of your hand or with a meat mallet, until about ⅛" thick.
3. Sprinkle meat with salt.
4. In a bowl, combine onions, nuts, ginger, and 3 peaches, chopped.
5. Divide peach mixture among the 6 thighs, placing it in the center of each one. Fold in the sides and bottom. Roll up each thigh, securing the bundles with toothpicks.
6. Place stuffed thighs in crock. If you need to make a second layer, stagger the pieces so they don't completely overlap.
7. Pour melted butter over thighs, including those on the bottom layer.
8. Cover. Cook on Low for 4 hours, or until an instant-read meat thermometer registers 160°-165° when stuck into the center of the meat.
9. Twenty minutes before the end of the cooking time, slice the remaining peaches into a saucepan. Stir in brown sugar, mustard, sour cream, and brandy.
10. Heat for 5 minutes, stirring frequently and making sure it doesn't boil.
11. Serve sauce over stuffed thighs.

Cornbread Chicken

Kaye Taylor
Florissant, MO

Makes 6 servings

Prep. Time: 15-20 minutes
Cooking Time: 4-5 hours
Ideal slow-cooker size: 4 or 5 qt.

8½-oz. pkg. cornbread mix
1 envelope dry ranch salad dressing mix
1 cup milk
6 boneless, skinless chicken thighs
1-2 Tbsp. oil

1. Grease interior of slow-cooker crock.
2. In large resealable plastic bag, combine cornbread mix and salad dressing mix.
3. Pour milk into shallow bowl.
4. Dip thighs, one at a time, in milk, then place in bag with dry mixes and shake to coat.
5. Place thighs in slow cooker. If you have to create a second layer, stagger them so they don't completely overlap.
6. Drizzle each with a bit of oil, lifting the top layer to drizzle the first layer, too.
7. Cover. Cook on Low for 4 hours, or until instant-read meat thermometer registers 160°-165° when inserted in thighs.
8. If you wish, place the thighs on a rimmed baking sheet and run under the broiler to allow chicken to brown. Watch carefully so it doesn't burn.

Creamy Italian Chicken

Jo Zimmerman
Lebanon, PA

Makes 4 servings

Prep. Time: 15 minutes
Cooking Time: 4 hours
Ideal slow-cooker size: 5 qt.

4 good-sized boneless, skinless chicken thighs
1 envelope dry Italian salad dressing mix
¼ cup water
8-oz. pkg. cream cheese, at room temperature
10.5-oz. can cream of chicken soup
2 cups sliced fresh mushrooms or 8-oz. can sliced mushrooms, drained

1. Grease interior of slow-cooker crock.
2. Place thighs in crock.
3. In a bowl, combine salad dressing mix and water. Pour over chicken.
4. Cover. Cook on Low for 3 hours.
5. Meanwhile, beat cream cheese and soup until well blended. Stir in mushrooms.
6. Pour over chicken.
7. Cover. Cook 1 hour longer on Low, or until instant-read meat thermometer registers 160°-165° when stuck in center of thighs.
8. Serve over rice.

Encore Dijon Chicken

Dorothy VanDeest
Memphis, TN

Makes 6 servings

Prep. Time: 10-15 minutes
Cooking Time: 4 hours
Ideal slow-cooker size: 5 qt.

¼ tsp. dried basil
¼ tsp. dried oregano
4 Tbsp. Dijon mustard
2 Tbsp. olive oil
2 tsp. minced garlic or 1 tsp. garlic powder
6 boneless, skinless chicken thighs

1. Grease interior of slow-cooker crock.
2. Mix basil, oregano, mustard, oil, and garlic in a large bowl.
3. Add chicken pieces one at a time, dredging each thigh in the mixture.
4. Place coated thighs in crock. If you need to make a second layer, stagger the pieces so they aren't directly on top of each other. Pour any remaining sauce over thighs.
5. Cover. Cook on Low for 4 hours, or until an instant-read meat thermometer registers 160°-165° when stuck into the thighs.

Honey Garlic Chicken

Donna Treloar
Muncie, IN

Makes 4 servings

Prep. Time: 10 minutes
Cooking Time: 4 hours
Ideal slow-cooker size: 5 qt.

4 boneless, skinless chicken thighs
⅓ cup honey
1 cup ketchup
2 Tbsp. soy sauce
4 garlic cloves, minced

1. Grease interior of slow-cooker crock.
2. Place chicken thighs in crock.
3. In a bowl, mix together honey, ketchup, soy sauce, and minced garlic. Pour over chicken.
4. Cover. Cook on Low 4 hours or until instant-read meat thermometer registers 160°-165° when inserted into center of thighs.
5. Serve chicken and sauce together.

Variations:

Add sliced onion to the bottom of the crock before putting chicken in.

Good go-alongs with this recipe:

Good served with rice.

Lemony Greek Chicken

Ruth Shank
Monroe, GA

Makes 6 servings

Prep. Time: 15 minutes
Cooking Time: 4 hours
Ideal slow-cooker size: 4 or 5 qt.

6 boneless, skinless chicken thighs
2 medium onions, cut in quarters
¼ cup lemon juice
2 tsp. dried oregano
½ tsp. garlic powder
¼ tsp. black pepper
2 Tbsp. olive oil

1. Grease interior of slow-cooker crock.
2. Place thighs in cooker. If you need to make a second layer, stagger the pieces so they don't completely overlap each other.
3. Tuck onion quarters in around the chicken pieces.
4. In a small bowl, mix together lemon juice, oregano, garlic powder, and pepper. Pour over chicken and onions, making sure that all of the pieces are coated with the glaze.
5. Drizzle thighs and onions with olive oil.
6. Cover. Cook on Low 4 hours, or until an instant-read meat thermometer shows 160°-165° when inserted in thickest part of thighs.

One hour on High in a slow cooker equals about 2½ hours on Low. But all cookers are different, so run a test in your own to make sure.

Tasty Ranch Chicken

Kathleen A. Rogge
Alexandria, IN

Makes 6 servings

Prep. Time: 15 minutes
Cooking Time: 4 or 5 hours
Ideal slow-cooker size: 4 or 5 qt.

½ cup ranch salad dressing
1 Tbsp. flour
6 boneless, skinless chicken thighs
½ cup shredded cheddar cheese
⅓ cup grated Parmesan cheese

1. Grease interior of slow-cooker crock.
2. Mix salad dressing and flour in a shallow bowl.
3. Coat each thigh with dressing-flour mixture. Place in slow cooker. If you need to make a second layer, stagger the pieces so they don't fully overlap each other.
4. Mix cheeses together in a small bowl. Sprinkle over chicken. Lift pieces on the second layer to sprinkle cheese over pieces in first layer.
5. Cover. Cook on Low for 4 hours, or until instant-read meat thermometer registers 160°-165° when inserted in thickest part of thighs.
6. If you wish, place chicken on rimmed baking sheet and run under the broiler to brown the cheese and chicken. But watch carefully so it doesn't burn.

Bacon Ranch Slow-Cooked Chicken

Lavina Hochstedler
Grand Blanc, MI

Makes 4 servings

Prep. Time: 10 minutes
Cooking Time: 4 hours
Ideal slow-cooker size: 4 qt.

¼ cup fried and crumbled bacon
1 garlic clove, minced
1 envelope dry ranch dressing mix
10.5-oz. can cream of chicken soup
1 cup sour cream
4 boneless, skinless chicken thighs
cooked noodles

1. Grease interior of slow-cooker crock.
2. Combine the bacon, garlic, dry dressing mix, soup, and sour cream. Mix together well.
3. Place chicken in crock.
4. Pour sauce over chicken.
5. Cover. Cook on Low 4 hours, or until instant-read meat thermometer registers 160°-165° when stuck in center of thighs.
6. Serve over hot noodles.

Variations:

This recipe is super easy. It tastes a little like an Alfredo sauce, and kids and adults alike enjoy it. I tend to use more bacon than it calls for!

Good go-alongs with this recipe:

Cole slaw, applesauce, and good dinner rolls.

Zesty Barbecued Chicken

Carol Eberly
Harrisonburg, VA

Makes 8-12 servings

Prep. Time: 10-15 minutes
Cooking Time: 4-5 hours
Ideal slow-cooker size: 6 qt.

8-12 boneless, skinless chicken thighs
3 Tbsp. ketchup
2 Tbsp. Worcestershire sauce
2 Tbsp. apple cider vinegar
2 Tbsp. soy sauce
3 Tbsp. brown sugar
1 tsp. spicy brown mustard
1 tsp. salt
1 tsp. black pepper

1. Grease interior of slow-cooker crock.
2. Lay thighs in crock. When you make a second layer, stagger the pieces so they don't directly overlap each other.
3. In a mixing bowl, stir together all other ingredients.
4. When well mixed, spoon over thighs, lifting up the pieces on the second layer so the bottom ones get topped with sauce, too.
5. Cover. Cook on Low 4-5 hours, or until instant-read meat thermometer registers 160°-165° when stuck into thighs.

Butter Chicken

Pat Bishop
Bedminster, PA

Makes 8 servings

Prep. Time: 20 minutes
Cooking Time: 6-8 hours
Ideal slow-cooker size: 5-6 qt.

2 onions, diced
3 cloves garlic, minced
3 Tbsp. butter, softened to room temperature
2 Tbsp. grated fresh ginger
2 Tbsp. packed brown sugar
2 tsp. chili powder
¾ tsp. ground coriander
¾ tsp. turmeric
½ tsp. ground cinnamon
½ tsp. ground cumin
½ tsp. salt
¼ tsp. black pepper
28-oz. can diced tomatoes, undrained
1 cup chicken broth
¼ cup peanut butter, almond butter, or cashew butter
3 lbs. boneless, skinless chicken thighs, halved
1 cup sour cream
2 Tbsp. chopped fresh cilantro

1. Grease interior of slow-cooker crock.
2. In crock combine onions, garlic, butter, fresh ginger, brown sugar, chili powder, coriander, turmeric, cinnamon, cumin, salt, pepper, and tomatoes.
3. In a bowl, whisk broth with nut butter. Pour into crock. Stir everything together until well blended.
4. Settle chicken thighs into sauce, submerging as much as possible.
5. Cover. Cook on Low for 4 hours, or until instant-read meat thermometer registers 160° when stuck in center of thigh pieces.
6. Remove chicken with slotted spoon and place in bowl. Cover and keep warm.
7. With immersion blender, puree sauce until smooth. Add chicken back into sauce.
8. Cover. Cook another 15 minutes, or until heated through.
9. Stir in sour cream.
10. Serve sprinkled with cilantro over basmati rice.

Smoky Mountain Chicken

Amber Swarey
Honea Path, SC

Makes 6 servings

Prep. Time: 10-15 minutes
Cooking Time: 4 hours
Ideal slow-cooker size: 4 or 5 qt.

1 medium onion
6 boneless, skinless chicken thighs
½ cup ketchup
½ cup maple syrup
¼ cup apple cider vinegar
2 Tbsp. prepared mustard, optional

1. Grease interior of slow-cooker crock.
2. Cut onion into thin slices. Scatter over bottom of cooker.
3. Arrange chicken over onion slices. If you need to create a second layer, stagger the pieces so they don't completely overlap each other.
4. Combine remaining ingredients in a small bowl. Pour over the chicken, coating all of the pieces as well as you can.
5. Cover. Cook on Low for 4 hours, or until a quick-read meat thermometer reads 160°-165° when inserted in thickest part of thighs.

Coq Au Vin

Bernadette Veenstra
Grand Rapids, MI

Makes 8 servings

Prep. Time: 35 minutes
Cooking Time: 4-6 hours
Ideal slow-cooker size: oval 6 qt.

3 slices bacon, cut into ¾"-wide pieces
8-10 oz. fresh mushrooms, cut in half
10-oz. pkg. frozen pearl onions
10 chicken thighs, skin removed
½ tsp. salt
¼ tsp. pepper
1 medium onion, chopped
1 large carrot, peeled and chopped
4 garlic cloves, chopped
1 cup dry red wine
2 Tbsp. tomato paste
1 bay leaf
¾ cup chicken broth

1. Grease interior of slow-cooker crock.
2. In a big non-stick skillet, cook bacon over medium heat until browned. Or place bacon pieces on a paper plate. Cover with a paper towel and microwave on High for 3 minutes.
3. Using a slotted spoon, transfer browned bacon to crock.
4. Gently stir mushroom pieces and pearl onions into bacon in crock.
5. Salt and pepper chicken thighs. Place on top of the vegetables in the crock. If you need to make two layers or more, stagger pieces so they don't directly overlap each other.
6. In a good-sized bowl, stir together onion, carrot, garlic, wine, tomato paste, bay leaf, and chicken broth, mixing well.
7. Spoon onion-carrot mixture over chicken pieces, lifting up thighs on top layer to add veggie mixture to tops of thighs underneath.
8. Cook for 4-6 hours on Low, or until instant-read meat thermometer registers 165° when stuck in center of thighs (but not touching a bone).
9. To serve, discard bay leaf. Serve chicken, vegetables, and sauce in shallow bowls.

Good go-alongs with this recipe:

Salad, crusty French bread, couscous.

Chicken in Alfredo Sauce

Phyllis Good
Lancaster, PA

Makes 6 servings

Prep. Time: 20 minutes
Cooking Time: 4 hours
Ideal slow-cooker size: 5 qt.

6 boneless, skinless chicken thighs
10-oz. pkg. frozen chopped spinach, thawed, or 3 cups fresh spinach, steamed, drained, and chopped
3 thin slices deli ham, each cut in half
½ small red bell pepper, cut in thin strips
2 cups Alfredo sauce from a jar
1½ Tbsp. fresh parsley, chopped

1. Grease interior of slow-cooker crock.
2. Spread open each thigh and flatten either with the heel of your hand or a meat mallet, until about ⅛" thick.
3. Squeeze as much moisture out of spinach as you can. Divide evenly over thighs.
4. Top each thigh with a half slice of ham and a few red pepper strips.
5. Fold in sides and bottom of each thigh and roll up carefully, keeping the spinach, ham, and pepper strips tucked inside. Secure each one with a toothpick.
6. Place stuffed thighs in crock. If you need to create a second layer, stagger the pieces so they aren't directly overlapping.
7. Spoon the Alfredo sauce evenly over each thigh, including those on the bottom layer.
8. Cover. Cook on Low for 4 hours, or until an instant-read meat thermometer registers 160°-165° when stuck into the center of the meat.
9. Baste thighs with sauce occasionally while they cook.
10. To serve, cut rolls in half. Place on a platter and top with sauce. Serve with rice or pasta.

Chicken with Feta

Susan Tjon
Austin, TX

Makes 6 servings

Prep. Time: 15 minutes
Cooking Time: 4 hours
Ideal slow-cooker size: 4 or 5 qt.

6 boneless, skinless chicken thighs
2 Tbsp. lemon juice, divided
3-4 oz. feta cheese, crumbled
1 red or green bell pepper, chopped

1. Grease interior of slow-cooker crock.
2. Place thighs on bottom of crock. If you need to create a second layer, stagger the thighs so they don't completely overlap each other.
3. Sprinkle with 1 Tbsp. lemon juice.
4. Crumble feta cheese evenly over thighs. (If you've made 2 layers, lift up the top layer and sprinkle cheese over those underneath.)
5. Top with remaining lemon juice.
6. Cover. Cook on Low for 4 hours, or until instant-read meat thermometer registers 160°-165° when inserted in thighs.
7. While chicken is cooking, chop bell pepper. Sprinkle chicken with pepper just before serving.

Easy Italian Chicken and Potatoes

Mary June Hershberger
Lynchburg, VA

Makes 4 servings

Prep. Time: 15 minutes
Cooking Time: 6-8 hours
Ideal slow-cooker size: 3 qt.

4 boneless, skinless chicken thighs
½ cup Italian salad dressing
½ tsp. dried oregano
½ tsp. dried basil
½ cup grated Parmesan cheese
4-6 medium potatoes, peeled and cut into wedges

1. Grease interior of slow-cooker crock.
2. Place chicken in bottom of crock.
3. In a bowl, mix together Italian dressing, oregano, basil, and Parmesan cheese.
4. Pour half of sauce over chicken.
5. Lay potatoes over top of chicken.
6. Pour the rest of dressing mixture over all.
7. Cook on Low 4 hours, or until instant-read meat thermometer registers 165° when stuck in center of thighs and potatoes are tender.

Roasted Herby Chicken

Phyllis Good
Lancaster, PA

Makes 4-6 servings

Prep. Time: 15-20 minutes
Cooking Time: 4-6 hours
Ideal slow-cooker size: oval 6 qt.

4-5-lb. whole chicken
1 tsp. dried parsley
1 tsp. dried sage
1 tsp. dried rosemary
1 tsp. dried thyme
1 medium onion, quartered
2 garlic cloves, 1 whole, 1 sliced
1 Tbsp. butter, softened
paprika to taste
salt to taste
coarsely ground black pepper to taste

1. Grease interior of slow-cooker crock.
2. Pat chicken dry.
3. Mix dried herbs together in small bowl. Rub herbs in cavity of bird.
4. Lift skin of chicken (being careful not to tear it) and rub any remaining herbs under the skin, all over the bird as well as you can.
5. Place quartered onion and whole and sliced garlic cloves into cavity.
6. Using skewers and cooking twine, tie the cavity opening closed.
7. Rub outside of chicken with softened butter. Sprinkle with paprika, salt, and pepper.
8. Place chicken in cooker, breast side down.
9. Cover. Cook on Low 4-5 hours, or until instant-read meat thermometer registers 160° when stuck in breast (don't get against a bone) or 170° when stuck in thighs (again, don't get against a bone).
10. Remove chicken from cooker and place on cutting board. Cover to keep warm. Allow to stand 15 minutes before carving.

Tips:

Leftover chicken makes good sandwiches, or added to fresh greens makes a tasty salad.

Country Chicken

Andrea O'Neil
Fairfield, CT

Makes 6-8 servings

Prep. Time: 15-20 minutes
Cooking Time: 4-5 hours
Ideal slow-cooker size: 6 qt.

4 medium potatoes, peeled or not, and cubed
1 lb. Italian sausage, sweet or hot, cut into 1" pieces
4 medium green bell peppers, chopped
1 large onion, quartered and separated into pieces
1¼ lbs. fresh green beans or 2 10-oz. pkgs. frozen green beans, thawed
½ cup water
½ tsp. salt
½ tsp. dried oregano
½ tsp. dried basil
6 boneless, skinless chicken thighs

1. Grease interior of slow-cooker crock.
2. Combine all ingredients in slow cooker, except chicken thighs. Mix together gently but well.
3. Place thighs in cooker, pushing them down into the mixture. If you need to make a second layer, stagger the pieces so they don't directly overlap each other. Spoon some of the mixture over all the thighs.
4. Cover. Cook on Low 4-5 hours, or until potatoes and beans are tender, and instant-read meat thermometer registers 160°-165° when stuck into the thighs.

Chicken with Red Onions, Potatoes, and Rosemary

Kristine Stalter
Iowa City, IA

Makes 8 servings

Prep. Time: 15 minutes
Cooking Time: 4-5 hours
Ideal slow-cooker size: 6 qt.

2 red onions, each cut into 10 wedges
1¼ lbs. new potatoes, unpeeled and cut into small chunks
2 garlic bulbs, separated into cloves, unpeeled
1 tsp. salt
½ tsp. black pepper
4 Tbsp. olive oil
2 Tbsp. balsamic vinegar
5-6 sprigs rosemary
8 boneless, skinless chicken thighs

1. Grease interior of slow-cooker crock.
2. Spread onions, potatoes, and garlic cloves over bottom of crock.
3. Scatter salt and pepper over top.
4. Pour oil and vinegar over. Add rosemary, leaving some sprigs whole and stripping leaves off the rest.
5. Toss veggies and seasonings together.
6. Tuck chicken thighs among veggies. If you need to create a second layer, spoon some of the veggies and seasonings over the second layer, too.
7. Cover. Cook on Low 4 hours. Check if veggies are tender and if an instant-read meat thermometer registers 160°-165° when stuck in the thighs.
8. If the vegetables and chicken aren't done, cover and continue baking another hour on Low. Test again. Continue cooking until veggies are done to your liking and chicken has reached 160°-165°.
9. To serve, place thighs in a deep serving dish. Surround with veggies.

Cheesy Chicken Thighs

Cheryl Lapp
Parkesburg, PA

Makes 6 servings

Prep. Time: 20 minutes
Cooking Time: 4-5 hours
Ideal slow-cooker size: 4 or 5 qt.

1½ cups herb stuffing crumbs
2 eggs
6 boneless, skinless chicken thighs
6 slices bacon
½ lb. sliced cheese of your choice

1. Grease interior of slow-cooker crock.
2. Crush stuffing crumbs with rolling pin to make them finer. Place stuffing crumbs in shallow dish.
3. Place eggs in shallow dish and beat.
4. Wrap a slice of bacon around each thigh. Secure in place with a toothpick.
5. Dip each piece of chicken in egg, and then in stuffing crumbs.
6. Lay each coated piece in slow cooker. If you need to make a second layer, stagger the pieces so they don't completely overlap each other.
7. Top each thigh with a slice or two of cheese, including those that are partially covered with another thigh.
8. Cover. Cook on Low for 4 hours, or until instant-read meat thermometer registers 160°-165° when inserted in thighs.
9. If you wish, place the chicken on a rimmed baking sheet. Run under broiler to brown. But watch carefully so it doesn't burn.

Easy Creamy Chicken

Colleen Heatwole
Burton, MI

Makes 6 servings

Prep. Time: 10 minutes
Cooking Time: 4 hours
Ideal slow-cooker size: 5 qt.

6 boneless, skinless chicken thighs
1 envelope dry onion soup mix
1 cup reduced-fat sour cream
10.75-oz. can cream of chicken soup

1. Grease interior of slow-cooker crock.
2. Place thighs in crock. If you need to make a second layer, stagger pieces so they don't directly overlap each other.
3. In a bowl combine dry soup mix, sour cream, and chicken soup until well mixed.
4. Pour over chicken, making sure to cover pieces on the bottom with sauce, too.
5. Cover. Cook on Low 4 hours, or until instant-read meat thermometer registers 165° when stuck in center of thighs.

Tips:

Serve with rice or noodles.

Variations:

If your family likes mushrooms, you can substitute cream of mushroom soup for the cream of chicken soup.

Creamy Chicken with Stuffing

Kayla Snyder
Saegertown, PA

Makes 6 servings

Prep. Time: 15 minutes
Cooking Time: 4 hours
Ideal slow-cooker size: 4 or 5 qt.

6 boneless, skinless chicken thighs
6 slices Swiss or provolone cheese
10.5-oz. can cream of mushroom soup
¼ cup milk
1 cup stuffing mix
¼ cup (½ stick) melted butter

1. Grease interior of slow-cooker crock.
2. Place chicken in crock. If you need to make a second layer, stagger pieces so they don't overlap each other.
3. Lay a slice of cheese on top of each thigh.
4. In a bowl, mix soup and milk together. Pour over cheese layer, making sure that any thighs on the bottom of the crock are partially covered with sauce, too.
5. In same bowl, toss stuffing mix and butter together.
6. Sprinkle on top of chicken and sauce.
7. Cover. Cook on Low 4 hours, or until instant-read meat thermometer registers 165° when stuck into center of thighs.

Variations:

If you want more stuffing, it's okay to add more on top of chicken. Add more butter proportionately.

Comforting Chicken and Stuffing

Elva Engel and Lauren Bailey
Gap, PA and Dillsburg, PA

Makes 10-12 servings

Prep. Time: 20-25 minutes
Cooking Time: 5-6 hours
Ideal slow-cooker size: 7-8 qt.

2½ cups chicken broth
1 cup (2 sticks) butter, melted
½ cup chopped onion
½ cup chopped celery
¼ cup dried parsley flakes
1½ tsp. rubbed sage
1 tsp. poultry seasoning
1 tsp. salt
1¼ tsp. coarsely ground black pepper
2 eggs
10.75-oz. can cream of chicken soup
12 cups day-old bread cubes, cut or torn into ½" pieces
5 cups cubed cooked chicken,* divided
***To make cooked chicken in a slow cooker, see recipe on page 267.**

1. Grease interior of slow-cooker crock.
2. In a bowl, combine chicken broth, melted butter, chopped onion and celery, parsley flakes, sage, poultry seasoning, salt, and pepper.
3. In another bowl, combine eggs and soup. Stir into broth mixture until smooth.
4. Put bread cubes in a large bowl. Pour broth-soup mixture over bread. Toss well until all bread cubes are dampened.
5. Layer ⅓ of bread mixture into crock.
6. Cover with half of cooked chicken.
7. Cover with half of remaining bread mixture.
8. Top with remaining chicken.
9. Cover with remaining bread mixture.
10. Cover. Cook on Low 3-4 hours. If you like a crusty finish to Stuffing, take lid off during last 45 minutes of cooking.
11. Serve with Chicken Gravy. See recipe on page 120.

Tips:

Serve with cranberry sauce and a green salad.

Variations:

I make a thick white sauce, with 3 tsp. of chicken base (aka "granulated bouillon") added, in place of the canned cream soup.

Chicken and Stuffing

Elva Engel
Gap, PA

Makes 12 servings

***Prep. Time:** 20-30 minutes*
***Cooking Time:** 4-5 hours*
***Ideal slow-cooker size:** 7 qt.*

12 good-sized boneless, skinless chicken thighs
1 loaf sturdy bread, whole wheat or multi-grain, torn into pieces
1 medium onion, diced
1 cup chopped celery
½ tsp. salt
1 tsp. curry powder
4 eggs, beaten
1 cup water

1. Grease interior of slow cooker crock.
2. Place thighs in crock. When you stack them, stagger the pieces so they don't directly overlap each other.
3. In large bowl, gently mix together the other ingredients in the order given.
4. When well mixed, spoon over chicken.
5. Cover. Cook on Low 4-5 hours, or until instant-read meat thermometer registers 160°-165° when stuck into the thighs. (Test several at different layers and positions within cooker to make sure all are finished.)
6. To serve, place stuffing on large platter, topped with thighs.

Excellent Chicken Dressing

Elsie Schlabach
Millersburg, OH

Makes 10-12 servings

***Prep. Time:** 25 minutes*
***Cooking Time:** 2-4 hours*
***Ideal slow-cooker size:** 6 or 7 qt.*

12 slices whole wheat bread
½ cup (1 stick) butter, melted
6 eggs, beaten
10.75-oz. can cream of celery soup
1½ cups chicken broth
1 tsp. chicken base or granulated bouillon
1 scant tsp. salt
½ tsp. seasoned salt
2 cups diced potatoes
1½ cups diced carrots
1½ cups chopped celery
1 cup diced sweet potatoes
3 cups diced cooked chicken

1. Grease interior of slow-cooker crock.
2. Cube bread and place in big bowl.
3. In a separate bowl, mix together butter, beaten eggs, soup, broth, bouillon, and seasonings.
4. Pour over bread cubes. Toss together gently.
5. Mix potatoes, carrots, celery, and sweet potatoes together. Fold into bread cubes.
6. Transfer to slow cooker.
7. Cover. Cook on Low 2-4 hours, or until vegetables are as tender as you like them.
8. Uncover during last 45 minutes of cooking time so top of Dressing dries and crisps.
9. Serve with Chicken Gravy (see recipe on page 120).

Tips:

This Dressing can be made ahead and frozen.

Good go-alongs with this recipe:

Applesauce is a nice side dish to serve with this.

If there's too much liquid collecting in the slow-cooker dish that you're cooking, vent the lid by sticking a toothpick—or even the handle of a wooden spoon—under the edge of the lid to tilt it slightly. That allows some moisture to escape.

Chicken Scarpariello

Bernadette Veenstra
Grand Rapids, MI

Makes 10 servings

Prep. Time: 30 minutes
Cooking Time: 4-6 hours
Ideal slow-cooker size: 6 qt.

1 lb. hot or sweet Italian sausage links, cut cross-wise into 1" pieces
1 medium onion, chopped
2 garlic cloves, minced
2 Tbsp. tomato paste
2 Tbsp. balsamic vinegar
1 tsp. Italian seasoning or dried thyme
10 chicken thighs (3½-4 lbs.), skin removed
¼ tsp. salt
¼ tsp. black pepper
1 pint cherry tomatoes
½ lb. fresh cremini mushrooms, sliced

1. Grease interior of slow-cooker crock.
2. In a 12" non-stick skillet, cook sausage pieces over medium heat, turning occasionally, until well browned, about 6 minutes.
3. Spoon browned sausage into slow-cooker crock.
4. Stir in onion and garlic.
5. Add tomato paste, vinegar, and Italian seasoning until well blended.
6. Sprinkle chicken pieces with salt and pepper.
7. Place chicken on top of sausage and sauce.
8. Spoon mushrooms and tomatoes over chicken.
9. Cover. Cook on Low 4-6 hours, or until instant-read meat thermometer registers 165° when stuck into center of thighs (but not against the bone).

Chicken Tikka Masala

Susan Kasting
Jenks, OK

Makes 6 servings

Prep. Time: 20 minutes
Cooking Time: 4¼ hours
Ideal slow-cooker size: 6 qt.

2 lbs. boneless, skinless chicken thighs
1 medium onion, chopped
3 cloves garlic, minced
1½ Tbsp. grated ginger
29-oz. can pureed tomatoes
1 Tbsp. olive oil
1 Tbsp. garam masala
½ tsp cumin
½ tsp. paprika
1 cinnamon stick
1 tsp. salt
1-1½ tsp. cayenne pepper, depending on how much heat you like
2 bay leaves
¾ cup Greek yogurt
½ cup cream
1½ tsp. cornstarch

1. Grease interior of slow-cooker crock.
2. Lay thighs in crock. If you need to make a second layer, stagger pieces so they don't directly overlap each other.
3. In a good-sized bowl, mix together onion, garlic, ginger, tomatoes, olive oil, garam masala, cumin, paprika, cinnamon stick, salt, cayenne pepper, and bay leaves.
4. Cover. Cook 4 hours on Low, or until instant-read meat thermometer registers 165° when inserted in center of thigh.
5. Remove thighs and keep warm on platter or bowl.
6. Mix Greek yogurt into sauce in cooker.
7. In a small bowl, combine cream and cornstarch until smooth. Mix into sauce in cooker.
8. Return chicken to cooker.
9. Cover. Cook an additional 15-20 minutes, or until sauce has thickened.

Tips:

Serve over rice.

Good go-alongs with this recipe:

Naan bread.

Indian Chicken Curry

Judy Buller
Bluffton, OH

Makes 6 servings

Prep. Time: 35 minutes
Cooking Time: 7½-8 hours
Ideal slow-cooker size: oval 6 qt.

2 Tbsp. curry powder
1 tsp. ground coriander
1 tsp. ground cumin
3 garlic cloves, minced
14-oz. can coconut milk
½ tsp. Tabasco sauce
1 Tbsp. tomato paste or ketchup
6 boneless, skinless chicken thighs
15-oz. can garbanzo beans, drained
1 medium onion, chopped
1 green or red bell pepper, chopped
1 cup sliced carrots
1 cup sliced celery
1 sweet potato, peeled and chopped

1. Grease interior of slow-cooker crock.
2. In the crock, combine curry, coriander, cumin, minced garlic, coconut milk, Tabasco, and tomato paste. Blend well.
3. Lay chicken thighs on top, pushing down into sauce.
4. Top thighs with beans, onion, bell pepper, carrots, celery, and sweet potato.
5. Cover. Cook on Low 7½-8 hours, or until instant-read meat thermometer registers 160° and vegetables are as tender as you like them.
6. Serve over cooked rice.

Good go-alongs with this recipe:

Fruit and bread.

Basic Meat Curry Sauce

Carol Eveleth
Hillsdale, WY

Makes 8 servings

Prep. Time: 20 minutes
Cooking Time: 3-4 hours on High
Ideal slow-cooker size: 3 qt.

2 onions, chopped
1-2 cloves garlic, minced
2 Tbsp. lemon juice
2-4 tsp. curry powder

Any one of the following ingredients:
3 lbs. cooked chicken thighs, cut in 1" chunks
2 lbs. cooked beef chunks
2 lbs. browned meatballs

1. Grease interior of slow-cooker crock.
2. Mix onions, garlic, lemon juice, and curry powder in crock.
3. Stir in your choice of meat until all pieces are well coated.
4. Cover. Cook on Low 2-3 hours, or until onions are as tender as you like them.
5. If you'd like a thickened sauce, mix 2 Tbsp. flour into meat and sauce at end of cooking time. Cook on High 10 minutes, or until sauce bubbles and thickens.
6. Serve over steamed rice.

Tips:

This is a great way to use leftover meat.

Flaming Chicken Bombay

Irene Dewar
Pickerington, OH

Makes 8 servings

***Prep. Time:** 15 minutes*
***Cooking Time:** 4 hours*
***Ideal slow-cooker size:** 5 qt.*

8 boneless, skinless chicken thighs
2 medium onions, chopped
1½ tsp. curry powder
1 tsp. salt
½ tsp. black pepper
¾ tsp. dried thyme
1 tsp. sugar
28-oz. can diced tomatoes, undrained
1 green bell pepper, diced
½ cup raisins
1½ cups uncooked instant rice
1 cup water

1. Grease interior of slow-cooker crock.
2. Lay thighs in cooker. If you need to create a second layer, stagger the pieces so they don't directly overlap each other.
3. In a bowl, mix together onions, curry powder, salt, pepper, thyme, sugar, and diced tomatoes with juice. Spoon over chicken, being sure to top each thigh with some of the sauce.
4. Cover. Cook on Low 3½ hours.
5. Remove thighs from cooker and place on platter. Cover to keep warm.
6. Stir chopped green pepper, raisins, rice, and water into sauce in cooker.
7. Put thighs back into cooker.
8. Cover and continue cooking another 30 minutes on High.
9. Check to see that rice is fully cooked and that an instant-read meat thermometer registers 160°-165° when stuck in thighs. If more time is needed, cook an additional 30 minutes and check again.
10. When ready to serve, place thighs in a deep platter or bowl and surround with rice and vegetables.

Yogurt Chicken Curry

Laverne Nafziger
Goshen, IN

Makes 10 servings

***Prep. Time:** 15 minutes*
***Cooking Time:** 4-5 hours*
***Ideal slow-cooker size:** 6 qt.*

2 lbs. (1 quart) plain yogurt
4 heaping tsp. curry powder
2 heaping tsp. turmeric
1 heaping tsp. ground coriander
8 boneless, skinless chicken thighs
1 large onion, chopped
5 garlic cloves, chopped
1" ginger root, grated or finely chopped
½ tsp. salt
1 medium raw potato, grated
1 cup sour cream
1 cup chopped cilantro, optional

1. Mix yogurt, curry powder, turmeric, and coriander in large non-metallic bowl.
2. Submerge chicken thighs in mixture. Cover and place in refrigerator to marinate 8 hours or overnight.
3. Grease interior of slow-cooker crock.
4. When ready to cook, remove chicken from sauce and set aside.
5. Put sauce into cooker. Add onion, garlic, ginger, salt, and raw potato. Mix together well.
6. Push thighs down into sauce. If you need to make a second layer, stagger the pieces so they don't directly overlap each other. Spoon sauce over thighs on both layers.
7. Cover. Cook on Low 4 hours. Check to see if chicken is fully cooked by inserting an instant-read meat thermometer into the thighs. If it registers 160°-165°, the chicken's finished. If not, continue cooking another hour on Low. Check again to see if it's reached the safe temperature. If not, continue cooking for 30-minute intervals, checking the temperature at the end of each.
8. When chicken is cooked, remove it to a platter.
9. Stir sour cream into sauce in cooker. Put chicken back into sauce in cooker. Cover and cook 30 more minutes on Low.
10. To serve, put chicken on platter. Pour sauce over. Top with cilantro just before serving. Pass a bowl of cooked rice, followed by the Yogurt Chicken Curry.

Chicken and Vegetable Curry

Rebekah Zehr
Lowville, NY

Makes 6 servings

Prep. Time: 15 minutes
Cooking Time: 4-6 hours
Ideal slow-cooker size: 5 or 6 qt.

1 lb. boneless, skinless chicken thighs
3-4 cups mixture of fresh vegetables, including onion, bell peppers, cauliflower, and fresh spinach
14-oz. can coconut milk
1-2 Tbsp. red curry paste, depending on how much you like curry
2 tsp. honey
1 Tbsp. lime juice
½ tsp. coarse salt
1 Tbsp. fish sauce

1. Grease interior of slow-cooker crock.
2. Place chicken in bottom of pot.
3. Place cut-up veggies on top of chicken, except for spinach. Leave cauliflower in big chunks; it will break down quickly if cut too small.
4. Mix all other ingredients together and pour over chicken and veggies.
5. Cook on Low 4-6 hours, or until vegetables are as tender as you like them, and instant-read meat thermometer registers 165° when stuck in center of thigh.
6. At end of cooking time mix in fresh spinach.

Tips:

1. If using frozen cauliflower, add 1 hour before end of cooking time. Otherwise it will break down if cooking 4-6 hours. 2. Serve over rice.

Mexican Stuffed Chicken

Karen Waggoner
Joplin, MO

Makes 6 servings

Prep. Time: 20 minutes
Cooking Time: 4-4½ hours
Ideal slow-cooker size: 5 qt.

6 boneless, skinless chicken thighs
6-oz. piece of Monterey Jack cheese, cut into 2″-long, ½″-thick sticks
2 4-oz. cans chopped green chilies, drained
½ cup dry bread crumbs
¼ cup grated Parmesan cheese
1 Tbsp. chili powder
½ tsp. salt
¼ tsp. ground cumin
¾ cup flour
1 stick (½ cup) butter, melted

1. Grease interior of slow-cooker crock.
2. Spread out the thighs and flatten each one, either with the heel of your hand or a mallet, until they're about ⅛″ thick.
3. Place a cheese stick in the middle of each thigh. Top with a mound of chilies. Roll up the thigh and tuck in ends. Secure with a toothpick. Set aside on a platter.
4. In a shallow bowl, mix bread crumbs, Parmesan cheese, chili powder, salt, and cumin.
5. In a second shallow bowl, coat chicken with flour.
6. Place melted butter in a third shallow bowl. Dip floured chicken into butter.
7. Then roll in crumb mixture.
8. Place seam side down in crock. If you need to make a second layer, stagger the pieces so they don't overlap directly.
9. Cover. Cook on Low 4-4½ hours, or until an instant-read meat thermometer registers 160°-165° when stuck into the center of the meat.
10. Take the toothpicks out of the rolls before serving, or warn the people you're serving.

Salsa Chicken with Veggies

Shelia Heil
Lancaster, PA

Makes 8 servings

Prep. Time: 20 minutes
Cooking Time: 5-6 hours on Low and 3 hours on High
Ideal slow-cooker size: 5 qt.

2 lbs. boneless, skinless chicken thighs
2 Tbsp., or 1 envelope, dry taco seasoning
1 cup salsa, your choice of heat
14.5-oz. can petite diced tomatoes, undrained
1 cup diced onions
½ cup shredded carrots
½ cup diced celery, optional
½ cup water
8 hamburger buns

1. Grease interior of slow-cooker crock.
2. Place chicken in crock. If you need to make another layer, stagger pieces so they don't directly overlap each other.
3. Sprinkle the taco seasoning over each piece, remembering to hit the pieces on the bottom.
4. Layer salsa and vegetables evenly over top chicken.
5. Pour water over mixture.
6. Cover. Cook on Low 4 hours, or until instant-read meat thermometer registers 165° when stuck into center of thighs.
7. Lift chicken into bowl. Shred with two forks.
8. Stir meat back into sauce and mix together well.
9. Serve on hamburger buns.

Mexican Chicken Bake

Gretchen H. Maust
Keezletown, VA

Makes 8 servings

Prep. Time: 15 minutes
Cooking Time: 4 hours
Ideal slow-cooker size: 6 qt.

½ cup raw brown rice
1⅓ cups water
2 14.5-oz. cans diced tomatoes, undrained
15-oz. can black beans, drained
1 cup corn, fresh, frozen, or canned
1 Tbsp. cumin
1 Tbsp. chili powder
½ tsp. salt
¼ tsp. black pepper
4 garlic cloves, minced
4 boneless, skinless chicken thighs
1 cup red bell pepper, diced
1 cup green bell pepper, diced
2 cups shredded cheddar cheese

1. Grease interior of slow-cooker crock.
2. Pour rice and water into crock.
3. Stir in tomatoes, beans, corn, cumin, chili powder, salt, pepper, and minced garlic. Mix together well.
4. Submerge chicken thighs in mixture.
5. Cover. Cook on Low for 3 hours.
6. Stir in diced red and green peppers. Cover and continue cooking 1 more hour on Low, or until instant-read meat thermometer registers 160°-165° when stuck into thighs.
7. Remove chicken and cut into bite-sized pieces. Stir back into mixture.
8. Sprinkle cheese over top. Allow cheese to melt, then serve.

Out of This World Chicken and Rice

Doris Slatten
Mt. Juliet, TN

Makes 8 servings

Prep. Time: 30 minutes
Cooking Time: 4 hours
Ideal slow-cooker size: 6 qt.

8 good-sized boneless, skinless chicken thighs
1 large onion, chopped
1 green bell pepper, chopped
1 red bell pepper, chopped
1 large garlic clove, sliced
1 lb. fresh mushrooms, sliced
12 oz. sliced black olives
½ tsp. salt
½ tsp. black pepper
½ tsp. dried oregano
½ tsp. dried rosemary
½ tsp. dried thyme
4 bay leaves
28-oz. can diced tomatoes with juice
8-oz. can tomato sauce
2 cups water
2 Tbsp. soy sauce
14-oz. box instant rice

1. Grease interior of slow-cooker crock.
2. Lay thighs in cooker. If you need to make a second layer, stagger the pieces so they don't directly overlap each other.
3. In a large bowl, mix together all other ingredients except rice.
4. Pour over thighs, making sure to spoon vegetables over all of them.
5. Cover. Cook on Low 4 hours, or until instant-read meat thermometer registers 160°-165° when stuck in thighs.
6. Thirty minutes before end of cooking time, lift thighs onto platter and cover to keep warm. Stir in rice.
7. Return thighs to cooker, pushing them down into the sauce. Cover and continue cooking 30 more minutes, or until rice is tender.
8. To serve, place chicken in a deep bowl or on a deep platter. Surround with rice and vegetables.

Magra's Chicken and Rice

Carolyn Spohn
Shawnee, KS

Makes 8 servings

Prep. Time: 20 minutes
Cooking Time: 5 hours
Ideal slow-cooker size: 6 qt.

2-3 medium carrots, chopped
1 medium onion, chopped
1 rib celery, chopped
2 cloves garlic, chopped
¼ tsp. dried rosemary, crumbled
3 cups chicken broth
8 boneless, skinless chicken thighs
1½ cups instant rice

1. Grease interior of slow-cooker crock.
2. Place carrots, onion, celery, garlic, rosemary, and chicken broth into slow cooker. Mix together well.
3. Put chicken into cooker, pushing it down into the broth. If you need to make a second layer, stagger the pieces so that they don't directly overlap each other. Spoon broth over top of second layer if you can't submerge those pieces in the liquid.
4. Cover. Cook on Low 4½ hours.
5. Lift thighs onto platter and cover. Stir rice into broth.
6. Return chicken to cooker, pushing pieces down in the broth as much as possible.
7. Cover. Cook 30 more minutes on Low, or until instant-read meat thermometer registers 160°-165° when stuck in the thighs.
8. To serve, place thighs in deep serving dish. Surround them with rice, vegetables, and broth.

Time-Saver Chicken and Rice

Elaine W. Good
Lititz, PA

Makes 6 servings

Prep. Time: 20 minutes
Cooking Time: 4 hours
Ideal slow-cooker size: 6 qt.

1½ cups uncooked brown rice
3 Tbsp. chopped onion
¼ cup chopped celery
½ cup white flour
¾ tsp. salt
½ stick (¼ cup) butter
3 cups water or chicken broth, or combination of the two
1¾ cups milk
6 good-sized boneless, skinless chicken thighs
seasoning salt, to taste

1. Grease interior of slow-cooker crock.
2. Cover bottom of crock evenly with uncooked rice.
3. Sprinkle evenly with chopped onion, chopped celery, flour, and salt.
4. Dot with chunks of butter.
5. Pour liquids over gently, being careful not to disturb the veggies, flour, and salt.
6. Arrange thighs on top, sprinkling each with seasoning salt before you put them in. If you need to make a second layer, stagger the pieces so they don't directly overlap each other.
7. Cover. Cook on Low 4 hours, or until rice is tender and instant-read meat thermometer registers 160°-165° when stuck into thighs.
8. Serve on deep platter or in a deep bowl, with the rice on the bottom and the chicken on top.

Chicken Tortilla Casserole

Edith Romano
Westminster, MD

Makes 6 servings

Prep. Time: 30 minutes
Cooking Time: 2-4 hours
Ideal slow-cooker size: 6 qt.

14.5-oz. can diced tomatoes, undrained
10.75-oz. can cream of chicken soup*
4-oz. can diced green chilies
¼-½ cup chopped cilantro, according to your taste preference
2 Tbsp. minute tapioca
12 torn-up corn tortillas, divided
2½-3 cups cubed chicken thighs, uncooked, divided
¾ cup diced onion, divided
2 cups grated cheddar cheese, divided
salsa
guacamole
sour cream

1. Grease interior of slow-cooker crock.
2. In a bowl, combine tomatoes, soup, green chilies, cilantro, and tapioca. Set aside.
3. Layer the following ingredients in crock in 3 layers: ⅓ of tortillas, ⅓ of chicken, ⅓ of reserved soup mixture, ⅓ of onions, ⅓ of cheese.
4. Repeat layers twice.
5. Cook on Low for 4 hours or on High for 2 hours.
6. Uncover. Allow to stand 10 minutes before serving to allow dish to firm up.
7. Serve with salsa, guacamole, and sour cream for each diner to add to top of individual serving.

Tips:

Leftover chicken is a good way to make this quick and easy.

Good go-alongs with this recipe:

Guacamole would be delicious with this recipe.

Buy dried herbs and spices in small amounts because they lose their flavor over time.

Taco Chicken Bowls

Kayla Snyder
Saegertown, PA

Makes 8 servings

Prep. Time: 15 minutes
Cooking Time: 3-4 hours
Ideal slow-cooker size: 4 qt.

1½ lbs. boneless, skinless chicken thighs
16-oz. jar salsa, as hot or mild as you like
15-oz. can black beans
½ lb. fresh or frozen corn
1 Tbsp. chili powder
½ Tbsp. cumin
1 Tbsp. minced garlic
1 tsp. dried oregano
¼ tsp. cayenne pepper
¼ tsp. salt
freshly ground black pepper to taste
¼ cup water
2 cups uncooked rice
2 cups shredded cheese
cilantro, chopped
favorite taco dressing

1. Grease interior of slow-cooker crock.
2. Place thighs in crock.
3. In a good-sized bowl, mix together salsa, beans, corn, chili powder, cumin, garlic, oregano, cayenne pepper, salt, black pepper, and water.
4. Spoon mixture over chicken.
5. Cover. Cook on Low 3-4 hours, or until instant-read meat thermometer inserted into center of thigh registers 160°-165°.
6. Near end of chicken's cooking time, cook 2 cups of rice in microwave or stove top, according to its package directions.
7. When chicken is done cooking, stir with a fork to shred meat. Or using a slotted spoon, lift chicken into large bowl and shred it with 2 forks. Stir back into sauce and keep warm.
8. Have each diner make a pile of rice on her/his plate. Top with taco chicken mixture, then shredded cheese, fresh cilantro, and dressing.

Wild Rice-Chicken-Sausage Bake

Carla Elliott
Phoenix, AZ

Makes 8-10 servings

Prep. Time: 30 minutes
Cooking Time: 4-5 hours
Ideal slow-cooker size: 6 qt.

1 lb. bulk sausage, regular, sweet Italian, or hot Italian
¾ cup uncooked wild rice
¾ cup uncooked brown rice
1 medium onion, chopped
1 cup diced celery
10.75-oz. can cream of mushroom soup
5 cups chicken broth
½ tsp. salt
½ tsp. black pepper
½ lb. fresh mushrooms, sliced, or 4-oz. can sliced mushrooms, drained
8 boneless, skinless chicken thighs

1. Brown sausage in skillet, stirring often to break up clumps, until no longer pink. Drain off drippings and discard.
2. Meanwhile, grease interior of slow-cooker crock.
3. With a slotted spoon, remove browned sausage from skillet and place in cooker.
4. Stir in uncooked wild rice and uncooked brown rice, onion, celery, cream of mushroom soup, chicken broth, salt, and pepper. Mix together well.
5. Stir in mushrooms.
6. Place thighs in cooker, pushing them down into the mixture. If you need to make a second layer, stagger the pieces so they don't directly overlap each other. Spoon some of the sauce over the top layer.
7. Cover. Cook on Low for 4 hours. Insert an instant-read meat thermometer into the thighs. If it registers 160°-165°, the chicken is finished. If it's done, remove the chicken to a large deep bowl, cover, and keep warm. If it is not, continue cooking another hour on Low, checking at the end to make sure it has reached the safe temperature.
8. Check that the rice is fully cooked. If not, it too can cook an additional hour. If the chicken is finished but the rice isn't, remove the chicken as instructed above, and allow the rice to continue cooking, covered, for another 30 minutes. Check it then. Continue cooking for 30-minute intervals and then checking, until the rice is tender.
9. To serve, place thighs in a deep bowl or platter and surround with the rice.

Edie's Paella

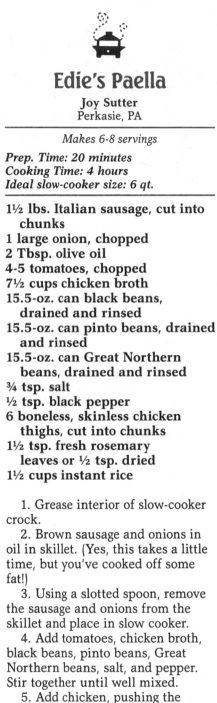

Joy Sutter
Perkasie, PA

Makes 6-8 servings

Prep. Time: 20 minutes
Cooking Time: 4 hours
Ideal slow-cooker size: 6 qt.

1½ lbs. Italian sausage, cut into chunks
1 large onion, chopped
2 Tbsp. olive oil
4-5 tomatoes, chopped
7½ cups chicken broth
15.5-oz. can black beans, drained and rinsed
15.5-oz. can pinto beans, drained and rinsed
15.5-oz. can Great Northern beans, drained and rinsed
¾ tsp. salt
½ tsp. black pepper
6 boneless, skinless chicken thighs, cut into chunks
1½ tsp. fresh rosemary leaves or ½ tsp. dried
1½ cups instant rice

1. Grease interior of slow-cooker crock.
2. Brown sausage and onions in oil in skillet. (Yes, this takes a little time, but you've cooked off some fat!)
3. Using a slotted spoon, remove the sausage and onions from the skillet and place in slow cooker.
4. Add tomatoes, chicken broth, black beans, pinto beans, Great Northern beans, salt, and pepper. Stir together until well mixed.
5. Add chicken, pushing the thighs down into the liquid.
6. Cover. Cook on Low 4 hours, or until instant-read meat thermometer registers 160°-165° when stuck into thighs.
7. Thirty minutes before end of cooking time, lift out thighs. Place on platter and cover with foil. Stir in rosemary and rice.
8. Put thighs back in cooker, pushing down into broth. Cover and continue cooking (see Step 6 above).
9. Let stand 10 minutes. Then remove chicken and cut it into bite-sized pieces. Stir back into mixture and serve.

Chicken and Tortellini Dinner

Susan Kasting
Jenks, OK

Makes 6-8 servings

Prep. Time: 15 minutes
Cooking Time: 4 hours
Ideal slow-cooker size: 6 qt.

1½ lbs. boneless, skinless chicken thighs
19-oz. bag cheese tortellini
10-oz. box frozen spinach, thawed and squeezed dry
8-oz. pkg. cream cheese
29-oz. can diced tomatoes
1 tsp. dried oregano
1 tsp. dried basil
2 cloves garlic, minced
grated Parmesan cheese, optional
hot pepper flakes, optional

1. Grease interior of slow-cooker crock.
2. Place thighs in crock. If you need to make a second layer, stagger the pieces so they don't directly overlap each other.
3. Scatter tortellini over chicken.
4. Cut cream cheese into cubes. Place in bowl.
5. Add all other ingredients, except Parmesan and pepper flakes, to cheese in bowl. Mix together well.
6. Spoon sauce over meat and tortellini in cooker.
7. Cover. Cook on Low 4 hours, or until instant-read meat thermometer registers 165° when stuck in center of thighs.
8. Pass Parmesan cheese and pepper flakes to diners to add to their dishes if they wish.

Good go-alongs with this recipe:

Ceasar salad.

Chicken-N-Noodles

Lavina Hochstedler
Grand Blanc, MI

Makes 8 servings

Prep. Time: 10 minutes
Cooking Time: 8 hours on Low
Ideal slow-cooker size: 6 or 7 qt.

4 good-sized boneless, skinless chicken thighs
2 10.5-oz. cans cream of chicken soup
6 cups chicken broth, or 32-oz. box, plus 15-oz. can, chicken broth
½ cup (1 stick) butter
16-oz. bag egg noodles

1. Grease interior of slow-cooker crock.
2. Place thighs in crock.
3. In a large bowl, mix soup and broth together.
4. Pour over thighs.
5. Cut butter into chunks and distribute over top of meat and sauce.
6. Cover. Cook on Low 3½ hours, or until instant-read meat thermometer registers 150° when stuck in center of thighs.
7. Stir noodles into sauce until noodles are submerged and mixed well throughout. (Lift thighs out with tongs into bowl and keep warm if you're having trouble mixing noodles and sauce. Then return thighs to crock, pushing down into sauce.)
8. Cook another 30-60 minutes, or until noodles are tender.

Variations:

Sometimes I add 1 cup frozen peas when I add the noodles. You may need to cook the dish a few minutes longer if you do that.

Good go-alongs with this recipe:

A good tossed salad, cole slaw, or applesauce.

Magical Chicken Pie

Marilyn Kurtz
Willow Street, PA

Makes 8-10 servings

Prep. Time: ½ hour
Cooking Time: 4-5 hours
Ideal slow-cooker size: 5 qt.

1 lb. fresh or frozen green beans (thawed if frozen)
2 cups potatoes, peeled or not, sliced
2 cups carrots, sliced
2 cups fresh, frozen (and thawed), or canned corn
¾ cup onion, chopped
2 lbs. boneless, skinless chicken thighs, cut in 1" cubes
½ tsp. salt
10.5-oz. can cream of celery soup
½ soup can, or ⅓ cup, of water

1. Grease interior of slow-cooker crock.
2. Put green beans, potatoes, carrots, corn, onion, and chicken cubes in crock in the order given.
3. In a bowl, blend together salt, soup, and water. When well mixed, pour over other ingredients in crock.
4. Cover. Cook on High for 3 hours, or until instant-read meat thermometer registers 160° when stuck in center of a chicken cube, and vegetables are as tender as you like them.
5. Serve. Or, if you're looking for a special touch, stir all ingredients together well. Then transfer to a greased 11x13 baking dish.
6. Top "Pie" with baked pie crust hearts, made ahead. Then serve.
7. To make hearts, use recipe for one 9" pie crust, rolled out and cut into heart shapes.
8. Put hearts on baking sheet and prick each with a fork.
9. Bake at 400° for about 10-12 minutes until lightly browned. Store in tightly covered container until ready to use.

My girlfriends and I get together for dinner once a month. We each bring along with us 4 frozen slow-cooker dinners, each for 6 people. Then we exchange our dinners, and each person goes home with 4 different dinners. It has been so much fun trying each other's recipes.
— Melanie Miller, Flemington, NJ

Chicken Gravy for a Buffet

Elsie Schlabach
Millersburg, OH

Makes 10-12 servings

Prep. Time: 20 minutes
Cooking Time: 1-2 hours
Ideal slow-cooker size: 1-2 qt.

4 Tbsp. cornstarch
3 Tbsp. flour
1 egg yolk
½ cup milk
4¼ cups chicken broth
1½ Tbsp. poultry seasoning
⅛ tsp. garlic powder

1. Using a whisk, blend cornstarch, flour, egg yolk, and milk together until smooth. Strain out any lumps.
2. In a medium saucepan, combine broth, seasoning, and garlic powder.
3. Bring to a boil. Turn back heat until broth just simmers.
4. Gradually stir cornstarch-flour mixture into hot broth.
5. Continue stirring until thickened.
6. Pour into small slow cooker to keep warm on your buffet.
7. Serve with waffles, biscuits, or chicken stuffing.

Chicken Cacciatore with Linguine

Phyllis Good
Lancaster, PA

Makes 6 servings

Prep. Time: 15 minutes
Cooking Time: 4 hours
Ideal slow-cooker size: 6 qt.

2 large onions, sliced thinly
3 lbs. chicken thighs, skin removed
2 garlic cloves, minced
28-oz. can stewed tomatoes
8-oz. can tomato sauce
1 tsp. salt
½ tsp. black pepper (coarsely ground is best)
2 tsp. dried oregano
1 tsp. dried basil
⅓ cup white wine
2 cups sliced fresh mushrooms

1. Grease interior of slow-cooker crock.
2. Place onions evenly over bottom of slow cooker.
3. Lay chicken thighs over onions. If you need to add a second layer, stagger the pieces so they don't directly overlap each other.
4. Combine remaining ingredients, except mushrooms, in a good-sized bowl. Pour over chicken.
5. Cover. Cook on Low 4 hours, or until instant-read meat thermometer registers 160°-165° when stuck in thighs.
6. Thirty minutes before end of cooking time, stir in sliced mushrooms. Cover and continue cooking.
7. Remove bay leaves before serving.
8. Serve over hot buttered linguine.

I cook a whole chicken on Sunday, and we have roast chicken and veggies for dinner. Leftovers are diced up for salads for lunch during the workweek and chicken noodle soup for supper. — Regina Martin, Brownstown, PA

Chicken Cacciatore with Vegetables

Marla Folkerts
Batavia, IL

Makes 4 servings

Prep. Time: 25 minutes
Cooking Time: 4 hours
Ideal slow-cooker size: 5 qt.

2 lbs. boneless, skinless chicken thighs
28-oz. can diced tomatoes
½ red bell pepper and ½ green bell pepper, cut lengthwise
½ large onion, chopped
1 tsp. dried oregano
1 bay leaf
salt and pepper to taste
3-4 large potatoes
1-lb. bag baby carrots

1. Grease interior of slow-cooker crock.
2. Lay chicken in crock. If you need to make a second layer, stagger the pieces so they don't directly overlap each other.
3. Mix all other ingredients together in a good-sized bowl.
4. Spoon vegetables and sauce over chicken, making sure that pieces on the bottom are covered, too.
5. Cover. Cook on Low for 4 hours, or until instant-read meat thermometer registers 160° when stuck into center of meat, and veggies are as tender as you like them.
6. Remove bay leaf before serving.

Cheesy Buffalo Chicken Pasta

Christina Gerber
Apple Creek, OH

Makes 6-8 servings

Prep. Time: 15 minutes
Cooking Time: High for 4 hours or Low for 8 hours
Ideal slow-cooker size: 6 qt.

3 cups chicken broth
½ cup buffalo wing sauce, divided
1 Tbsp. dry ranch dressing mix
¾ teaspoon garlic powder
½ tsp. salt
⅛ tsp. black pepper
1½ lbs. boneless, skinless chicken thighs
8-oz. pkg. cream cheese, cubed
1 cup shredded sharp cheddar cheese
1 Tbsp. cornstarch plus 1 Tbsp. water
1 lb. linguine
chopped cilantro, optional

1. Grease interior of slow-cooker crock.
2. Mix broth, ¼ cup buffalo sauce, and seasonings in crock.
3. Submerge chicken in sauce.
4. Scatter cubed cream cheese and shredded cheese over chicken.
5. Cover. Cook on Low 4 hours.
6. When chicken is fully cooked, remove to bowl and shred with 2 forks. (Cover crock to keep sauce warm.)
7. Add remaining ¼ cup buffalo sauce to shredded chicken and toss to coat. Set aside but keep warm.
8. In a small bowl, stir cornstarch and water together until smooth. Stir into warm sauce in crock until sauce smooths out and thickens.
9. Break noodles in half and place in crock.
10. Top with shredded chicken and cover.
11. Cook on High 30-60 minutes, or just until noodles are fully cooked. Stir 3-4 times during cooking.
12. If you need more liquid for noodles to cook, add water ¼ cup at a time.
13. Garnish with cilantro if you wish, and serve immediately.

Tips:

This is a great one-pot meal. No extra pan needed to cook the pasta!

Cheesy Chicken Tator Tot Casserole

Jennifer Archer
Kalona, IA

Makes 8-10 servings

***Prep. Time:** 10-15 minutes*
***Cooking Time:** 4 hours*
***Ideal slow-cooker size:** 4 qt.*

32-oz. bag Tator Tots,* divided
½ lb. bacon, fried and crumbled, divided
2 cups shredded cheddar cheese, divided
1 lb. boneless, skinless chicken thighs, cubed
salt and pepper to taste
¾ cup milk
***To make your own Hash Browns (or big Tater Tots, which can be cut up), see page 269.**

1. Grease interior of slow-cooker crock.
2. Layer half of Tator Tots on bottom of crock.
3. Sprinkle with ⅓ of bacon and then ⅓ of cheese.
4. Top with all of chicken and seasoning.
5. Layer on half of remaining bacon and then half of remaining cheese.
6. Top with the rest of the Tator Tots.
7. Finish with remaining bacon and cheese.
8. Pour milk over top. Do not stir.
9. Cover. Cook on Low 4 hours, or until completely hot in center.

Tips:

This is a great potluck dish!

Barbecued Chicken Pizza

Susan Roth
Salem, OR

Makes 4 to 6 servings

***Prep. Time:** 20-25 minutes*
***Cooking Time:** 2½-3 hours*
***Standing Time:** 2 hours before you begin*
***Ideal slow-cooker size:** 6 qt.*

8- or 12-oz. pkg. prepared pizza dough, depending how thick you like your pizza crust
1 cup barbecue sauce, teriyaki flavored, or your choice of flavors
2 cups cooked, chopped chicken (your own leftovers, rotisserie chicken, or canned chicken)
20-oz. can pineapple tidbits, drained, optional
½ cup green bell pepper, chopped, optional
¼ cup red onion, diced or sliced, optional
2 cups shredded mozzarella cheese

1. If the dough's been refrigerated, allow it to stand at room temperature for 2 hours.
2. Grease interior of slow-cooker crock.
3. Stretch the dough into a large circle so that it fits into the crock, covering the bottom and reaching up the sides by an inch or so the whole way around. (If the dough is larger than the bottom of the cooker, fold it in half and stretch it to fit the bottom and an inch up the sides. This will make a thicker crust.)
4. Bake crust, uncovered, on High 1 hour.
5. Spread barbecue sauce over hot crust.
6. Drop chopped chicken evenly over sauce.
7. If you wish, spoon pineapple, chopped peppers, and onion over chicken.
8. Sprinkle evenly with cheese.
9. Cover. Cook on High for about 2 hours, or until the crust begins to brown around the edges.
10. Uncover, being careful not to let the condensation on the lid drip onto the pizza.
11. Let stand for 10 minutes. Cut into wedges and serve.

Tips:

From the tester: I refrigerated the leftovers, and they tasted great on the second day. We reheated it in the microwave at 60% power.

—Gladys Voth

Sweet-and-Sour Chicken Wings

Linda Roberta Pond
Los Alamos, NM

Makes 4-6 servings

Prep. Time: 20 minutes
Cooking Time: 4-5 hours
Ideal slow-cooker size: 5 qt.

10-12 chicken wings
14-oz. bottle ketchup
8-oz. can tomato sauce
1 cup apple cider vinegar
1 cup white sugar
1 tsp. dry mustard
1 tsp. ground ginger

1. Grease interior of slow-cooker crock.
2. Use kitchen scissors or a sharp sturdy knife to cut through the 2 joints on each wing. Discard the wing tip. Place the other 2 pieces into the crock. If you have to create more than one layer, stagger the wings so they don't directly overlap each other.
3. In a bowl, mix together all other ingredients.
4. Pour over wings, lifting them to make sure that all are coated with the sauce.
5. Cover. Cook on Low 4-5 hours, or until tender.

Nacho Chicken and Cheese Wraps

Lavina Hochstedler
Grand Blanc, MI

Makes 10 servings

Prep. Time: 10 minutes
Cooking Time: 4 hours
Ideal slow-cooker size: 4-5 qt.

10.75-oz. can cheddar cheese soup
1 cup water
2 cups picante sauce
2 lbs. boneless, skinless chicken thighs, cut into 1½" cubes
1¼ cups uncooked instant rice
10 10" flour tortillas

1. Grease interior of slow-cooker crock.
2. Stir soup, water, picante sauce, and chicken thighs together in crock.
3. Cover. Cook on Low 3½ hours, or until instant-read meat thermometer registers 155° when stuck into thigh.
4. Stir in rice.
5. Cover. Cook on High 20-30 minutes, or until rice is tender.
6. Spoon about 1 cup chicken mixture down the center of each tortilla. Fold the tortilla around the filling and serve.

Good go-alongs with this recipe:

Tossed salad.

Chicken Tacos

Susan Kasting
Jenks, OK

Makes 6-8 servings

Prep. Time: 10 minutes
Cooking Time: 6 hours on Low
Ideal slow-cooker size: 6 qt.

4 large boneless, skinless chicken thighs
1 envelope dry taco seasoning
1 cup salsa, your choice of heat
10.5-oz. can cream of chicken soup, or 8-oz. pkg. cream cheese

1. Grease interior of slow-cooker crock.
2. Holding thighs over crock, sprinkle each one, top and bottom, with taco seasoning.
3. Place seasoned thighs in crock.
4. In bowl, mix salsa and soup, or salsa and cubed cream cheese, together. Pour over chicken.
5. Cover. Cook on Low 4 hours, or until instant-read meat thermometer registers 160° when stuck in center of thighs.
6. When chicken is done, lift into deep bowl and shred with 2 forks.
7. Stir shredded chicken back into sauce. Stir together well.
8. Serve with tortillas.

Variations:

1. I top these with sour cream, grated cheese, and chopped cilantro.
2. You can also add a can of corn, drained, or black beans, drained, to the sauce in Step 4.

BBQ Chicken Sandwiches

Sarah Herr
Goshen, IN

Makes 8 servings

Prep. Time: 15 minutes
Cooking Time: 4 hours
Ideal slow-cooker size: 5 qt.

3 lbs. boneless, skinless chicken thighs
1 onion, chopped
½ cup brown sugar
½ cup apple cider vinegar
½ cup ketchup
1 tsp. ground mustard
1 tsp. cumin
1 Tbsp. chili powder
½ tsp. black pepper
8 hamburger buns

1. Grease interior of slow-cooker crock.
2. Place chicken into crock. If you need to make a second layer, stagger the pieces so they don't directly overlap each other.
3. Mix other ingredients together well in a bowl.
4. Spoon over thighs. Make sure the ones on the bottom layer get covered, too.
5. Cover. Cook on Low 4 hours, or until instant-read meat thermometer registers 160° when stuck in center of thighs.
6. Lift cooked chicken out of crock and shred with 2 forks.
7. Stir shredded meat back into sauce in crock.
8. Serve on hamburger buns.

Tips:

Good with dill pickles and chips or fries.

Orange-Glazed Turkey Thighs

Rosemarie Fitzgerald
Gibsonia, PA

Makes 6 servings

Prep. Time: 10 minutes
Cooking Time: 4-5 hours
Ideal slow-cooker size: 5 qt.

1½ lbs. turkey thighs
¾ tsp. salt
½ tsp. black pepper
½ tsp. cinnamon
½ cup orange marmalade
¼ tsp. nutmeg
¼ tsp. ground ginger

1. Grease interior of slow-cooker crock.
2. Cut thighs into 3"-4" pieces and place in cooker.
3. Mix all other ingredients together in a small saucepan.
4. Heat, stirring frequently, until marmalade melts.
5. Pour over thighs.
6. Cover. Cook on Low 4-5 hours, or until instant-read meat thermometer registers 160°-165° when stuck into thighs.
7. Place meat on platter and spoon marmalade sauce over top.

Parsley, Sage, Ginger Turkey

Connie Butto
Lititz, PA

Makes 6 servings

Prep. Time: 20 minutes
Cooking Time: 4 hours
Ideal slow-cooker size: 5 qt.

2½-3 lbs. boneless, skinless turkey thighs
½ tsp. dried sage
1 tsp. dried parsley
¼-½ tsp. ground ginger, according to taste
⅔ cup chicken broth
½ cup white wine
¼ cup chopped onions

1. Grease interior of slow-cooker crock.
2. Cut thighs into 6-8 pieces. Place in slow cooker.
3. Mix all other ingredients together in a bowl.
4. Spoon over turkey.
5. Cover. Cook on Low 4-5 hours, or until instant-read meat thermometer registers 160°-165° when stuck into meat.
6. Serve with broth.

For Thanksgiving, I always use a slow cooker for mashed potatoes that I cook and mash the night before. In the morning, I take them out of the fridge and put them on Warm until dinner. And I also use 4 other slow cookers: for yams, pumpkin pie, hot fudge pudding cake, and wassail.
— Colleen Larson, Plain City, UT

Amazing Turkey

Theresa Leppert
Schellsburg, PA

Makes 10 servings

Prep. Time: 10 minutes
Cooking Time: 6 hours
Ideal slow-cooker size: 6-7 qt.

8-lb. turkey breast
1 tsp. salt
¼-½ tsp. black pepper, according to taste
1 stick (½ cup) butter

Gravy (multiply amounts proportionately if you have more than 1 cup drippings and broth):
1 cup drippings and broth
¼ cup cold water
3 Tbsp. flour

1. Grease interior of slow-cooker crock.
2. Using your hands, rub butter under skin of turkey breast.
3. Place buttered turkey breast in crock.
4. Sprinkle with salt and pepper.
5. Cover. Cook on High for 1 hour.
6. Turn cooker to Low and cook 6 more hours, covered.
7. Using sturdy tongs or 2 metal spatulas, lift turkey out of crock and place on cutting board. Cover to keep warm.
8. To make gravy, pour drippings from crock into saucepan. Bring to boil.
9. Place water and flour in a jar with a tight-fitting lid. Shake vigorously until well mixed and without lumps. Shake the jar several times just to make sure that ingredients have mixed thoroughly.
10. With broth near boiling, pour in water-flour mixture in a thin stream, stirring continuously. Continue stirring until broth thickens into gravy. Keep warm.
11. Carve turkey and serve with gravy.

Variations:

My family likes garlic so I use ½ tsp. garlic powder mix in the butter.

Quick and Savory Turkey Breast

Lauren Bailey
Dillsburg, PA

Makes 6-8 servings

Prep. Time: 10 minutes
Cooking Time: 5-6 hours
Ideal slow-cooker size: 6-8 qt.

5-6-lb. turkey breast, bone in
1 envelope dry onion soup mix
salt and pepper to taste
15-oz. can whole cranberry sauce

1. Grease interior of slow-cooker crock.
2. Sprinkle salt and pepper all over turkey breast.
3. Do the same with envelope of onion soup mix.
4. Place breast in crock.
5. Break up cranberry sauce in a bowl, so you can drop it evenly over breast.
6. Cover. Cook on Low 5-6 hours, or until instant-read meat thermometer registers 165° in center of breast (not touching bone).

Tips:

Delicious served with mashed potatoes and a green salad.

Put your slow-cooker meal together the night before you're going to cook it. Stick it in the fridge overnight. Then pull it out the next morning, and flip it on just before you go out the door. No reason to add pressure and panic to your morning rush.

Savory Turkey and Mushrooms

Clara Newswanger
Gordonville, PA

Makes 6-8 servings

Prep. Time: 20 minutes
Cooking Time: 4-4½ hours
Ideal slow-cooker size: 5 qt.

1 medium onion, chopped
½ stick (¼ cup) butter
3 cups fresh mushrooms, sliced
4 Tbsp. cornstarch
1 cup beef broth
2 Tbsp. soy sauce
2½ lbs. boneless, skinless turkey thighs, cut in 4" cubes
salt and pepper, optional

1. Sauté chopped onion in butter in saucepan.
2. Stir in mushrooms and cornstarch until well mixed.
3. Stir in beef broth and soy sauce. Bring to a boil, stirring continuously so mixture thickens but doesn't stick.
4. Grease interior of slow-cooker crock.
5. Place cut-up turkey evenly over bottom of crock. Pour sauce over meat.
6. Cover. Cook on Low 4-4½ hours, or until turkey is tender when pierced with a fork.
7. Taste broth and season with salt and pepper if you wish.
8. Serve over cooked rice or noodles.

Turkey Loaf

Dottie Schmidt
Kansas City, MO

Makes 5-6 servings

Prep. Time: 15 minutes
Cooking Time: 3-4 hours
Ideal slow-cooker size: 4 or 5 qt.

1¼ lbs. ground turkey
½ cup dry bread crumbs
½ cup finely chopped celery
1 egg, beaten
2 green onions, finely chopped
¼ tsp. salt
⅛ tsp. black pepper
1 Tbsp. Worcestershire sauce
2 Tbsp. ketchup
1-2 Tbsp. sesame seeds

1. Grease interior of slow-cooker crock.
2. Make a tin foil sling for your slow cooker so you can lift the cooked Turkey Loaf out easily. Begin by folding a strip of tin foil accordion-fashion so that it's about 1½"-2" wide, and long enough to fit from the top edge of the crock, down inside and up the other side, plus a 2" overhang on each side of the cooker. Make a second strip exactly like the first.
3. Place the one strip in the crock, running from end to end. Place the second strip in the crock, running from side to side. The two strips should form a cross in the bottom of the crock.
4. Combine all ingredients except ketchup and sesame seeds in bowl, mixing together gently but well.
5. Form into 6"-long loaf and place in crock, centering loaf where foil strips cross.
6. Spread ketchup over top of loaf. Sprinkle with sesame seeds.
7. Cover. Cook on Low for 3-4 hours, or until instant-read meat thermometer registers 150°-155° when stuck in center of loaf.
8. Using foil handles, lift loaf out of crock and onto cutting board. Cover and keep warm for 10 minutes. Then slice and serve.

Sloppy Party Sliders

Bob Coffey
New Windsor, NY

Makes 10 servings

Prep. Time: 25 minutes
Cooking Time: 3 hours
Ideal slow-cooker size: 5 qt.

1 large onion, chopped finely
1 large green bell pepper, chopped finely
1 lb. ground turkey
¾ cup ketchup
¾ cup plain yellow mustard
10 slider rolls

1. Grease interior of slow-cooker crock.
2. Place chopped onions and bell peppers into cooker. Crumble in ground turkey. Mix together well.
3. Stir in ketchup and mustard. Mix together until well combined.
4. Cover. Cook on Low for 3 hours, or until vegetables are as tender as you like them.
5. When guests arrive, spoon mixture onto slider rolls and serve.

Tips:

These are great for parties because they can be made well ahead of time. The cleanup is minimal and can wait until everyone leaves. I've never had any leftovers when I've served these!

Mexican Meatballs

Janie Steele
Moore, OK

Makes 10-12 servings

Prep. Time: 30 minutes
Cooking Time: 3-4 hours
Ideal slow-cooker size: 4 qt.

2 cups crumbled cornbread
10-oz. can enchilada sauce, divided
1½ lbs. ground turkey
8-oz. can tomato sauce
½ cup shredded Mexican cheese

1. Grease interior of slow-cooker crock.
2. In a bowl, combine cornbread, ½ cup enchilada sauce, and ground turkey. Form into 1" meatballs.
3. Brown slightly in non-stick skillet in several batches so they brown and don't just steam in each other's juices.
4. Spoon browned meatballs into crock.
5. Add rest of enchilada sauce and tomato sauce to meatballs in crock. Stir together gently.
6. Cover. Cook 3-4 hours on Low.
7. Sprinkle with cheese before serving.

Turkey Kielbasa and White Beans

Lucille Amos
Greensboro, NC

Makes 6-8 servings

Prep. Time: 20 minutes
Cooking Time: 3 hours
Ideal slow-cooker size: 5 qt.

1 cup chopped onions
2 12-oz. pkgs. turkey kielbasa sausage, cut into 3"pieces
3 15.5-oz. cans Great Northern beans, drained
14.5-oz. can diced tomatoes
1 cup red wine or beef broth
½ tsp. dried basil
½ tsp. dried oregano
1 tsp. chopped garlic
½ tsp. black pepper
⅓ cup cooked, crumbled bacon

1. Grease interior of slow-cooker crock.
2. Place all ingredients in cooker except bacon. Stir together well.
3. Cover. Cook on Low 2 hours.
4. If the dish is juicier than you like, continue cooking another hour uncovered. If you like the consistency, cover the cooker and continue cooking another hour.
5. While the dish is cooking, fry the bacon until crispy. Drain on paper towels. Crumble when cooled.
6. Taste the finished dish and add seasonings if you wish.
7. Top individual servings with crumbled bacon.

Good go-alongs with this recipe:

Cornbread.

Zucchini and Turkey Dish

Dolores Kratz
Souderton, PA

Makes 6 servings

Prep. Time: 25 minutes
Cooking Time: 8-9 hours
Ideal slow cooker size: 3- or 4-qt.

3 cups sliced zucchini
1 small onion, chopped
¼ tsp. salt
1 cup cubed cooked turkey
2 fresh tomatoes, sliced, *or* 14½-oz. can diced tomatoes
½ tsp. dried oregano
1 tsp. dried basil
¼ cup freshly grated Parmesan cheese
6 Tbsp. shredded provolone cheese
¾ cup Pepperidge Farms stuffing

1. Combine zucchini, onion, salt, turkey, tomatoes, oregano, and basil in slow cooker. Mix well.
2. Top with cheeses and stuffing.
3. Cover. Cook on low 8-9 hours.

I soak dry beans in my slow cooker overnight. In the morning, I rinse them, add more water, and turn it on.
— Becky Price, Dallas, PA

My family lives in the Southwest, and I use slow cookers for our annual Christmas Eve fiesta. Family members, friends, and neighbors gather at our house for a relaxing time during the hectic holiday season. Guests can help themselves to an array of Mexican dishes on a wintry evening. My large slow cookers keep my green chile stew and posole warm on our festivelydecorated buffet table. I use my small slow cookers to keep sauces warm for guests to pour over my chicken olé casserole. Beef and beans are ready to go in slow cookers for a build-your-own taco bar. Another slow cooker keeps my chile con queso dip warm for guests at our appetizer table. We enjoy a relaxing evening filled with interesting conversations while we play board games, and make homemade ornaments.
— Cathy Fraser, Albuquerque, NM

The week after my husband and I were married in 1974, we attended a reception for his older brother and new wife. My mother-in-law served these killer meatballs. I asked for the recipe and she gave it to me. Later, she submitted the recipe as her contribution to a church cookbook they were publishing. Now, I have become well known for these meatballs, but I always give my mother-in-law credit, as it was originally her recipe. Even my husband's co-workers ask for these meatballs, so my husband hauls the slow cooker in to work. Recently, I made the meatballs for Thanksgiving dinner appetizers with my husband's family, and my mother-in-law asked me for the recipe! I told her it wasn't mine, but hers, but that thanks to her, I was well known for my excellent meatballs. She didn't believe me or remember them from the wedding reception 30-some years prior. I didn't convince her until I pulled the church cookbook off her kitchen shelf and showed her her own submission!
— Sandy Olson, Turton, SD

Beef Main Dishes

Savory Roast Beef

Sylvia High
Ephrata, PA

Makes 6 to 8 servings

Prep. Time: 20 minutes
Cooking Time: 6-8 hours
Ideal slow-cooker size: 4 qt.

3-4-lb. boneless beef chuck
1 onion, sliced
2 cups rich beef broth
¼ cup flour
¼ cup brown sugar
¼ cup apple cider vinegar
2 tsp. salt
1 tsp. dry mustard
1 tsp. Worcestershire sauce

1. Grease interior of slow-cooker crock.
2. Place meat in crock. Drop sliced onions over meat.
3. Blend together remaining ingredients in a bowl. Pour over meat, but without disturbing onions.
4. Cover. Cook 6-8 hours on Low, or until an instant-read meat thermometer inserted into center of roast registers 145°.
5. Remove roast from cooker with 2 sturdy metal spatulas. Place on cutting board and cover to keep warm. Let stand 10-15 minutes before slicing or cutting into chunks.
6. Serve on a deep platter with the rich gravy over top. Pass any extra gravy in a bowl for diners to add to their individual servings.

Marinated Chuck Roast

Susan Nafziger
Canton, KS

Makes 7-8 servings

Prep. Time: 15 minutes
Cooking Time: 6-7 hours
Marinating Time: 2-3 hours
Ideal slow-cooker size: oval 5 qt.

1 cup olive oil
1 cup soy sauce
¼ cup red wine vinegar
½ cup chopped onions
⅛ tsp. garlic powder
¼ tsp. ground ginger
½ tsp. black pepper (coarsely ground is best)
½ tsp. dry mustard
3-4 lb. boneless chuck roast

1. Mix all ingredients, either by whisking together in a bowl or whirring the mixture in a blender.
2. Place roast in a low baking or serving dish and pour marinade over top. Cover and refrigerate for 2-3 hours.
3. Grease interior of slow-cooker crock.
4. Place roast in crock. Pour marinade over top.
5. Cover. Cook on Low 5-6 hours, or until instant-read meat thermometer registers 140°-145° when stuck into center of meat.
6. When finished cooking, use a sturdy pair of tongs, or 2 metal spatulas, to move roast onto a cutting board. Cover to keep warm and allow to stand 15 minutes.
7. Cut into slices or chunks. Top with marinade and serve.

Savory Sweet Roast

Marie Hostetler
Nappanee, IN

Makes 8-10 servings

Prep. Time: 20 minutes
Cooking Time: 6-7 hours
Ideal slow-cooker size: oval 5 or 6 qt.

3-4-lb. boneless beef chuck roast
1-2 Tbsp. olive oil
1 medium onion, chopped
10.75-oz. can cream of mushroom soup
½ cup water
1 tsp. prepared mustard
2 tsp. salt
¼ cup cider vinegar
¼ cup sugar
1 tsp. Worcestershire sauce

1. Grease interior of slow-cooker crock.
2. In a large skillet, brown roast on all sides in olive oil.
3. Meanwhile, in a mixing bowl, blend together all other ingredients.
4. When roast is browned, place in slow cooker.
5. Pour all other ingredients over meat.
6. Cover. Cook on Low 6-7 hours, or until instant-read meat thermometer registers 140°-145°.
7. Using a sturdy pair of tongs, or 2 metal spatulas, remove roast and place on cutting board. Cover to keep warm. Let stand for 15-20 minutes.
8. Slice and serve with sauce.

Tips:

1. The sauce from this roast makes a succulent gravy. Serve over the meat, and over potatoes, rice or pasta.
2. I like to cut potato wedges (peeled or unpeeled) and place them on top of the meat before switching on the slow cooker. I like to do the same with julienned carrot sticks.

Either or both of those combinations gives you a good meal all in one container.

Whole Meal Pot Roast

Naomi Fast,
Hesston, KS

Makes 6-8 servings

Prep. Time: 25 minutes
Cooking Time: 6 hours
Ideal slow-cooker size: oval 6 or 7 qt.

1 onion, chopped finely
4 carrots, finely chopped
1 lb. red-skinned potatoes, cut in ½" pieces
1½ cups beef stock
1 cup tomato sauce
1 garlic clove, crushed
3 fresh thyme sprigs
1 bay leaf
3-4-lb. boneless beef rump roast
1 tsp. salt
½ tsp. coarsely ground black pepper
¼ cup all-purpose flour
1 Tbsp. olive oil
¼ cup sour cream

1. Grease interior of slow-cooker crock.
2. Put onions, carrots, potatoes, stock, tomato sauce, garlic, thyme, and bay leaf in crock.
3. Put salt, pepper, and flour in large bowl. Mix together well. Add roast, and toss to coat evenly with seasoned flour.
4. In large skillet or sauté pan over medium heat, heat olive oil until smoking. Add roast and brown all sides, 3-4 minutes total.
5. Put roast in crock.
6. Cover. Cook 6 hours on Low, or until instant-read meat thermometer registers 140°-145° when stuck in center.
7. Remove roast from cooker with 2 metal spatulas onto cutting board. Allow to rest 10 minutes, covered with foil, before slicing.
8. Meanwhile, stir sour cream into vegetables and sauce in crock until well blended. Cover and keep warm while preparing roast for serving.
9. Serve on a deep platter, surrounded and topped with vegetables.

Good go-alongs with this recipe:

Serving this pot roast and vegetables with beet salad, rolls, and fruit cups makes a hearty meal.

My tricks for getting my slow cooker to do its best work:

Milk, cream, and sour cream break down in extended cooking. As much as possible, add them in the last hour of cooking, or use condensed soups.

Classic Pot Roast

Jenny Unternahrer
Wayland, IA

Makes 8-10 servings

Prep. Time: 30 minutes
Cooking Time: 6-8 hours
Ideal slow-cooker size: oval 6 qt.

3 Tbsp. canola or olive oil
3-4-lb. boneless chuck roast
salt
pepper
¼ cup flour
2 Tbsp. tomato paste or ketchup
½ cup dry red wine
1½ cups beef or chicken broth
1 Tbsp. Worcestershire sauce
1 or more medium onions, thinly sliced, depending on how much you like onions
½-1 lb. baby carrots
2 small ribs celery, thinly sliced
3 cloves garlic, diced
½ tsp. dried thyme
6-8 small potatoes, quartered

1. Heat oil in good-sized skillet, ideally not non-stick. Sprinkle roast with salt and pepper.
2. Brown roast on all sides over high heat until browned, approximately 10 minutes.
3. Grease interior of slow-cooker crock.
4. Place roast in slow cooker.
5. Stir flour and tomato paste into skillet over medium heat and cook for 1 minute. Add wine, broth, and Worcestershire sauce. Use a wooden spoon to scrape bits off the bottom of skillet.
6. Pour sauce over roast.
7. Mix onions, carrots, celery, garlic, and thyme in bowl. Spoon into crock, alongside and on top of meat.
8. Cover. Cook on Low 4 hours.
9. Add quartered potatoes to crock. Cover. Cook another 2-4 hours, or until vegetables are as tender as you like them, and instant-read meat thermometer registers 140°-145° when stuck in center of roast.
10. Cut roast into chunks. Place meat, vegetables, and broth together in deep serving bowl. Stir together gently.

Tips:

Yukon gold potatoes keep their shape with long cooking. They're a good choice for this recipe.

Herbed Pot Roast

Sarah Herr
Goshen, IN

Makes 6 servings

Prep. Time: 20 minutes
Cooking Time: 6-8 hours on Low
Ideal slow-cooker size: oval 6 qt.

2 lbs. boneless beef chuck roast
3 medium potatoes, peeled or not, cut into small chunks
1 Tbsp. olive oil
3 carrots, peeled and cut into small chunks
2 ribs celery, cut into small chunks
½ tsp. salt
½ tsp. dried rosemary
½ tsp. dried thyme
¼ tsp. garlic powder
¼ tsp. onion powder
¼ tsp. paprika
¼ tsp. coarsely ground pepper
3 Tbsp. balsamic vinegar

1. Grease interior of slow-cooker crock.
2. Place roast in crock.
3. Toss potatoes in olive oil to keep them from discoloring.
4. Place potatoes and other veggies around roast.
5. Sprinkle herbs and spices evenly over all.
6. Drizzle balsamic vinegar over top.
7. Cover. Cook on Low 6-8 hours.

Beef Roast with Homemade Ginger-Orange Sauce

Beverly Hummel
Fleetwood, PA

Makes 8 servings

Prep. Time: 20 minutes
Cooking Time: 8 hours
Ideal slow-cooker size: 7 qt.

3-lb. boneless chuck roast
salt and pepper to taste

Ginger-Orange Sauce:
2 cups soy sauce
½ cup brown sugar
½ cup white sugar
¼ cup minced onion
1 Tbsp. ground ginger
1 clove garlic, minced
½ cup orange juice

1. Grease interior of slow-cooker crock.
2. Holding roast over crock, salt and pepper it on all sides.
3. Place roast in cooker. Cover. Cook on Low 4-6 hours, or until an instant-read meat thermometer registers 150°-160° when stuck in center of roast.
4. While roast is cooking, combine all ingredients for Sauce in saucepan. Stir together until well mixed.
5. Simmer 15 minutes, stirring occasionally so it doesn't stick.
6. Using sturdy tongs or 2 metal spatulas, lift cooked roast into big bowl. Shred with 2 forks.
7. Drain drippings and broth out of slow cooker. Save for gravy or soup.
8. Return shredded meat to crock. Stir in 1 cup Ginger-Orange Sauce.
9. Cover. Cook on Low 30 minutes, or until heated through.
10. Serve over mashed potatoes or rice. Or serve in sandwiches.

Tips:

We found this sauce while vacationing on the West Coast, but could find nothing like it where we live on the East Coast. My children asked for it often, so I came up with this homemade sauce that's comparable.

Good go-alongs with this recipe:

Mashed potatoes and green bean casserole.

Guiness Corned Beef

Bob Coffey
New Windsor, NY

Makes 10 servings

Prep. Time: 5 minutes
Cooking Time: 8+ hours
Ideal slow-cooker size: 5.5 qt.

3-4-lb. corned beef with seasoning packet
14.9-oz. can Guinness beer
¾ cup water
1 bay leaf
¼ tsp. mustard seeds
¼ tsp. caraway seeds
¼ tsp. peppercorns
1-lb. bag baby carrots
½ cup chopped onions
4 cups chopped cabbage

1. Grease interior of slow-cooker crock.
2. Remove seasoning packet from meat and place beef in crock.
3. Pour beer and ¾ cup water over meat.
4. Lay bay leaf on meat.
5. In a small bowl, mix together mustard and caraway seeds, peppercorns, and ingredients of seasoning packet. Spoon over meat.
6. Cover. Cook on Low 8 hours, or until instant-read thermometer registers 145° when stuck in center of meat.
7. One hour before end of cooking time, add carrots and onions.
8. Thirty minutes before end of cooking time, add chopped cabbage.
9. To serve, lift beef and vegetables out of liquid. (Save liquid for soup or cooking dried beans.) Discard bay leaf.

Tips:

There's nothing wrong with the small seasoning packet that comes with store-bought corned beef. It's just not nearly enough to season a full slow cooker. That's why I supplement with the seasonings above.

Good go-alongs with this recipe:

Serve with mashed potatoes and coarse mustard or horseradish for the beef.

Corned Beef Brisket

Karen Ceneviva
Seymour, CT

Makes 6-8 servings

Prep. Time: 15 minutes
Cooking Time: 5-11 hours
Ideal slow-cooker size: oval 7 qt.

5-lb. corned beef brisket, rinsed
salt and pepper to taste
½ head green cabbage, cored and quartered
10-12 carrots, peeled and chopped into 1" pieces
1½ cups lager beer

1. Grease interior of slow-cooker crock.
2. Holding brisket over crock, salt and pepper on all sides. Place in crock.
3. Lay cabbage quarters and carrots around meat and on top.
4. Pour beer over all.
5. Cover. Cook on Low 9-11 hours or on High 5-7 hours, or until instant-read meat thermometer registers 140°-145° when stuck in center of brisket.
6. Remove meat from cooker with sturdy tongs or 2 metal spatulas. Let stand on cutting board, covered, for 15 minutes to allow juices to re-gather.
7. Slice across the grain. Place on deep platter. Surround and top with vegetables.

Tips:

Serve with a cruet of white vinegar. A light pour over everything really enhances the flavor of this dish. Also serve with mashed potatoes.

Good go-alongs with this recipe:

Soda bread and bread pudding for dessert.

Barbecued Brisket

Dorothy Dyer
Lee's Summit, MO

Makes 9-12 servings

Prep. Time: 15 minutes
Cooking Time: 4-8 hours
Marinating Time: 12 hours
Ideal slow-cooker size: oval 6 qt.

3-4-lb. beef brisket
⅓ cup Italian salad dressing
1½ tsp. liquid smoke
⅓ cup + 2 tsp. brown sugar, packed
½ tsp. celery salt
½ tsp. salt
1 Tbsp. Worcestershire sauce
½ tsp. black pepper (coarsely ground is best)
¼ tsp. chili powder
½ tsp. garlic powder
1¼ cups barbecue sauce

1. Pierce meat all over with fork. Place meat in good sized sturdy plastic bag with no holes.
2. Combine all remaining ingredients, except barbecue sauce, in bowl.
3. Pour marinade into bag with meat. Swirl around so meat is immersed in sauce. Tie shut. Place in long, shallow dish and refrigerate for 12 hours.
4. When ready to cook, grease interior of slow-cooker crock.
5. Place meat in cooker. Pour marinade over top.
6. Cover. Cook on Low for 6-8 hours, or on High 4-5 hours, or until instant-read meat thermometer registers 140°-145° when stuck in center of meat.
7. Using sturdy tongs or 2 metal spatulas, lift meat onto cutting board. Cover with foil to keep warm. Let stand 20 minutes.
8. Slice diagonally, across grain, into ½"-thick slices. Place slices in long baking dish.
9. Pour barbecue sauce over sliced meat. Broil for 5 minutes or so, to brown. Watch carefully so it doesn't burn.

The slow cooker does force me to plan ahead for meals, but I love that once I prepare the meal in the slow cooker, I can pretty much "forget it." I like to have cooked ground beef on hand in the freezer so that I can easily pull it out to make chili or spaghetti sauce in the slow cooker. — Addie Calvitt, Durham, NC

Brisket with Tomatoes and Sauerkraut

Alyce C. Kauffman
Gridley, CA

Makes 6-8 servings

Prep. Time: 15 minutes
Cooking Time: 4-7 hours
Ideal slow-cooker size: 5 qt.

15.5-oz. can stewed tomatoes, cut up and undrained
8-oz. can sauerkraut, undrained
1 cup applesauce
2 Tbsp. brown sugar
2½-3½-lb. beef brisket
2 Tbsp. cold water
2 Tbsp. cornstarch
sprigs of fresh parsley

1. Grease interior of slow-cooker crock.
2. Mix together tomatoes, sauerkraut, applesauce, and brown sugar.
3. Place brisket in crock.
4. Pour tomato-sauerkraut sauce over top.
5. Cover. Cook on Low 6-7 hours, or on High 4-5 hours, or until instant-read meat thermometer registers 140°-145° when stuck in center of meat.
6. Uncover and lift brisket onto cutting board using sturdy tongs or 2 metal spatulas. Cover to keep warm. Let stand 15 minutes.
7. Meanwhile, turn cooker to High. Combine cold water and cornstarch until smooth. Stir into sauce in crock. Continue stirring until sauce thickens and bubbles.
8. Cut brisket into chunks or slices. Spoon some of sauce over meat. Serve remaining sauce as gravy.
9. Just before serving, garnish meat with parsley.

Aunt Iris's Barbecued Brisket

Carolyn Spohn
Shawnee, KS

Makes 6 servings

Prep. Time: 20-30 minutes
Cooking Time: 4-8 hours
Marinating Time: 8 hours or overnight
Ideal slow-cooker size: oval 6 qt.

3-lb. beef brisket
½ tsp. garlic powder
½ tsp. onion powder
½ tsp. celery salt
4 Tbsp. liquid smoke
2 tsp. Worcestershire sauce

Barbecue Sauce:
½ cup honey
⅔ cup soy sauce
⅔ cup ketchup
½ tsp. Tabasco
1 tsp. dry mustard
1 tsp. paprika
1 cup apple cider vinegar
1 cup orange juice
1 tsp. salt

1. In a small bowl, mix together garlic and onion powders, celery salt, and liquid smoke.
2. Rub on all sides of brisket. Place brisket in large bowl or roaster.
3. Cover tightly and refrigerate 8 hours or overnight.
4. Grease interior of slow-cooker crock.
5. Drain off liquid that's gathered while meat marinated. Place meat in crock, sprinkling each side with Worcestershire sauce.
6. Cover. Cook on Low 7-8 hours or on High 4-6 hours, or until instant-read meat thermometer registers 140°-145° when stuck in center of meat.
7. While beef cooks, make Sauce by combining all its ingredients in saucepan.
8. Cook uncovered, stirring occasionally until Sauce comes to a boil.
9. Simmer uncovered for 30 minutes, or until sauce thickens and reduces down.
10. When meat is finished, use sturdy tongs or 2 metal spatulas to lift it onto a cutting board. Cover to keep warm. Let stand 10-15 minutes before slicing.
11. Serve Sauce alongside or spooned over sliced brisket.

Caesar Stew

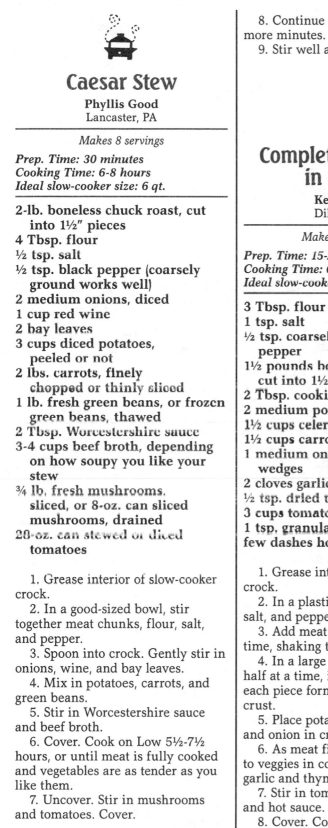

Phyllis Good
Lancaster, PA

Makes 8 servings

Prep. Time: 30 minutes
Cooking Time: 6-8 hours
Ideal slow-cooker size: 6 qt.

2-lb. boneless chuck roast, cut into 1½" pieces
4 Tbsp. flour
½ tsp. salt
½ tsp. black pepper (coarsely ground works well)
2 medium onions, diced
1 cup red wine
2 bay leaves
3 cups diced potatoes, peeled or not
2 lbs. carrots, finely chopped or thinly sliced
1 lb. fresh green beans, or frozen green beans, thawed
2 Tbsp. Worcestershire sauce
3-4 cups beef broth, depending on how soupy you like your stew
¾ lb. fresh mushrooms, sliced, or 8-oz. can sliced mushrooms, drained
28-oz. can stewed or diced tomatoes

1. Grease interior of slow-cooker crock.
2. In a good-sized bowl, stir together meat chunks, flour, salt, and pepper.
3. Spoon into crock. Gently stir in onions, wine, and bay leaves.
4. Mix in potatoes, carrots, and green beans.
5. Stir in Worcestershire sauce and beef broth.
6. Cover. Cook on Low 5½-7½ hours, or until meat is fully cooked and vegetables are as tender as you like them.
7. Uncover. Stir in mushrooms and tomatoes. Cover.
8. Continue cooking on High 30 more minutes.
9. Stir well and serve.

Complete Beef Stew in a Crock

Kelly Bailey
Dillsburg, PA

Makes 6-8 servings

Prep. Time: 15-20 minutes
Cooking Time: 6-8 hours
Ideal slow-cooker size: 5 or 6 qt.

3 Tbsp. flour
1 tsp. salt
½ tsp. coarsely ground black pepper
1½ pounds boneless beef chuck cut into 1½" cubes
2 Tbsp. cooking oil
2 medium potatoes, cubed
1½ cups celery
1½ cups carrots, chunked
1 medium onion, cut into 8 wedges
2 cloves garlic, sliced
½ tsp. dried thyme
3 cups tomato sauce
1 tsp. granulated beef bouillon
few dashes hot sauce, to taste

1. Grease interior of slow-cooker crock.
2. In a plastic bag combine flour, salt, and pepper.
3. Add meat cubes, a few at a time, shaking to coat.
4. In a large skillet, brown meat, half at a time, in hot oil, just until each piece forms a deep brown crust.
5. Place potatoes, celery, carrots, and onion in crock.
6. As meat finishes browning add to veggies in cooker. Gently stir in garlic and thyme.
7. Stir in tomato sauce, bouillon, and hot sauce.
8. Cover. Cook on Low 6-8 hours.

Tips:

Serve with fresh homemade bread, rolls, or muffins.

Make sure your ingredients are of equal sizes for even cooking. — Judy Faro, Dallas, GA

Beef-N-Sherry

Carole Bolatto
Marseilles, IL

Makes 8 servings

Prep. Time: 10 minutes
Cooking Time: 6 hours
Ideal slow-cooker size: 6 qt.

3 lbs. boneless chuck roast, cut into bite-sized cubes
1½ 10.75-oz. cans cream of mushroom soup
½ envelope dry onion soup mix
¾ cup sherry
¼ lb. fresh mushrooms, sliced, or 4-oz. can sliced mushrooms

1. Grease interior of slow-cooker crock.
2. Mix all ingredients together in crock.
3. Cook on Low for 6 hours.
4. Serve over cooked rice or pasta or over mashed potatoes.

Good go-alongs with this recipe:

Adding a salad and dinner rolls makes this a wonderful meal.

Beef Burgundy with Mushrooms

Rosemarie Fitzgerald
Gibsonia, PA

Makes 6 servings

Prep. Time: 15 minutes
Cooking Time: 5¼-6¼ hours
Ideal slow-cooker size: 5 qt.

2-3-lb. boneless chuck roast, cut into 1½" pieces
1 cup onions, chopped
2 cloves garlic
2 cups burgundy
¼-½ tsp. marjoram, according to your taste preference
½ lb. fresh mushrooms, sliced, or canned and drained
6-oz. can tomato paste
dash of sugar

1. Grease interior of slow-cooker crock.
2. Mix beef cubes, onions, and garlic together in crock.
3. Pour in burgundy. Cover and cook on Low 4½-5½ hours.
4. Stir in marjoram and mushrooms. Cover and continue cooking 30 more minutes.
5. Stir in tomato paste and sugar. Cook another 10-15 minutes, uncovered, to allow sauce to thicken.
6. Serve over cooked noodles, rice, or potatoes.

Let a roast that you've just lifted out of the cooker stand 10-15 minutes before slicing or carving it so it can re-gather its juices and firm up. Cover it and keep it warm while it's resting.

Beer-Braised Short Ribs

Willard Roth
Elkhart, IN

Makes 6 servings

Prep. Time: 15 minutes
Cooking Time: 4 hours
Ideal slow-cooker size: 4 or 5 qt.

2 lbs. boneless beef short ribs
2 tsp. sea salt
2 tsp. pepper
1 Tbsp. canola oil
2 12-oz. cans Guinness draught
2 cups beef broth
2 carrots, cut in 2" chunks
2 parsnips, cut in 1½" chunks
2 onions, peeled and quartered
2 ribs celery, cut in 1½" chunks
8 cloves garlic, peeled
1 Tbsp. brown sugar
½ cup dried cranberries, or raisins
2 bay leaves

1. Grease interior of slow-cooker crock.
2. Season ribs with salt and pepper. Add oil to large skillet over high heat.
3. When oil is hot, add ribs, turning occasionally until browned, about 10 minutes. Transfer to slow cooker, and set on High.
4. Pour beer into hot skillet. Using a wooden spoon, scrape up any brown bits. Pour beer with bits over ribs.
5. Stir in remaining ingredients.
6. Cover. Cook on High 4 hours.
7. Fish out bay leaves before serving.

Good go-alongs with this recipe:

I like to serve these ribs over colcannon (mashed potatoes, mixed with either chopped kale or cabbage) or polenta (whisk ¾ cup cornmeal into 4 cups simmering water; stir until thick, about 15 minutes). Top complete dish with gremolata (½ cup chopped fresh parsley, 1 minced clove garlic, zest of 1 orange and 1 lemon, mixed together).

Beef Short Ribs in Red Wine

Patricia Howard
Green Valley, AZ

Makes 4-6 servings

Prep. Time: 15 minutes
Cooking Time: 7¼-9¼ hours
Ideal slow-cooker size: 6 qt.

4 lbs. bone-in beef short ribs
¼ tsp. salt
¼ tsp. pepper
2 Tbsp. olive oil
14.5-oz. can stewed tomatoes, undrained
2 Tbsp. tomato paste
1 medium onion, chopped
¾ cup red wine
¾ cup beef broth
1 Tbsp. Worcestershire sauce
¼ cup water
2 Tbsp. cornstarch

1. Grease interior of slow-cooker crock.
2. Season ribs with salt and pepper. Brown short ribs in olive oil in a large skillet.
3. Place tomatoes, tomato paste, and onion in cooker. Stir together well.
4. Stir in wine, broth, and Worcestershire sauce.
5. Settle ribs into cooker, pushing down into sauce.
6. Cover. Cook on Low 7-9 hours, or until meat begins to fall off the bones.
7. When done, remove ribs and bones from cooker, spoon off any fat, and increase heat to High. (Cover ribs and keep warm.)
8. In small bowl, mix water and cornstarch until smooth. Then stir into sauce in cooker until smooth.
9. Cover cooker and cook 10-15 minutes, or until mixture thickens.
10. Serve sauce over ribs.

Variations:

Dissolve 2 beef bouillon cubes in ¾ cup water and use instead of beef broth.

Good go-alongs with this recipe:

Good with mashed potatoes!

Butterfly Steaks

Mary Louise Martin
Boyd, WI

Makes 8-10 servings

Prep. Time: 30 minutes
Cooking Time: 2-4 hours
Standing Time: 2 hours
Ideal slow-cooker size: oval 7 qt.

4-lb. butt beef, or venison, tenderloin
4½ tsp. garlic powder, divided
2 tsp. celery seeds
1 tsp. black pepper
1 Tbsp. salt
½ cup cider vinegar
¾ cup canola oil
½ cup soy sauce
⅓ cup olive oil
1 tsp. ground ginger
1 tsp. dry mustard
½ tsp. garlic powder

1. Cut tenderloin into ¾"-1"-thick slices. Cut each slice through the center but not the whole way through. Flatten into a butterfly-shaped steak and lay in large glass baking dish.
2. In a bowl, mix 4 tsp. garlic powder, celery seeds, pepper, salt, vinegar, and canola oil for marinade. Pour over steaks in a glass pan.
3. Cover, and marinate in fridge for 2 hours, stirring occasionally.
4. Meanwhile, grease interior of slow-cooker crock.
5. Place marinated steaks on broiler pan and broil at 400° just until lightly browned. Place steaks in slow cooker. Stagger the pieces so they don't directly overlap each other.
6. Mix soy sauce, olive oil, ginger, dry mustard, and remaining ½ tsp. garlic powder. Pour over meat, making sure to spoon sauce on any steaks on the bottom layer.
7. Cook on Low 2-4 hours.
8. Serve with rice.

Slow-Cooked Swiss Steak

Sharon Wantland
Menomonee Falls, WI

Makes 6 Servings

Prep. Time: 20-30 minutes
Cooking Time: 3-8 hours
Ideal slow-cooker size: 4 or 5 qt.

1 medium onion, cut into ¼"-thick slices
2 Tbsp. flour
½ tsp. salt
¼ tsp. black pepper
2-2½ lbs. boneless beef chuck roast, cut into 6 pieces of nearly equal size
1 rib celery, cut into ½"-thick slices
2 8-oz. cans tomato sauce

1. Grease interior of slow-cooker crock.
2. Distribute onion slices in bottom of crock.
3. In a large resealable plastic bag, combine flour, salt, and pepper.
4. Add beef, one piece at a time, and toss to coat. Lay beef over onions as you finish flouring each piece.
5. Spoon celery and tomato sauce over meat.
6. Cover. Cook on Low for 6-8 hours or on High for 3-4 hours, or until instant-read meat thermometer registers 140°-145° when stuck in center of pieces of meat.
7. Serve meat topped with onions, celery, and tomato sauce.

Hungarian Beef with Paprika

Maureen Csikasz
Wakefield, MA

Makes 9 servings

Prep. Time: 15 minutes
Cooking Time: 3-6 hours
Ideal slow-cooker size: oval 5 or 6 qt.

3-lb. boneless chuck roast
2-3 medium onions, coarsely chopped
5 Tbsp. sweet paprika
¾ tsp. salt
¼ tsp. black pepper
½ tsp. caraway seeds
1 clove garlic, chopped
½ green bell pepper, sliced
¼ cup water
½ cup sour cream
fresh parsley

1. Grease interior of slow-cooker crock.
2. Place roast in crock.
3. In a good-sized bowl, mix all ingredients together, except sour cream and parsley.
4. Spoon evenly over roast.
5. Cover. Cook on High 3-4 hours, or on Low 5-6 hours, or until instant-read meat thermometer registers 140°-145° when stuck in center of meat.
6. When finished cooking, use sturdy tongs or 2 metal spatulas to lift meat to cutting board. Cover with foil to keep warm. Let stand 10-15 minutes.
7. Cut into chunks or slices.
8. Just before serving, dollop with sour cream. Garnish with fresh parsley.
9. Serve with buttered noodles or potatoes.

Sauerbraten

Phyllis Good
Lancaster, PA

Makes 10-12 servings

Prep. Time: 30 minutes
Cooking Time: 5-9 hours
Ideal slow-cooker size: oval 6 or 7 qt.

5-6-lb. bottom round roast
2 cups red wine vinegar
2 cups water
¼ cup brown sugar
1 Tbsp. salt
1 bay leaf
½ tsp. black pepper
3 medium onions, chopped
2 large carrots, diced
1½ cups celery, diced

Gravy:
½ stick (4 Tbsp.) butter
10 gingersnap cookies, crushed
4 cups broth

1. Place roast in large bowl.
2. In another bowl, mix together vinegar, water, brown sugar, salt, bay leaf, pepper, onions, carrots, and celery.
3. Pour over roast. Cover bowl. Place in refrigerator for 2-3 days, turning roast several times.
4. Grease interior of slow-cooker crock.
5. Remove meat from marinade and pat dry.
6. Place roast in cooker. Pour marinade over top.
7. Cover. Cook on Low 7-9 hours, or on High 4-6, or until instant-read meat thermometer registers 140°-145° when stuck in center of roast.
8. Remove meat from cooker and place on cutting board, using sturdy tongs or 2 metal spatulas. Cover to keep warm. Allow to stand 15 minutes.
9. Pour marinade from cooker through a strainer, collecting broth in a 4-cup measure. Keep broth hot.
10. Meanwhile, melt butter in saucepan. Stir in crushed cookies, stirring constantly until hot.
11. Stir in hot broth, stirring continuously until gravy thickens because of the cookies.
12. Cut meat into chunks or slices. Serve with gravy and mashed potatoes.

Braised Beef with Cranberries

Audrey L. Kneer
Williamsfield, IL

Makes 4-5 servings

Prep. Time: 20 minutes
Cooking Time: 4-8 hours
Ideal slow-cooker size: 4 or 5 qt.

½ cup unpeeled, chopped potato
1 medium onion, chopped
1 medium carrot, chopped
1 rib celery, cut finely
1 green bell pepper, chopped
1 Tbsp. garlic powder
2-lb. chuck roast
½ tsp. cayenne pepper
1 cup apple juice
1 cup fresh or frozen (thawed) cranberries
1 Tbsp. sherry or red wine
1 bay leaf
2 sprigs fresh parsley

1. Grease interior crock of slow cooker.
2. Mix chopped potato, onion, carrot, celery, bell pepper, and garlic powder together.
3. Put half of vegetable mixture into crock.
4. Rub beef all over with red pepper.
5. Lay on top of veggies.
6. Spread remaining vegetables over meat.
7. Mix together apple juice, cranberries, sherry, and bay leaf in a bowl. Spoon over vegetables and meat.
8. Cover. Cook on Low 7-8 hours or on High 4-6 hours, or until instant-read meat thermometer registers 140°-145° when stuck into center of meat and veggies are tender.
9. Slice meat and top with sauce to serve.

A Whole Dinner in a Crock

Judy Diller
Bluffton, OH

Makes 4 servings

Prep. Time: 20 minutes
Cooking Time: 4¼-5¼ hours
Ideal slow-cooker size: 4 qt.

1 lb. ground beef
1 cup sliced carrots
1 cup sliced potatoes
1 onion, chopped
1 cup chopped celery
1 can tomato soup mixed with 1 can water
1 cup peas

1. Grease interior of slow-cooker crock.
2. Slice carrots into crock.
3. Slice potatoes into crock.
4. Scatter in chopped onions and celery.
5. If you have time, brown ground beef in skillet. Using a slotted spoon, lift beef into crock, spreading it around evenly over vegetables.
6. If you don't have time, crumble beef over vegetables.
7. In a bowl, blend soup and water. Pour over meat and vegetables. Do not stir.
8. Cover. Cook on Low 4-5 hours, or until vegetables are as tender as you like them.
9. Fifteen minutes before end of cooking time, scatter peas over top.
10. Cover. Cook 10 more minutes on High.

Tips:

The amounts of vegetables are very flexible. Use whatever amount you have, and add more if you want to stretch this meal further.

Good go-alongs with this recipe:

Great with bread and salad.

I always flour, season, and sear my meat before putting it in the slow cooker. I reserve the drippings for whatever liquid I am using—it makes a huge difference in the flavor of the dish. —Nancy Looby, Hometown, IL

Lazy Cabbage Rolls

Janie Steele
Moore, OK

Makes 6-8 servings

Prep. Time: 36 minutes
Cooking Time: 2-5½ hours
Ideal slow-cooker size: 6 or 7 qt.

1½-2 lbs. ground beef
1 large onion, chopped
1 clove garlic, minced
1½-lb. small cabbage head, chopped into 1" squares
¾ cup uncooked brown rice
2 14.5-oz. cans diced tomatoes, undrained
16-oz. can tomato sauce
salt and pepper to taste

1. Grease interior of slow-cooker crock.
2. Crumble beef over bottom of cooker. Season each layer with salt and pepper, except tomatoes and tomato sauce.
3. Add a layer of onions. Follow that with garlic, and then cabbage.
4. Spread uncooked rice over cabbage.
5. Pour tomatoes and sauce on top. Cook on High 2-3 hours or on Low 4-5½ hours, or until cabbage and rice are tender.
6. Let stand 15 minutes before serving to let the dish firm up.

Un-Stuffed Peppers

Pat Bechtel
Dillsburg, PA

Makes 6 servings

Prep. Time: 10-15 minutes
Cooking Time: 4¼ hours
Ideal slow-cooker size: 4 or 5 qt.

1 lb. ground beef
28-oz. jar your favorite spaghetti sauce
2 Tbsp. barbecue sauce
2 large green bell peppers (3-4 cups), coarsely chopped
1¼ cups water
1 cup instant rice

1. Grease interior of slow-cooker crock.
2. If you have time, brown beef in skillet, stirring frequently and breaking up the clumps of meat. Using a slotted spoon, remove to slow cooker. If you don't have time to brown the meat, crumble it directly into the crock.
3. Stir in all remaining ingredients except rice.
4. Cover. Cook on Low 4 hours, or until meat is cooked through and peppers are as soft as you like them.
5. Stir in rice. Cover. Cook on High 20-30 minutes, or until rice is tender.

Variations:

If you don't have spaghetti sauce, you can substitute 4 cups tomato juice or V-8.

—Sharon Miller

Kodiak Casserole

Bev Beiler
Gap, PA

Makes 8-10 servings

Prep. Time: 20-25 minutes
Cooking Time: 4 hours
Ideal slow-cooker size: 5 qt.

1 lb. ground beef
1-2 cups diced onions, depending on how much you like onions
½ tsp. minced garlic
3 medium bell peppers, chopped, your choice of colors
1 cup barbecue sauce
10.75-oz. can cream of tomato soup, undiluted
¾ cup salsa, as mild or hot as you like
15-oz. can black beans, drained
½ cup fresh mushrooms, sliced, or 4-oz. can mushrooms, undrained
1 Tbsp. Worcestershire sauce
1 cup cheddar cheese, shredded

1. Grease interior of slow-cooker crock.
2. If you have time, brown beef, onions, and garlic together in a skillet. Using a slotted spoon, lift beef and vegetables out of drippings and place in crock. If you don't have time, place beef in bowl and use a sturdy spoon to break it up into small clumps. Mix in onions and garlic.
3. Stir in all other ingredients except grated cheese. Spoon into crock.
4. Cover. Cook on Low 3¾ hours, or until dish is bubbly and hot in the center.
5. Sprinkle Casserole with cheese. Cover. Continue cooking 15 more minutes.

Potato Haystacks

Anita Troyer
Fairview, MI

Makes 6-8 servings

Prep. Time: 30 minutes
Cooking Time: 3-4 hours
Ideal slow-cooker size: 6 qt.

1 lb. ground beef
1 medium onion, chopped
½ envelope dry taco seasoning
32-oz. bag frozen cooked, shredded potatoes*
½ envelope dry ranch seasoning mix
2 Tbsp. sour cream
2 cups milk, divided
10.75-oz. can cream of mushroom soup
crushed nacho chips
*** To make your own Frozen Hash Browns, see recipe on page 269.**

1. Grease interior of slow-cooker crock.
2. If you have time, brown hamburger and onion in skillet. Stir in dry taco seasoning. Set aside.
3. If you don't have time, crumble ground beef in a bowl. Stir in onion and dry taco seasoning. Set aside.
4. In another bowl, mix together potatoes, ranch seasoning, sour cream, and 1 cup milk.
5. Put half the meat and onions in bottom of crock.
6. Cover with a layer of potato mixture.
7. Repeat layers.
8. Mix soup with remaining cup of milk in bowl where you've mixed potatoes and other ingredients. Pour over layers in crock.
9. Cover. Cook on Low 3-4 hours, or until potatoes are cooked through and tender.
10. Pass crushed nachos for individuals to add to their Haystacks.

German Supper

Lizzie Ann Yoder
Hartville, OH

Makes 6 servings

Prep. Time: 20 minutes
Cooking Time: 4 hours
Ideal slow-cooker size: 4 or 5 qt.

1 lb. ground beef
¾ cup onions, chopped
¼ cup green bell pepper, finely diced
15-oz. can sauerkraut, undrained
½ cup water
¼ cup beef broth
8-oz. can tomato sauce
¼ tsp. black pepper
½ cup instant rice

1. Grease interior of slow-cooker crock.
2. If you have time, brown beef and onions together in a skillet. Using a slotted spoon, lift beef and onions out of drippings and place in good-sized bowl. If you don't have time, place beef in bowl and use a sturdy spoon to break it up into small clumps. Mix in onions.
3. Stir in diced green peppers, sauerkraut and its juices, water, and beef broth.
4. Place in crock. Pour tomato sauce over top. Sprinkle with black pepper.
5. Cover. Cook on Low 3½ hours.
6. Stir in rice so that it's submerged in other ingredients.
7. Cover. Cook on High 20-30 minutes, or until rice is tender.

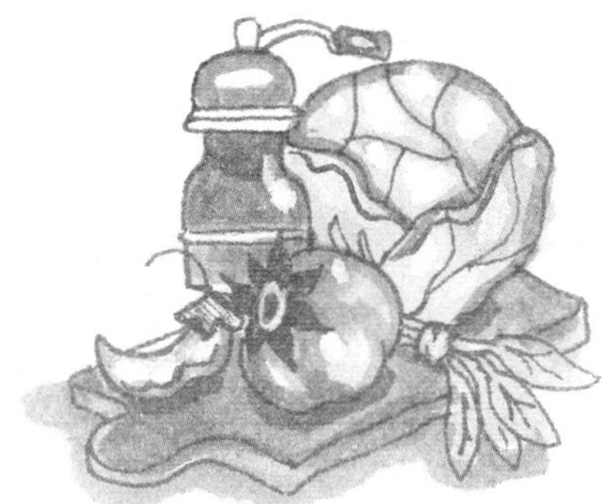

Peppy Peppers

Susie Nisley
Millersburg, OH

Makes 6 servings

Prep. Time: 20 minutes
Cooking Time: 4 hours
Ideal slow-cooker size: 4 qt.

1 large green bell pepper, diced
1 lb. ground beef
1 tsp. salt
1 quart tomato juice
1 envelope dry taco seasoning
1 cup instant rice
1 lb. creamy cheese of your choice, cubed

1. Grease interior of slow-cooker crock.
2. Scatter chopped pepper over bottom of crock.
3. If you have time, brown beef in a skillet. Stir in salt and pepper. Using a slotted spoon, lift beef and onions out of drippings and spread over green pepper pieces. If you don't have time, place beef in bowl and use a sturdy spoon to break up into small clumps. Stir in salt. Scatter over green pepper in crock.
4. Mix tomato juice and taco seasoning together in a bowl.
5. Pour over meat and chopped pepper.
6. Cover. Cook on Low 3½ hours.
7. Stir in rice. Cover. Cook on High 20-30 minutes, or until rice is tender.
8. Top with cheese. Allow to stand 10 minutes, or until cheese melts.

Cottage Pie

Ruthie Schiefer
Vassar, MI

Makes 4 servings

Prep. Time: 20 minutes
Cooking Time: 4 hours
Ideal slow-cooker size: 4 or 5 qt.

1 Tbsp. vegetable oil
1 medium onion, diced
1 lb. ground beef
1 beef bouillon cube or 1 tsp. beef base
¾ cup beef broth
1-2 tsp. Worcestershire sauce, according to taste
½ tsp. salt
¼-½ tsp. black pepper, according to taste
1 cup fresh, frozen, or canned corn
1 cup fresh or frozen peas
1 cup shredded sharp cheddar cheese
3 cups mashed potatoes or 24-oz. pkg. prepared mashed potatoes
pinch of paprika

1. Grease interior of slow-cooker crock.
2. If you have time, heat oil in large skillet over high heat. Add onion and ground beef and sauté until meat is browned.
3. If you don't have time, scatter onion and crumble ground beef into crock. (You won't need the oil.)
4. Add beef bouillon, beef broth, Worcestershire sauce, salt, and pepper. Stir together.
5. Stir in corn and peas.
6. Top with cheddar cheese.
7. Spread mashed potatoes evenly over top of all.
8. Sprinkle with paprika.
9. Cover. Cook on Low 3½ hours.
10. Uncover. Cook on High an additional 30 minutes so potatoes get crusty on top.

Seven-Layer Dinner with Rice

Jere Zimmerman
Reinholds, PA

Makes 6 servings

Prep. Time: 20-30 minutes
Cooking Time: 4 hours
Ideal slow-cooker size: 4 qt.

4 strips bacon, cut in half
1 cup frozen or canned whole-kernel corn, drained
½ cup onions, chopped
½ cup green bell pepper, chopped
¾ lb. ground beef
1 tsp. salt
½ tsp. black pepper
2 8-oz. cans tomato sauce
¾ cup water
1 cup instant rice

1. Grease interior of slow-cooker crock.
2. Fry bacon in skillet until crisp. Drain on paper towels until needed.
3. Scatter corn over bottom of crock.
4. Top with onions and green pepper.
5. If you have time, brown ground beef in a skillet. Using a slotted spoon, lift beef out of drippings and spoon evenly over vegetables in crock. If you don't have time, place beef in bowl and use a sturdy spoon to break up into small clumps. Then scatter over vegetables.
6. In a bowl, mix together salt, pepper, tomato sauce, and water. When blended, pour over ingredients in crock.
7. Cover. Cook on Low 3½ hours, or until meat is cooked through and vegetables are as tender as you like them.
8. Spoon rice into crock, pushing it down into the liquid.
9. Cover. Cook on High 20-30 minutes, or until rice is tender.
10. Just before serving, top with bacon strips.

Pizza Rice Casserole

Mary June Hershberger
Lynchburg, VA

Makes 6 servings

Prep. Time: 20 minutes
Cooking Time: 3-5 hours
Ideal slow-cooker size: 3 qt.

1 cup uncooked brown rice
2 cups water
2 cups cottage cheese
½ lb. hamburger
1 onion, chopped
2 cups pizza sauce
1-1¼ tsp. salt, according to taste
¼-½ tsp. black pepper, according to taste
1 cup shredded cheddar cheese

1. Grease interior of slow-cooker crock.
2. Combine rice with water and cottage cheese in crock. Spread out over bottom.
3. If you have time, brown beef with onion in skillet. Mix in pizza sauce. Or mix uncooked beef, onion, and pizza sauce together.
4. Spoon beef/sauce over rice mixture.
5. Scatter cheese over top.
6. Cover. Cook 3 hours on High or until rice is tender.

Beef and Potato Loaf

Deb Martin
Gap, PA

Makes 4-5 servings

Prep. Time: 20-30 minutes
Cooking Time: 6-7 hours
Ideal slow-cooker size: oval 5 or 6 qt.

4 cups raw, thinly sliced potatoes, peeled or not
½ cup cheddar cheese, grated
½ tsp. salt
¼ tsp. black pepper
1 lb. ground beef
¾ cup tomato juice, or evaporated milk
½ cup dry quick oats
½ cup onions, chopped
dash of black pepper
1 tsp. seasoning salt
¼-½ cup ketchup

1. Grease interior of slow-cooker crock.
2. Arrange potatoes evenly over bottom of crock.
3. Layer grated cheese across potatoes.
4. Sprinkle with ½ tsp. salt and ¼ tsp. pepper.
5. In a bowl, mix together ground beef, tomato juice, dry oats, onions, ketchup, pepper, and seasoning salt.
6. When well blended, crumble meat mixture evenly over potatoes and cheese.
7. Drizzle with ketchup.
8. Cover. Cook on Low 6-7 hours, or until potatoes and onions are as tender as you like them.

BBQ Meat Loaf

Marjorie Nolt
Denver, PA

Makes 10 servings

Prep. Time: 30 minutes
Cooking Time: 5-6 hours
Ideal slow-cooker size: oval 6 qt.

2 lbs. lean ground beef
1 lb. lean ground pork
½ cup finely chopped onion
½ cup almond, or all-purpose, flour
1 tsp. salt
1 tsp. black pepper
1 tsp. garlic powder
2 large eggs
1 cup of your favorite barbecue sauce

1. Grease interior of slow-cooker crock.
2. Make a tin foil sling for your slow cooker so you can lift the cooked Meat Loaf out easily. Begin by folding a strip of tin foil accordion-fashion so that it's about 1½"-2" wide, and long enough to fit from the top edge of the crock, down inside and up the other side, plus a 2" overhang on each side of the cooker. Make a second strip exactly like the first.
3. Place the one strip in the crock, running from end to end. Place the second strip in the crock, running from side to side. The 2 strips should form a cross in the bottom of the crock.
4. In a large bowl, mix all ingredients together, except barbecue sauce. Mix well with your hands until fully combined.
5. Place loaf into crock, centering it where the 2 foil strips cross.
6. Cover. Cook on Low 3-4 hours.
7. Thirty minutes before end of cooking time, brush top and sides of loaf with about ⅓ cup barbecue sauce.
8. Use foil handles to lift Meat Loaf out of the crock and onto a serving platter. Let stand 10-15 minutes to allow meat to gather its juices.
9. Slice and serve with remaining barbecue sauce.

Marvelous Mini-Meat Loaves

Krista Hershberger
Elverson, PA

Makes 6 servings

Prep. Time: 20 minutes
Cooking Time: 3 hours
Ideal slow-cooker size: oval 6 or 7 qt.

1 lb. extra-lean ground beef
6-oz. pkg. stuffing mix
1 cup water
½ tsp. dried basil
½ tsp. dried oregano
¾ cup spaghetti or pizza sauce
¾ cup shredded mozzarella cheese

1. Grease interior of 6 individual muffin tins or sturdy ramekins.
2. Mix meat, stuffing mix, water, and herbs together in a bowl with clean hands.
3. Divide mixture into 6 pieces. Roll each into a ball.
4. Flatten and fit each one into a tin or ramekin, covering the bottom and pushing the meat up the sides a bit.
5. Make an indentation in each with a spoon.
6. Spoon sauce into center of each mini-meat loaf, dividing sauce evenly among the containers.
7. Place filled containers on floor of crock.
8. Cover. Cook on Low 2-3 hours, or until meat is cooked through.
9. Scatter shredded cheese evenly over mini-loaves. Cover cooker and continue heating for 10 minutes, or until cheese has melted.
10. Use sturdy tongs, or a metal spatula and spoon, to lift out the filled containers.
11. Let stand for 10 minutes so the meat can firm up. Then serve.

Cheesy Beef and Pork Meat Loaf

Jean Turner
Williams Lake, British Columbia

Makes 8 servings

Prep. Time: 15-20 minutes
Cooking Time: 4 hours
Ideal slow-cooker size: 5 qt.

½ cup onions, chopped
½ cup green bell pepper, chopped
8-oz. can tomato sauce
2 eggs, beaten
1 cup white cheddar cheese, shredded
1 cup soft bread crumbs
1 tsp. salt
dash black pepper
¼ tsp. dried thyme
1½ lbs. ground beef
½ lb. ground pork

1. Grease interior of slow-cooker crock.
2. Make a tin foil sling for your slow cooker so you can lift the cooked Meat Loaf out easily. Begin by folding a strip of tin foil accordion-fashion so that it's about 1½"-2" wide, and long enough to fit from the top edge of the crock, down inside and up the other side, plus a 2" overhang on each side of the cooker. Make a second strip exactly like the first.
3. Place the one strip in the crock, running from end to end. Place the second strip in the crock, running from side to side. The 2 strips should form a cross in the bottom of the crock.
4. Combine all Meat Loaf ingredients in a bowl. Shape into a loaf and place it in the crock, centering it where the 2 foil handles cross.
5. Cover. Cook on Low 4-5 hours, or until Meat Loaf is cooked in the center.
6. Using the foil handles, lift the Loaf out of the crock and onto a cutting board. Allow to stand 15 minutes.
7. Cut into slices and serve.

Meat Loaf with Sweet Tomato Glaze

Phyllis Good
Lancaster, PA

Makes 6-8 servings

Prep. Time: 15-20 minutes
Cooking Time: 4 hours
Ideal slow-cooker size: oval 5 qt.

Meat Loaf:
1½ lbs. ground beef
1 medium onion, chopped finely
1 cup dry bread crumbs
1 cup tomato juice
1 large egg or 2 small eggs
1 tsp. salt
scant ¼ tsp. black pepper

Glaze:
3 Tbsp. brown sugar
¼ cup ketchup
1 tsp. dry mustard

1. Grease interior of slow-cooker crock.
2. Make a tin foil sling for your slow cooker so you can lift the cooked Meat Loaf out easily. Begin by folding a strip of tin foil accordion-fashion so that it's about 1½"-2" wide, and long enough to fit from the top edge of the crock, down inside and up the other side, plus a 2" overhang on each side of the cooker. Make a second strip exactly like the first.
3. Place the one strip in the crock, running from end to end. Place the second strip in the crock, running from side to side. The 2 strips should form a cross in the bottom of the crock.
4. Combine all Meat Loaf ingredients in a bowl. Shape into a loaf and place it in the crock, centering it where the 2 foil handles cross.
5. Mix all Glaze ingredients together.
6. Spoon half the Glaze over the Meat Loaf. Reserve the rest for later.
7. Cover. Cook on Low 4-5 hours.
8. Using the foil handles, lift Meat Loaf out of cooker. Place on rimmed baking sheet.
9. Spoon remaining Glaze over top.
10. Place meat on rimmed baking sheet under broiler for 2-4 minutes. Keep watch so it browns and bubbles but doesn't burn.
11. Let stand for 10 minutes. Then slice and serve.

Taco Meat Loaf

Tammy Smith
Dorchester, WI

Makes 8 servings

Prep. Time: 20 minutes
Cooking Time: 4 hours
Ideal slow-cooker size: oval 5 or 6 qt.

3 eggs, lightly beaten
½ cup crushed tomatoes
¾ cup crushed tortilla chips
1 medium onion, finely chopped
2 garlic cloves, minced
3 tsp. taco seasoning
2 tsp. chili powder
1 lb. ground beef
1 lb. ground pork
½ tsp. salt
¾ tsp. black pepper

1. Grease interior of slow-cooker crock.
2. Make a tin foil sling for your slow cooker so you can lift the cooked Meat Loaf out easily. Begin by folding a strip of tin foil accordion-fashion so that it's about 1½"-2" wide, and long enough to fit from the top edge of the crock, down inside and up the other side, plus a 2" overhang on each side of the cooker. Make a second strip exactly like the first.
3. Place one strip in crock, running from end to end. Place second strip in crock, running from side to side. The 2 strips should form a cross in bottom of the crock.
4. In a large bowl, combine all ingredients well.
5. Shape into a loaf. Place into crock so that the center of loaf sits where the 2 strips of foil cross.
6. Cover. Cook for 4 hours on Low.
7. Using the foil handles, lift Loaf onto platter. Cover to keep warm. Let stand for 10-15 minutes before slicing.

Cheesy Meat Loaf

Judi Manos
West Islip, NY

Makes 8 servings

Prep. Time: 15-20 minutes
Cooking Time: 4 hours
Ideal slow-cooker size: 4 qt.

2 lbs. ground beef
6-oz. pkg. stuffing mix for chicken or pork
½ cup water
2 eggs, beaten
1 onion, chopped
½ cup ketchup
1 Tbsp. your favorite prepared mustard
1 cup shredded cheddar or mozzarella cheese

1. Grease interior of slow-cooker crock.
2. Make a tin foil sling for your slow cooker so you can lift the cooked Meat Loaf out easily. Begin by folding a strip of tin foil accordion-fashion so that it's about 1½"-2" wide, and long enough to fit from the top edge of the crock, down inside and up the other side, plus a 2" overhang on each side of the cooker. Make a second strip exactly like the first.
3. Place the one strip in the crock, running from end to end. Place the second strip in the crock, running from side to side. The 2 strips should form a cross in the bottom of the crock.
4. Mix all ingredients together, except cheese, just until blended. Form into round loaf.
5. Center loaf in crock where the 2 foil strips cross.
6. Cover. Cook on High 4 hours, or until instant-read meat thermometer registers 160° when stuck into center of loaf.
7. Top with shredded cheese. Let stand, covered, until cheese melts, about 5 minutes.
8. Use foil handles to remove Meat Loaf from slow cooker before slicing to serve.

Tips:

You can spray the foil handles with cooking spray to be sure meat does not stick to them.

Variations:

Before cooking, layer baby carrots around Meat Loaf in crock. Cut up potatoes and put around edges with carrots.

Creamy, Spicy Meatballs

Sherlyn Hess
Millersville, PA

Makes 4-5 servings

Prep. Time: 20-30 minutes
Cooking Time: 4 hours
Ideal slow-cooker size: 5 qt.

Meatballs:
1 lb. ground beef
½ lb. hot Italian sausage, squeezed out of its casing
½ cup fine dry bread crumbs
1 egg
½ cup onions, chopped
½ tsp. salt

Sauce:
10.75-oz. can golden mushroom soup
¼ cup water
1 clove garlic, minced
¼ tsp. dried oregano

1. Grease interior of slow-cooker crock.
2. In a good-sized mixing bowl, combine beef, sausage, bread crumbs, egg, onions, and salt.
3. Place Meatballs in crock. If you need to make a second layer, stagger Meatballs so they don't directly overlap each other.
4. In a saucepan combine soup, water, garlic, and oregano. Stir occasionally, cooking until mixture comes to a boil.
5. Pour over Meatballs, spooning Sauce over all Meatballs, including those on the bottom.
6. Cover. Cook on Low 4 hours, or until Meatballs are cooked through but aren't dry.

Cranberry Ginger Meatballs

Bea Gagliano
Lakewood, NJ

Makes 4-6 servings

Prep. Time: 20-30 minutes
Cooking Time: 4 hours
Ideal slow-cooker size: 5 qt.

1½ lbs. ground beef
1 Tbsp. + 1 tsp. raw instant rice
1 egg
½ tsp. salt
¼ tsp. black pepper
½ tsp. paprika

Sauce:
1 onion, chopped
8-oz. can tomato sauce
½ cup brown sugar, packed
2-3 Tbsp. lemon juice
⅓ cup raisins
3 gingersnaps, crushed
1 cup whole cranberry sauce

1. Grease interior of slow-cooker crock.
2. In a bowl, mix together ground beef, rice, egg, salt, pepper, and paprika.
3. When well mixed, form into small balls.
4. Place Meatballs in crock. If you need to make a second layer, stagger the Meatballs so they don't directly overlap each other.
5. Mix all Sauce ingredients together in a bowl. Pour over Meatballs in crock. Be sure to spoon Sauce over all Meatballs on bottom layer, as well as top.
6. Cover. Cook on Low 4 hours, or until instant-read meat thermometer registers 140°-145° when stuck in center of several Meatballs.

Bacon Beef Rolls

Susan Nafziger
Canton, KS

Makes 10-12 servings

Prep. Time: 30 minutes
Cooking Time: 4-5 hours
Ideal slow-cooker size: 5 or 6 qt.

12 slices bacon
1 cup cheddar cheese, shredded
1 cup coarse cracker crumbs
½ cup chopped onions
1 cup milk
2 Tbsp. ketchup or barbecue sauce
1 tsp. salt
¼ tsp. black pepper
¼ tsp. celery salt
¼ cup brown sugar
2 lbs. ground beef

1. Fry bacon in skillet or in microwave until it begins to crisp slightly but is still bendy. You're cooking it a bit so it gives up some of its fat. Set aside on paper towels to drain.
2. Grease interior of slow-cooker crock.
3. Mix all remaining ingredients well.
4. On a cutting board, spread meat mixture into a 9x12 rectangle.
5. Divide into 12 equal pieces by cutting down the center, and then lengthwise across 6 times. Shape each piece into a log.
6. Wrap each log with a slice of bacon. Fasten with a toothpick.
7. Lay in crock seam side down. If you need to make a second layer, stagger the logs so they don't directly overlap each other.
8. Cover. Cook on Low 4-5 hours, or until logs are cooked through.
9. Using tongs, remove logs and place on a rimmed baking sheet.
10. Run under broiler until log and bacon brown but don't burn.
11. Flip each log over and broil for another minute or so.

Barbecued Meatballs

Jolene Schrock
Millersburg, OH

Makes 8-12 servings

Prep. Time: 15-20 minutes
Cooking Time: 4-5 hours
Ideal slow-cooker size: 6 qt.

Meatballs:
12-oz. can evaporated milk
2 cups dry quick oats
2 eggs
1 cup onions, chopped
2 tsp. salt
½ tsp. black pepper
2 tsp. chili powder
3 lbs. ground beef

Topping:
1 cup brown sugar
½ cup onions, chopped
1 cup ketchup
1 cup bottled barbecue sauce

1. Grease interior of slow-cooker crock.
2. Mix all Meatball ingredients together well.
3. Shape into 24 balls. Lay in crock. If you need to make a second layer, stagger the balls so they don't directly overlap each other.
4. Mix Topping ingredients together well.
5. Pour over Meatballs, making sure to spoon sauce over all of them, including those on the bottom.
6. Cover. Cook 4-5 hours on Low, or until the Meatballs are all cooked through but aren't dry.

Variations:

Use 2 lbs. ground beef and 1 lb. bulk sausage instead of 3 lbs. ground beef.

—Katie Stoltzfus

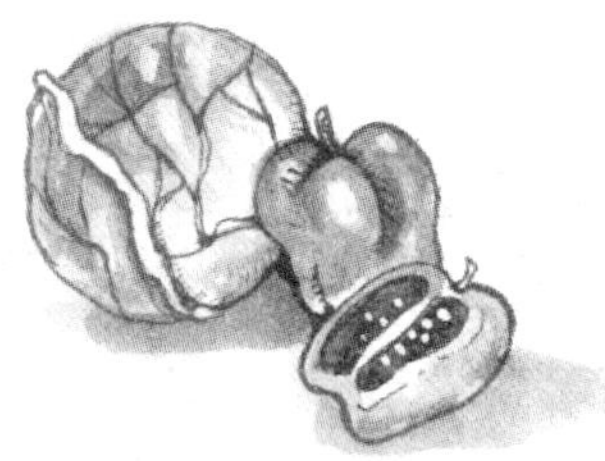

Reuben in a Crock

Joleen Albrecht
Gladstone, MI

Makes 8-10 servings

Prep. Time: 25-30 minutes
Cooking Time: 4-5 hours
Ideal slow-cooker size: 5 or 6 qt.

1½ cups Thousand Island salad dressing
1 cup sour cream
1 Tbsp. minced onions
12 slices dark rye bread, cubed, divided
1 lb. sauerkraut, drained
1½ lbs. deli corned beef, thinly sliced
2 cups shredded Swiss cheese
½ stick (¼ cup) butter, melted

1. Grease interior of slow-cooker crock.
2. In a bowl, mix together dressing, sour cream, and onions. Set aside.
3. Place half the bread cubes in crock.
4. Top with sauerkraut, spread out evenly over bread.
5. Add layer of corned beef, distributed evenly over sauerkraut.
6. Spread dressing mixture over corned beef.
7. Scatter shredded cheese over top.
8. Top with remaining bread cubes.
9. Drizzle with melted butter.
10. Cover and cook on Low 3½ hours, or until mixture is heated through.
11. Remove cover. Cook on Low 30 more minutes to allow moisture to escape.

Slow-Cooker Beef Stroganoff

Orpha Herr
Andover, NY

Makes 12 servings

Prep. Time: 20 minutes
Cooking Time: 5-7 hours
Ideal slow-cooker size: 5 qt.

1 large onion, chopped
10.75-oz. can cream of mushroom soup
10.75-oz. can cream of onion soup
½ tsp. salt
¼-½ tsp. coarsely ground black pepper, according to taste
¼ tsp. dried thyme
2-3-lb. boneless beef chuck roast, cut into 1" cubes
8-oz. can sliced mushrooms, drained, or 1 lb. fresh mushrooms, sliced
½ 8-oz. block of cream cheese, room temperature
8 oz. sour cream, room temperature
6 cups hot cooked noodles or rice, for serving

1. Grease interior of slow-cooker crock.
2. Mix onion, soups, salt, pepper, and thyme in crock.
3. Gently stir in beef cubes and sliced mushrooms.
4. Cover. Cook on Low 5-7 hours.
5. Stir in cream cheese and sour cream. Cook an additional 10-20 minutes until heated through and cream cheese is totally melted.
6. Serve on hot noodles or rice.

Meatball Stroganoff

Shannon D. Lear
Middleton, MA

Makes 6 servings

Prep. Time: 35 minutes
Cooking Time: 4¼-5¼ hours
Ideal slow-cooker size: 4 or 5 qt.

Meatballs:
1½ lbs. ground beef
¾ cup dry bread crumbs
1 tsp. salt
¼ tsp. black pepper
⅛ tsp. garlic powder
¾ cup chopped onions
1 Tbsp. Worcestershire sauce
1 egg
½ cup milk
3 Tbsp. cooking oil

Sauce:
3 Tbsp. tomato paste
1 tsp. Worcestershire sauce
¼ tsp. salt
¼ cup flour
1½ cups beef broth
¼ cup sherry or white wine, optional
1 cup sour cream

1. Grease interior of slow-cooker crock.
2. Combine beef, bread crumbs, salt, pepper, garlic powder, onions, Worcestershire sauce, egg, and milk.
3. Mix well. Shape into 1" balls.
4. Brown meatballs in cooking oil in skillet. Using a slotted spoon, lift meatballs out of skillet and place in slow cooker. Reserve drippings in skillet.
5. Stir tomato paste, Worcestershire sauce, salt, and flour into drippings in skillet over low heat until smooth.
6. Stir in broth over medium heat until mixture becomes thickened and bubbly.
7. Blend in sherry. Fold in sour cream.
8. Pour over meatballs.
9. Cover cooker. Cook on Low 4 hours.
10. Serve over buttered noodles or cooked rice.

Heart-Healthy Meatballs & Spaghetti

Shirley Unternahrer
Wayland, IA

Makes 8 servings

Prep. Time: 50 minutes
Cooking Time: 3 hours
Ideal slow-cooker size: 4-6 qt.

2 lbs. lean ground beef
½ tsp. dried basil
½ tsp. dried oregano
¼ tsp. garlic powder
¼ tsp. onion powder
⅛ tsp. black pepper
1 egg
1 lb. pasta, regular or gluten-free
24- or 30-oz. jar low-salt spaghetti sauce
27-oz. can no-salt-added tomato sauce

1. Grease interior of slow-cooker crock.
2. Using your hands, mix together ground beef, basil, oregano, garlic and onion powders, pepper, and egg.
3. Shape into balls the size of walnuts and place on sprayed jelly-roll pan or baking sheet with sides.
4. Bake meatballs for 30 minutes at 400°.
5. While meatballs bake, empty jar of spaghetti sauce and can of tomato sauce into crock.
6. Remove baked meatballs from pan and add to sauce in crock.
7. Cook for 3 hours on Low.
8. Serve over cooked pasta.

Tips:

Set cayenne pepper, garlic powder, and oregano on the table when serving so diners can add more flavor if they wish.

Good go-alongs with this recipe:

Garden salad.

Brown the ground beef or sausage before you put it in the cooker if you can. Sure, it's an extra step and an extra pan to wash, but you've cooked off the fat and drippings rather than consume them.

Mushroom-Herb Pasta Sauce

Phyllis Good
Lancaster, PA

Makes 4 servings

Prep. Time: 20-30 minutes
Cooking Time: 3 hours
Ideal slow-cooker size: 5 qt.

1 lb. ground beef
½ cup onions, chopped, or 4 chopped shallots
3 cloves garlic, minced
⅛ tsp. black pepper
1½ Tbsp. butter
2 Tbsp. mushrooms, chopped
1½ Tbsp. flour
¾ cup milk
1 cup tomato sauce
¼ tsp. chili powder
1 cup sliced mushrooms
3 Tbsp. dried parsley
2 tsp. dried basil
1 tsp. dried oregano
⅓ tsp. dried thyme
scant ¼ tsp. dried rosemary
½ lb. dry spaghetti
½ cup grated Parmesan cheese
fresh whole basil leaves

1. Grease interior of slow-cooker crock.
2. If you have time, brown beef, onions, and garlic together in a skillet. Using a slotted spoon, lift beef and veggies out of drippings and place in crock. If you don't have time, place beef in bowl and use a sturdy spoon to break it up into small clumps. Mix in onions and garlic. Spoon into crock.
3. In a small saucepan, melt butter. Sauté chopped mushrooms in butter until tender, stirring frequently.
4. Add flour and stir until smooth.
5. Over low heat, stir in milk, stirring continuously until mixture begins to bubble and thicken.
6. Add sauce to beef, along with tomato sauce and chili powder. Stir until well mixed.
7. Gently stir in sliced mushrooms and all herbs.
8. Cover. Cook on Low 3 hours.
9. As cooking time nears the end, cook spaghetti according to package directions.
10. Pour sauce over spaghetti. Top with Parmesan cheese and fresh whole basil leaves.

Pizza in a Crock

Donna Treloar
Muncie, IN

Makes 6+ servings

Prep. Time: 15-20 minutes
Cooking Time: 2-4 hours
Ideal slow-cooker size: 6 or 7 qt.

1 lb. bulk sausage of your choice
1 lb. ground beef
1 large onion, diced
1 large green pepper, diced
1 pkg. sliced mushrooms
1 tsp. garlic powder
1 tsp. salt
1 tsp. black pepper
16 oz. ricotta cheese
4 cups mozzarella cheese, shredded
28-oz. jar pizza sauce, divided
3-4 cups uncooked pasta, rotini, spiral, your choice, divided
5-oz. pkg. sliced pepperoni, optional, divided

1. Grease interior of slow-cooker crock.
2. In a good-sized skillet, brown sausage and ground beef together. Drain off drippings.
3. Add onion, green pepper, and mushrooms. Cook another 5 minutes.
4. Stir garlic powder, salt, and pepper into meat-veggie mixture.
5. In a good-sized bowl, mix cheeses together.
6. Spoon about 1½ cups pizza sauce in bottom of crock.
7. Layer in half the pasta.
8. Follow that with half the meat-vegetable mixture.
9. Top with half the pepperoni, if you wish, followed by half the cheese mixture.
10. Start a new layer, beginning with remaining pizza sauce, then the remaining pasta, meat-vegetable mixture, pepperoni if you wish, and remaining cheeses.
11. Cover. Cook 2-4 hours on Low, or until pasta is tender.

Variations:

1. Use cottage cheese instead of ricotta. 2. Use turkey sausage and turkey pepperoni if you wish.

Pizza with Macaroni Crust

Dorothy Hess
Willow Street, PA

Makes 8 servings

Prep. Time: 20 minutes
Cooking Time: 3¼ hours
Ideal slow-cooker size: 5 qt.

10.75-oz. can tomato soup
28-oz. jar pizza sauce
1 Tbsp. sugar
½ lb. uncooked macaroni
1 egg, beaten
½ cup milk
2 lbs. ground beef
1 onion, chopped
15-oz. can tomato sauce
½ tsp. dried basil
½ tsp. dried oregano
1 tsp. salt
½ tsp. black pepper
4 oz. grated cheddar cheese
8 oz. grated mozzarella cheese

1. In a large bowl, stir together tomato soup (undiluted), pizza sauce, and sugar. Stir in beaten egg and milk.
2. Stir uncooked macaroni into tomato mixture.
3. Grease interior of slow-cooker crock.
4. Spoon macaroni-tomato mixture into crock, spreading it evenly over the bottom and up the sides as much as possible.
5. Cover. Cook on High for 3 hours.
6. Twenty minutes before end of cooking time, brown ground beef and onion in a saucepan. Drain off drippings.
7. Stir tomato sauce, basil, oregano, salt, and pepper into beef and onion mixture. Cover saucepan and keep warm over low heat.
8. Check that macaroni are tender. If so, spoon beef-tomato mixture over macaroni.
9. Cover cooker. Cook on High 10 minutes.
10. Scatter cheeses over beef and macaroni. Cover. Cook on High 5 more minutes.

Variations:

Instead of 2 lbs. ground beef, use 1 lb. ground beef and 1 lb. sausage squeezed out of casings.

Slow-Cooker "Pizza"

Judy Diller
Bluffton, OH

Makes 6 servings

Prep. Time: 20 minutes
Cooking Time: 4 hours
Ideal slow-cooker size: 5 qt.

8 oz. noodles or other pasta, cooked just until very al dente, and drained
1 lb. ground beef
1 small onion, chopped
4 oz. pepperoni
1 tsp. garlic salt
30-oz. jar pizza or spaghetti sauce
¼ lb. fresh mushrooms or 4-oz. can sliced mushrooms, drained
2 cups shredded mozzarella cheese

1. Grease interior of slow-cooker crock.
2. If you have time, brown beef and onion in skillet. Using a slotted spoon, lift meat and onion out of drippings and into crock.
3. If you don't have time, crumble beef into crock. Mix in onions.
4. Add all other ingredients and stir together gently.
5. Cover. Cook 4 hours on Low.

Tips:

From the tester: A very family-friendly and delicious dish. Everyone loved it!

—Joleen Albrecht

Variations:

1. Use different pasta shapes for variety. 2. Stir in other pizza toppings as you like, such as chopped sweet or hot peppers and olives. 3. You can use sausage in place of the ground beef.

Good go-alongs with this recipe:

I often serve this Sunday afternoon after church with garlic bread and salad.

Upside-Down Pizza

Julia Rohrer
Aaronsburg, PA

Makes 8-10 servings

Prep. Time: 30 minutes
Cooking Time: 5-6 hours
Ideal slow-cooker size: 6 qt.

2 lbs. ground beef
1 medium onion, chopped
1 medium red or green bell pepper, chopped
1 tsp. dried basil
1 tsp. dried oregano
1 cup pizza or spaghetti sauce
¼ lb. fresh mushrooms or 4-oz. can chopped mushrooms, drained
2 cups grated mozzarella cheese
sprinkling of dried oregano
sprinkling of grated Parmesan cheese

Batter:
3 eggs
1½ cups milk
1½ Tbsp. oil
½ tsp. salt
1 tsp. baking soda
1¾ cups flour

1. Grease interior of slow-cooker crock.
2. If you have time, brown beef, onions, and peppers together in a skillet. Using a slotted spoon, lift beef and veggies out of drippings and place in good-sized bowl. If you don't have time, place beef in bowl and use a sturdy spoon to break it up into small clumps. Mix in onions and chopped peppers.
3. Spoon beef and vegetables into crock.
4. Stir in herbs, sauce, and mushrooms.
5. Cover. Cook on Low 4 hours, or until hot in center.
6. Thirty minutes before end of cooking time, prepare batter by beating eggs, milk, and oil together in good-sized mixing bowl.
7. Add salt, baking soda, and flour, stirring just until mixed.
8. Uncover crock. Top beef and vegetables with grated mozzarella cheese.
9. Spoon batter over top, spreading it out evenly. Do not stir.
10. Sprinkle with oregano and Parmesan cheese.
11. Cover. Cook on High 1 hour, or until toothpick inserted in center of dough comes out clean.

Variations:

Add a layer of sliced pepperoni, plus a layer of sliced black olives, immediately after Step 8—on top of the cheese layer and under the dough.

—Joyce Cox

Cabbage Lasagna

Sylvia Eberly
Reinholds, PA

Makes 4-5 servings

Prep. Time: 30 minutes
Cooking Time: 5 hours
Ideal slow-cooker size: 5 qt.

1 medium to large head cabbage, about 6" in diameter
1 lb. ground beef
2 garlic cloves, minced or pressed
1 medium onion, chopped
1 green sweet bell pepper, chopped
6-oz. can tomato paste
8-oz. can tomato sauce
1-3 tsp. dried oregano, according to your taste preference
2 tsp. dried basil, optional
1 tsp. black pepper
1 cup mozzarella cheese, grated, divided
½ cup ricotta or cottage cheese, divided
½ cup Parmesan cheese, grated

1. Wash cabbage and remove tough outer leaves. Cut head in half and slice thinly.
2. Arrange finely sliced cabbage in a steamer basket and steam about 3-5 minutes. (You might need to do this in 2 batches.)
3. Drain cabbage well. Set aside.
4. Grease interior of slow-cooker crock.
5. If you have time, brown beef, garlic, onions, and green pepper together in a skillet. Drain off any drippings. If you don't have time, place beef in bowl and use a sturdy spoon to break up into small clumps. Mix in garlic, onions, and green pepper.
6. Add tomato paste, tomato sauce, and seasonings to beef mixture. Combine well.
7. Drain cabbage again.
8. Make layers in crock, starting with half the cabbage leaves, half the meat mixture, ⅓ of the mozzarella, and half the ricotta.
9. Repeat layers, using remaining cabbage and meat mixture, half the remaining mozzarella, and all of the ricotta.
10. Top with remaining mozzarella.
11. Cover. Cook on Low 5 hours, or until vegetables are as tender as you like them.
12. Uncover. Sprinkle with Parmesan cheese.
13. Let stand 10 minutes so that Parmesan cheese can melt and Lasagna firms up.

Zucchini and Beef Lasagna

Carolyn Snader
Ephrata, PA

Makes 4 servings

Prep. Time: 15-20 minutes
Cooking Time: 4 hours
Ideal slow-cooker size: 4 or 5 qt.

6 cups sliced, unpeeled zucchini
1 lb. ground beef
½ tsp. dried basil
½ tsp. dried oregano
⅛ tsp. garlic powder
6-oz. can tomato paste
1 cup cottage cheese
1 egg
2 cups mozzarella cheese, shredded, divided

1. Grease interior of slow-cooker crock.
2. If you have time, brown beef in a skillet. Using a slotted spoon, lift beef out of drippings and place in good-sized bowl. If you don't have time, place beef in bowl and use a sturdy spoon to break into small clumps.
3. Mix basil, oregano, and garlic powder with beef.
4. Stir tomato paste into beef mixture.
5. In a separate bowl, combine cottage cheese, egg, and 1 cup mozzarella.
6. Cover bottom of crock with half the zucchini slices.
7. Top with half the meat mixture.
8. Spoon half the cheese mixture over meat.
9. Repeat layers.
10. Cover. Cook on Low 4 hours, or until zucchini is as tender as you like.
11. Uncover crock. Sprinkle in remaining mozzarella cheese. Allow to stand 10 minutes so cheese can melt and Lasagna can firm up.

Zucchini-Hamburger Bake

Linda Overholt
Abbeville, SC

Makes 6 servings

Prep. Time: 20-30 minutes
Cooking Time: 4 hours
Ideal slow-cooker size: 5 qt.

1 lb. ground beef
1 small onion, chopped
½ tsp. salt
¼ tsp. black pepper
2 cups pizza sauce
4 cups zucchini, peeled or not, and cubed
1½ cups water, divided
½ cup instant rice
¾ cup mozzarella cheese, shredded

1. Grease interior of slow-cooker crock.
2. If you have time, brown beef and onions together in a skillet. Using a slotted spoon, lift beef and onions out of drippings and place in crock. If you don't have time, place beef in bowl and use a sturdy spoon to break up into small clumps. Mix in onions. Place in crock.
3. Stir in salt and pepper, pizza sauce, zucchini, and ¾ cup water. Mix well.
4. Cover. Cook on Low 3½ hours, or until beef is cooked through and vegetables are as tender as you like them.
5. Stir in rice and remaining water.
6. Cover. Cook on High 20-30 minutes, or until rice is tender.
7. Remove lid. Sprinkle grated cheese over top.
8. Allow to stand until cheese is melted. Then serve.

Lentil and Lamb Curry

Bob Coffey
New Windsor, NY

Makes 12 servings

Prep. Time: 20-30 minutes
Cooking Time: 6-8 hours
Ideal slow-cooker size: 5.5 qt.

1¼ lbs. dried lentils, picked through for debris and rinsed
3 stalks celery, diced
4 large carrots, diced
2 large onions, diced
4 garlic cloves, smashed and chopped
2 cups chicken broth
4+ cups water
2-lb. boneless leg of lamb, cut into bite-sized pieces*
2 tsp. curry powder
1 tsp. turmeric
1 tsp. salt
1 bunch fresh cilantro, rinsed and chopped
***If you can't find that size boneless leg of lamb, buy what's available, cut off a 2-lb. piece, and freeze the rest.**

1. Grease interior of slow-cooker crock.
2. Add all ingredients except cilantro into slow cooker. Make sure everything is covered with water. Stir together well.
3. Cover. Cook on Low for 6-8 hours, or until instant-read meat thermometer registers 160° when stuck in center of a cube.
4. While cooking, stir once or twice to check the doneness of the lentils. Add some water if they aren't done but are beginning to cook dry.
5. Stir in cilantro 10 minutes before serving

Tips:

1. If you like curry, you may want to add a little more powder in the final minutes of cooking. Taste, too, to see if dish needs more salt.
2. This freezes well and is even better when eaten later.

Good go-alongs with this recipe:

Traditional naan bread is a treat alongside this curry.

Mild Indian Curry

Vic and Christina Buckwalter
Keezletown, VA

Makes 4-6 servings

Prep. Time: 20 minutes
Cooking Time: 4 hours
Ideal slow-cooker size: 4 qt.

1 lb. ground beef
1 onion, chopped
3 garlic cloves, finely chopped
½ tsp. ground ginger
2 tsp. coriander
2 tsp. cumin
1 tsp. turmeric
¼ tsp. ground cloves
¼ tsp. cayenne pepper
¾ cup tomato sauce
2 tsp. salt
2 Tbsp. sugar
¼ cup plain yogurt
cooked basmati rice
topping options: grated cheeses; chopped fresh onions; orange sections; sliced bananas; chopped papaya, mango, and/ or tomatoes; peanuts; raisins

1. Grease interior of slow-cooker crock.
2. If you have time, brown beef, onions, and garlic together in a skillet. Using a slotted spoon, lift beef and vegetables out of drippings and place in crock. If you don't have time, crumble beef into crock. Scatter onions and garlic over top.
3. Mix in ginger, coriander, cumin, turmeric, ground cloves, and cayenne pepper.
4. Stir in tomato sauce, salt, and sugar.
5. Cover. Cook on Low 4 hours, or until the beef is cooked through and everything is hot.
6. Just before serving, blend in yogurt.
7. Serve over basmati rice.
8. Send bowls of each topping that you choose around the table after rice and curry have been passed.

Tips:

We picked up this recipe while living in East Africa. It brings back memories of the Swahili Coast.

East Africa Beef Curry

Joyce Hedrick
Lederach, PA

Makes 6-8 servings

Prep. Time: 20-30 minutes
Cooking Time: 4 hours
Ideal slow-cooker size: 4 qt.

1½-2 lbs. boneless chuck, cut into 1" cubes
1 medium onion, diced
2-3 Tbsp. curry powder
⅓ cup fresh mushrooms, sliced, or 4-oz. can sliced mushrooms, drained
1 tomato, diced
1 large garlic clove, minced
2 tsp. salt
2 tsp. sugar
2 cups (more or less) water
2 Tbsp. cornstarch
2 Tbsp. water
3 cups cooked rice

Condiments:
diced onion
diced tomatoes
peanuts
diced hard-boiled eggs
chopped cauliflower
diced oranges
pickle relish
chutney
raisins
chopped dates
diced bananas
chopped green bell peppers
shredded coconut
shredded cabbage
diced cucumbers
diced pineapple
shredded carrots
diced apples
grated cheese

1. Grease interior of slow-cooker crock.
2. Place cubed beef, diced onions, and curry powder in slow cooker. Mix together well.
3. Stir in sliced mushrooms, diced tomato, minced garlic, salt, and sugar.
4. Add enough water to barely cover beef and vegetables (about 2 cups).
5. Cover. Cook on Low 4 hours, or until meat and vegetables are as tender as you like them.
6. In a small bowl, mix together cornstarch and 2 Tbsp. water until smooth.
7. Add to slow cooker, stirring until sauce thickens and bubbles.
8. Serve meat, veggies, and sauce over cooked rice.
9. Prepare as many condiments as you wish as the curry is cooking. Put in individual bowls in center of table and pass to everyone to choose their own toppings.

Tips:

You can make the meat and vegetables a day or two ahead of serving, as long as it is refrigerated. The curry and other flavors steep well. It's a great socializing meal.

Spicy Beef and Black Bean Salsa

Harriette Johnson
Spring Valley, WI

Makes 10 servings

Prep. Time: 10-15 minutes
Cooking Time: 5-10 hours
Ideal slow-cooker size: oval 6 or 7 qt.

3-4-lb. boneless chuck roast
1 tsp. cayenne pepper
1 tsp. chili powder
½ tsp. red pepper flakes
½ tsp. ground cumin
1 Tbsp. oil
¼ cup water
14.5-oz. can spicy black beans, undrained
1 cup red onion, chopped
⅓ cup lemon juice
½-¾ cup chopped fresh cilantro
salt to taste
black pepper to taste
2 fresh tomatoes, diced, or 8-10 tomatillos, diced

1. Grease interior of slow-cooker crock.
2. In a small bowl, mix together cayenne pepper, chili powder, red pepper flakes, and cumin, dampened with oil. Rub over roast on all sides.
3. Place roast in cooker. Pour ¼ cup water down along sides of cooker so as not to wash off the rub.
4. Cover. Cook on Low 7-8 hours, or on High 4-5 hours, or until instant-read meat thermometer registers 140°-145° when inserted in center of roast.
5. While roast is cooking, combine beans, chopped onion, and lemon juice.
6. When well mixed, stir in cilantro, salt, pepper, and tomatoes.
7. When roast is done cooking, use sturdy tongs or 2 metal spatulas to lift it onto a cutting board. Cut into chunks or slices.
8. Top with salsa to serve.

Mexican Lasagna

Marcia S. Myer
Manheim, PA

Makes 12 servings

Prep. Time: 30 minutes
Cooking Time: 3-4 hours
Ideal slow-cooker size: 5 or 6 qt.

1 lb. ground beef
15-oz. can corn, drained
15-oz. can tomato sauce
1 cup picante sauce or hot salsa, if you want more kick
1 Tbsp. chili powder
1½ tsp. cumin
16-oz. carton cottage cheese
2 eggs, slightly beaten
¼ cup Parmesan cheese
1 tsp. dried oregano
½ tsp. garlic salt
12 corn tortillas, divided
1 cup (4 oz.) cheddar cheese, shredded
chopped cilantro
2 chopped green onions
chopped lettuce
chopped tomatoes

1. Grease interior of slow-cooker crock.
2. In a large skillet, brown ground beef. Drain off drippings.
3. Add corn, tomato sauce, picante sauce or hot salsa, chili powder, and cumin to beef in skillet. Stir together well.
4. In a bowl, blend together cottage cheese, eggs, Parmesan cheese, oregano, and garlic salt.
5. Arrange 4 tortillas over bottom of crock, overlapping and breaking to fit as needed.
6. Top with half of meat/vegetable mixture.
7. Arrange 4 more tortillas over mixture, overlapping and breaking to fit as needed.
8. Top with all of cheese/egg mixture.
9. Arrange remaining 4 tortillas over cheese, overlapping and breaking to fit as needed.
10. Spoon remaining meat/vegetable mixture over tortillas.
11. Cover. Cook on Low 3-4 hours, or until heated through.
12. Fifteen minutes before end of cooking time, remove lid and scatter shredded cheese over top.
13. Cover and continue cooking for 15 more minutes.
14. Remove lid. Let stand 10 minutes before serving.
15. Top individual servings with chopped cilantro, green onions, lettuce, and tomatoes.

Lasagna Mexicana

Barbara Walker
Sturgis, SD

Makes 6 servings

Prep. Time: 20 minutes
Cooking Time: 4 hours
Ideal slow-cooker size: 5 qt.

1 lb. ground beef
16-oz. can refried beans
2 tsp. dried oregano
1 tsp. ground cumin
¾ tsp. garlic powder
9 uncooked lasagna noodles, divided
1 cup salsa, as hot or as mild as you like
1 cup water
2 cups sour cream
2.25-oz. can sliced ripe olives, drained
1 cup Mexican blend cheese, shredded
½ cup sliced green onions

1. Grease interior of slow-cooker crock.
2. If you have time, brown beef in a skillet. Using a slotted spoon, lift beef out of drippings and place in good-sized bowl. If you don't have time, place beef in bowl and use a sturdy spoon to break up into small clumps.
3. Stir in beans and seasonings.
4. Place three uncooked noodles in bottom of crock, breaking and overlapping to fit.
5. Cover with half of meat/vegetable mixture.
6. Repeat layers of noodles and meat/vegetables.
7. Top with remaining noodles.
8. Combine salsa and water in a bowl. Pour over noodles.
9. Cover. Cook on Low 4 hours, or until noodles are tender.
10. Spread Lasagna with sour cream.
11. Sprinkle with olives, cheese, and green onions.

Saucy Tacos

Sarah Herr
Goshen, IN

Makes 8 servings

Prep. Time: 20 minutes
Cooking Time: 6-8 hours
Ideal slow-cooker size: 4 qt.

2 lbs. flank steak
1 green bell pepper, chopped
1 onion, chopped
1 cup salsa (I use peach flavored, which is less tomatoey)
2 Tbsp., or 1 envelope, taco seasoning

1. Grease interior of slow-cooker crock.
2. Place steak in crock.
3. Mix all other ingredients in a bowl. Spoon over meat.
4. Cover. Cook 6-8 hours on Low, or until instant-read meat thermometer registers 140°-145° when stuck in center.
5. Shred meat with 2 forks, or slice thinly. Mix with vegetables and juice.
6. Serve with tortillas or taco shells. Or drain and include in a taco salad.

Good go-alongs with this recipe:

Serve with beans, lettuce, tomato, cheese, sour cream, black olives, and your other favorite taco toppings.

Quick and Easy Tacos

Audrey Romonosky
Austin, TX

Makes 4 servings

Prep. Time: 10 minutes
Cooking Time: 4 hours
Ideal slow-cooker size: 4 qt.

1 lb. ground beef
1 cup corn, fresh, frozen, or canned
½-1 cup salsa or picante sauce, according to your taste preference
10-12 tortillas
guacamole, optional
1½ cups grated cheddar cheese, optional

1. Grease interior of slow-cooker crock.
2. If you have time, brown the ground beef in a skillet, stirring to break up clumps. When browned, use a slotted spoon to remove the beef and put it in the crock. If you don't have time, crumble the beef directly into the cooker.
3. Stir corn and salsa into beef.
4. Cover. Cook on Low 4 hours, or until beef is fully cooked.
5. Spoon into tortillas and garnish with guacamole and cheese, if you wish.

Tostadas

Jenny Unternahrer
Wayland, IA

Makes 8-10 servings

Prep. Time: 15 minutes
Cooking Time: 6-8 hours
Ideal slow-cooker size: 5 qt.

¼ cup lime juice, divided
3 garlic cloves, finely chopped
1 jalapeño, seeded and finely chopped
1 large onion, chopped
1 Tbsp. chili powder, or a combination of cumin, garlic powder, onion powder, and cayenne pepper
¼ tsp. cumin
⅛ tsp. cayenne pepper
1½ lbs. boneless beef chuck roast
½ tsp. salt
½ tsp. coarsely ground black pepper
hard or soft tortillas
toppings: refried beans, cooked onions and bell peppers, chopped lettuce, shredded Mexican-blend cheese, salsa, guacamole, sour cream, and more

1. Grease interior of slow-cooker crock.
2. Place 3 tablespoons of lime juice, all the garlic, jalapeño, onion, chili powder, cumin, and cayenne into crock. Mix together well.
3. Holding roast over crock, salt and pepper on all sides. Lay meat on top of sauce.
4. Cover. Cook on Low for 6-8 hours, or until instant-read meat thermometer registers 145°-150° when stuck in center of roast.
5. Remove beef to a cutting board and when cool enough to handle, shred with fingers or 2 forks.
6. Place shredded beef in large bowl. Strain remaining liquid in slow cooker over bowl or measuring cup, discarding solids.
7. Add strained liquid and remaining 1 Tbsp. lime juice to beef in bowl. Stir to combine.
8. Cover and keep warm until ready to serve in either hard or soft tortillas, along with your favorite toppings.

Variations:

You can also use a pork butt or goat roast instead of the beef chuck.

Enchilada Pie

Arlene Leaman Kliewer
Lakewood, CO

Makes 8 servings

Prep. Time: 30 minutes
Cooking Time: 4 hours

2 lbs. ground beef
1 small onion, chopped
1 small can sliced black olives, drained
2 cups tomato sauce
15.5-oz. can Mexican-style beans, undrained
18 corn tortillas, divided
2 lbs. your favorite creamy cheese, cubed or shredded
1 cup beef broth

1. Grease interior of slow-cooker crock.
2. If you have time, brown beef and onions together in a skillet. Using a slotted spoon, lift beef and onions out of drippings and place in good-sized bowl. If you don't have time, place beef in bowl and use a sturdy spoon to break it up into small clumps. Mix in onions.
3. Stir in olives, tomato sauce, and beans.
4. Place half of tortillas in crock, breaking to fit, distributing evenly over the bottom.
5. Spoon in half the meat/vegetable mixture evenly over the tortillas.
6. Top with half the cheese.
7. Repeat layers, ending with cheese.
8. Pour broth over all.
9. Cover. Cook on Low 4 hours.
10. Allow to stand 10 minutes before serving.

Fabulous Fajitas

Phyllis Good
Lancaster, PA

Makes 4 servings

***Prep. Time:** 15 minutes*
***Cooking Time:** 3½ hours*
***Ideal slow-cooker size:** 4 qt.*

1-1½ lbs. flank steak, cut across grain in ½"-thick strips
2 Tbsp. lemon juice
1 garlic clove, minced
1½ tsp. cumin
½ tsp. red pepper flakes
1 tsp. seasoning salt
2 Tbsp. Worcestershire sauce
1 tsp. chili powder
1 green bell pepper, cut in strips
1 yellow onion, sliced
6-8 warmed tortillas, for serving
favorite toppings: sour cream, chopped fresh cilantro, salsa, shredded cheese, etc.

1. Grease interior of slow-cooker crock.
2. Place beef strips in crock.
3. Stir in lemon juice, garlic, cumin, red pepper flakes, seasoning salt, Worcestershire sauce, and chili powder.
4. Cook on Low 2½ hours, or until beef is nearly tender.
5. Stir in peppers and onion.
6. Cover. Cook for another hour on Low or until vegetables are as tender as you like them.
7. Spoon mixture into warm tortillas. Top with favorite toppings.

Enchilada Stack-Up

Sally Holzem
Schofield, WI

Makes 8 servings

***Prep. Time:** 30 minutes*
***Cooking Time:** 4 hours*
***Ideal slow-cooker size:** 5 qt.*

1 lb. ground beef
1 cup chopped onion
½ cup chopped red, yellow, or orange bell peppers
1 tsp. olive oil
15-oz. can kidney beans, rinsed and drained
15-oz. can black beans, rinsed and drained
14.5-oz. can diced tomatoes and green chilies
1½ tsp. cumin
¼ tsp. black pepper
6 8" tortillas
2 cups shredded cheddar cheese

1. Cut 3 (25x3) strips of heavy-duty foil. Criss-cross strips so they resemble spokes of a wheel inside bottom and up sides of crock. Spray with cooking spray.
2. In skillet, brown ground beef, onions, and bell peppers in olive oil.
3. Drain off drippings and discard.
4. Stir black beans, kidney beans, tomatoes, cumin, and black pepper into beef-veggie mixture in skillet.
5. Lay 1 tortilla in bottom of crock (and over top of the foil strips). Spoon ¾ cup bean mixture over top. Sprinkle with ⅓ of cheese.
6. Repeat layers 5 times.
7. Cover and cook on Low 4-5 hours, until very hot in the middle.
8. Use foil strips as handles to remove stack from slow cooker to platter.
9. Gently ease foil strips out from underneath stack, or bend them over so they're out of the way.
10. Cover stack to keep warm. Allow to stand 10-15 minutes to firm up. Then cut into wedges and serve.

Tips:

This is a great game-day meal.

Good go-alongs with this recipe:

Fresh fruit to cool the palate and sherbet for dessert.

California Tacos

Mary June Hershberger
Lynchburg, VA

Makes 6-8 servings

Prep. Time: 20 minutes
Cooking Time: 3 hours
Ideal slow-cooker size: 2 qt.

1 lb. ground beef
1 medium onion, chopped
1 green bell pepper, chopped
1 envelope, or 4 Tbsp., dry taco seasoning
2 cups salsa, your choice of heat
15.5-oz. can pinto beans, rinsed and drained
salt and pepper to taste

1. Grease interior of slow-cooker crock.
2. If you have time, brown beef in skillet. Drain off drippings and place meat in crock.
3. If you don't have time, crumble beef over bottom of crock.
4. Stir in onion and bell pepper, taco seasoning, salsa, and pinto beans.
5. Cover. Cook on Low for 3 hours.

Tips:

Serve in tortillas, or on top of lettuce with chopped fresh tomatoes, sliced cucumbers, grated cheese, black olives, and your favorite salad dressing. Top with crushed tortilla chips.

Good go-alongs with this recipe:

Garlic bread.

Open-Face Italian Beef Sandwiches

Edith Romano
Westminster, MD

Makes 10 servings

Prep. Time: 20-30 minutes
Cooking Time: 6-8 hours
Ideal slow-cooker size: 5 or 6 qt.

3 lbs. boneless beef chuck roast, partially frozen
1½ cups sliced onions
19-oz. can tomato-basil soup
2 Tbsp. cornstarch
2 Tbsp. brown sugar
¼ tsp. dried oregano
¼ tsp. dried basil
⅛ tsp. cayenne pepper
2 Tbsp. Worcestershire sauce
10 ½"-thick slices Italian bread
10 slices provolone cheese
2 Tbsp. chopped fresh parsley

1. Grease interior of slow-cooker crock.
2. Cut beef diagonally across grain into thin slices. Place beef in crock, along with onions.
3. In medium bowl, combine soup, cornstarch, brown sugar, oregano, basil, cayenne pepper, and Worcestershire sauce. Mix until smooth.
4. Pour sauce over beef and onions. Stir well so all pieces of meat are covered with sauce.
5. Cover. Cook on Low 6-8 hours, or until beef is tender.
6. Stir occasionally to keep beef that touches sides of crock from getting too dry.
7. To serve, place 1 slice of bread on plate. Top with 1 slice of cheese. Spoon about ¾ cup beef mixture over cheese. Sprinkle with parsley and serve immediately.

Tips:

I lost this recipe for about a year and just recently found it. I'd been using a similar recipe, but this is by far the best.

Good go-alongs with this recipe:

Coleslaw.

Beef and Salsa Burritos

Joyce Shackelford
Green Bay, WI

Makes 8 servings

***Prep. Time:** 10 minutes*
***Cooking Time:** 3 hours*
***Ideal slow-cooker size:** 4 qt.*

1¼ lbs. ground beef
1½ Tbsp. chili powder
1½ Tbsp. cumin
½ tsp. salt
¼-½ tsp. coarsely ground black pepper, according to taste
3 cups fresh spinach, chopped, or 10-oz. pkg. frozen chopped spinach, thawed
1¼ cups chunky salsa, as hot or mild as you like
1 cup shredded cheddar cheese
sliced green onions, optional
sour cream, optional
8 medium-sized flour tortillas, warmed

1. Grease interior of slow-cooker crock.
2. Place ground beef, chili powder, cumin, salt, and pepper in crock. Break up beef into fine chunks, while mixing all ingredients together well.
3. Cover. Cook on High for 2-3 hours, or until beef browns well.
4. Meanwhile, wash fresh spinach. Shake off a bit of the water and place it in a microwave-safe bowl. Heat on High for 1½ minutes. Drain well. Allow to cool enough to chop.
5. Or if you're using frozen spinach, squeeze it dry after it's thawed.
6. Mix spinach and salsa into seasoned beef.
7. Cover. Cook 20 minutes on High, or until heated through.
8. Stir cheese into mixture.
9. Spoon about ½ cup beef mixture into center of each tortilla.
10. If you wish, scatter green onions over top and drop on a spoonful of sour cream.
11. Fold bottom up and fold sides into center and serve.

Italian Cheesesteak Sandwiches

Jennifer Archer
Kalona, IA

Makes 8-10 servings

***Prep. Time:** 10 minutes*
***Cooking Time:** 10-12 hours*
***Ideal slow-cooker size:** 6 qt.*

3-lb. boneless beef chuck roast
1 envelope dry Italian dressing mix
2-3 bay leaves
1 Tbsp. dried basil
1 Tbsp. dried oregano
2-3 tsp. garlic powder, according to taste
1-2 cups beef broth
¼-½ tsp. coarsely ground black pepper, according to taste
8 or 10 steak rolls
8 or 10 provolone or mozzarella cheese slices

1. Grease interior of slow-cooker crock.
2. Place roast in slow cooker.
3. In a bowl, mix together dry dressing mix, bay leaves, basil, oregano, garlic powder, broth, and pepper.
4. Pour sauce ingredients over roast.
5. Cover. Cook 6-8 hours on Low, or until instant-read meat thermometer registers 145°-150° when stuck in center of roast.
6. Lift roast out of crock with 2 sturdy metal spatulas onto cutting board. Use 2 forks to shred. Fish out bay leaves.
7. Return shredded meat to crock and stir into sauce.
8. Place rolls open-faced on baking sheet. Using a slotted spoon, pile each roll with beef and slice of cheese. Place under broiler for 2-3 minutes, until cheese is bubbly.

Tips:

You can freeze the cooked beef. You'll want leftovers!

Coney Dogs

Anita Troyer
Fairview, MI

Makes 8 servings

Prep. Time: 30 minutes
Cooking Time: 3 hours
Ideal slow-cooker size: 4 qt.

1½ lbs. ground beef
1½ cups diced onions
1 garlic clove, crushed
2 Tbsp. chili powder
1 Tbsp. prepared mustard
16-oz. can tomato sauce
½ cup water
2 lbs. hot dogs, or fresh or smoked sausage, cut into 5″ lengths
hot dog rolls or cooked pasta

1. Grease interior of slow-cooker crock.
2. If you have time, brown beef, onion, and garlic together in a skillet.
3. When browned, place in crock.
4. If you're using fresh sausage, brown in drippings in skillet. Place in crock.
5. Stir chili powder, mustard, tomato sauce, and water into meat in crock. Mix well.
6. Cover. Cook on Low for 2 hours.
7. Stir in hot dogs or fresh sausage. Cook on Low another hour, uncovered so sauce can reduce.
8. Serve in rolls or over pasta.

Variations:

If you wish, add 15.5-oz. can kidney beans, drained and rinsed, to Step 6.

—Marilyn Kurtz

Beef and Pepperoncini Hoagies

Donna Treloar
Muncie, IN

Makes 10 servings/varies w/ roast size

Prep. Time: 15 minutes
Cooking Time: 8-10 hours on Low
Ideal slow-cooker size: 5 or 6 qt.

3-5-lb. boneless chuck roast (inexpensive cuts work fine)
16-oz. jar of pepperoncini peppers, mild or medium, depending on your preference
1 garlic clove, minced, or 1 tsp. garlic powder
salt and pepper, to taste
hoagie rolls or buns of your choice
20 slices provolone cheese

1. Grease interior of slow-cooker crock.
2. Trim roast of fat.
3. Salt and pepper to taste, holding over crock.
4. If using garlic powder, sprinkle on all sides of beef over crock. Place beef in crock.
5. If using minced garlic, scatter over beef in crock.
6. If the pepperoncini peppers are whole and have stems, remove peppers from jar and cut up. Reserve liquid.
7. Scatter cut-up peppers over meat.
8. Pour liquid from peppers down along side of crock interior so you don't wash off the seasonings.
9. Cover. Cook on low 7½-9½ hours, or until beef registers 160° on an instant-read meat thermometer when stuck in center of roast.
10. Lift roast into a big bowl and shred with 2 forks.
11. Stir shredded meat back into juices in crock.
12. Cover. Cook another 30 minutes on Low.
13. When ready to serve, use a slotted spoon to drain meat well.
14. Spoon well-drained meat onto a hoagie roll and top each sandwich with 2 slices cheese.

Tips:

This is an all-time favorite that I've made for years. Everyone asks for this recipe! My original recipe said to cook 7-8 hours, but 10 hours is even better if you have the time. Warming the hoagie rolls is nice, too.

Variations:

This is excellent as is . . . but I frequently add chopped onions to Step 7 . . . just because we love onions. You can also add a package of dry Italian dressing mix and a cup or two of beef broth to Steps 7 and 8. Or you can add a package of Lipton Onion Soup mix along with beef and chicken broth. It's hard to hurt this recipe!

Good go-alongs with this recipe:

Sweet potato fries.

Beef, Bacon, and Beans

Janeen Troyer
Fairview, MI

Makes 8 servings

Prep. Time: 30 minutes
Cooking Time: 2-3 hours
Ideal slow-cooker size: 6 qt.

1 lb. ground beef
½ lb. chopped bacon
⅓ cup chopped onion
15.5-oz. can pork and beans, undrained
15.5-oz. can kidney beans, drained
2 Tbsp. molasses
½ tsp. salt
¼ tsp. pepper
½ tsp. chili powder
¼ cup ketchup
½ cup your favorite barbecue sauce
2 Tbsp. prepared mustard
¾ cup brown sugar

1. Grease interior of slow-cooker crock.
2. Browning beef and bacon before adding them to the crock cooks off a lot of fat and leaves it behind in a skillet. So, if you have time, brown ground beef, bacon, and onion together in a good-sized skillet for a healthier dish. Using a slotted spoon, lift mixture out of drippings and place in crock.
3. If you don't have time to do the browning, crumble ground beef into crock. Stir in chopped bacon and onions.
4. In a good-sized bowl mix together 2 kinds of beans, molasses, salt and pepper, chili powder, ketchup, barbecue sauce, mustard, and brown sugar.
5. Add sauce to meat and bean mixture in crock and mix well.
6. Cover. Cook on Low for 2 hours if you've browned the beef, bacon, and onion ahead of time. Cook on Low for 3 hours if you haven't done the browning.

Good go-alongs with this recipe:

This goes well with cornbread.

Chuck Roast Beef Barbecue

Helen Heurich
Lititz, PA

Makes 20 servings

Prep. Time: 30-40 minutes
Cooking Time: 5-10 hours
Ideal slow-cooker size: oval 6 qt.

3-lb. boneless beef chuck roast
⅔ cup sriracha, ketchup, or barbecue sauce
1¼ cups traditional tomato ketchup
3 Tbsp. lemon juice
2 Tbsp. Worcestershire sauce
2 Tbsp. brown sugar
1½ tsp. spicy brown prepared mustard
3 Tbsp. apple cider vinegar, optional
1-2 medium onions, chopped
3-4 ribs celery, chopped

1. Grease interior of slow-cooker crock.
2. Place roast in crock.
3. Mix all other ingredients together in big bowl.
4. Spoon mixture over roast.
5. Cover. Cook on Low 8-10 hours, or on High 5-6 hours.
6. Using 2 forks, pull the meat apart until it's shredded. Do this in the cooker, or lift out the roast and do it on a good-sized cutting board or big bowl.
7. Return the shredded meat to the cooker and mix the sauce through it.
8. Serve immediately on rolls, or cover and set cooker on Low if you'll eat soon.

I only cook with the leanest ground meats, and get no grease from them, so even if I don't precook the meat, I am not adding grease to my food. Plus, I think that ground meats cooked in liquid are more tender, and keep more of the natural meat flavors and juices. — Donna Davis, Horse Cave, KY

Beef Chuck Barbecue

Frances Kruba
Baltimore, MD

Makes 12 servings

***Prep. Time:** 10-15 minutes*
***Cooking Time:** 6½-8½ hours*
***Ideal slow-cooker size:** 5 qt.*

3-lb. boneless beef chuck roast
1 cup of your favorite barbecue sauce
½ cup apricot jam
⅓ cup chopped green or red bell pepper
1 small onion, chopped
1 Tbsp. Dijon, or your favorite spicy, mustard
1 Tbsp. brown sugar
12 sandwich rolls

1. Grease interior of slow-cooker crock.
2. Cut roast into quarters. Place in crock.
3. In a bowl, combine barbecue sauce, jam, green peppers, onions, mustard, and brown sugar.
4. Pour sauce over roast.
5. Cover. Cook on Low for 6-8 hours, or until meat is tender and instant-read meat thermometer registers 145° when stuck in center of roast.
6. Remove roast from crock with sturdy tongs or 2 metal spatulas. Place on cutting board and slice thinly.
7. Return meat to crock and stir gently into sauce.
8. Cover. Cook 20-30 minutes longer on Low.
9. Serve beef and sauce on rolls.

Beef Barbecue

Carol Eveleth
Hillsdale, WY

Makes 4 servings

***Prep. Time:** 20 minutes*
***Cooking Time:** 3 hours*
***Ideal slow-cooker size:** 3 qt.*

1 Tbsp. oil, optional
2 lbs. lean ground beef
½ cup chopped onions
¾ cup chopped celery
1 Tbsp. prepared mustard
2 Tbsp. brown sugar
2 Tbsp. Worcestershire sauce
¾ cup ketchup
1 tsp. salt
8 hamburger rolls

1. Grease interior of slow-cooker crock.
2. If you have time, brown beef in oil, along with onions and celery, in skillet. Break up the meat into small chunks as it cooks.
3. If you don't have time, crumble meat into crock. Stir in onions and celery. (You won't need the oil.)
4. Add remaining ingredients and mix together well.
5. Cover. Cook on Low 3 hours, or until meat is cooked through and onions and celery are as tender as you like them.
6. Serve on hamburger rolls.

Variations:

Add a slice of cheese to each sandwich.

I use my slow cooker most often when I have guests. It's helpful to prepare the main dish and then concentrate on the rest of the meal. I don't feel pressured, so I'm able to relax and enjoy relating to the friends we are entertaining.
— Arianne Hochstetler, Goshen, IN

Sloppy Joes

Joyce Cox
Port Angeles, WA

Makes 4-6 servings

Prep. Time: 15 minutes
Cooking Time: 3-4 hours
Ideal slow-cooker size: 4 qt.

1 lb. ground beef
1 cup chopped onion
¾ cup ketchup
2 Tbsp. chili sauce
1 Tbsp. Worcestershire sauce
1 Tbsp. prepared mustard
1 Tbsp. apple cider vinegar
4-6 hamburger rolls
butter

1. Grease interior of slow-cooker crock.
2. If you have time, brown beef and onion in saucepan. Use a slotted spoon to lift browned beef and onions into crock, draining off fat and discarding.
3. If you don't have time, crumble beef into crock. Scatter onions over top.
4. In a bowl, mix together ketchup, chili sauce, Worcestershire sauce, mustard, and vinegar.
5. Pour over beef and onions. Mix together well.
6. Cover. Cook on Low 3-4 hours.
7. Open rolls and butter tops and bottoms. Place open face on baking sheet. Toast in 350° oven until lightly crispy on top.
8. Fill rolls with beef mixture and serve immediately.

Tips:

Serve with your favorite green or grain salad.

My tips for converting oven and stove-top recipes into good slow cooker recipes:

Rule of thumb is 1 hour of High heat is equal to about 2-2½ hours of cooking time on Low heat.

So-Good Sloppy Joes

Judy Diller
Bluffton, OH

Makes 18 servings

Prep. Time: 20 minutes
Cooking Time: 4-5 hours
Ideal slow-cooker size: 5 or 6 qt.

3 lbs. ground beef
1 medium onion, chopped
1 green bell pepper, diced
10.75-oz. can tomato soup
1 cup ketchup (use a lively one if you like some kick)
2 Tbsp. prepared mustard (use a spicy variety if you want some extra zest)
2 Tbsp. apple cider vinegar
1 Tbsp. brown sugar
2 Tbsp. Worcestershire sauce
18 burger rolls

1. Grease interior of slow-cooker crock.
2. If you have time, brown beef in large skillet. Using a slotted spoon, lift beef out of drippings and place in crock. If you don't have time, place beef in crock and use a sturdy spoon to break it up into small clumps.
3. Stir in all remaining ingredients except rolls.
4. Cover. Cook on Low 4-5 hours, or until beef is fully cooked and veggies are as tender as you like them.
5. Serve in rolls. Turn the cooker to Warm and serve the Sloppy Joes over a several-hour period if you wish.

During April 2011, the South was devastated by tornadoes. We were without power for weeks. Those of us who wanted to feed families that had lost everything plugged power strips into a generator, plugged the slow cookers into that, and cooked so we had hot food to serve to people. Never expected that I would use my slow cooker like that! – Joy York, Wildwood, GA

I made barbecued pulled pork in my slow cooker for a Christmas party at work. The flavors and the tenderness were perfect. I started the cooking process the night before and then the next day took my slow cooker with me to work. Everyone who walked past wanted to know what I made and what time we were eating. My slow cooker was empty before the fancy finger sandwiches were even half gone. – Melody Rauscher, Wantage, NJ

Lemon Sweet Pork Chops

Doris Slatten
Mt. Juliet, TN

Makes 8 servings

Prep. Time: 15 minutes
Cooking Time: 5-7 hours
Ideal slow-cooker size: oval 7 qt.

8 bone-in, ¾"-thick, blade-cut pork chops
¼ tsp. salt
¼ tsp. coarsely ground black pepper
½ tsp. dried oregano
½ tsp. dried chives
⅛ tsp. dried dill
½ tsp. minced garlic
8 lemon slices
4 Tbsp. ketchup
4 Tbsp. brown sugar

1. Grease interior of slow-cooker crock.
2. In a small bowl, mix together salt, pepper, oregano, chives, dill, and garlic.
3. Sprinkle over both sides of each chop, then lay chop in crock. If you need to make a second layer, stagger the pieces so they don't directly overlap each other.
4. Place lemon slice on each chop.
5. In same small bowl, mix together ketchup and brown sugar. Drop a Tbsp. of mixture on top of each chop.
6. Cover. Cook on Low 5-7 hours, or until instant-read meat thermometer registers 145° when stuck into center of chops (but not against bone).

Pork on Sweet Potatoes

Dottie Schmidt
Kansas City, MO

Makes 5 servings

Prep. Time: 15-20 minutes
Cooking Time: 4½-5 hours
Ideal slow-cooker size: oval 6 or 7 qt.

2 medium sweet potatoes, peeled and cut into ½"-thick slices
1 small onion, chopped
2 apples, cored, peeled or not, and sliced
1 Tbsp. brown sugar
¼ tsp. ground cinnamon
¼ tsp. salt
⅛ tsp. coarsely ground black pepper
5 blade-cut, bone-in pork chops, about ¾" thick
15-oz. can sauerkraut, drained

1. Grease interior of slow-cooker crock.
2. Arrange sweet potato slices over bottom of slow cooker.
3. Sprinkle chopped onions over potatoes.
4. Cover with apple slices.
5. In a small bowl, stir together brown sugar, cinnamon, salt, and pepper. Sprinkle over apple slices.
6. Top with pork chops. If you must make a second layer, stagger the pieces so they don't directly overlap each other.
7. Spoon drained sauerkraut over top of all chops, including any on the bottom layer.
8. Cover. Cook on Low 4½-5 hours or on High 2-3 hours, or until instant-read meat thermometer registers 145°-150° when stuck in center of chops (but not against bone).

Pork Chops and Friends

Phyllis Good
Lancaster, PA

Makes 6 servings

Prep. Time: 20 minutes
Cooking Time: 5-7 hours
Ideal slow-cooker size: oval 6 qt.

6 strips bacon
1 lb. sauerkraut, drained
6 bone-in, ¾"-thick, blade-cut pork chops
3 onions, sliced into rings
4 medium potatoes, peeled and sliced
20-oz. can stewed tomatoes, undrained
½ tsp. salt
¼ tsp. coarsely ground pepper
caraway seeds

1. Grease interior of slow-cooker crock.
2. Line bottom of crock with bacon.
3. Cover with sauerkraut.
4. Place chops on top. If you need to create a second layer, stagger chops so they don't directly overlap each other.
5. Pour tomatoes over everything.
6. Sprinkle with salt, pepper, and caraway seeds.
7. Cover. Cook on Low 5-7 hours, or until instant-read meat thermometer registers 145°-150° when stuck into center of chops (but not against bone).
8. Serve chops on a deep platter, topped with bacon, sauerkraut, onions, potatoes, and tomatoes.

Pork Chops and Apples

Arlene M. Kopp
Lineboro, MD

Makes 6 servings

Prep. Time: 15 minutes
Cooking Time: 2-3 hours
Ideal slow-cooker size: oval 6 or 7 qt.

4 good-sized baking apples, cored and sliced, peeled or not
¼ cup brown sugar
1 tsp. cinnamon
6 ¾"-thick bone-in, blade-cut pork chops
salt
pepper

1. Grease interior of slow-cooker crock.
2. Scatter apple slices over bottom of crock.
3. Sprinkle with brown sugar and cinnamon.
4. Salt and pepper each chop on both sides. Place on top of apples.
5. Cover. Cook on Low 2-3 hours, or until instant-read thermometer registers 140°-145°.
6. Serve on platter, topped with apples.

Pork Chops with Apple Pie Filling and Stuffing

Judi Robb
Manhattan, KS

Makes 4 servings

Prep. Time: 20-30 minutes
Cooking Time: 2-7 hours
Ideal slow-cooker size: oval 6 or 7 qt.

21-oz. can apple pie filling
4 ¾"-thick bone-in, blade-cut pork chops
salt and pepper to taste
1 box pork-flavored, or any other flavored, stuffing mix

1. Grease interior of slow-cooker crock.
2. Spread apple pie filling over bottom of crock.
3. Salt and pepper both sides of each chop. Then lay them on top of pie filling, overlapping the chops as little as possible.
4. Prepare stuffing according to directions on box.
5. Layer prepared stuffing over chops.
6. Cover. Cook on Low 5-7 hours, or on High 2-3 hours, or until instant-read meat thermometer registers 140°-145° when stuck into chops (being careful not to get against the bone).
7. Make sure to serve all three layers to everyone at the table.

New Mexican Pork Chops

John D. Allen
Rye, CO

Makes 6 servings

Prep. Time: 5 minutes
Cooking Time: 2¼-7¼hours
Ideal slow-cooker size: oval 6 or 7 qt.

6 ¾"-thick bone-in, blade-cut pork chops
salt and pepper to taste
¼ cup water
8-oz. jar salsa, your choice of heat

1. Grease interior of slow-cooker crock.
2. Salt and pepper top and bottom of each pork chop.
3. Arrange in crock, overlapping chops as little as possible.
4. Pour water down the side of the crock so as not to wash the seasoning off the chops.
5. Cover. Cook on Low 4-7 hours, or on High 2-3 hours, or until instant-read meat thermometer registers 140°-145° when stuck into center of chops (being careful not to get against any bones).
6. Top each chop with salsa. Cover. Cook on Low 10-15 more minutes, just enough to warm the salsa.

Pork Chops with Asian Flair

Shirley Unternahrer
Wayland, IA

Makes 4 servings

Prep. Time: 15 minutes
Cooking Time: 2-3 hours
Ideal slow-cooker size: 4-6 qt.

½ cup orange juice
½ cup orange marmalade
2 cloves garlic, minced
3 Tbsp. soy sauce
2 Tbsp. brown sugar
2 Tbsp. rice vinegar, or 1 Tbsp. white vinegar
2 tsp. Asian-style chili paste
4 6-7-oz. bone-in, blade-cut pork chops
8 oz. angel hair pasta
8 oz. snow peas, or broccoli

1. Grease interior of slow-cooker crock.
2. Mix orange juice, orange marmalade, minced garlic, soy sauce, brown sugar, vinegar, and chili paste in rectangular glass dish that will hold the pork chops in one layer.
3. Place chops in sauce to marinate for 1 hour. Place covered dish in fridge. Turn chops over once halfway through marinating time.
4. Place chops in slow cooker. Spoon marinade over top.
5. Cover. Cook 2-3 hours on Low, or until instant-read meat thermometer registers 145°-150° when stuck in center of chops (but not against bone).
6. Near end of cooking time for chops, cook pasta according to package directions.
7. Two minutes before end of pasta cooking time, stir snow peas into water with pasta. When done cooking, drain and keep warm.
8. Place chops on platter.
9. Toss pasta and snow peas with sauce in crock. Spoon onto serving platter next to chops. Serve.

I brown my pork ribs in the broiler first before putting them in the slow cooker. It cooks off some of the fat. — Audrey Romonosky, Austin, TX

Chicken Lickin' Good Pork Chops

Jennifer Freed
Harrisonburg, VA

Makes 6-8 servings

Prep. Time: 30 minutes
Cooking Time: 4 hours
Ideal slow-cooker size: oval 6 or 7 qt.

½ cup flour
1 tsp. salt
1½ tsp. dry mustard
½ tsp. garlic powder
2 Tbsp. oil
1 can golden mushroom soup
1 can chicken and rice soup
6-8 bone-in pork chops, about ¾" thick

1. Grease interior of slow-cooker crock.
2. Combine flour, salt, dry mustard, and garlic powder. Place in Ziploc bag.
3. Put pork chops in bag, one at a time. Toss to coat.
4. Place oil in good-sized skillet. Brown chops, a few at a time, over high heat, just for a couple of minutes. Don't crowd skillet, or the chops will steam and not brown.
5. As they finish browning, place in cooker. If you have to add a second layer, stagger the chops so they don't directly overlap each other.
6. Mix soups together in bowl. Spoon over all chops.
7. Cover cooker. Cook on Low 4-6 hours, or on High 2-3 hours, or until instant-read meat thermometer registers 145° when stuck in center of chop (but not against bone).

Tips:

These chops smell delicious as they cook.

Chops in the Crock

Lavina Hochstedler
Grand Blanc, MI

Makes 4 servings

Prep. Time: 15-20 minutes
Cooking Time: 2½-3½ hours
Ideal slow-cooker size: 6 or 7 qt.

4 ¾"-thick bone-in, blade-cut pork chops
salt and pepper to taste
2 medium onions, chopped
2 ribs celery, chopped
1 large green bell pepper, sliced
14.5-oz. can stewed tomatoes, undrained
½ cup ketchup
2 Tbsp. cider vinegar
2 Tbsp. brown sugar
2 Tbsp. Worcestershire sauce
1 Tbsp. lemon juice
1 beef bouillon cube
2 Tbsp. cornstarch
2 Tbsp. water
cooked rice

1. Grease interior of slow-cooker crock.
2. Holding chops over crock, salt and pepper tops and bottoms. Lay in cooker.
3. Scatter chopped onions, sliced celery and peppers, and stewed tomatoes over chops.
4. In a bowl, mix together ketchup, vinegar, brown sugar, Worcestershire sauce, and lemon juice. When well mixed, add bouillon cube. Spoon over vegetables and chops.
5. Cover. Cook on Low 2-3 hours, or until instant-read meat thermometer registers 145° when stuck into center of chops.
6. In small bowl, mix cornstarch and water together until smooth. Stir into sauce in crock.
7. Cover. Cook 30 more minutes, until sauce thickens.
8. Serve over cooked rice.

Roast Pork and Sauerkraut

Susan Alexander
Baltimore, MD

Makes 4-6 servings

Prep. Time: 15 minutes
Cooking Time: 6-8 hours
Ideal slow-cooker size: oval 6 qt.

1-2 lbs. fresh or canned sauerkraut, depending on how much you like sauerkraut
1 Tbsp. caraway seeds
1 large onion, sliced
3-4-lb. boneless pork butt roast
1 lb. fresh or canned sauerkraut
12-oz. can Coke (soda)
2 cups water
1 envelope dry onion soup mix

1. Grease interior of slow-cooker crock.
2. Place sauerkraut in bottom of crock. Sprinkle with caraway seeds.
3. Lay sliced onion over sauerkraut and seeds.
4. Place pork roast on sliced onions.
5. Pour water and soda over meat.
6. Sprinkle onion soup mix over roast.
7. Cover. Cook on Low 6-8 hours, or until instant-read meat thermometer registers 150° when stuck in center of roast.
8. Cut meat into chunks and serve topped with sauerkraut, onions, seeds, and broth.

Tips:

We like this served with mashed potatoes, green beans, and cornbread.

Savory Pork Roast

Mary Louise Martin
Boyd, WI

Makes 4-6 servings

Prep. Time: 15 minutes
Cooking Time: 3½-4½ hours
Ideal slow-cooker size: oval 6 qt.

4-lb. boneless pork butt roast
1 tsp. ground ginger
1 Tbsp. fresh minced rosemary
½ tsp. mace
1 tsp. coarsely ground black pepper
2 tsp. salt
2 cups water

1. Grease interior of slow-cooker crock.
2. Place roast in slow cooker.
3. In a bowl, mix spices and seasonings together. Sprinkle half on top of roast, pushing down on spices to encourage them to stick.
4. Flip roast and sprinkle with rest of spices, again, pushing down to make them stick.
5. Pour 2 cups water around the edge, being careful not to wash spices off meat.
6. Cover. Cook on Low 3½-4½ hours, or until instant-read meat thermometer registers 140° when stuck into center of roast.

Brown Sugar and Dijon-Marinated Pork Roast

J. B. Miller
Indianapolis, IN

Makes 4-6 servings

Prep. Time: 10 minutes
Cooking Time: 3-3½ hours
Marinating Time: 2-3 hours
Ideal slow-cooker size: oval 5 qt.

½ cup soy sauce
¼ cup sherry vinegar
½ tsp. Dijon mustard
¼ cup brown sugar
2-lb. pork loin roast, short and wide in shape

1. Mix soy sauce, sherry vinegar, mustard, and brown sugar in large, Ziploc plastic bag. Squeeze bag to mix marinade.
2. Place roast in marinade and close bag tightly. Surround meat with marinade, place the bag in a long dish, and refrigerate for 2-3 hours.
3. Grease interior of slow-cooker crock.
4. Remove meat from bag and place in crock fat side up. Pour marinade over top.
5. Cover. Cook on Low for 3-3½ hours, or until an instant-read meat thermometer registers 140°.
6. Slice and serve.

Tomato-Glazed Pork with Grilled Corn Salsa

Janet Melvin
Cincinnati, OH

Makes 6-8 servings

Prep. Time: 45 minutes
Cooking Time: 3-4 hours
Ideal slow-cooker size: 5 qt.

Tomato Glaze:
2 Tbsp. dry mustard
1 Tbsp. ground ginger
1 Tbsp. ground fennel
1 Tbsp. minced garlic
¼ cup mayonnaise
1 cup ketchup
¼ cup honey
1 Tbsp. Worcestershire sauce
¼ cup grated fresh horseradish
3 Tbsp. white wine mustard
2 Tbsp. minced capers
1 Tbsp. Tabasco sauce

Salsa:
3 ears sweet corn, husked and silked, or 4 cups frozen or canned corn
½ cup olive oil
¼ cup chopped sun-dried tomatoes
1 clove garlic, minced
½ cup wild mushrooms, sliced
2 Tbsp. chopped fresh cilantro
2 Tbsp. fresh lime juice
1 chipotle pepper in adobo sauce, finely chopped
½ tsp. salt
2-lb. boneless pork loin roast, short and wide in shape

1. Grease interior of slow-cooker crock.
2. Prepare glaze by mixing together dry mustard, ginger, fennel, garlic, and mayonnaise.
3. When well blended, stir in remaining glaze ingredients.
4. Place pork in slow cooker, fat side up. Cover with glaze.
5. Cover. Cook on Low 3-4 hours, or until instant-read meat thermometer registers 140° when stuck into center of roast.
6. While roast is cooking, brush ears of corn with olive oil. Wrap in foil.
7. Bake at 350° for 15 minutes. Unwrap and grill or broil until evenly browned.
8. Cool. Cut kernels from cob.
9. Combine corn with rest of salsa ingredients.
10. Cover and refrigerate until ready to use.
11. When pork is finished cooking, remove from cooker to cutting board. Cover with foil and let stand for 10 minutes.
12. Slice and serve on top of grilled corn salsa.

Pork Tenderloin with Mustard Sauce

Bobbie Jean Weidner Muscarella
State College, PA

Makes 10-12 servings

Prep. Time: 20 minutes
Cooking Time: 3-4 hours
Marinating Time: 2-3 hours
Ideal slow-cooker size: oval 6 or 7 qt.

Roast Pork:
½ cup soy sauce
½ cup bourbon
¼ cup brown sugar
3-lb. boneless pork loin roast (wide and short; not skinny and long)

Mustard Sauce:
1 Tbsp. dry mustard
¼ cup Dijon mustard
2 Tbsp. sugar
½ tsp. salt
2 Tbsp. apple cider vinegar
4 egg yolks, beaten
1 cup cream

1. Grease interior of slow-cooker crock.
2. In a bowl, mix together soy sauce, bourbon, and brown sugar.
3. Place pork in bowl. Pour marinade over it. Cover.
4. Marinate at room temperature for 2-3 hours, turning meat over occasionally.
5. Place meat in crock. Pour marinade over top.
6. Cover. Cook on Low 3-4 hours, or until instant-read meat thermometer registers 140°-145° when stuck into center.
7. While roast is cooking, place dry mustard, Dijon mustard, sugar, salt, vinegar, and egg yolks in top of double boiler.
8. Cook over simmering water, stirring constantly until thickened.
9. Cool slightly. Then stir in cream. Set aside. (You can serve it at room temperature or heated slightly.)
10. Lift roast out of cooker with sturdy tongs or 2 sturdy metal spatulas onto cutting board. Cover and keep warm. Let stand 10 minutes.
11. Slice into thin, diagonal slices and serve with mustard sauce.

Tips:

You can make the Mustard Sauce ahead of time and keep it in the fridge for up to 3 days. The sauce is also delicious on ham.

Garlic Pork Roast in the Slow-cooker

Earnie Zimmerman
Mechanicsburg, PA

Makes 10 servings

Prep. Time: 15-20 minutes
Cooking Time: 7-8 hours
Ideal slow-cooker size: 6-8 qt.

3-lb. boneless pork loin roast, short and wide rather than long and narrow
1 Tbsp. butter or olive oil, optional
1 tsp. salt
½ tsp. coarsely ground black pepper
1 medium onion, sliced
6 cloves garlic, peeled
8 strips (each 3″ long, ½″ wide) fresh lemon peel
1½ lbs. red potatoes, cut in ½″-thick slices
1 lb. baby carrots
½ tsp. dried thyme
1 cup chicken broth

1. Grease interior of slow-cooker crock.
2. If you have time, heat butter in 12″ skillet over medium-high heat until hot. Place pork roast in skillet and brown on all sides. Move meat to crock.
3. If you don't have time, place pork in crock directly.
4. Sprinkle all over with salt and pepper.
5. In a large bowl, mix together onion, garlic, lemon peel, potatoes, carrots, and thyme. Stir in chicken broth.
6. Spoon mixture into crock alongside meat and over top.
7. Cover. Cook on Low 4 hours, or until instant-read meat thermometer registers 140°-145° when stuck in center of roast. Remove roast to cutting board. Cover to keep warm. Let stand for 10 minutes.
8. Check if onions, potatoes, and carrots are as tender as you like them. If not, cover crock and continue cooking another 30-60 minutes, or until veggies are as done as you want.
9. Slice pork into ½″-thick slices. Place on deep platter. Serve topped with vegetables and broth.

Tips:

Serve with rice or couscous and a salad.

Honey-Orange Pork Roast

Earnie Zimmerman
Mechanicsburg, PA

Makes 8-10 servings

Prep. Time: 15 minutes
Cooking Time: 4-8½ hours
Ideal slow-cooker size: oval 6 or 7 qt.

4-lb. boneless pork butt roast
1 cup orange juice
¼-½ cup honey
1 cup fresh, frozen, or dried cranberries
2 good-sized tart apples, cored and quartered
4-5 good-sized sweet potatoes

1. Grease interior of slow-cooker crock.
2. Place roast in crock.
3. In a bowl, mix together orange juice, honey, and cranberries. Spoon over roast.
4. Cover. Cook on High 2-2½ hours, or on Low 4 hours.
5. While roast is cooking, peel sweet potatoes and cut into 1″-thick chunks. Place alongside and on top of roast.
6. Cover. Continue cooking 1 more hour on High, or 3 more hours on Low.
7. While roast and sweet potatoes are cooking, prepare apples.
8. Place apples alongside and on top of sweet potatoes.
9. Cover. Continue cooking another hour on High, or another 1-1½ hours on Low.
10. Insert instant-read meat thermometer into center of roast. When it reaches 150°-160°, roast is finished.
11. Check if sweet potatoes and apples are as tender as you like them. If not, remove roast to platter, cover, and keep warm. Continue cooking potatoes and apples another 30-60 minutes, or until done.
12. Slice roast against grain. Place slices of meat, sweet potatoes, and apples, along with broth, in deep platter or bowl to serve.

Tips:

We like this served with rice and a green veggie.

Barbecue Roast of Pork

Phyllis Good
Lancaster, PA

Makes 6-8 servings

Prep. Time: 10 minutes
Cooking Time: 8-9 hours
Ideal slow-cooker size: oval 6 qt.

3-5-lb. Boston butt shoulder-blade roast
10.75-oz. can tomato soup
⅓ cup chopped onion
⅓ cup chopped celery
1 clove garlic, minced
2 Tbsp. brown sugar
2 Tbsp. Worcestershire sauce
2 Tbsp. lemon juice
2 tsp. prepared mustard
4 drops Tabasco sauce

1. Grease interior of slow-cooker crock.
2. Place roast in crock.
3. Cover. Cook on Low 7-8 hours, or until instant-read meat thermometer registers 135° when stuck in center of roast.
4. While roast is cooking, mix soup, onions, celery, garlic, brown sugar, Worcestershire sauce, lemon juice, mustard, and Tabasco sauce together in a bowl.
5. Pour over roast.
6. Cover. Continue cooking 1 more hour on Low.
7. Using sturdy tongs or 2 strong metal spatulas, lift roast out of crock and onto cutting board. Cover and keep warm, while standing for 10 minutes.
8. Carve into chunks or slice. Spoon sauce over top to serve.
9. Put extra sauce in bowl and serve to diners along with meat.

Sunny Ham

Shelia Heil
Lancaster, PA

Makes 12-15 servings

Prep. Time: 20 minutes
Cooking Time: 3-4 hours on High or 6-8 hours on Low
Ideal slow-cooker size: oval 6 or 7 qt.

4-6-lb. cured, bone-in ham
12-oz. can ginger ale or 7-Up
15-oz. can crushed pineapple with juice
2 cups brown sugar

1. Grease interior of slow-cooker crock.
2. Cut slits an inch deep here and there all over ham so the sauce infuses it.
3. Place ham in crock.
4. In a bowl, mix together soda, pineapple with its juice, and sugar.
5. Pour mixture over ham.
6. Cover. Cook on Low 5-6 hours, or until instant-read meat thermometer registers 100° when stuck into center of ham, but not against bone.
7. Using 2 sturdy metal spatulas, lift ham onto cutting board. Cover and keep warm for 10-15 minutes to allow meat to re-gather its juices.
8. Carve into chunks or slices. Top with pineapple sauce when serving.

Easy and Elegant Ham

Frances Kruba
Baltimore, MD

Makes 18-20 servings

Prep. Time: 10-15 minutes
Cooking Time: 5-6 hours
Ideal slow-cooker size: oval 7 qt.

2 20-oz. cans sliced pineapple, divided
6-lb. bone-in, cured ham
½ cup dried cherries
12-oz. jar orange marmalade

1. Grease interior of slow-cooker crock.
2. Drain pineapple slices, reserving juice. (Set juice aside.) Place half of pineapple slices in bottom of crock.
3. Place ham on top of pineapple slices.
4. Place remaining pineapple slices on top of ham and around its base.
5. In a bowl, combine reserved pineapple juice, cherries, and marmalade. Stir until well mixed.
6. Spoon over ham and pineapple slices.
7. Cover. Cook on Low 5-6 hours, or until instant-read meat thermometer registers 100° when stuck into center of ham.
8. Using 2 sturdy metal spatulas, remove ham and place on cutting board. Cover to keep warm. Let stand 10-15 minutes so it can re-gather its juices before slicing.
9. Serve topped with fruit. Pass sauce in bowl so diners can add more to their individual plates.

Glazed Holiday Ham

Jennifer Archer
Kalona, IA

Makes 8-10 servings

Prep. Time: 5 minutes
Cooking Time: 6-8 hours on Low
Ideal slow-cooker size: oval 6 or 7 qt.

4-5-lb. bone-in, cured ham
½ cup apple juice
½ cup orange juice
½ cup brown sugar
½ cup honey

1. Grease interior of slow-cooker crock.
2. Place ham in crock.
3. In a bowl, mix remaining ingredients until combined.
4. Pour over ham.
5. Cover. Cook on Low 4-5 hours, or until instant-read meat thermometer registers 100° when stuck into center of ham (but not against bone).
6. If you're home and available, baste ham with glaze every hour or so.
7. Using 2 sturdy metal spatulas, lift cooked ham onto cutting board. Cover and keep warm for 15 minutes, so it can gather its juices.
8. Cut into slices or chunks. Spoon glaze over top.
9. Pass additional glaze in a bowl to diners to add more to their individual servings.

Tips:

This is a great option for holiday dinners when you need your oven for other dishes.

Honey-Baked Ham

Nicole Koloski
East Sandwich, MA

Makes 6-7 servings

Prep. Time: 20 minutes
Cooking Time: 5¼ hours
Ideal slow-cooker size: oval 6 or 7 qt.

5-lb. fully cooked ham
½ cup brown sugar
¼ cup dry sherry
3 Tbsp. honey
3 Tbsp. Dijon mustard
¼ tsp. coarsely ground black pepper
½ cup pineapple chunks
½ cup fresh cranberries

1. Grease interior of slow-cooker crock.
2. Using a sharp knife, score surface of ham into diamond shapes, cutting about ¼" deep. Place ham in crock.
3. Cover cooker. Cook on Low 3 hours.
4. While ham is cooking, blend together brown sugar, sherry, honey, mustard, and black pepper.
5. Brush ham with glaze. Cover and continue cooking.
6. After ham has cooked 2 more hours (for a total of 5 hours), brush again with glaze.
7. Using toothpicks, decorate ham with pineapple chunks and cranberries, spreading pieces over ham evenly.
8. Cover and cook on High another 15 minutes.
9. When ham is heated through, remove from cooker with sturdy tongs and metal spatulas supporting. Slice meat.
10. Place slices on deep platter, covering them with glaze.
11. Put any remaining glaze, and any pineapples and cranberries that have fallen off, in a bowl to pass around the table for diners to add more to their individual plates.

Savory Orange-Glazed Ham

Ruthie Schiefer
Vassar, MI

Makes 6-8 servings

Prep. Time: 15 minutes
Cooking Time: 4-5 hours
Ideal slow-cooker size: 6 qt.

3-lb. boneless ham
⅓ cup finely diced red onion
⅔ cup chicken broth
½ cup orange marmalade
1 Tbsp. Dijon, or brown, mustard
1 Tbsp. cornstarch

1. Grease interior of slow-cooker crock.
2. Place ham in slow cooker and sprinkle with diced onion.
3. In a bowl, whisk together remaining ingredients and pour over ham.
4. Cover. Cook on Low 4-5 hours, or until sauce is thickened and ham is warmed throughout.

Variations:

Add can of pineapple chunks, drained, in last hour of cooking.

Raspberry-Glazed Ham

Elizabeth Miller
Walnut Creek, OH

Makes 8-10 servings

Prep. Time: 15-20 minutes
Cooking Time: 8-10 hours
Ideal slow-cooker size: oval 7 qt.

4-5-lb. boneless, fully cooked ham
¼ cup apple juice or dry white wine
2 Tbsp. lemon juice
1½ Tbsp. cornstarch
⅓ cup seedless raspberry jam, divided
1 Tbsp. butter
watercress, fresh parsley, or other greens

1. Grease interior of slow-cooker crock.
2. Using a sharp knife, score surface of ham into diamond shapes, cutting about ¼" deep. Place ham in crock.
3. Cover cooker. Cook on Low 3 hours.
4. While ham is cooking, in a saucepan blend apple juice or wine with lemon juice, cornstarch, and half the jam. Cook, stirring continuously until jam melts and sauce thickens.
5. Stir in remaining jam and butter. Heat, stirring until both melt.
6. Brush ham with glaze. Cover and continue cooking.
7. After ham has cooked 2 more hours (for a total of 5 hours), brush again with glaze.
8. When ham is heated through, remove from cooker with sturdy tongs and metal spatulas supporting. Slice meat.
9. Place slices on deep platter, covering them with glaze. Garnish ham with choice of greens and serve.
10. Put any remaining glaze in a bowl to pass around the table for diners to add more to their individual plates.

Ham, Potatoes, and Green Beans

Phyllis Good
Lancaster, PA

Makes 6 servings

Prep. Time: 15-20 minutes
Cooking Time: 4-5 hours
Ideal slow-cooker size: 5 qt.

3-lb. bone-in, cured ham
4 good-sized potatoes, peeled or not, and cut in chunks
1-2 lbs. frozen green beans
black pepper to taste
½ cup water

1. Grease interior of slow-cooker crock.
2. Place ham in crock.
3. Surround with potato chunks and green beans.
4. Sprinkle meat and vegetables with pepper.
5. Pour in water along sides of crock.
6. Cover. Cook on Low 4-5 hours, or until vegetables are as tender as you like them, and instant-read meat thermometer registers 100° when stuck in center of ham.
7. Lift ham onto cutting board with 2 sturdy metal spatulas. Cut into chunks.
8. Place on deep platter or into big bowl, surrounded by potatoes and green beans.

Good go-alongs with this recipe:

My grandma, and then my mother, made this dish when green beans were in season. Each of them always served it with coleslaw.

Using a slow cooker saves busy people that frantic "what's for dinner?" rush at the end of the day. Five minutes or so in the morning will have a delightful meal on the table for your hungry family in the evening with no stress. — Angel Barnes, Kinderhook, IL

Barbecued Ham Steaks

Phyllis Good
Lancaster, PA

Makes 4 servings

Prep. Time: 15 minutes
Cooking Time: 3-4 hours
Ideal slow-cooker size: oval 6 or 7 qt.

1 small onion, chopped
7-oz. bottle 7-Up, Sprite, or ginger ale
¼ cup ketchup
1 tsp. dry mustard
1 tsp. salt
⅛ tsp. black pepper
4 whole cloves
2 lbs. ham steaks

1. Grease interior of slow-cooker crock.
2. Mix together chopped onion, soda, ketchup, mustard, salt, pepper, and whole cloves in crock.
3. Submerge steaks in sauce. Overlap steaks if you must, but as little as possible.
4. Cover.
5. Cook on Low 3-4 hours, or until meat is heated through but not dry.
6. Fish out cloves and discard.
7. Cut each steak into smaller pieces and serve topped with barbecue sauce.

Ham 'n' Apple Cheese Pie

Phyllis Good
Lancaster, PA

Makes 6-8 servings

Prep. Time: 20-25 minutes
Cooking Time: 3 hours
Ideal slow-cooker size: oval 6 or 7 qt.

2 lbs. ham slices, ¾" thick
2-3 tart apples, pared, cored, and sliced
2 Tbsp. (¼ stick) butter, melted
⅓ cup flour
½ cup brown sugar
6 8 slices mild cheese of your choice
1 cup sour cream

1. Grease interior of slow-cooker crock.
2. Cut ham slices into serving-sized pieces. Arrange over bottom of crock. If you need to create a second layer, stagger pieces so they don't directly overlap each other.
3. Arrange apple slices over each piece of ham, including those that might be partly covered.
4. In a bowl, mix together melted butter, flour, and brown sugar.
5. Crumble over apples, again making sure that ham pieces on bottom layer get crumbs, too.
6. Top each ham piece with slice of cheese.
7. Cover. Cook on Low 3 hours, or until ham is heated through but not dry.
8. Ten minutes before end of cooking time, spoon a dollop of sour cream on each piece of ham. Continue cooking uncovered.

A slow cooker does its best work when it's at least half full and no more than 2/3 full. When it's packed full, it may not cook evenly throughout. And when there's a relatively small amount in a cooker, the food tends to dry out. These are near-miracle appliances, but understanding how they work helps them to produce better food!

Creamy Ham and Red Beans over Rice

Phyllis Good
Lancaster, PA

Makes 6 servings

Prep. Time: 20 minutes
Cooking Time: 5-11 hours
Standing Time: 1 hour
Ideal slow-cooker size: 6 qt.

1 lb. dried red-skinned kidney beans
2 Tbsp. oil
2 cups diced onions
1½-2 cups diced celery
1 cup diced green bell pepper
4 large garlic cloves, minced
1 Tbsp. Creole seasoning
4 bay leaves
1 tsp. dried thyme
2 quarts water
2½ lbs. meaty ham hocks
salt and pepper, optional
6 cups cooked rice

1. Place dried beans in stockpot. Cover with water by 3″.
2. Bring to a boil and cook 2 minutes.
3. Cover. Remove from heat and let stand 1 hour. Drain.
4. Grease interior of slow cooker.
5. Pour beans into slow cooker.
6. Stir in oil, diced vegetables, Creole seasoning, bay leaves, and thyme.
7. Submerge ham hocks in mixture.
8. Cover. Cook on Low 9-11 hours or on High 5-7 hours, or until beans are tender and meat is falling off the bone.
9. Using tongs or a slotted spoon, remove ham hocks from cooker. Fish out bay leaves, too.
10. Allow meat to cool enough to pull or cut into bite-sized pieces.
11. Stir meat chunks back into bean mixture. Heat 15 minutes.
12. Place 1 cup or so cooked rice in each individual serving bowl. Top with creamy ham and beans.

Variations:

1. Instead of using dried kidney beans, use 3 14.5-oz. cans kidney beans. Skip Steps 1-4 above. Add canned beans halfway through cooking time. 2. Instead of using store-bought Creole seasoning, make your own: ⅔ tsp. paprika, 1 tsp. salt, 1 tsp. garlic powder, ½ tsp. black pepper, ½ tsp. onion powder, ½ tsp. cayenne pepper, ½ tsp. dried oregano, ½ tsp. dried thyme. Stir together well. Store any leftovers in a dry, tightly covered container.

Ham Loaf with Glaze

Starla Kreider
Mohrsville, PA

Makes 6-8 servings

Prep. Time: 20-30 minutes
Cooking Time: 3-4 hours
Ideal slow-cooker size: oval 5 or 6 qt.

¾ lb. ground ham
¾ lb. ground pork
1 egg
¼ cup finely chopped onions
½ cup cracker crumbs
½ cup milk
¼ tsp. black pepper

Glaze:
½ cup brown sugar
1 Tbsp. dry mustard
¼ cup apple cider vinegar

1. Grease interior of slow-cooker crock.
2. Make a tin foil sling for your slow cooker so you can lift the cooked Ham Loaf out easily. Begin by folding a strip of tin foil accordion-fashion so that it's about 1½″-2″ wide, and long enough to fit from the top edge of the crock, down inside and up the other side, plus a 2″ overhang on each side of the cooker. Make a second strip exactly like the first.
3. Place the one strip in the crock, running from end to end. Place the second strip in the crock, running from side to side. The 2 strips should form a cross in the bottom of the crock.
4. In a large mixing bowl, combine ham, pork, egg, onions, cracker crumbs, milk, and pepper until well blended.
5. Form into a loaf. Place in crock, centering loaf over the spot where the 2 foil strips cross in the bottom.
6. Make glaze by mixing brown sugar, dry mustard, and vinegar together in a bowl until smooth.
7. Pour glaze over loaf in crock.
8. Cover. Cook on Low 3-4 hours, or until instant-read meat thermometer registers 150° when stuck in center of loaf.
9. When loaf is finished cooking, use foil handles to lift it onto a cutting board. Cover and keep warm for 10-15 minutes so it can re-gather its juices.
10. Slice. Serve topped with warm glaze.

Terrific Tenders

Carol Turner
Mountain City, GA

Makes 8 servings

Prep. Time: 15-20 minutes
Cooking Time: 3-4 hours
Marinating Time: 8 hours or overnight
Ideal slow-cooker size: oval 6 or 7 qt.

3-4-lb. boneless pork loin roast, wide and short (not skinny and long)
7-9 garlic cloves, halved or quartered lengthwise
salt to taste
pepper to taste
2-2½ cups opal basil, raspberry or blackberry vinegar, or your favorite fruity vinegar
1 Tbsp. butter
2 Tbsp. oil
1 Tbsp. chopped shallots
1½ tsp. dried tarragon
1½ tsp. Dijon mustard
fresh parsley sprigs

1. Pierce roast with knife about ½″ deep at 2″ intervals. Insert piece of garlic in each slit.
2. Place roast in covered container to marinate. Sprinkle all over with salt and pepper.
3. Pour in enough vinegar to come at least halfway up sides of roast.
4. Cover. Refrigerate for 8 hours or overnight. Turn meat over a couple of times in marinade.
5. Grease interior of slow-cooker crock.
6. Remove meat from marinade. If you have time, brown in butter and oil on all sides in large skillet. Using strong tongs or 2 metal spatulas, lift out of skillet and place in crock.
7. If you don't have time, place roast straight from marinade into crock. (Reserve marinade.)
8. Cover cooker. Cook on Low 3-4 hours, or until instant-read meat thermometer registers 145° when stuck in center of roast.
9. Near end of roast's cooking time, melt butter in skillet. Sauté shallots until softened. Stir in tarragon and mustard. Mix well.
10. Stir 1½-2 cups reserved marinade into mixture in skillet. Reduce heat and cook until slightly thickened and creamy. Set aside, but keep warm until serving time.
11. Remove roast from cooker to cutting board. Cover and keep warm. Let stand 10 minutes. Then slice.
12. Place slices in deep platter. Cover with warm sauce. Garnish with parsley sprigs and serve.

Sunday Pork Loin

Jessalyn Wantland
Paris, TX

Makes 8 servings

Prep. Time: 5 minutes
Cooking Time: 3-8 hours
Ideal slow-cooker size: 5 qt.

1½ Tbsp. seasoned salt
3-4-lb. boneless pork picnic shoulder roast
1 bottle of Lawry's Herb and Garlic Marinade
4 Tbsp. A1 Garlic and Herb Rub
1 tsp. coarsely ground black pepper

1. Grease interior of slow-cooker crock.
2. Scatter seasoned salt over bottom of slow cooker.
3. Put roast on top of salt.
4. Pour bottle of marinade over roast.
5. Sprinkle Garlic and Herb Rub on top of roast.
6. Sprinkle pepper over roast.
7. Cover. Cook on Low 6-8 hours or on High 3-4 hours, or until instant-read meat thermometer registers 145°-150° when stuck in center.

Good go-alongs with this recipe:

Baked or mashed potatoes.

Pork Thai Stew

Marilyn Mowry
Irving, TX

Makes 6 servings

Prep. Time: 15-30 minutes
Cooking Time: 2½-3 hours
Ideal slow-cooker size: 4 qt.

2 lbs. pork tenderloin
2 cloves garlic, sliced
2 cups sliced red bell pepper
¼ cup rice vinegar
½ cup teriyaki sauce
1-2 tsp. red pepper flakes, according to your taste preference
¼-½ cup creamy peanut butter
cooked rice
chopped peanuts
chopped green onions

1. Grease interior of slow-cooker crock.
2. Cut meat into 1½" cubes.
3. Place in slow cooker.
4. Top with sliced garlic cloves and red pepper strips.
5. Stir in vinegar, sauce, and red pepper flakes.
6. Cook until meat is tender, 2-2½ hours on Low.
7. Shred meat with 2 forks.
8. Stir in peanut butter. Continue cooking for 30 more minutes, until heated through.
9. Serve over cooked rice.
10. Pass bowls of chopped peanuts and sliced green onions for each diner to add as they wish.

Good go-alongs with this recipe:

Egg drop soup.

Sweet 'n' Sour Ribs

Frances Kruba
Baltimore, MD

Makes 8 servings

Prep. Time: 20 minutes
Cooking Time: 5-8 hours
Ideal slow-cooker size: oval 6 qt.

3-4 lbs. spare ribs
20-oz. can pineapple tidbits, undrained
2 8-oz. cans tomato sauce
½ cup thinly sliced onions
½ cup thinly sliced green bell pepper
½ cup packed brown sugar
¼ cup cider vinegar
¼ cup tomato paste or ketchup
2 Tbsp. Worcestershire sauce
1 garlic clove, minced
salt and pepper to taste

1. Place ribs in ungreased crock. As you add layers, stagger the pieces so they don't directly overlap each other.
2. Combine remaining ingredients in a bowl.
3. Pour over ribs, making sure that those on lower levels also get covered with sauce.
4. Cover. Cook on Low 5-8 hours or until meat is tender.
5. Remove ribs from sauce. Cut into individual serving sizes. If serving immediately, keep warm.
6. Using a good-sized spoon, lift layer of grease off sauce and discard. Or refrigerate sauce, allowing fat to harden. Then remove with spoon.
7. After removing grease, heat sauce and serve with ribs.

Tips:

From the tester: After removing the grease, I would cook some rice in that yummy sauce!
—Colleen Heatwole

Good go-alongs with this recipe:

Mashed potatoes.

Saucy Spareribs

Phyllis Good
Lancaster, PA

Makes 4 servings

Prep. Time: 15 minutes
Cooking Time: 4-5 hours
Ideal slow-cooker size: 6 qt.

3-4 lbs. country-style pork spareribs, cut into serving-sized pieces
¾ cup ketchup
1-2 Tbsp. sriracha sauce, depending how much heat you like, optional
3 Tbsp. packed brown sugar
¼ cup honey
¼ cup lemon juice
2 Tbsp. soy sauce
¾ tsp. ground ginger
¼ tsp. chili powder
¼ tsp. ground mustard
¼ tsp. garlic powder
¼ tsp. black pepper (coarsely ground is best)

1. Place cut-up ribs into slow cooker.
2. Mix all remaining ingredients together in a bowl until well combined.
3. Pour over ribs.
4. Cover. Cook on Low 4-6 hours, or until the meat begins to fall off the bones.

Variations:

Double the amount of sauce if you like a lot to eat with the ribs, or if you're serving them with pasta, rice, or potatoes and want to spoon sauce over top.

Boneless Barbecued Pork Ribs

Jessalyn Wantland
Paris, TX

Makes 4-6 servings

Prep. Time: 10 minutes
Cooking Time: 5-6 hours
Ideal slow-cooker size: 5 or 6 qt.

3-4 lbs. boneless pork ribs
1 onion, sliced
2 cups your favorite barbecue sauce
2 tsp. lemon juice

1. Grease interior of slow-cooker crock.
2. Place ribs in crock. If you need to make a second layer, stagger the pieces so they don't directly overlap each other.
3. Combine sliced onions, barbecue sauce, and lemon juice in bowl. Mix together well.
4. Pour over ribs, covering any that are on the bottom layer, too.
5. Cover cooker. Cook on Low 5-6 hours, or until instant-read meat thermometer registers 150° when stuck in center of ribs.

Tips:

From tester: We loved the sauce over brown rice.

—Gladys Voth

Good go-alongs with this recipe:

Serve with macaroni salad, baked beans, and potato chips.

Country-Style Ribs

Patricia Howard
Green Valley, AZ

Makes 6-8 servings

Prep. Time: 10-15 minutes
Cooking Time: 4-7 hours
Ideal slow-cooker size: 6 qt.

4-5 lbs. pork shoulder ribs
¾ cup ketchup
¾ cup water
1 tsp. salt
1 tsp. coarsely ground black pepper
dash cayenne pepper
1 Tbsp. chopped dried chili pepper
2 Tbsp. apple cider vinegar
2 Tbsp. Worcestershire sauce

1. Grease interior of slow-cooker crock.
2. Place ribs in crock. If you need to make a second layer, stagger pieces so they don't directly overlap each other.
3. Mix together all other ingredients in a bowl.
4. Spoon mixture over ribs, making sure that those on the bottom get covered with some sauce, too.
5. Cover. Cook on Low 5-7 hours, or on High 3-4 hours, or until instant-read meat thermometer registers 145°-150° when stuck in center of ribs (but not against bone).

Good go-alongs with this recipe:

Potato salad and baked beans.

Barbecued Pulled Pork

Sue Hertzler Schrag
Beatrice, NE

Makes 10-12 servings

Prep. Time: 30 minutes
Cooking Time: 4-18 hours
Ideal slow-cooker size: 5 qt.

3-4-lb. boneless pork picnic shoulder roast
salt and pepper to taste
½ cup water
½ tsp. salt
1½ Tbsp. Worcestershire sauce
¼ cup chopped onion
¼ cup brown sugar, packed
1 cup ketchup
¼ cup white vinegar
⅛ tsp. black pepper
1 Tbsp. prepared mustard
10-12 hamburger rolls

1. Grease interior of slow-cooker crock.
2. Salt and pepper all sides of roast liberally.
3. Place in slow cooker. Pour ½ cup water down along the side of the cooker so you don't wash the seasonings off the meat.
4. Cover. Cook on Low 7½-8 hours, or on High 4-6 hours, or until instant-read meat thermometer stuck into center of roast registers 145°-150°.
5. Meanwhile, mix all other ingredients together in a bowl. Set aside.
6. When roast is cooked, place it on a cutting board or in a roomy bowl. Using 2 forks, pull the pork apart, shredding it.
7. Return shredded pork to cooker. Stir in sauce and mix together well.
8. Cover. Cook on High 20-30 minutes, or until mixture reaches a boil.
9. Serve in hamburger rolls. (Keep the meat warm in the cooker by putting it on the Warm setting. Stir occasionally.)

Basic Pulled Pork

Jenny Unternahrer
Wayland, IA

Makes 12-15 servings

Prep. Time: 15 minutes
Cooking Time: 6-8 hours
Ideal slow-cooker size: 5 qt.

3-lb. boneless pork butt roast
1 onion, sliced, divided
salt and pepper
½ cup water

1. Grease interior of slow-cooker crock.
2. Put half of sliced onions in bottom of cooker.
3. If roast is wrapped in netting, cut it off and discard. Trim off and discard any pieces of fat.
4. Holding roast over crock with onions, salt and pepper meat on all sides.
5. Place in cooker. Top with remaining onions, sprinkling them with salt and pepper, too.
6. Cover. Cook on Low 6-8 hours or until instant-read meat thermometer registers 150° when stuck in center of roast.
7. Pull out chunks of meat with tongs and place in bowl. Shred with 2 forks or your fingers.
8. Return shredded meat to cooker and mix with onions and broth.
9. To serve, mix with barbecue sauce (homemade or bottled) and enjoy as a sandwich or as a pizza topping. Or stir in cumin, chili powder, cayenne pepper and make tostadas.

Tips:

This freezes well. From the tester: This is so easy to jazz up with some barbecue sauce.

—Jessalyn Wantland

Good go-alongs with this recipe:

When eating this as sandwiches, we enjoy it with creamy coleslaw as a condiment and baked sweet potato fries.

My tricks for getting my slow cooker to do its best work:

It doesn't matter what size pork roast you get so long as it fits in the crock. If I buy a really big one, sometimes I cut it in half and cook the two pieces together.

Pulled Pork with Dr. Pepper

Christina Gerber
Apple Creek, OH

Makes 6-8 sandwiches

Prep. Time: 20-25 minutes
Cooking Time: 4-8 hours
Ideal slow-cooker size: 6 qt.

1 medium onion, cut in eighths
2½-3-lb. boneless pork butt roast
2 12-oz. cans Dr. Pepper
1 garlic clove, minced
1½ tsp. dry mustard
¼-½ tsp. cayenne pepper, according to taste
1 tsp. salt
1 tsp. ground black pepper
¼ cup apple cider vinegar
3 Tbsp. Worcestershire sauce
your favorite barbecue sauce
your favorite rolls or buns

1. Grease interior of slow-cooker crock.
2. Place cut-up onions on bottom of crock.
3. Place pork roast on top of onions.
4. Pour Dr. Pepper over top.
5. In a bowl, mix together garlic, ground mustard, cayenne pepper, salt, black pepper, vinegar, and Worcestershire sauce.
6. Spoon sauce over roast, patting it on with your hands to help it stick.
7. Cover. Cook on Low 6-7 hours, or on High 3-4 hours, or until instant-read meat thermometer registers 145°-150° when stuck into center of roast.
8. Using 2 sturdy metal spatulas, remove meat from crock and place on large cutting board. Using 2 forks, shred pork.
9. Place shredded pork back into crock. Mix well with sauce.
10. Cover. Cook 1 more hour on Low.
11. Using a slotted spoon, lift shredded meat and onions out of crock and into large bowl.
12. Stir barbecue sauce into meat and onions, ¼ cup at a time, until you get the sauciness you like.
13. Serve in rolls or buns.

Good go-alongs with this recipe:

Coleslaw and oven fries.

Italian Barbecue Sandwiches

Pat Bishop
Bedminster, PA

Makes 8-10 servings

***Prep. Time:** 10 minutes*
***Cooking Time:** 6-7 hours*
***Ideal slow-cooker size:** 5 qt.*

1 lb. bulk sausage, or 1 lb. regular sausage squeezed out of its casings
1 lb. flank steak
4 large onions, cut in rings
28-oz. jar spaghetti sauce
1 Tbsp. dried oregano
2 medium-sized green bell peppers, sliced
½ lb. fresh mushrooms, sliced, or 4-oz. can sliced mushrooms, drained
salt to taste
8-10 hoagie rolls

1. Grease interior of slow-cooker crock.
2. Break up sausage with your hands and scatter into crock.
3. Lay in flank steak.
4. Cover with onion rings.
5. Pour in sauce. Sprinkle oregano over top.
6. Cover. Cook on Low 4 hours. Then add pepper strips and mushroom slices, pushing them down into the liquid.
7. Cover and continue cooking another 2 or 3 hours on Low, or until steak is tender.
8. Taste. Add salt if needed.
9. Using 2 sturdy metal spatulas, lift steak out and onto cutting board. Cover and let stand for 10 minutes so it can re-gather its juices. Then slice across the grain into ¼"-thick slices.
10. Stir meat back into sauce.
11. Serve on hoagie rolls.

Tasty Pork Tacos

Donna Suter
Pandora, OH

Makes 6 servings

***Prep. Time:** 20 minutes*
***Cooking Time:** 6 hours*
***Ideal slow-cooker size:** 4 qt.*

3-lb. boneless pork butt roast
juice and zest of 2 limes
1-2 tsp. garlic powder, or 1 tsp. minced garlic
½ tsp. salt
1-2 tsp. cumin
1 cup fresh chopped cilantro, divided
tortillas
salsa
chopped onions
chopped fresh tomatoes
sliced black olives
torn lettuce
shredded cheese
chopped jalapeño peppers
sour cream

1. Grease interior of slow-cooker crock.
2. Place pork in crock.
3. In a bowl, mix together juice and zest of limes, garlic powder, salt, cumin, and ½ cup chopped cilantro.
4. Pour sauce over roast.
5. Cover. Cook on Low 6 hours, or until instant-read meat thermometer registers 145°-150° when inserted in center of roast.
6. Remove roast from crock and place in good-sized bowl. Shred, using 2 forks.
7. Stir shredded meat back into crock. Add remainder of chopped cilantro.
8. Fill tortillas and add your favorite toppings.

Snow on the Mountain

Marilyn Kurtz
Willow Street, PA

Makes 6-8 servings

Prep. Time: 30 minutes
Cooking Time: 8-10 hours
Ideal slow-cooker size: 5 qt.

26-oz. can, or 3 10.75-oz. cans, cream of mushroom soup
1½ cups water
1½ cups chopped onion
2 cloves garlic, chopped
1½ Tbsp. curry powder
½ tsp. black pepper
3 Tbsp. flour
2½-3 lbs. boneless pork picnic shoulder roast
cooked rice for 6-8 servings
pineapple tidbits
chopped apples
craisins
grated carrots
sliced celery
chopped peanuts
grated coconut, creating the "snow on the mountain!"

1. Grease interior of slow-cooker crock.
2. Pour soup and water into crock. Mix together until well blended.
3. Stir in chopped onion and garlic, curry powder, black pepper, and flour, mixing well.
4. Settle roast into sauce.
5. Cover. Cook on Low 8-10 hours, or until instant-read meat thermometer registers 145°-150° when stuck into center of roast.
6. Cook rice toward end of meat's cooking time.
7. Prepare individual bowls for condiments—pineapple, apples, craisins, grated carrots, sliced celery, chopped peanuts, and grated coconut.
8. Cut meat into chunks and serve in sauce.
9. Pass condiments so diners can add what they want to their individual servings.

Tips:

Both the curry and rice heat up well as leftovers, so I like to make this in a large amount.

Variations:

From the tester: You can also top this great pork dish with shredded cheddar cheese, almond slivers, chopped green onions, diced tomatoes, diced green and black olives, chopped celery, and chow mein noodles!

—Carol Eveleth

Sausage Town

Kathy Hertzler
Lancaster, PA

Makes 4-6 servings

Prep. Time: 15 minutes
Cooking Time: 9-10 hours
Ideal slow-cooker size: 5 qt.

1 cup chopped onions
¾ cup dry lentils, rinsed well and picked clean
¾ cup shredded cheddar cheese
2 cloves garlic, crushed
½ tsp. dried thyme
½ tsp. dried basil
½ tsp. dried oregano
⅛ tsp. dried sage
¼ tsp. salt
freshly ground black pepper to taste
1-2 lbs. sausage of your choice, squeezed out of casing and broken into small chunks
4 14.5-oz. cans chicken broth
¾ cup uncooked long-grain brown rice

1. Grease interior of slow-cooker crock.
2. Place onions, lentils, cheese, garlic, thyme, basil, oregano, sage, salt, black pepper, sausage, and chicken broth into crock. Stir together well.
3. Cover. Cook on Low 6-7 hours.
4. Stir in uncooked rice.
5. Cover. Continue cooking on Low another 3 hours, or until both rice and lentils are as tender as you like them.
6. If dish is juicier than you want, uncover during last 30 minutes of cooking and turn cooker to High.
7. Stir well and serve.

There's a trick to lifting a slow-cooker lid. Because a lot of moisture collects on the underside of your slow cooker's lid, tilt it quickly away from the food when you lift it off. Otherwise, you'll be diluting what you've carefully prepared in your slow cooker.
— Phyllis Pellman Good, Lancaster, PA

Pumpkin Breakfast Custard, page 27

Banana Chocolate Chip Bars, page 252

Bratwurst and Red Cabbage, page 191

Autumn Sweet Potatoes, page 233

Sausage and Corn Supper

Jean Shenk
Mt. Joy, PA

Makes 4 servings

***Prep. Time:** 10-20 minutes*
***Cooking Time:** 3 hours*
***Ideal slow-cooker size:** 4 qt.*

1 lb. bulk sausage or link sausage squeezed out of its casing
1 quart fresh or frozen corn (thawed), or 2 15.5-oz. cans canned corn, drained
4 eggs, well beaten
1 cup soft bread crumbs
1 tsp. salt
1 Tbsp. chopped onion
ketchup

1. Grease interior of slow-cooker crock.
2. If you have time, brown sausage in skillet, breaking it up into small clumps. When browned, use slotted spoon to lift meat out of drippings and into crock.
3. If you don't have time, break up sausage in crock.
4. Stir in corn, beaten eggs, bread crumbs, salt, and onion. Mix together well.
5. Spread ketchup over all.
6. Cover. Cook on Low 3 hours, or until the dish is set but not dry.

Sausage, Sauerkraut, and Cabbage

Susanne Nobrega
Duxbury, MA

Makes 4-6 servings

***Prep. Time:** 15-20 minutes*
***Cooking Time:** 3-6 hours*
***Ideal slow-cooker size:** 5 qt.*

1-lb. bag or can sauerkraut
1 lb. (about 4 cups) fresh cabbage, shredded
1 Tbsp. caraway seeds, optional
1 lb. fresh sausage, bulk or cut into ¾"-thick chunks
½ cup beer
¼-½ cup water, optional

1. Grease interior of slow-cooker crock.
2. Mix sauerkraut, shredded cabbage, and caraway seeds if you wish in crock.
3. Place sausage chunks, or crumble bulk sausage, over top.
4. Pour beer over top, but don't stir.
5. Add water if you want a more soupy finished dish.
6. Cover. Cook on Low 4-6 hours, or on High 2-3 hours, or until sausage is cooked through and cabbage is as tender as you like it.

Polish Kraut and Apples

Frances Kruba
Baltimore, MD

Makes 4 servings

***Prep. Time:** 10-15 minutes*
***Cooking Time:** 2-4 hours*
***Ideal slow-cooker size:** 5 qt.*

14.5-oz. can sauerkraut, drained, divided
1 lb. fully cooked Polish sausage, cut in 1"-thick pieces
3 medium tart apples, peeled and cut into eighths
½ cup packed brown sugar
½ tsp. caraway seeds
⅛ tsp. coarsely ground black pepper
¾ cup apple juice

1. Grease interior of slow-cooker crock.
2. Place half of sauerkraut in crock.
3. Arrange all of sausage and apples over top.
4. Crumble brown sugar over meat and apples. Sprinkle with caraway seeds and pepper.
5. Spoon remaining sauerkraut over top.
6. Pour apple juice over all.
7. Cover. Cook on Low 4-5 hours or on High 2-2½ hours, or until apples are tender and everything is heated through.

Sweet-and-Sour Kielbasa

Phyllis Good
Lancaster, PA

Makes 8-10 servings

***Prep. Time:* 15 minutes**
***Cooking Time:* 4 hours**
***Ideal slow-cooker size:* 5 or 6 qt.**

3 lbs. kielbasa
1 bottle chili sauce
20-oz. can crushed pineapple, undrained
½ cup brown sugar

1. Grease interior of slow-cooker crock.
2. Cut kielbasa into 1″-thick slices.
3. Mix all ingredients in slow-cooker crock.
4. Cover. Cook on Low 4 hours, or until kielbasa is fully cooked.
5. Serve over cooked rice, pasta, or potatoes.

Red Beans and Sausage

Joyce Cox
Port Angeles, WA

Makes 6 servings

***Prep. Time:* 1 hour**
***Cooking Time:* 2-2½ hours**
***Ideal slow-cooker size:* 4 qt.**

1 lb. (about 2 cups) dried kidney beans
water to cover
2 tsp. olive oil
1 cup finely chopped onion
½ tsp. chopped garlic
1 lb. smoked sausage, cut in thin slices
3 bay leaves
6 cups water

1. Pick over dried beans and discard any stones. Place in saucepan and cover with water.
2. Cover pan and bring to boil. Simmer until beans are tender, about 1 hour.
3. While beans are cooking, sauté onion in oil in skillet.
4. When onions are nearly tender, add garlic and sauté briefly. Set aside.
5. Grease interior of slow-cooker crock.
6. When beans are done cooking, drain off liquid.
7. Pour beans into crock. Stir in onion, garlic, and sausage.
8. Add bay leaves and 6 cups water. Stir until well mixed.
9. Cover. Cook on High for 1 hour.
10. Turn cooker to Low and cook 1½ hours.
11. Remove bay leaves before serving.

Good go-alongs with this recipe:

Hot crusty bread and fresh butter.

Hearty Sausage and Beans

Sharon Shank
Bridgewater, VA

Makes 12 servings

***Prep. Time:* 10 minutes**
***Cooking Time:* 2-4 hours**
***Ideal slow-cooker size:* 6 qt.**

2 quarts sauerkraut, drained, with ½ cup juice reserved
1 lb. smoked sausage, cut into small pieces
½ medium onion, chopped
3 15.5-oz. cans pinto or navy beans
¼ cup brown sugar
½ cup ketchup
¼-½ tsp. coarsely ground pepper

1. Grease interior of slow-cooker crock.
2. Place all ingredients in crock. Stir gently together until well mixed.
3. Cover. Cook on Low for 4 hours or on High 2 hours.

Jiffy Jambalaya

Carole M. Mackie
Williamsfield, IL

Makes 6 servings

Prep. Time: 30 minutes
Cooking Time: 4-5 hours
Ideal slow-cooker size: 5 qt.

1 onion, chopped
½ cup chopped green bell pepper
1 lb. smoked sausage
28-oz. can diced tomatoes, undrained
½ cup water
1 Tbsp. sugar
1 tsp. paprika
½ tsp. dried thyme
½ tsp. dried oregano
¼ tsp. garlic powder
3 drops hot pepper sauce
1½ cups uncooked instant rice

1. Grease interior of slow-cooker crock.
2. Place all ingredients except uncooked rice in crock. Stir together well but gently.
3. Cover. Cook on Low 3 hours, or until vegetables are as tender as you like them.
4. Stir in rice. Cover. Cook on High 20-30 minutes, or until rice is tender and fully cooked.
5. Stir and serve.

Sausage Sweet Potato De-lish

Cathy Boshart
Lebanon, PA

Makes 4-6 servings

Prep. Time: 20-30 minutes
Cooking Time: 2-6 hours
Ideal slow-cooker size: 5 qt.

4 large raw sweet potatoes, or 29-oz. can cooked sweet potatoes, drained and reserved
salt to taste, optional
1 lb. smoked sausage, or kielbasa, cut in ¼"-thick slices
4 large apples, peeled or not
¼ cup water or reserved sauce from canned sweet potatoes
½ cup brown sugar

1. Grease interior of slow-cooker crock.
2. If using raw sweet potatoes, peel and cut into ¼"-½"-thick rounds.
3. Place half of sweet potato slices in cooker, distributing them evenly.
4. Salt if you wish.
5. Cover with sausage slices.
6. Top with sliced apples, peeled or not.
7. Cover with remaining sweet potatoes.
8. Salt if you wish.
9. Drizzle with water or sauce from canned sweet potatoes.
10. Crumble brown sugar over top.
11. Cover. Cook on Low 4-6 hours, or on High 2-3 hours, or until potatoes are as tender as you like them.

Bratwurst and Red Cabbage

Esther Porter
Minneapolis, MN

Makes 4 servings

Prep. Time: 15 minutes
Cooking Time: 2-3 hours
Ideal slow-cooker size: 5 qt.

1 small head red cabbage
4 fresh, uncooked bratwurst
3 Tbsp. currant jam
1 cup apple juice or cider
1 Tbsp. apple cider vinegar
1 tsp. juniper berries, optional

1. Grease interior of slow-cooker crock.
2. Shred or chop cabbage coarsely. Scatter over bottom of crock.
3. Settle bratwurst into cabbage in crock.
4. Put jam in a small bowl and microwave on High for 20 seconds, or until it melts.
5. Stir in apple juice, vinegar, and juniper berries if you wish. Blend together well.
6. Pour over bratwurst and cabbage.
7. Cover. Cook on Low 2-3 hours, or until bratwurst is done and cabbage is as tender as you like it.

Tips:

Serve with your favorite grainy mustard.

Italian Sausage, Peppers, and Potatoes

Maryann Markano
Wilmington, DE

Makes 4 servings

Prep. Time: 15-20 minutes
Cooking Time: 2-6 hours
Ideal slow-cooker size: 5 qt.

1 lb. sweet or hot Italian sausage, cut on the diagonal in 1" lengths
1 lb. small red potatoes, each cut in half
1 large onion, cut into 12 wedges
2 red or yellow bell peppers, or 1 of each color, cut into strips

1. Grease interior of slow-cooker crock.
2. Put sausage, potatoes, and onion into crock. Stir together well.
3. Gently stir in bell pepper strips.
4. Cover. Cook on Low 4-6 hours, or on High 2-3 hours, or until sausage is cooked through and potatoes and onions are as tender as you like them.

Sausage Tortellini

Christie Detamore-Hunsberger
Harrisonburg, VA

Makes 8 servings

Prep. Time: 25-30 minutes
Cooking Time: 2½-3 hours
Ideal slow-cooker size: 6 qt.

1 lb. sausage of your choice, cut into ½"-thick slices
1 cup chopped onions
2 cloves garlic, minced
5 cups beef or chicken broth
½ cup water
½ cup red wine
2 14-oz. cans diced tomatoes, undrained
1 cup thinly sliced carrots
½ tsp. dried basil
½ tsp. dried oregano
16-oz. can tomato sauce
½ cup sliced zucchini, optional
16-oz. pkg. tortellini
3 Tbsp. chopped fresh parsley

1. Grease interior of slow-cooker crock.
2. If you have time, brown sausage in its own drippings in a skillet. When lightly browned, stir in onions and garlic and cook just until softened.
3. Using a slotted spoon, lift meat and veggies out of drippings (to be discarded) and put into crock.
4. Add broth, water, wine, tomatoes, carrots, basil, oregano, and tomato sauce to crock. Stir together well.
5. Add zucchini if you wish, and tortellini.
6. Cover. Cook on High 1½-2½ hours, or until pasta is as tender as you like it, but not mushy.
7. Stir in parsley and serve.

Herby Italian Sausage Pasta Sauce

Karen Sander
Robinson, IL

Makes 4-6 servings

Prep. Time: 15 minutes
Cooking Time: 3-4 hours
Ideal slow-cooker size: 4 qt.

1 lb. Italian sausage, sweet or hot, squeezed out of its casing
1 quart canned tomatoes or 1 29-oz. can whole tomatoes with juice
6-oz. can tomato paste
pinch of salt or 2 Tbsp. dried summer savory
2 Tbsp. honey
2 tsp. dried basil
2 tsp. dried oregano
2 tsp. dried Italian parsley
2 tsp. dried thyme
coarsely ground black pepper, to taste

1. Grease interior of slow-cooker crock.
2. If you have time, brown sausage in skillet, breaking it up into small chunks. Using a slotted spoon, lift browned sausage out of its drippings and place in crock.
3. If you don't have time, break up sausage in crock.
4. Stir into crock canned tomatoes, tomato paste, salt or savory, honey, basil, oregano, parsley, thyme, and black pepper. Mix together well.
5. Cover. Cook on Low 3-4 hours.
6. Serve over 1 lb. cooked pasta of your choice.

Italian-Style Red Sauce

Barb Perry
Huron, TN

Makes 8 servings

Prep. Time: 20-25 minutes
Cooking Time: 3-3½ hours
Ideal slow-cooker size: 6 qt.

4-6 garlic cloves, minced
1 lb. bulk pork sausage or link sausage squeezed out of its casing
3 large onions, chopped
1 tsp. cayenne pepper
2 quarts tomato puree or 2 29-oz. cans and 1 15.5-oz. can crushed tomatoes
1 quart whole tomatoes with juice, or 1 29-oz. can whole tomatoes with juice
1 Tbsp. dried basil
1 Tbsp. dried oregano
1 Tbsp. dried sage
1 Tbsp. dried parsley
3 bay leaves
2 tsp. dried rosemary
2 tsp. dried winter savory
2 tsp. dried thyme
2 tsp. dried bee balm
2 large green bell peppers, chopped
½ cup Chianti or other red wine, optional
¼ cup honey, optional
1-2 tsp. salt, optional

1. Grease interior of slow-cooker crock.
2. If you have time, brown sausage in skillet, breaking it into small chunks as it browns.
3. Using a slotted spoon, remove meat from skillet and place in cooker.
4. Sauté onions in drippings until softened. Lift out of skillet with slotted spoon and add to pork in crock.
5. Stir cayenne pepper, tomato puree, whole tomatoes and juice, basil, oregano, sage, parsley, bay leaves, rosemary, winter savory, thyme, and bee balm into crock.
6. Cover. Cook on Low 2 hours.
7. Stir in chopped green peppers.
8. Cover. Continue cooking another 30 minutes.
9. Stir in wine and honey if you wish.
10. Cover. Continue cooking another 30-60 minutes, or until vegetables are as soft as you like them.
11. Taste. Add salt if needed.
12. Serve over pasta, or use as a sauce for pizza, lasagna, or baked ziti.

Tips:

1. This freezes well.
2. Eliminate meat for a hearty vegetarian sauce.
3. Vary the meat as you like—use ground chuck, cubed chuck roast, fresh pork, venison, or Italian sausage.

I love to use my slow cooker to cook any kind of dried beans. I buy organic in bulk and have very yummy beans with bean stock leftover. I just put beans in the cooker, add enough water to cover by 2 inches, a swirl of olive oil, and 1 bay leaf. I quarter an onion and throw that in. I cover the crock and put it on High for 4 hours and my beans are perfect and ready to go. Plus, once I strain it, the juice left over is a very yummy broth or stock that can be used or frozen for soups or to mix in hummus, etc. — Amy Schultz, Lancaster, PA

I hosted a get-together for about 40 people. It was themed "Beans & Greens" and I cooked 4 different types of beans: pintos, navy, black-eyed peas, and limas. I also cooked 8 full-sized bags of turnip and mustard greens, cornbread, and all the trimmings. I used the slow cookers to keep everything hot after it was finished cooking. I could not have pulled it off without my slow cookers! Everyone had a great time, and I didn't have to worry about anything burning or boiling over. — Joy York, Wildwood, GA

Pasta, Grains Meatless, and Seafood Main Dishes

Fresh Veggie Lasagna

Deanne Gingrich
Lancaster, PA

Makes 4-6 servings

Prep. Time: 30 minutes
Cooking Time: 4 hours
Ideal slow-cooker size: 4 or 5 qt.

1½ cups shredded mozzarella cheese
½ cup ricotta cheese
⅓ cup grated Parmesan cheese
1 egg, lightly beaten
1 tsp. dried oregano
¼ tsp. garlic powder
3 cups marinara sauce, divided, plus more for serving
1 medium zucchini, diced, divided
4 uncooked lasagna noodles
4 cups fresh baby spinach, divided
1 cup fresh mushrooms, sliced, divided

1. Grease interior of slow-cooker crock.

2. In a bowl, mix together mozzarella, ricotta and Parmesan cheeses, egg, oregano, and garlic powder. Set aside.

3. Spread ½ cup marinara sauce in crock.

4. Sprinkle with half the zucchini.

5. Spoon ⅓ of cheese mixture over zucchini.

6. Break 2 noodles into large pieces to cover cheese layer.

7. Spread ½ cup marinara over noodles.

8. Top with half the spinach and then half the mushrooms.

9. Repeat layers, ending with cheese mixture, and then sauce. Press layers down firmly.

10. Cover. Cook on Low 4 hours, or until vegetables are as tender as you like them and noodles are fully cooked.

11. Let stand 15 minutes so Lasagna can firm up before serving.

Classic Spinach Lasagna

Bernice Esau
North Newton, KS

Makes 10 servings

Prep. Time: 30 minutes
Cooking Time: 4-5 hours
Ideal slow-cooker size: 6 or 7 qt.

1 small onion, chopped
1 medium garlic clove, minced
3 14.5-oz. cans diced or stewed tomatoes, undrained
2 6-oz. cans tomato paste
¾ cup dry red wine
1 tsp. dried basil
½ tsp. salt
½ tsp. dried oregano
¼ tsp. coarsely ground black pepper
2 16-oz. containers ricotta cheese
3 large eggs, divided
2 10-oz. pkgs. frozen chopped spinach, thawed and squeezed dry
8 oz. uncooked lasagna noodles
16 oz. mozzarella cheese, sliced or shredded, divided
¼ cup grated Parmesan cheese

1. Grease interior of slow-cooker crock.
2. In a large bowl, gently mix together onion, garlic, tomatoes, tomato paste, red wine, basil, salt, oregano, and black pepper.
3. In a separate bowl, mix ricotta with 2 eggs.
4. In another bowl, mix spinach with 1 egg.
5. Spoon 2 cups tomato mixture into crock.
6. Arrange half the noodles over sauce, overlapping and breaking to fit.
7. Spoon half ricotta mixture over noodles.
8. Top with half the mozzarella, half the spinach mixture, and half the remaining tomato sauce.
9. Repeat layers, ending with sauce.
10. Sprinkle with Parmesan cheese.
11. Cover. Cook on Low 4-5 hours, or until noodles are fully cooked.
12. Let stand 10-15 minutes so Lasagna can firm up before serving.

Easy Spinach Lasagna

LaRee Eby
Portland, OR

Makes 6-8 servings

Prep. Time: 30 minutes
Cooking Time: 4 hours
Chilling Time: 8 hours or overnight
Standing Time: 15 minutes
Ideal slow-cooker size: 5 or 6 qt.

28-oz. jar spaghetti sauce
8-oz. can tomato sauce
¼ cup water
1 tsp. dried basil
1 tsp. dried oregano
¾ lb. fresh spinach, chopped, lightly steamed and squeezed dry, or 10-oz. box frozen chopped spinach, thawed and squeezed dry
16-oz. container cottage cheese
1 egg, slightly beaten
¼ tsp. black pepper (coarsely ground is best)
8 oz. uncooked lasagna noodles
2 cups (8 oz.) mozzarella cheese, grated, divided
½ cup Parmesan cheese, grated

1. Grease interior of slow-cooker crock.
2. In large bowl, mix together spaghetti sauce, tomato sauce, water, basil, oregano, and spinach.
3. In a separate bowl, mix together cottage cheese, egg, and black pepper.
4. Spoon about ⅓ of the spaghetti sauce mixture over bottom of crock.
5. Cover that with 4 uncooked lasagna noodles, breaking to make them fit.
6. Spread with half the cottage cheese-egg mixture.
7. Sprinkle with ⅓ of the mozzarella.
8. Spoon over half the remaining spaghetti sauce mixture.
9. Cover with remaining 4 lasagna noodles.
10. Spread with remaining cottage cheese-egg mix.
11. Sprinkle with half the remaining mozzarella.
12. Spoon over last of spaghetti sauce mixture.
13. Scatter with last of mozzarella cheese.
14. Spread evenly with grated Parmesan cheese.
15. Cover. Put in fridge for 8 hours or overnight.
16. When ready to cook, cover. Set on Low for 4-4½ hours, or until lasagna is hot in the center and noodles are fully cooked.
17. Let stand 15 minutes before serving to allow lasagna to firm up.

Variations:

1. Add 1 chopped onion to Step 1.
2. Add 1 tsp. salt to Step 1.

Easy Black Bean Lasagna

Kristen Leichty
Ames, IA

Makes 12-15 servings

Prep. Time: 30 minutes
Cooking Time: 5 hours
Ideal slow-cooker size: 6 or 7 qt.

15-oz. can black beans, rinsed and drained
2 29-oz. can crushed tomatoes
15-oz. can refried beans
¾ cup chopped onions
½ cup chopped green bell pepper
¾ cup medium salsa
1 tsp. chili powder
½ tsp. ground cumin
8 oz. cottage cheese
¼ tsp. garlic powder
2 eggs
¾ tsp. salt
½ tsp. black pepper
10 uncooked lasagna noodles
1½ cups shredded cheddar cheese, divided
1½ cups shredded mozzarella cheese, divided

1. Grease interior of slow-cooker crock.
2. In a large bowl, combine black beans, tomatoes, refried beans, onions, green peppers, salsa, chili powder, and cumin. Mix together well.
3. In a small bowl, combine cottage cheese, garlic powder, eggs, salt, and pepper.
4. Spread 2 cups tomato mixture in bottom of crock.
5. Top with half the noodles, overlapping and breaking to fit.
6. Top with half the remaining tomato mixture.
7. Spoon cottage cheese mixture over top.
8. Top with half the shredded cheeses.
9. Put in remaining noodles, again overlapping and breaking to fit.
10. Spoon remaining tomato mixture over noodles.
11. Top with rest of shredded cheeses.
12. Cover. Cook on Low 5 hours, or until noodles are fully cooked.
13. Let stand 15 minutes so Lasagna can firm up before serving.

Sweet Sausage Lasagna Sauce

Sally Holzem
Schofield, WI

Makes 8 servings

Prep. Time: 20 minutes
Cooking Time: 4 hours
Ideal slow-cooker size: 4 or 5 qt.

1 lb. sweet Italian sausage, squeezed out of casing, or ground beef
1 medium onion, chopped finely
2 cloves garlic, chopped finely
2 11-oz. cans tomato puree
14.5-oz. can crushed Italian tomatoes
15-oz. can tomato sauce
6-oz. can tomato paste
black pepper to taste
3 bay leaves
1½ Tbsp. dry basil
1½ Tbsp. dry oregano
black sliced olives, optional

1. Grease interior of slow-cooker crock.
2. Brown sausage or beef with onion and garlic in good-sized skillet.
3. Using a slotted spoon, drain off drippings while putting browned meat and veggies into crock.
4. Stir in tomato puree, crushed tomatoes, tomato sauce, tomato paste, black pepper, bay leaves, dry basil and oregano, and black olives if you wish.
5. Cover. Cook on Low for 4 hours.
6. Use in your favorite lasagna recipe.

Tips:

I use brown rice lasagna noodles with this sauce.

Pasta with Tomatoes, Olives, and Two Cheeses

Diane Clement
Rogers, AR

Makes 6-8 servings

Prep. Time: 30 minutes
Cooking Time: 3 hours
Ideal slow-cooker size: 5 or 6 qt.

1½ cups chopped onion
1 tsp. minced garlic
3 28-oz. cans Italian plum tomatoes, drained
2 tsp. dried basil
¼-½ tsp. red pepper flakes, according to the amount of heat you like
2 cups chicken broth
salt and black pepper to taste
1 lb. uncooked penne or rigatoni
3 Tbsp. olive oil
2½ cups Havarti cheese
⅓ cup sliced, pitted, brine-cured olives (such as Kalamata)
⅓ cup grated Parmesan cheese
¼ cup finely chopped fresh basil

1. Grease interior of slow-cooker crock.
2. Place onion, garlic, tomatoes, dried basil, and red pepper flakes in crock. Stir together well, breaking up tomatoes with back of spoon.
3. Stir in chicken broth.
4. Season with salt and pepper.
5. Cover. Cook on High 2 hours.
6. Uncover. Continue cooking on High 1 hour, or until sauce is reduced to the consistency you like.
7. During last 30 minutes of cooking, prepare pasta according to package directions in a large stockpot until al dente.
8. Drain pasta and stir in olive oil. Cover and keep warm.
9. When sauce is done cooking, pour over pasta and toss to blend.
10. Stir in Havarti cheese and allow to melt.
11. Spoon into serving bowl. Top with olives and Parmesan cheese.
12. Sprinkle with fresh basil, then serve immediately.

Creamy Ziti in the Crock

Judi Manos
West Islip, NY

Makes 8 servings

Prep. Time: 20 minutes
Cooking Time: 2-3 hours
Ideal slow-cooker size: 5-6 qt.

4 cups uncooked ziti pasta, divided
5 cups spaghetti or marinara sauce, divided
8-oz. pkg. cream cheese, cubed, room temperature
1 tsp. dried basil
⅛ tsp. pepper
14.5-oz. can diced tomatoes, undrained
1 cup mozzarella cheese, divided
⅓ cup grated Parmesan cheese

1. Grease interior of slow-cooker crock.
2. Heat 1-2 cups spaghetti sauce in saucepan or microwave. Add cream cheese cubes and stir until melted.
3. Add remaining spaghetti sauce, basil, pepper, and diced tomatoes to warmed creamy sauce.
4. Put ⅓ of tomato sauce mixture in bottom of crock.
5. Add 2 cups ziti, topped with ½ cup mozzarella.
6. Add half of remaining tomato mixture.
7. Layer in final 2 cups of ziti and ½ cup mozzarella.
8. Spoon on remaining tomato mixture. Sprinkle with Parmesan.
9. Cover. Cook on High for 2-3 hours, until pasta is al dente and sauce is bubbling at edges.

Variations:

Add some spinach leaves, sliced black olives, chopped kielbasa, or sliced mushrooms as you make layers. Just keep the sauce and pasta proportions the same so there is enough liquid for the pasta.

Good go-alongs with this recipe:

Green salad and Italian bread.

Fresh Vegetables Pasta Sauce

Dorothy Lingerfelt
Stonyford, CA

Makes 8-10 servings

Prep. Time: 35-45 minutes
Cooking Time: 5 hours
Ideal slow-cooker size: 6 or 7 qt.

3 medium onions, chopped
1 medium green bell pepper, chopped
1 medium red bell pepper, chopped
5 garlic cloves, minced
3 medium yellow summer squash, peeled or unpeeled and chopped
3 medium tomatoes, chopped
½ tsp. salt
½ tsp. coarsely ground black pepper
½ lb. fresh mushrooms, sliced
2 28-oz. cans crushed tomatoes
6-oz. can tomato paste
2 2.25-oz. cans sliced ripe olives, drained
2 Tbsp. dried rosemary
1 tsp. dried oregano
1 tsp. dried basil
3 Tbsp. chopped fresh oregano
¼ cup chopped fresh basil
cooked pasta

1. Grease interior of slow-cooker crock.
2. Place all ingredients in crock, except fresh oregano, fresh basil, and cooked pasta.
3. Stir together gently until well mixed.
4. Cover. Cook on Low 4 hours.
5. Remove lid and continue cooking another hour to thicken sauce.
6. Ten minutes before end of cooking time, stir in fresh oregano and fresh basil.
7. Serve over just-cooked pasta.

Lotsa Veggies Spaghetti

Jean M. Butzer
Batavia, NY

Makes 4-5 servings

Prep. Time: 15 minutes
Cooking Time: 2-3 hours
Ideal slow-cooker size: 5 qt.

1 cup chopped onions
½ cup chopped celery
1 garlic clove, minced
24-oz. jar meatless pasta sauce
15-oz. can garbanzo beans, rinsed and drained
14.5 oz. can diced tomatoes with garlic and onions, undrained
1 tsp. sugar
½-¾ tsp. salt, according to taste
½ tsp. dried oregano
1 bay leaf
1 lb. spaghetti
¼ cup grated Parmesan cheese

1. Grease interior of slow cooker.
2. Place all ingredients, except spaghetti and cheese, into slow cooker. Stir together until well mixed.
3. Cover. Cook on Low 2-3 hours, or until vegetables are as tender as you like them and the flavors are well blended.
4. Remove the bay leaf. Serve sauce over cooked spaghetti.
5. Top individual servings with grated cheese.

Cherry Tomato Spaghetti Sauce

Beverly Hummel
Fleetwood, PA

Makes 8-10 servings

Prep. Time: 20 minutes
Cooking Time: 4-5 hours
Ideal slow-cooker size: 6 qt.

4 quarts cherry tomatoes
1 onion, chopped
2 cloves garlic, minced
3 tsp. sugar
1 tsp. dried rosemary
2 tsp. dried thyme
1 tsp. dried oregano
1 tsp. dried basil
1 tsp. salt
½ tsp. coarsely ground black pepper
cooked spaghetti

1. Grease interior of slow-cooker crock.
2. Stem tomatoes and cut them in half. Place in slow cooker.
3. Add chopped onions and garlic to cooker.
4. Stir in sugar, herbs, and seasonings, mixing well.
5. Cover. Cook on Low 4-5 hours, or until the veggies are as tender as you like them.
6. For a thicker sauce, uncover the cooker for the last 30-60 minutes of cooking time.
7. Serve over just-cooked spaghetti.

Southern Italy Sauce

Monica Wagner
Quarryville, PA

Makes 8-10 servings

Prep. Time: 30 minutes
Cooking Time: 4-5 hours
Ideal slow-cooker size: 6 qt.

½ cup pitted Kalamata olives, divided
3 28-oz. cans stewed tomatoes, undrained
6-oz. can tomato paste
1 large onion, chopped
4 cloves garlic, minced
1 Tbsp., plus 1 tsp., dried parsley
2 Tbsp. capers, drained
2 tsp. dried basil
¼ tsp. cayenne pepper
¼ tsp. salt
¼ tsp. coarsely ground black pepper
cooked pasta or rice
Parmesan cheese, shaved or grated, optional

1. Grease interior of slow-cooker crock.
2. Chop ¼ cup olives. Place in slow cooker.
3. Halve remaining olives. Set aside.
4. Cut up stewed tomatoes so they're in small chunks. Add, along with their juice, to the cooker.
5. Add all remaining ingredients to slow cooker, except halved olives, cooked pasta or rice, and cheese. Mix together well.
6. Cover. Cook on Low 4-5 hours.
7. Stir in halved olives.
8. Serve over just-cooked pasta or rice. If you wish, shave Parmesan cheese over individual servings.

I slightly skew the top if I don't want too much liquid to build up, especially for the last couple of hours. Do that if you want your spaghetti sauce to reduce down and get thicker. Do it, too, if you are roasting meat and want some of the broth that has gathered to cook off.
— Beth Moss, Clio, MI

Mushroom Spaghetti Sauce

Natalia Showalter
Mt. Solon, VA

Makes 10 servings

Prep. Time: 30-45 minutes
Cooking Time: 3-4 hours
Ideal slow-cooker size: 5 qt.

4 medium onions, chopped
6 garlic cloves, minced
4 large bell peppers, chopped, your choice of colors
¾-1 lb. fresh mushrooms, sliced
4 cups tomato sauce
8 cups chunky tomatoes, fresh or canned
1½ tsp. salt
¼ cup evaporated cane juice or sugar
2 Tbsp. honey
6 bay leaves
1 tsp. garlic powder
1 tsp. dried thyme
1 tsp. dried oregano
1 tsp. dried basil
1 tsp. black pepper
1 tsp. chili powder
½ tsp. ground cumin
½ tsp. cayenne pepper or to taste
2 Tbsp. dried parsley flakes
cooked spaghetti
freshly ground Parmesan cheese, optional

1. Grease interior of slow-cooker crock.
2. Place all ingredients in crock. Mix together well.
3. Cover. Cook on Low 2-4 hours, or until vegetables are as tender as you like them.
4. Serve over cooked spaghetti. Sprinkle with cheese if you wish.

Rich with Veggies Pasta Sauce

Natalia Showalter
Mt. Solon, VA

Makes 10 servings

Prep. Time: 30 minutes
Cooking Time: 3-4 hours
Ideal slow-cooker size: 5 qt.

4 medium onions, chopped
4 large sweet bell peppers, chopped
3-6 garlic cloves, minced, according to your taste preference
½ lb. fresh mushrooms, sliced
1 quart tomato juice
2 quarts whole tomatoes, drained and cut up
6 bay leaves
1 tsp. dried thyme
1 tsp. dried oregano
1 tsp. dried basil
1 tsp. black pepper
1 tsp. chili powder
½ tsp. cumin
½ tsp. cayenne
2 Tbsp. dried parsley
¼ cup sugar, optional
2 Tbsp. honey, optional

1. Grease interior of slow-cooker crock.
2. Place all ingredients in slow cooker.
3. Cover. Cook on Low 4 hours, or until vegetables are as tender as you like them.
4. Fish out bay leaves. Serve over cooked pasta.

Variations:

1. Add ½ tsp. dried rosemary and 2 Tbsp. red wine vinegar in Step 2.
2. Substitute 1 lb. ground beef in place of sliced mushrooms. Or add it as an extra ingredient and keep mushrooms.

—Deborah Heatwole

As a nurse, I worked the night shift for years. Nothing better than coming home, throwing supper in the slow cooker, going to bed, and having dinner ready when you wake up! I never had enough left to freeze a meal ahead.
—Sandy Olson, Turton, SD

Veggie Macaroni and Cheese

Dorothy Lingerfelt
Stonyford, CA

Makes 8-10 servings

Prep. Time: 15 minutes
Cooking Time: 4-4½ hours
Ideal slow-cooker size: 6 qt.

8 oz. uncooked elbow macaroni
3½ cups milk
3 cups chopped broccoli, fresh or frozen (and thawed)
2 cups chopped cauliflower, fresh or frozen (and thawed)
3 carrots, sliced thinly
1 medium onion, chopped
¼ tsp. black pepper
¾ tsp. salt
¼ tsp. paprika
1 Tbsp. Dijon mustard
4 cups shredded cheddar cheese

1. Grease interior of slow-cooker crock.
2. Gently mix all ingredients together in crock, making sure that everything gets distributed well.
3. Cover. Cook on Low 4 hours, or until vegetables and macs are as tender as you like them.
4. If you find water around the edges of the dish at end of cooking time, cook on High, uncovered, for 20 minutes. That will also make the top slightly crusty and crunchy.

Macaroni and Cheese with Ham and Peas

Marcia S. Myer
Manheim, PA

Makes 6-8 servings

Prep. Time: 20 minutes
Cooking Time: 2-3 hours
Ideal slow-cooker size: 4 or 5 qt.

2 10.75-oz. cans cream of celery or mushroom soup
2 soup cans, or 2½ cups, milk
½ tsp. garlic powder
2 cups cooked ham, cubed
2 cups uncooked elbow macaroni
¼ lb. your favorite creamy cheese, cubed
1 cup frozen peas
2 Tbsp. (¼ stick) melted butter
2 slices torn bread

1. Grease interior of slow-cooker crock.
2. Whisk together soup and milk in crock until smooth. Stir in garlic powder, ham, uncooked macaroni, and cubed cheese.
3. Cover. Cook on Low 2-3 hours, or until macaroni are set and soft.
4. Twenty minutes before end of cooking time, stir in peas. Cover and continue cooking.
5. If you like a crusty top, or if water has gathered at the edges, uncover crock and cook on High another 15-20 minutes.
6. While macaroni are cooking, melt butter in skillet.
7. Whirl torn bread in food processor just until coarse crumbs form. Stir crumbs into melted butter and toast, stirring often, until browned.
8. Before serving Macaroni and Cheese, top with browned crumbs.

I normally put together my slow-cooker dish before I clean up the dinner dishes. That way, I only have to clean the kitchen one time. The completed dish stays in the fridge overnight, covered in plastic wrap, and goes into the electrical unit in the morning. — Becky Thompson, San Antonio, TX

Horseradish Macaroni and Cheese

Phyllis Good
Lancaster, PA

Makes 4-6 servings

Prep. Time: *10-15 minutes*
Cooking Time: *4 hours*
Ideal slow-cooker size: *4 or 5 qt.*

8 oz. uncooked elbow macaroni
12-oz. can evaporated milk
1½ cups milk, your choice of whole, skim, or in between
1 Tbsp., plus 1 tsp., horseradish mustard
¾ tsp. salt
¼ tsp. black pepper
1½ cups shredded horseradish or cheddar cheese, divided
1½ cups shredded Swiss cheese

1. Grease interior of slow-cooker crock.
2. Combine all ingredients in crock, except ¾ cup shredded horseradish or cheddar cheese.
3. Sprinkle top with remaining ¾ cup grated cheese.
4. Cover. Cook on Low 4 hours, or until macs are tender but not overcooked.
5. If there's water around the edges at end of cooking time, turn cooker to High for 20 minutes and continue cooking, uncovered.

Creamy Mac and Cheese

Renee Hankins
Narvon, PA

Makes 6 servings

Prep. Time: *5 minutes*
Cooking Time: *3 hours on Low*
Ideal slow-cooker size: *5 qt.*

12 oz. uncooked elbow macaroni
2 cups milk
12-oz. can evaporated milk
1 small onion, chopped
½ tsp. salt
¼ tsp. black pepper
1 cup grated Gouda cheese
1½ cups grated cheddar cheese

1. Grease interior of slow-cooker crock.
2. Mix all ingredients, except Gouda and cheddar cheeses, in crock.
3. Cover. Cook on Low 3-4 hours, or until macaroni are as soft as you like them.
4. Thirty minutes before end of cooking time, stir in cheeses. Cover and continue cooking.
5. If you want a crispy top, or if water has gathered around the edges, uncover during last 30 minutes of cooking time.

"Baked" Macaroni and Cheese

Lorna Rodes
Port Republic, VA

Makes 8 servings

Prep. Time: 30 minutes
Cooking Time: 3-4 hours
Ideal slow-cooker size: 4 qt.

8 oz. uncooked elbow macaroni
12 oz. evaporated milk
½ cup milk
1 tsp. salt
pepper to taste
2 eggs, beaten
3 cups shredded cheese of your choice
¼ cup (½ stick) melted butter
4 slices of your favorite cheese

1. Grease interior of slow-cooker crock.
2. Cook macaroni according to package directions, just until al dente. Drain.
3. Pour barely cooked macaroni into crock. Mix in all remaining ingredients, except slices of cheese.
4. Top with 4 slices of your favorite cheese.
5. Cover. Cook on Low 2-3 hours, just until macaroni are tender but not mushy.

Tips:

From the tester: Seven-year-old Tommy's absolute favorite food is macaroni and cheese, and he thought this was as good as the from-scratch macaroni and cheese that Grandma usually makes for him.

—Colleen Heatwole

Extra Cheesy Macaroni and Cheese

Linda Thomas
Sayner, WI

Makes 4 servings

Prep. Time: 10 minutes
Cooking Time: 2-2½ hours
Ideal slow-cooker size: 4 qt.

½ cup sour cream
10.5-oz. can cheddar cheese soup
1 cup milk
3 eggs, slightly beaten
½ tsp. salt
½ tsp. coarsely ground black pepper
½ tsp. dry mustard
1½ cups uncooked elbow macaroni
2½ cups shredded sharp cheddar cheese

1. Grease interior of slow-cooker crock.
2. Mix together sour cream, cheddar cheese soup, milk, eggs, salt, pepper, and dry mustard.
3. Stir in uncooked macaroni and shredded cheese.
4. Cover. Cook on Low for 2-2½ hours, until macaroni is soft and set.
5. If there's water at the edges that you don't like, turn cooker to High and cook uncovered another 15-20 minutes.

Double Corn Tortilla Bake

Kathy Keener Shantz
Lancaster, PA

Makes 4 servings

Prep. Time: *15 minutes*
Cooking Time: *2-3 hours*
Ideal slow-cooker size: *3 or 4 qt.*

8 corn tortillas, divided
1½ cups shredded Monterey Jack cheese, divided
1 cup corn, fresh, frozen, or canned (drained of juice), divided
4 green onions, sliced, about ½ cup, divided
2 eggs, beaten
1 cup buttermilk
4 oz. can diced green chilies

1. Grease interior of slow-cooker crock.
2. Tear 4 tortillas into bite-sized pieces. Scatter evenly over bottom of crock.
3. Top with half the cheese, half the corn, and half the green onions.
4. Repeat layers.
5. In a mixing bowl, stir together eggs, buttermilk, and chilies. Gently pour over tortilla mixture.
6. Cover. Cook on Low 2-3 hours, or until knife inserted in center comes out clean.

Chili Rellenos Casserole

Darla Sathre and Becky Harder
Baxter, MN and Monument, CO

Makes 6 servings

Prep. Time: *10 minutes*
Cooking Time: *1½ hours*
Ideal slow-cooker size: *4 qt.*

6 eggs, beaten slightly
1½ cups low-fat cottage cheese
20 buttery crackers, crushed
4-oz. can chopped green chilies, or 18-20 mild chili peppers
¾ cup shredded cheddar cheese, divided
¾ cup shredded Monterey Jack cheese, divided

1. Grease interior of slow-cooker crock.
2. In a bowl, mix together eggs, cottage cheese, crackers, chilies, and half the cheddar and Monterey Jack cheeses.
3. Cover. Cook on High for 1¼ hours. Check to see if mixture is set. If not, cook another 15 minutes and check again.
4. Uncover and sprinkle dish with remaining cheese.
5. Cook, uncovered, until cheese melts.
6. Let stand 5 minutes before serving.

Good go-alongs with this recipe:

Sour cream and Spanish rice. Hominy, salad, and tortillas. Rice and beans, salad.

I always give the side a quick touch a few minutes after turning the slow cooker on just to make sure it is really on and plugged in. There have been several times I have come home and it is plugged in, but not turned on, or turned on and not plugged in. My husband just shakes his head and laughs. But the quick touch has saved me from this issue on several occasions. — Jennifer McClain, Hughesville, PA

Rice and Beans Bake

Jane Meiser
Harrisonburg, VA

Makes 6 servings

Prep. Time: 20 minutes
Cooking Time: 4 hours
Ideal slow-cooker size: 5 qt.

1 lb. ground beef
¾ cup onions, chopped
½ cup green bell pepper, chopped
3 cups salsa, as mild or hot as you like, divided
½ cup water
15-oz. can refried beans
1 Tbsp. ground cumin
¾ cup raw instant rice

1. Grease interior of slow-cooker crock.
2. If you have time, brown beef, onions, and green pepper together in a skillet. Using a slotted spoon, lift beef and veggies out of drippings and place in good-sized bowl. If you don't have time, place beef in bowl and use a sturdy spoon to break it up into small clumps. Mix in onions and green pepper chunks.
3. Spoon beef and vegetables into crock.
4. Stir in all remaining ingredients except rice.
5. Cover. Cook on Low 3½ hours, or until mixture is hot and bubbly.
6. Stir in rice, pushing it down into the liquid.
7. Cover. Cook on High 20-30 minutes, or until rice is tender.

Jamaican Rice and Beans

Lorraine Pflederer
Goshen, IN

Makes 4 servings

Prep. Time: 10 minutes
Cooking Time: 2 hours
Ideal slow-cooker size: 3 qt.

14-oz. can light coconut milk
½ cup water
scant ½ tsp. allspice
½ tsp. salt
3 fresh thyme sprigs, or 1 tsp. dried thyme
1 garlic clove, crushed
15-oz. can dark red kidney beans, drained and rinsed
1 cup uncooked instant rice

1. Grease interior of slow-cooker crock.
2. Stir all ingredients into the crock except uncooked rice.
3. Cover. Cook on Low 1½ hours.
4. Stir rice into cooker.
5. Cover. Cook on High 20-30 minutes, or until rice is tender but not dry.
6. Stir and serve.

Mexican Rice and Beans

Helen Schlabach
Winesburg, OH

Makes 6-8 servings

Prep. Time: 10 minutes
Cooking Time: 2-3 hours
Ideal slow-cooker size: 4 qt.

15-oz. can black beans, rinsed and drained
10-oz. pkg. frozen whole-kernel corn
1 cup raw long-grain brown rice
16-oz. jar thick and chunky mild or medium salsa
1½ cups vegetable, cocktail, or tomato juice
½ tsp. dried cumin
½ tsp. dried oregano
½ tsp. salt
¼ tsp. black pepper
¾ cup shredded cheddar cheese

1. Grease interior of slow-cooker crock.
2. Combine all ingredients, except cheese, in crock.
3. Cover. Cook on High 2-3 hours, until rice is tender, stirring once halfway through.
4. Scatter cheese over Rice and Beans.
5. Allow to stand, uncovered, until cheese melts.

Slow-Cooker Lasagna

Frances Kruba
Baltimore, MD

Makes 6-8 servings

Prep. Time: 30 minutes
Cooking Time: 4-5 hours
Ideal slow-cooker size: 5 qt.

1 lb. ground beef
1 large onion, chopped
2 garlic cloves, minced
29-oz. can tomato sauce
1 cup water
6-oz. can tomato paste
1 tsp. salt
1 tsp. dried oregano
8 oz. regular lasagna noodles, uncooked
4 cups (16 oz.) shredded mozzarella cheese
1½ cups (12 oz.) small-curd cottage cheese
½ cup grated Parmesan cheese

1. Grease interior of slow-cooker crock.
2. In a skillet, cook beef, onion, and garlic over medium heat until meat is no longer pink. Drain off drippings and discard.
3. Stir tomato sauce, water, tomato paste, salt, and oregano into meat mixture.
4. Spoon ¼ of meat-tomato mixture in crock.
5. Arrange ⅓ of noodles over sauce, breaking noodles to fit.
6. Combine 3 cheeses.
7. Spoon ⅓ of cheese mixture over noodles.
8. Repeat layers twice. Top with remaining meat sauce.
9. Cover. Cook on Low for 4-5 hours or until noodles are tender.
10. Let stand 15 minutes before serving to allow Lasagna to firm up.

Summer Squash Lasagna

Natalia Showalter
Mt. Solon, VA

Makes 12 servings

Prep. Time: 30-45 minutes
Cooking Time: 4-5 hours
Ideal slow-cooker size: 6-7 qt.

2 medium zucchini squash, unpeeled and sliced thinly
2 medium yellow squash, unpeeled and sliced thinly
8 oz. portobello mushrooms, sliced
1 large onion, diced
1 red sweet bell pepper, chopped
4 cups fresh tomatoes, chopped
6-oz. can tomato paste
1 Tbsp. minced garlic
½ tsp. dried basil
1 Tbsp. brown sugar
½ tsp. salt
½ tsp. dried oregano
½ tsp. coarsely ground black pepper
15 oz. ricotta cheese or 12 oz. cottage cheese
8-oz. pkg. cream cheese, softened
2 large eggs, beaten
1 tsp. dried parsley
6 uncooked lasagna noodles, divided
2-4 cups shredded mozzarella cheese
2 cups shredded Colby cheese or Italian cheese blend, divided

1. Grease interior of slow-cooker crock.
2. Place green and yellow squash, mushrooms, onions, sweet pepper, tomatoes, tomato paste, garlic, basil, brown sugar, salt, oregano, and pepper into large bowl. Mix together gently but well.
3. In a separate bowl, combine ricotta, cream cheese, eggs, and parsley until well blended. Set aside.
4. Spread half of vegetable mixture in bottom of crock.
5. Top with 3 noodles, breaking them to fit and cover the vegetables.
6. Spread with half the ricotta mixture.
7. Sprinkle with half the mozzarella and Colby cheeses.
8. Repeat layers.
9. Cover. Cook on Low 4-5 hours, or until vegetables are as tender as you like them and noodles are fully cooked.
10. Let stand 10-15 minutes to allow Lasagna to firm up before serving.

Vegetarian Lasagna

Margaret W. High
Lancaster, PA

Makes 8-10 servings

Prep. Time: 25 minutes
Cooking Time: 4 hours
Ideal slow-cooker size: 6 qt.

3 cups grated mozzarella
1½ cups ricotta cheese or cottage cheese
5 cups spaghetti sauce, the more herbs the better, divided
½ lb. sliced fresh mushrooms, divided
½ lb. chopped fresh spinach, divided
1½ cups ricotta cheese or cottage cheese
¼ cup water (if your sauce is on the thin side, skip the water)
¼ cup freshly grated Parmesan

1. Grease interior of slow-cooker crock.
2. In a bowl, mix together grated mozzarella and ricotta cheeses. Set aside.
3. Put 1 cup spaghetti sauce on bottom of crock.
4. Put ⅓ of mushrooms on top.
5. Add ⅓ of noodles on top, breaking as necessary to fit them in, and covering the mushrooms as completely as possible.
6. Spread ⅓ of cheese mixture over noodles.
7. Top with half the spinach, then ⅓ of remaining sauce, half the remaining mushrooms, half the noodles, and half the cheese.
8. Make another whole set of layers, ending with a layer of sauce on top.
9. Sprinkle with Parmesan. Pour water down the side if your sauce is really thick.
10. Cover. Cook on Low for 4 hours, until noodles are al dente.
11. Let stand 10-15 minutes before serving to allow cheeses to firm up.

Tips:

Use a metal serving spoon to cut out servings, but be careful not to scrape/scratch the ceramic crock. I never try to fuss with squares of lasagna with this recipe. It's absolutely delicious and really easy because you don't have to cook the noodles first.

Variations:

Add other veggies and subtract some spinach and mushrooms. I sometimes add sliced black olives or artichokes. And I sub in Swiss chard for the spinach.

Good go-alongs with this recipe:

Green salad and French bread dipped in olive oil with salt and pepper.

Cornbread-Topped Frijoles

Andy Wagner
Quarryville, PA

Makes 8-10 servings

Prep. Time: 20-30 minutes
Cooking Time: 3 hours
Ideal slow-cooker size: 5 qt.

1 medium onion, chopped
1 medium green bell pepper, chopped
2 garlic cloves, minced
16-oz. can kidney beans, rinsed and drained
15-oz. can pinto beans, rinsed and drained
14.5-oz. can diced tomatoes, undrained
8-oz. can tomato sauce
1 tsp. chili powder
½ tsp. coarsely ground black pepper
¼ tsp. hot pepper sauce

Cornbread Topping:
½ cup flour
½ cup yellow cornmeal
2 tsp. sugar
1 tsp. baking powder
¼ tsp. salt
1 egg, lightly beaten
¾ cup skim milk
½ cup cream-style corn
1½ Tbsp. canola oil

1. Grease interior of slow-cooker crock.
2. Stir onion, green pepper, garlic, both beans, tomatoes, tomato sauce, chili powder, black pepper, and hot sauce together in crock.
3. Cover. Cook on High 1 hour.
4. While Frijoles are cooking, in a large bowl, mix together flour, cornmeal, sugar, baking powder, and salt.
5. In another bowl, combine egg, milk, corn, and oil.
6. Add wet ingredients to dry, mixing well.
7. Spoon evenly over Frijoles in crock. Do not stir.
8. Cover. Cook on High 2 more hours, or until a toothpick inserted in center of cornbread comes out clean.

Creamy Black-Eyed Peas

Margaret W. High
Lancaster, PA

Makes 6-8 servings

Prep. Time: 20 minutes
Cooking Time: 5-7 hours
Ideal slow-cooker size: 4 qt.

2 cups dry black-eyed peas
5 cups water
1 onion, chopped
2 bay leaves
½ tsp. dried thyme
1 Tbsp. brown sugar
2 Tbsp. butter
1 tsp. salt
2 Tbsp. flour
½-1 cup whole milk, room temperature
hot cornbread, for serving

1. Combine black-eyed peas, water, onion, bay leaves, thyme, brown sugar, and butter in slow cooker.
2. Cover and cook on Low for 4-6 hours, until peas are tender.
3. Remove bay leaves. Add salt.
4. Separately, whisk flour and milk together. Decide how much milk to use depending how soupy your peas are or how saucy you want them.
5. Whisk milk mixture into beans. Cover and cook again on Low for 30-45 minutes, until creamy and thickened. Taste and adjust salt.
6. Serve over cornbread.

Variations:

Serve over rice or biscuits.

Good go-alongs with this recipe:

Great with Southern food like cooked collard greens, fried fish, biscuits and jam, and peach cobbler. I usually include something spicy, too, since the black-eyed peas are creamy and mild.

Refried Beans

Gail Shetler
Goshen, IN

Makes 8-10 servings

Prep. Time: 15 minutes
Cooking Time: 5-11 hours
Ideal slow-cooker size: 5 qt.

1 medium onion, peeled and halved
3 cups dry pinto beans, washed and sorted
½ fresh jalapeño pepper, seeded and chopped, or 1 Tbsp. canned jalapeño, chopped
2-3 cloves garlic, minced
1 tsp. black pepper
¼ tsp. ground cumin
9 cups water
3 or so tsp. salt

1. Grease interior of slow-cooker crock.
2. Combine all ingredients in crock, except salt. (Salt can prevent or slow down cooking dried beans soft.)
3. Cover. Cook on High 5-7 hours or on Low 9-11 hours, or until beans are as soft as you like them.
4. Drain off a few cups of liquid. Save liquid.
5. Mash beans in crock with potato masher. Add some of saved liquid to reach consistency you like.
6. Stir in salt to taste.

Tips:

1. Beans will absorb more liquid as they cool. You may want to save any reserved liquid to reheat leftovers.
2. These refried beans freeze well.
3. Depending on how hot the jalapeños are, you might want to use more or less.

Sweet Pepper Burritos

Anita King
Bellefontaine, OH

Makes 6 servings

Prep. Time: 35 minutes
Cooking Time: 2 hours
Standing Time: 5 minutes
Ideal slow-cooker size: 5 qt.

¾ cup raw brown rice
1¼ cups water
1 medium onion, chopped
2 tsp. ground cumin
½ tsp. black pepper
2 medium sweet red bell peppers, diced
1 medium sweet yellow bell pepper, diced
1 medium sweet green bell pepper, diced
1½ cups cheddar cheese, shredded
3-oz. pkg. cream cheese, cubed
6 whole wheat tortillas, about 6" in diameter
salsa, as mild or hot as you like, optional

1. Grease interior of slow-cooker crock.
2. Place raw brown rice, water, onion, cumin, and black pepper in crock. Stir until well mixed.
3. Cover. Cook on High for 1¾ hours, or until rice is nearly tender.
4. While rice is cooking, dice sweet bell peppers.
5. Stir in at end of cooking time, along with cheddar and cream cheeses.
6. Cover. Continue cooking on High 30 more minutes, or until rice and peppers are as tender as you like them.
7. Spoon ⅔ cup rice-pepper-cheese mixture onto lower half of each tortilla. Fold in the sides. Then bring up the bottom and roll up.
8. Place each burrito, seam side down, in greased 9x13 baking pan.
9. Cover. Bake at 425° 10-15 minutes.
10. Let stand 4 minutes. Serve with salsa if you wish.

Black Bean Burritos

Esther Nafziger
La Junta, CO

Makes 6-8 servings

Prep. Time: 20 minutes
Cooking Time: 6-10 hours
Ideal slow-cooker size: 5 qt.

2 cups dried black beans
7 cups water
hot chilies, diced, to taste
½ cup chopped onion
⅓ cup salsa, as hot or mild as you like
3 cloves garlic, minced
1 tsp. dried oregano
1 tsp. chili powder
2 tsp. salt
¼ tsp. black pepper
6-8 flour tortillas
chopped lettuce
fresh tomatoes, chopped, or salsa
1½ cups shredded cheese of your choice

1. Grease interior of slow-cooker crock.
2. Sort and rinse dried beans.
3. Place in crock. Add water.
4. Cover. Cook on Low 9-10 hours, or on High 6-7 hours, or until beans are as tender as you like them.
5. Drain off any cooking liquid.
6. Stir hot chilies, onion, salsa, garlic, oregano, chili powder, salt, and pepper into cooked beans in crock.
7. Cover. Cook on High 1 hour, or on Low 2 hours, or until veggies are as tender as you want.
8. Spoon filling down center of each tortilla. Top with lettuce, tomatoes, or salsa and cheese.
9. Fold top and bottom of each tortilla over filling. Roll up to serve.

Tips:

Leftover filling freezes well.

Good go-alongs with this recipe:

Spanish rice.

Salsa Lentils

Karen Stanley
Amherst, VA

Makes 4 servings

Prep. Time: 15 minutes
Cooking Time: 2-4 hours
Ideal slow-cooker size: 4 or 5 qt.

2 cups dry green lentils, picked over for any stones and rinsed
4 cups water
2 cups chopped onions
¼ cup chopped garlic
2 cups salsa, mild, medium, or hot
1-3 jalapeño peppers, seeded and chopped
1.25-oz. pkg. dry taco seasoning
½ tsp. salt
1 cup chopped fresh cilantro
cooked rice or corn chips
chopped lettuce
diced fresh tomatoes
grated cheese of your choice
sour cream

1. Grease interior of slow-cooker crock.
2. Place lentils, water, chopped onions and garlic, salsa, jalapeño peppers, taco seasoning, and salt in crock. Stir together until well mixed.
3. Cover. Cook on Low 3-4 hours or on High 2-3 hours, or until lentils are tender.
4. Just before serving, stir in chopped cilantro.
5. Serve over rice or corn chips.
6. Top with remaining ingredients.

Lentils Swiss-Style

Lenore Waltner
North Newton, KS

Makes 6 servings

Prep. Time: 20-30 minutes
Cooking Time: 4-6 hours
Ideal slow-cooker size: 5 qt.

1¾ cups dry lentils, picked over for any stones and rinsed
2 cups water
1 whole bay leaf
2 tsp. salt
¼ tsp. coarsely ground black pepper
½ tsp. dried marjoram
½ tsp. dried sage
½ tsp. dried thyme
2 large onions, chopped
2-4 cloves garlic, minced
2 cups home-canned tomatoes, or 1 14.5-oz. can diced or stewed tomatoes
2 large carrots, sliced thinly
½ cup celery, sliced thinly
1 green bell pepper, chopped, optional
¼ cup chopped fresh parsley
¼ cup sherry
3 cups shredded Swiss or cheddar cheese

1. Grease interior of slow-cooker crock.
2. Place lentils, water, bay leaf, salt, black pepper, marjoram, sage, thyme, onions, garlic, tomatoes, carrots, and celery in slow cooker. Stir together until well mixed.
3. Cover. Cook on Low 4-6 hours, or on High 2-3 hours, or until lentils and raw vegetables are as tender as you like them.
4. Twenty minutes before end of cooking time, stir in chopped green pepper, if you wish.
5. Just before serving, stir in parsley and sherry. Sprinkle with cheese. When cheese has melted, serve.

Variations:

Start thawing a 10-oz. pkg. of frozen spinach. Break the block in half when it's thawed enough to do that. Place half back in the freezer. Allow the other half to thaw completely. Squeeze it dry and then stir spinach into lentil mixture in Step 4.

—Zoë Rohrer

Good go-alongs with this recipe:

Fresh fruit and rolls.

Make your slow cooker your summertime friend. Put your dinner in your cooker, and then take your kids to the pool or their sports practice. Or work in your flower beds and garden as long as you want.

Herbed Rice and Lentil Bake

Peg Zannotti
Tulsa, OK

Makes 4 servings

Prep. Time: 15 minutes
Cooking Time: 2-4 hours
Ideal slow-cooker size: 4 qt.

2⅔ cups vegetable broth or water
¾ cup dried green lentils, picked over for any stones and rinsed
¾ cup chopped onions
½ cup uncooked brown rice
¼ cup dry white wine or water
½ tsp. dried basil
¼ tsp. dried oregano
¼ tsp. dried thyme
⅛ tsp. garlic powder
½ cup shredded Italian-mix cheese or cheddar cheese

1. Grease interior of slow-cooker crock.
2. Place everything in the crock, except cheese. Stir together until well mixed.
3. Cover. Cook on Low 3-4 hours, or on High 2-3 hours, or until lentils and rice are both as tender as you like them.
4. Just before serving, sprinkle top with cheese. Allow to melt, and then serve.

Variations:

1. Add ½ tsp. salt in Step 2 if you wish.
2. Before adding cheese, top mixture with ½ cup Italian-flavored panko bread crumbs. Cook, uncovered, 5-10 minutes. Sprinkle with cheese. Allow cheese to melt, and then serve.

Curried Lentils

Susan Kasting
Jenks, OK

Makes 4-6 servings

Prep. Time: 15 minutes
Cooking Time: 3½-5½ hours
Ideal slow-cooker size: 4-5 qt.

1 large onion, chopped
5 tsp. curry powder
¼ tsp. cayenne pepper
5½ cups vegetable broth
1 lb. dried lentils, picked over for any stones and rinsed
15-oz. can garbanzo beans, rinsed and drained
10-oz. pkg. frozen chopped spinach, thawed and squeezed dry
½ cup plain yogurt

1. Grease interior of slow-cooker crock.
2. Add chopped onion, curry powder, cayenne, broth, and lentils to crock. Mix together well.
3. Cover. Cook on Low 4-5 hours, or on High 3-4 hours, or until onions and lentils are as tender as you like them.
4. Stir in beans and spinach. Cover. Continue cooking on either Low or High another 30 minutes, or until dish is thoroughly hot.
5. Serve, adding a dollop of yogurt to each individual dish.

Good go-alongs with this recipe:

Pita bread.

Baked Lentils with Cheese

Kay Nussbaum
Salem, OR

Makes 4 main-dish, or 8 side-dish, servings

Prep. Time: 25-30 minutes
Cooking Time: 3-8 hours
Ideal slow-cooker size: 5 qt.

1¾ cups raw lentils, rinsed and picked clean
2 cups water
1 whole bay leaf
½ tsp. salt
¼ tsp. black pepper
⅛ tsp. dried marjoram
⅛ tsp. dried sage
⅛ tsp. dried thyme
2 large onions, chopped
2 cloves garlic, minced
2 cups, or 14.5-oz. can, stewed tomatoes
2 large carrots, sliced thinly
½ cup celery, sliced thinly
1 sweet bell pepper, chopped, optional
2 Tbsp. dried parsley
1 cup cheddar cheese, grated

1. Grease interior of slow-cooker crock.
2. Mix all ingredients together in crock, except sweet pepper, parsley, and grated cheese.
3. Cover. Cook on Low 6-8 hours, or on High 3-5 hours, or until lentils and vegetables are as tender as you like them.
4. Twenty minutes before end of cooking time, stir in chopped peppers if you wish, and parsley.
5. Just before serving, uncover crock and scatter grated cheese over top. Serve when it's melted.

Quinoa and Black Beans

Gloria Frey
Lebanon, PA

Makes 6-8 servings

Prep. Time: 15-20 minutes
Cooking Time: 2-3 hours
Ideal slow-cooker size: 4 qt.

1 medium onion, chopped
3 cloves garlic, chopped
1 red bell pepper, chopped
1½ cups vegetable broth
1 tsp. ground cumin
¼ tsp. cayenne pepper
½ tsp. salt
¼ tsp. coarsely ground black pepper
1 cup fresh, frozen, or canned corn, drained
2 15-oz. cans black beans, rinsed and drained
¾ cup uncooked quinoa
½ cup fresh cilantro, chopped

1. Grease interior of slow-cooker crock.
2. Mix all ingredients, except quinoa and cilantro, in crock.
3. Cover. Cook on Low 2 hours, or until veggies are as tender as you like.
4. Stir in quinoa. Cover and continue cooking on Low 20-30 more minutes, or until quinoa is tender.
5. Just before serving, stir in cilantro.

Vegetables and Red Quinoa Casserole

Gladys Voth
Hesston, KS

Makes 6-8 servings

Prep. Time: 20 minutes
Cooking Time: 1½-4 hours
Ideal slow-cooker size: 4 qt.

4 cups cubed (¾" in size) butternut squash
2 cups cubed beets (¾" in size)
2 cups sliced celery (½" thick), about 2 stalks
6 cloves garlic
1½ cups vegetable broth
3 Tbsp. dried basil
1 cup uncooked red quinoa, rinsed
Mixed Berry Almond non-dairy yogurt, for topping
½ cup cashew nuts, for topping

1. Grease interior of slow-cooker crock.
2. Peel butternut squash. Remove seeds. Cut into ¾" pieces. Place in crock.
3. Peel beets. Cut into ¾" pieces. Place in crock.
4. Wash celery stalks. Slice into ½"-thick slices. Place in crock.
5. Coarsely chop garlic cloves. Place in crock.
6. Pour vegetable broth over ingredients in slow cooker.
7. Crush dried basil between fingers while adding to slow cooker.
8. Stir everything together well.
9. Cover. Cook on High 1½-2 hours or on Low 3-4 hours.
10. Thoroughly rinse quinoa in a colander in cold water to remove bitterness. Drain. Set aside.
11. Twenty to 30 minutes before end of cooking time, stir in quinoa. Cover and cook on High 20-30 minutes.
12. Serve hot or at room temperature.
13. Top each serving with non-dairy yogurt and a sprinkling of cashews.

Tips:

This red dish is fun to include on a Valentine's Day or Christmas menu.

Variations:

Quinoa, an ancient seed food, is gaining popularity in North America. It is chewy, mildly nutty, and high in protein. It is gluten free and cholesterol free.

Good go-alongs with this recipe:

A fresh fruit, pineapple, and banana salad lends eye appeal to the plate while adding a contrast in flavors.

Barley with Mushrooms

Rosemary Martin
Bridgewater, VA

Makes 4 servings

Prep. Time: 10-15 minutes
Cooking Time: 3-6 hours
Ideal slow-cooker size: 3 qt.

¾ cup uncooked pearl barley
½ cup diced onions
1 clove garlic, minced
14.5-oz. can vegetable broth
3 cups chopped fresh mushrooms, or 4-oz. can mushrooms, with juice
½ cup slivered almonds, optional
pinch cayenne pepper or black pepper, to taste
⅓ cup shredded sharp cheddar cheese, optional

1. Grease interior of slow-cooker crock.
2. Place all ingredients in slow cooker except cheese.
3. Cover. Cook on Low 5-6 hours, or on High 3-4 hours, or until barley and onions are as tender as you like them.
4. Just before serving, uncover and sprinkle with cheese. Allow cheese to melt, and then serve.

Moroccan Sweet Potato Medley

Pat Bishop
Bedminster, PA

Makes 6 servings

Prep. Time: 20 minutes
Cooking Time: 2¼-4¼ hours
Ideal slow-cooker size: 5 qt.

1 medium onion, sliced
2 cloves garlic, minced
1½ tsp. ground coriander
1½ tsp. cumin
¼-½ tsp. black pepper, coarsely ground, according to taste
2 medium sweet potatoes, peeled and cubed, or 1-lb. can sweet potatoes, cubed and drained
14.5-oz. can stewed tomatoes, undrained
¾ cup uncooked bulgur
2¼ cups water
15-oz. can garbanzo beans, rinsed and drained
½ cup raisins
1 cup cilantro leaves, chopped

1. Grease interior of slow-cooker crock.
2. Place sliced onion, garlic, coriander, cumin, pepper, sweet potatoes, tomatoes, bulgur, and water in slow cooker.
3. Cover. Cook on Low 2 hours if you're using canned sweet potatoes, or 4 hours if you're using raw sweet potatoes, or until vegetables are done to your liking and bulgur is tender.
4. Stir in beans and raisins.
5. Cover. Cook 15 more minutes.
6. Serve, topping each individual plate or bowl with a scattering of chopped cilantro leaves.

Thai Veggie Curry

Christen Chew
Lancaster, PA

Makes 4-5 servings

Prep. Time: 30 minutes
Cooking Time: 5-6 hours
Ideal slow-cooker size: 4 or 5 qt.

2 large carrots, thinly sliced
1 medium onion, chopped
3 cloves garlic, chopped
2 large potatoes, peeled or not, and diced
15.5-oz. can garbanzo beans, rinsed and drained
14.5-oz. can diced tomatoes, undrained
2 Tbsp. curry powder
1 tsp. ground coriander
1 tsp. cayenne pepper
2 cups vegetable stock
½ cup frozen green peas
½ cup coconut milk
salt to taste
cooked rice

1. Grease interior of slow-cooker crock.
2. Stir all ingredients except peas, coconut milk, salt, and cooked rice into crock. Mix together well, making sure seasonings are distributed throughout.
3. Cover. Cook on Low 5-6 hours, or until vegetables are as tender as you like them.
4. Just before serving, stir in peas and coconut milk. Season with salt to taste.
5. Serve over cooked rice.

Wild Rice Casserole

Edith Romano
Westminster, MD

Makes 6 servings

Prep. Time: 30 minutes
Cooking Time: 2½ hours
Ideal slow-cooker size: 6 qt.

1½ cups uncooked long-grain rice
½ cup uncooked wild rice
1 envelope dry onion soup mix
4 cups water
¼ cup chopped green onions
8 oz. fresh or canned sliced mushrooms
¼ cup (½ stick) melted butter
1-3 Tbsp. cut-up fresh parsley

1. Grease interior of slow-cooker crock.
2. Combine all ingredients, except parsley, in crock.
3. Cover. Cook on High for 2-2½ hours, or until rice is tender but not dry.
4. Ten minutes before end of cooking time, stir in parsley.

Tips:

From the tester: I've added this recipe to my keeper file. It's much tastier than plain rice but requires very little additional effort.
—Kelly Bailey

Good go-alongs with this recipe:

This is good with chicken.

Spinach Rice Bake

Esther Porter
Minneapolis MN

Makes 4 servings

Prep. Time: 10-15 minutes
Cooking Time: 1-2 hours
Ideal slow-cooker size: 3 qt.

10-oz. pkg. frozen chopped spinach
¾ cup grated cheese of your choice
½ tsp. garlic salt
1 Tbsp. diced onion
⅓ cup uncooked instant rice
1 egg, beaten
1 cup milk

1. Grease interior of slow-cooker crock.
2. Thaw spinach. Squeeze it as dry as you can. Place in crock.
3. Stir grated cheese, garlic salt, onion, and rice into spinach, mixing well.
4. Mix in egg and milk.
5. Cook on Low 1-2 hours, or until set in the middle. (Stick the blade of a knife into the center. If it comes out clean, the Bake is done. If it doesn't, cover and continue cooking another 15 minutes.)

Good go-alongs with this recipe:

Baked sweet potatoes or baked squash.

Brown Rice Vegetable Dinner

Judy Buller
Bluffton, OH

Makes 6-8 servings

Prep. Time: 20-30 minutes
Cooking Time: 3-6 hours
Ideal slow-cooker size: 5 qt.

3 cups vegetable broth
3 Tbsp. soy sauce
1½ cups uncooked brown rice
2 cups chopped onions, divided
2 garlic cloves, minced
½ tsp. dried thyme
1 medium carrot, cut in thin sticks
1 cup broccoli florets
1 cup cauliflower florets
1 cup sliced zucchini, peeled or not
1 cup sliced yellow squash, peeled or not
1 medium red bell pepper, cut in strips
1 cup cashews
2 cups shredded cheddar cheese

1. Grease interior of slow-cooker crock.
2. Place broth, soy sauce, uncooked rice, onions, garlic, thyme, carrot, broccoli, and cauliflower in crock.
3. Cover. Cook on High 2 hours or on Low 3-4 hours, or until vegetables are nearly tender.
4. Stir in zucchini, yellow squash, and pepper strips.
5. Cover. Cook on High another hour or on Low 2 more hours, or until all vegetables are as tender as you like them.
6. Just before serving, sprinkle dish with cashews and cheese. When cheese has melted, serve.

Variations:

Use any vegetable in season. Remember that denser veggies need to cook longer than more delicate ones.

Sunshine Casserole

Abigail Zuck
Manheim, PA

Makes 4 main-dish, or 6-8 side-dish, servings

Prep. Time: 10-30 minutes
Cooking Time: 2-3 hours
Ideal slow-cooker size: 4 qt.

2 cups shredded carrots (shred your own, or pick up a pkg. in your grocery store)
2 cups cream-style, or whole-kernel, corn
2 eggs
1½ cups sharp cheese, cubed
¼ cup milk
1 Tbsp. butter, melted
¼ tsp. ground mustard, optional
¼ cup finely chopped onion
½ tsp. salt
¼ tsp. black pepper
⅔ cup uncooked instant rice
1⅓ cups water

1. Grease interior of slow-cooker crock.
2. Mix all ingredients, except rice and water, in crock.
3. Cover. Cook on Low 2-3 hours, or until veggies are as tender as you like them.
4. Stir in uncooked rice and water.
5. Cover. Cook on High 20-30 minutes, or until rice is fully cooked.

Risotto in the Crock

Carolyn Spohn
Shawnee, KS

Makes 3-4 servings

Prep. Time: 20 minutes
Cooking Time: 1½-2½ hours
Ideal slow-cooker size: 3 or 4 qt.

½ medium onion, chopped
1 Tbsp. olive oil
1 cup uncooked Arborio rice
⅓ cup grated Parmesan cheese
2½ cups chicken or vegetable broth
salt and pepper to taste

1. Grease interior of slow-cooker crock.
2. In skillet, sauté onion in olive oil until soft.
3. Add rice and sauté until rice becomes somewhat translucent around the edges.
4. Meanwhile, heat broth just to boiling point.
5. Put rice-onion mix in crock.
6. Stir 2 cups hot broth into rice.
7. Cover. Cook on High 1½-2½ hours, or until rice is just tender. Stir once or twice during cooking time.
8. When rice is cooked but still a bit firm, stir in grated cheese and enough reserved broth to reach the consistency you want.
9. Taste before serving. Add salt and pepper as needed.

Tips:

This makes a good side dish to take the place of potatoes or regular rice.

Polenta in a Crock

Carolyn Spohn
Shawnee, KS

Makes 4 servings

Prep. Time: 10-15 minutes
Cooking Time: 2-5 hours
Ideal slow-cooker size: 2 qt.

1 cup coarsely ground cornmeal
3 cups boiling water
½-1 tsp. salt
1 Tbsp. butter or olive oil
¼-½ cup grated Parmesan cheese

1. Grease interior of slow-cooker crock.
2. Place cornmeal, boiling water, and salt in crock. Stir together well until there are no lumps.
3. Cover. Cook on High 2-3 hours or on Low 4-5 hours.
4. When cornmeal is cooked and thick, stir in butter or oil and grated cheese.
5. Serve.

Tips:

This is delicious as is, or great, too, topped with a spicy bean sauce.

Herbal Apple Cheese Dish

Jane D. Look
Mapleton, IL

Makes 4 servings

Prep. Time: 20 minutes
Cooking Time: 2 hours
Ideal slow-cooker size: 6 qt.

2 cups chopped tart apples, peeled or not
½ cup chopped onion
¼ tsp. garlic powder
¼ tsp. dried thyme or ¾ tsp. chopped fresh thyme
¼ tsp. dried marjoram or ¾ tsp. chopped fresh marjoram
3 Tbsp. butter
4 Tbsp. flour
1 tsp. salt
1 cup milk
1 cup grated cheddar cheese
¼ cup chopped walnuts
2 strips fried bacon, crumbled
4 egg yolks
6 egg whites
¼ tsp. cream of tartar

1. In a saucepan or skillet fry bacon until crisp. Remove from pan and drain on paper towels. Crumble bacon when cool.
2. Sauté apples, onion, garlic powder, thyme, and marjoram in bacon drippings and butter for 3 minutes.
3. Gradually stir in flour, salt, and milk over low heat. Continue stirring until sauce thickens and bubbles.
4. Stir in cheese, nuts, and bacon.
5. Beat egg yolks well and stir in.
6. Beat whites with cream of tartar until stiff. Fold into mixture.
7. Pour mixture into lightly greased baking dish that will fit into your slow cooker. Set dish on a small trivet or jar rings in the crock.
8. Cover cooker and cook on High for 2 hours, or until eggs are set.
9. Using sturdy tongs, or a metal spatula in one hand and a spoon in the other, lift out the baking dish. Allow to stand for 10 minutes before cutting into wedges and serving.

Filled Acorn Squash

Teresa Martin
New Holland, PA.

Makes 4 servings

Prep. Time: *20-30 minutes*
Cooking Time: *5-10 hours*
Ideal slow-cooker size: *oval 7 qt.*

2 medium acorn squash, about 1¼ lbs. each
2 Tbsp. water
15-oz. can black beans, rinsed and drained
½ cup pine nuts, raw, or toasted if you have time
1 large tomato, coarsely chopped
2 scallions, sliced thinly
1 tsp. ground cumin
½ tsp. coarsely ground black pepper, divided
2 tsp. olive oil
½-¾ cup shredded Monterey Jack cheese

1. Grease interior of slow-cooker crock.
2. Place washed whole squashes in slow cooker.
3. Spoon in water.
4. Cover. Cook on High for 4-6 hours or on Low for 7-9 hours, or until squashes jag tender when you pierce them with a fork.
5. While squashes are cooking, mix together beans, pine nuts, tomato, scallions, cumin, and ¼ tsp. black pepper. Set aside.
6. Use sturdy tongs, or wear oven mitts, to lift squashes out of cooker. Let cool until you can cut them in half.
7. Scoop out seeds.
8. Brush cut sides and cavity of each squash half with olive oil.
9. Sprinkle all 4 cut sides with remaining black pepper.
10. Spoon heaping ½ cup of bean mixture into each halved squash, pressing down gently to fill cavity.
11. Return halves to slow cooker. Cover. Cook on High another hour, or on Low another hour or 2, until vegetables are as tender as you like them and thoroughly hot.
12. Uncover and sprinkle with cheese just before serving. When cheese has melted, put a filled half squash on each diner's plate.

Tips:

I enjoy serving this recipe in the fall when I can buy squash at our local farmers market or at roadside stands where they are plentiful and inexpensive. This dish is high in protein and fiber and low in fat.

Scalloped Spinach

Susan Segraves
Lansdale, PA

Makes 3-4 main-dish, or 8 side-dish, servings

Prep. Time: *10-15 minutes*
Cooking Time: *2¼ hours*
Ideal slow-cooker size: *3 or 4 qt.*

2 10-oz. pkgs. frozen chopped spinach, or 1½ lbs. fresh spinach
3 eggs, beaten
half an 8-oz. pkg. cream cheese, softened
½ stick (¼ cup) butter, softened
¾ cup milk
dash black pepper
dash nutmeg
¼ cup finely chopped onions
1½ cups crushed wheat crackers
½ cup shredded cheddar cheese

1. Grease interior of slow-cooker crock.
2. If you're using frozen spinach, thaw it completely. Then squeeze dry and place in good-sized bowl.
3. If you're using fresh spinach, wash it and place it in a large stock-pot. Cover and cook over medium heat. Stir frequently, stirring up from the bottom so it steams evenly. When it's all steamed and soft, drain off water. Then squeeze dry in bunches and chop as you go. Place in good-sized bowl after chopping.
4. Stir in eggs.
5. Melt cream cheese and butter either in microwave or on stovetop, stirring frequently to keep it from sticking or burning.
6. When melted, mix in milk, pepper, nutmeg, and onion. Stir into spinach/egg mixture.
7. In a separate bowl, mix together crushed crackers and shredded cheese.
8. Place half of spinach mixture into slow cooker.
9. Top with half the crumbs.
10. Spoon remaining spinach over top.
11. Cover. Cook on Low 2 hours, or until hot.
12. Uncover. Top with remaining crumb-cheese mixture.
13. Cook 15 more minutes on Low.

Crustless Spinach Quiche

Barbara Hoover
Landisville, PA

Makes 8 servings

Prep. Time: 15 minutes
Cooking Time: 2-4 hours
Ideal slow-cooker size: 3 or 4 qt.

2 10-oz. pkgs. frozen chopped spinach
2 cups cottage cheese
½ stick (¼ cup) butter, cut into pieces
1½ cups sharp cheese, cubed
3 eggs, beaten
¼ cup flour
1 tsp. salt

1. Grease interior of slow-cooker crock.
2. Thaw spinach completely. Squeeze as dry as you can. Then place in crock.
3. Stir in all other ingredients and combine well.
4. Cover. Cook on Low 2-4 hours, or until quiche is set. Stick blade of knife into center of quiche. If blade comes out clean, quiche is set. If it doesn't, cover and cook another 15 minutes or so.
5. When cooked, allow to stand 10-15 minutes so mixture can firm up. Then serve.

Variations:

1. Double the recipe if you wish. Cook it in a 5-quart slow cooker.
2. Omit cottage cheese. Add 1 cup milk, 1 tsp. baking powder, and increase flour to 1 cup instead.
3. Reserve sharp cheese and sprinkle on top. Allow to melt before serving.

—Barbara Jean Fabel

Zucchini Torte

Mary Clair Wenger
Kimmswick, MO

Makes 8 servings

Prep. Time: 25 minutes
Cooking Time: 4-5 hours
Ideal slow-cooker size: 4 qt.

5 cups diced zucchini
1 cup grated carrots
1 small onion, diced finely
1½ cups biscuit baking mix
½ cup grated Parmesan cheese
4 eggs, beaten
¼ cup olive oil
2 tsp. dried marjoram
½ tsp. salt
pepper to taste

1. Mix together all ingredients. Pour into greased slow cooker.
2. Cover and cook on Low for 4-5 hours, until set. Remove lid last 30 minutes to allow excess moisture to evaporate.
3. Serve hot or room temperature.

Zucchini Quiche

Anita Troyer
Fairview, MI

Makes 4-6 servings

Prep. Time: 20 minutes
Cooking Time: 1½-2 hours
Ideal slow-cooker size: 3 qt.

2 cups finely diced zucchini
½ cup chopped onion
2 Tbsp. (¼ stick) butter
4 eggs, beaten
1 cup buttermilk baking mix (like Bisquick)
½ cup milk or half-and-half
⅓ cup grated Parmesan cheese
½ tsp. dried basil
½ tsp. dried oregano
1 tsp. seasoning salt
½ tsp. garlic powder
1 Tbsp. olive oil

1. Grease interior of slow-cooker crock.
2. If you have time, sauté zucchini and onion in butter in a skillet until clear. Or microwave zucchini and onion with 2 Tbsp. water (and no butter) on High for 3 minutes. Drain off moisture before placing vegetables in crock. If you don't have time, place chopped zucchini and onion straight into crock, and skip the butter and water.
3. Add eggs, baking mix, milk, grated cheese, basil, oregano, seasoning salt, garlic powder, and oil to veggies. Stir together gently but well.
4. Cover. Cook on High for 1½-2 hours, or until crust begins to brown around edges.
5. Uncover, being careful not to let condensation on lid drip onto Quiche.
6. Let stand for 15 minutes before cutting into wedges and serving to allow Quiche to firm up.

Variations:

Add 3 fried slices of bacon, crumbled, to Step 3.

Summer Veggie Bake

Eone Riales
Nesbit, MS

Makes 8-10 servings

Prep. Time: 30 minutes
Cooking Time: 4½ hours
Ideal slow-cooker size: 4 qt.

3 medium-sized green zucchini, sliced in thin coins, divided
3 ears of yellow sweet corn, kernels sliced off, divided
3 large red tomatoes, diced, divided
1 small onion, sliced in rings, divided
½ red bell pepper, sliced thinly, divided
¼ cup fresh basil leaves, divided
3 Tbsp. olive oil, divided
salt and pepper, to taste
1 cup small-curd cottage cheese
1½ cups saltine cracker crumbs
¾ cup shredded sharp cheddar cheese, divided

1. In lightly greased crock, layer ⅓ of each vegetable: zucchini, corn, tomatoes, onion, bell pepper, and basil leaves. Drizzle with 1 Tbsp. olive oil. Sprinkle lightly with salt and pepper.
2. Separately, combine cottage cheese, cracker crumbs, and ½ cup cheddar.
3. Dollop ⅓ of mixture over vegetables.
4. Make another layer of vegetables the same way, another layer of cheese mixture, and a final layer of vegetables.
5. Sprinkle remaining ¼ cup cheddar over top.
6. Cover and cook on Low for 4 hours. Remove lid and cook another 30 minutes to allow excess moisture to evaporate.

Tips:

Serve with crusty bread and olive oil for dipping.

Baked Tomato Rarebit

Edwina Stoltzfus
Lebanon, PA

Makes 6 servings

Prep. Time: 25 minutes
Cooking Time: 4-5 hours
Ideal slow-cooker size: 3 qt.

4 cups fresh bread cubes
1½ cups grated sharp cheddar cheese
3 eggs, beaten
½ tsp. dry mustard
1½ tsp. salt
pinch pepper
3 cups stewed tomatoes with peppers and onions

1. In lightly greased slow cooker, make layers of bread cubes and cheese.
2. Separately, whisk together eggs, mustard, salt, and pepper.
3. Pour egg mixture over bread and cheese layers.
4. Pour stewed tomatoes evenly over all.
5. Cover and cook on Low for 4-5 hours, until bubbling and edges are browning.

Apricot Salsa Salmon

Sue Hamilton
Benson, AZ

Makes 2 servings

Prep. Time: 5 minutes
Cooking Time: 1-1½ hours
Ideal slow-cooker size: 4 qt.

12 oz. frozen salmon fillets . . . do NOT thaw
¼ cup apricot jam
¼ cup roasted salsa verde*

1. Grease interior of slow-cooker crock.
2. Remember not to thaw the salmon! Place frozen salmon skin side down in bottom of cooker.
3. Mix together jam and salsa. Spread mixture over salmon.
4. Cover. Cook on Low for 1-1½ hours or until an instant-read meat thermometer registers 135° when stuck into center of fillet.

Tips:

1. Pass extra salsa to add to salmon while eating.
2. *From the tester: If you'd like to make your own salsa verde, here's a great recipe:

2 large oranges
¼ cup olive oil
¼ cup fresh lemon juice (about 2 large lemons)
½ cup chopped fresh flat-leaf parsley
2 scallions, finely sliced
3 Tbsp. chopped fresh mint leaves
2 Tbsp. capers, rinsed and drained
2 Tbsp. orange zest
1 tsp. lemon zest
½-1 tsp. crushed red pepper flakes
optional: coarse salt, and coarsely ground black pepper.

1. Peel oranges. Cut along the membrane on both sides of each segment and slide segments into medium bowl.
2. Stir in olive oil, lemon juice, parsley, scallions, mint, capers, orange zest, lemon zest, and red pepper flakes.
3. Chop with immersion blender or in food processor.

—Catherine Boshart

Variations:

You can easily change the flavor of the jam and the salsa to fit your taste. If you want to avoid sugar, you can use no-sugar jam.

Red Clam Sauce with Pasta

Carol Sherwood
Batavia, NY

Makes 3-4 servings

Prep. Time: 15 minutes
Cooking Time: 3 hours
Ideal slow-cooker size: 3 or 4 qt.

1 medium onion, chopped
2 garlic cloves, minced
14.5-oz. can diced tomatoes, undrained
6-oz. can tomato paste
1 bay leaf
1 tsp. sugar
1 tsp. dried basil
½ tsp. dried thyme
2 6.5-oz. cans chopped clams, undrained
¼ cup minced fresh parsley
linguine, cooked and drained

1. Grease interior of slow-cooker crock.
2. Put onions, garlic, diced tomatoes, tomato paste, bay leaf, sugar, basil, and thyme into crock.
3. Cover. Cook on Low for 2 hours, or until onions are as tender as you like them.
4. Stir in tomatoes, tomato paste, parsley, bay leaf, sugar, basil, and thyme.
5. Cover and cook on Low for 3 hours or until onions are tender.
6. Stir in clams and their juice and fresh parsley.
7. Cover. Let stand for 5 minutes.
8. Fish out bay leaf before serving over linguine.

Good go-alongs with this recipe:

Garlic bread and salad.

Fruited Wild Rice with Pecans

Dottie Schmidt
Kansas City, MO

Makes 8 servings

Prep. Time: 15 minutes
Cooking Time: 1½-2 hours
Ideal slow-cooker size: 4-qt.

½ cup chopped onions
1 Tbsp. canola oil
6-oz. pkg. long-grain and wild rice
seasoning packet from wild rice pkg.
1½ cups hot water
⅔ cup apple juice
1 large tart apple, chopped
¼ cup raisins
¼ cup coarsely chopped pecans

1. Combine all ingredients except pecans in slow cooker sprayed with non-fat cooking spray.
2. Cover. Cook on high 2-2½ hours.
3. Stir in pecans. Serve.

Always check the harder veggies with a fork 1 hour before the earliest time that the recipe says they are done. If the recipe says 8-10 hours on Low, I check it at 7 hours. —Nancy Eaton, Manchester, CT

Vegetables and Side Dishes

Aunt Twila's Beans

Mary Louise Martin
Boyd, WI

Makes 10-12 servings

Prep. Time: 15 minutes
Cooking Time: 10 hours
Ideal slow-cooker size: 5 qt.

5 cups dry pinto beans
2 tsp. ground cumin
1 medium yellow onion, minced
4 minced garlic cloves
9 cups water
3 tsp. salt
3 Tbsp. lemon juice

1. Combine beans, cumin, onion, garlic, and water in slow cooker.
2. Cook on Low for 8 hours.
3. Add salt and lemon juice. Stir. Cook on Low for another 2 hours.

Tips:

Serve on rice with Mexican toppings. Mash cooked beans as for refried beans, and use as a filling in tacos or burritos.

Bean Hot Dish

Linda Thomas
Sayner, WI

Makes 8 servings

Prep. Time: about 30 minutes
Cooking Time: 4 hours
Ideal slow-cooker size: 6 qt.

½ lb. bacon
1½ lbs. ground beef or turkey
1 medium onion, chopped
3 garlic cloves, chopped finely
¾ cup brown sugar
½ cup ketchup
2 Tbsp. cider vinegar
2 28-oz. cans Bush's baked beans
16-oz. can butter beans, drained
16-oz. can pork-n-beans, drained
16-oz. can B & M baked beans

1. Fry bacon in skillet until crisp. Set aside on paper towels.
2. Fry ground beef and onion in bacon grease. Drain off drippings.
3. Transfer beef and onion to slow cooker.
4. Add rest of ingredients except bacon.
5. Cover and cook on Low for 4-6 hours. Crumble bacon pieces on top before serving.

Variations:

You can add more cans of beans as well as more hamburger to stretch it to feed a bigger group. The bacon should be held until it is ready to serve, or else it won't be crispy.

Curried Beans

Anita Troyer
Fairview, MI

Makes 6-8 servings

***Prep. Time:** 20 minutes*
***Cooking Time:** 4-5 hours*
***Ideal slow-cooker size:** 3 qt.*

3 slices bacon
½ cup chopped onion
31-oz. can pork and beans
1 medium apple, peeled and diced
¼ cup ketchup
2 Tbsp. molasses
2 tsp. prepared mustard
1-2 tsp. curry powder
1 tsp. Worcestershire sauce

1. Fry bacon and onions in a skillet, draining away grease when fully cooked. Crumble bacon.
2. Transfer bacon to slow cooker.
3. Add rest of ingredients.
4. Cook on Low for 4-5 hours.

Ranch Beans

Jo Zimmerman
Lebanon, PA

Makes 8-10 servings

***Prep. Time:** 10 minutes*
***Cooking Time:** 3-4 hours*
***Ideal slow-cooker size:** 3 qt.*

16-oz. can kidney beans, rinsed and drained
16-oz. can pork and beans
15-oz. can lima beans, rinsed and drained
14-oz. can cut green beans, drained
12-oz. bottle chili sauce
⅔ cup brown sugar, packed
1 small onion, chopped

1. Combine all ingredients in slow cooker. Mix.
2. Cover and cook on High 3-4 hours.

Slow-Simmered Kidney Beans

Frances Kruba
Baltimore, MD

Makes 16 servings

***Prep. Time:** 20 minutes*
***Cooking Time:** 6-8 hours*
***Ideal slow-cooker size:** 5 qt.*

6 bacon strips, diced
½ lb. smoked sausage, chopped
3 16-oz. cans kidney beans, rinsed and drained
28-oz. can diced tomatoes, drained
2 medium red bell peppers, chopped
1 large onion, chopped
1 cup ketchup
½ cup brown sugar, packed
¼ cup honey
¼ cup molasses
1 Tbsp. Worcestershire sauce
1 tsp. salt
¼ tsp. ground pepper
1 tsp. ground mustard
2 medium unpeeled red apples, cored and cut into ½" pieces

1. Fry bacon in skillet. Transfer bacon and drippings to slow cooker.
2. Add rest of ingredients to cooker except apples.
3. Cover and cook on Low for 4-6 hours.
4. Stir in apples. Cover and cook on Low 2 more hours.

Super Bowl Beans

Rebekah Zehr
Lowville, NY

Makes 6-8 servings

Prep. Time: *15 minutes*
Cooking Time: *6-8 hours*
Ideal slow-cooker size: *3 qt.*

2 Tbsp. butter
2 large green peppers, chopped
1 medium sweet onion, chopped
1 lb. sliced bacon, crisply fried and crumbled
54-oz. can Grandma Brown's Baked Beans
2 tsp. dry mustard
¾ cup bottled chili sauce
1 cup brown sugar
Tabasco sauce, to taste

1. In skillet, melt butter. Sauté peppers and onion in butter until tender.
2. Transfer pepper, onion, and butter to slow cooker.
3. Add rest of ingredients.
4. Cover and cook on Low 6-8 hours.

Good go-alongs with this recipe:

Great with chicken wings and a football game!

Basil Refried Beans

Jacqueline Swift
Perrysburg, NY

Makes 6-8 servings

Prep. Time: *20 minutes*
Cooking Time: *5-7 hours*
Ideal slow-cooker size: *3 qt.*

2 Tbsp. butter
1½ cups diced onion
4 cups cooked pinto beans
½ cup vegetable broth
2 cloves garlic, minced
1 tsp. cumin
2 tsp. dried basil
½ tsp. dried rosemary
pinch cayenne pepper, or to taste
1 tsp. salt
½ cup shredded sharp cheddar cheese

1. Combine butter and onions in slow cooker.
2. Cover and cook on High for 1 hour.
3. Add beans, broth, garlic, cumin, basil, rosemary, cayenne, and salt.
4. Cover and cook on Low for 4-6 hours.
5. Mash beans with potato masher. Stir in cheese until melted. Taste for seasoning before serving.

Homemade Refried Beans

Emily Fox
Bethel, PA

Makes 15 servings

Prep. Time: *15 minutes*
Cooking Time: *8 hours*
Ideal slow-cooker size: *5 qt.*

1 onion, peeled and halved
3 cups dry pinto or black beans, rinsed
½ fresh or frozen jalepeño, chopped
2 cloves garlic
3-4 tsp. salt
1¾ tsp. black pepper
⅛ tsp. ground cumin
9 cups water

1. Place all ingredients in slow cooker and stir to combine.
2. Cook on High for 8 hours.
3. Drain off liquid, reserving it. Mash beans with potato masher, adding liquid as needed to get consistency you want.

Tips:

Much better than canned! Eat alone or with rice and tortillas, or use in recipes.

Simple Black Beans

Carolyn Spohn
Shawnee, KS

Makes 6 servings

Prep. Time: 10 minutes
Cooking Time: 4-6 on High, depending on age of slow cooker.
Standing Time: 6-10 hours
Ideal slow-cooker size: 5 qt.

2 cups dry black beans
¼ cup chopped onion
1-2 cloves garlic, chopped
1 Tbsp. brown sugar
1 Tbsp. olive oil
4 cups water or chicken broth
salt, to taste

1. Place beans in bowl and cover with water about 2″ over beans. Soak for 6-10 hours.
2. Drain off water. Put soaked beans in slow cooker.
3. Add rest of ingredients to slow cooker except salt.
4. Cover and cook on High for 4-6 hours, until beans are soft. Add salt.

Good go-alongs with this recipe:

Rice or other mild-flavored grain to make a complete protein.

Lima Beans Catalance

Judy Keas
Rowley, MA

Makes 4 servings

Prep. Time: 20 minutes
Cooking Time: 2-3 hours
Ideal slow-cooker size: 4 qt.

16-oz. pkg. frozen limas
½ cup finely chopped chorizo
¼ cup diced onion
1 clove garlic, minced
1 bay leaf
1 tsp. dried mint
½ tsp. salt
freshly ground pepper
2 Tbsp. butter, melted
¼ cup cooking sherry
¼ cup chopped fresh parsley

1. Combine limas, still frozen, in slow cooker with chorizo, onion, garlic, bay leaf, mint, salt, pepper, butter, and sherry.
2. Cover and cook on Low for 2-3 hours until limas are tender.
3. Remove bay leaf. Stir in parsley.

Baked Potatoes

Shelia Heil
Lancaster, PA

Makes 4 servings

Prep. Time: 5 minutes
Cooking Time: 3-8 hours
Ideal slow-cooker size: 3-4 qt.

4 baking potatoes, well scrubbed

1. Prick each potato with a fork. Wrap each potato in foil.
2. Placed wrapped potatoes in slow cooker.
3. Cover and cook on Low 6-8 hours or High 3 hours, until potatoes are tender when poked. Cooking time depends on size and variety of potatoes.
4. Unwrap potatoes to serve with favorite toppings.

Easiest Baked Potatoes

Carrie Fritz
Meridian, ID

Makes 6 servings

Prep. Time: 5 minutes
Cooking Time: 6-8 hours
Ideal slow-cooker size: 6 qt.

6 large baking potatoes, scrubbed and dried
butter or shortening

1. Pierce the potatoes with a sharp knife.
2. Rub potatoes with butter or shortening.
3. Place greased potatoes in lightly greased slow cooker.
4. Cover and cook on Low 6-8 hours, until potatoes are as tender as you like them when poked with a fork.

Tips:

Good with cheese, sour cream, and green onions.

Cabbage and Potatoes

Deb Kepiro
Strasburg, PA

Makes 4 servings

Prep. Time: 15 minutes
Cooking Time: 3-6 hours
Ideal slow-cooker size: 4 qt.

1 small head green cabbage, sliced thinly
14 small red-skinned potatoes, cut in 1" chunks
1 small onion, diced
3 Tbsp. olive oil
2 Tbsp. balsamic vinegar
1 tsp. kosher salt
½ tsp. black pepper

1. Put all ingredients in slow cooker. Mix well.
2. Cover and cook on High for 3 hours, until potatoes are as tender as you like them.

Good go-alongs with this recipe:

Bratwurst in buns with good mustard.

Colcannon

Margaret W. High
Lancaster, PA

Makes 6-8 servings

Prep. Time: 20 minutes
Cooking Time: 4-6 hours
Ideal slow-cooker size: 6 qt.

6 cups chopped kale, ribs removed
6 cups chopped potatoes, peeled or not
2 leeks, chopped
1½ tsp. salt
¼ tsp. black pepper
1 cup chicken stock
3 Tbsp. butter
3 Tbsp. olive oil

1. Combine kale, potatoes, leeks, salt, pepper, and chicken stock in slow cooker.
2. Cover and cook on Low for 4-6 hours, until potatoes are tender.
3. Add butter and olive oil. Mash well with potato masher.

Tips:

Colcannon is an Irish version of mashed potatoes. It's often served on St. Patrick's Day, and some people use cabbage instead of kale and serve it with additional butter melted on top.

Scalloped Potatoes

Betty Moore
Avon Park, FL

Makes 8 servings

Prep. Time: 15 minutes
Cooking Time: 3-4 hours
Ideal slow-cooker size: 4 qt.

3 lbs. sliced potatoes
1 onion, chopped
1 cup shredded sharp cheddar cheese
salt and pepper, to taste
½ cup milk
10-oz. can cheddar cheese soup
1 tsp. dry mustard
½ cup Parmesan cheese

1. Layer potatoes, onions, and cheddar cheese in greased slow cooker, adding salt and pepper to each layer.
2. Separately, mix milk, cheese soup, and dry mustard. Pour over layers in slow cooker.
3. Sprinkle with Parmesan.
4. Cover and cook on High 3-4 hours, until potatoes are tender.

Sour Cream Potatoes with Ham

Janeen Troyer
Fairview, MI

Makes 4-6 servings

Prep. Time: 15 minutes
Cooking Time: 2-3 hours
Ideal slow-cooker size: 3 qt.

2 Tbsp. butter
1 small onion, chopped
1 lb. shredded potatoes
1 cup chopped ham
10-oz. can cream of mushroom soup
½ cup shredded sharp cheese
1 cup sour cream

1. In small skillet, sauté onion in butter until well browned.
2. In greased slow cooker, combine onion/butter with rest of ingredients.
3. Cover and cook on High for 2-3 hours, stirring every 30 minutes, until potatoes are tender.

Tips:

You can freeze the mixture after Step 2 and cook it later. Just be sure it is thawed before putting it in the slow cooker.

Bacon Onion Potato Bake

Janie Steele
Moore, OK

Makes 4 servings

Prep. Time: 30 minutes
Cooking Time: 3-4 hours
Ideal slow-cooker size: 3 qt.

1 pkg. dry onion soup mix
10-12 baby red potatoes, thinly sliced
12 slices cooked, crumbled bacon
1 small onion, diced
salt and pepper, to taste
2 Tbsp. butter

1. Mix potatoes with dry soup.
2. Layer potatoes in slow cooker with bacon and onion, adding salt and pepper to taste.
3. Pour melted butter over top.
4. Cover and cook on High 3-4 hours, until potatoes are tender.

Tips:

Add 1 cup shredded cheese with the other layers. May serve with sour cream at the table.

Cottage Potatoes

Margaret W. High
Lancaster, PA

Makes 6-8 servings

***Prep. Time:** 15 minutes*
***Cooking Time:** 3 hours*
***Ideal slow-cooker size:** 5 qt.*

5-6 large cooked potatoes, diced (peel if you want to—I don't)
1 onion, diced
½ green bell pepper, diced, optional
2 cups diced bread, preferably dry and stale
2 cups diced sharp cheese
¾ tsp. salt
¼ tsp. pepper
1 tsp. dried rosemary
¼ cup (½ stick) butter, melted

1. In lightly greased slow cooker, combine all ingredients except melted butter. Stir gently.
2. Pour melted butter over all.
3. Cover and cook on High 2½ hours. Remove lid and cook uncovered an additional 30 minutes.

Tips:

I make extra baked potatoes at one meal in order to have enough for this dish later in the week.

Good go-alongs with this recipe:

We eat this as a vegetarian main dish with a green vegetable and cranberry applesauce on the side. It's also wonderful with baked ham.

Ranch Potatoes

Janette Fox
Honey Brook, PA

Makes 6 servings

***Prep. Time:** 10 minutes*
***Cooking Time:** 6 hours*
***Ideal slow-cooker size:** 4 qt.*

2 lbs. red potatoes, diced
10-oz. can cream of chicken soup
1 cup sour cream
1-oz. pkg. ranch dressing mix

1. Mix all ingredients in slow cooker.
2. Cook on Low for 6 hours, until potatoes are tender.

Variations:

I use any potatoes I have. Red-skinned just add color.

Slow-Cooker Mashed Potatoes

Marilyn Mowry
Irving, TX

Makes 8-10 servings

***Prep. Time:** 20 minutes*
***Cooking Time:** 4 hours*
***Ideal slow-cooker size:** 6 qt.*

3 lbs. Yukon gold potatoes, peeled and cut into 1" chunks
2 lbs. russet potatoes, peeled and cut into 1" chunks
12 Tbsp. (1½ sticks) unsalted butter, cut into ½" cubes
1 Tbsp. Kosher salt
½ tsp. freshly ground pepper
¾ cup chicken broth
½-1 cup milk, divided
½ cup sour cream

1. Layer the potatoes in slow cooker in layers, adding butter, salt, and pepper to each layer.
2. Pour broth and ½ cup milk over all.
3. Cover and cook on High until potatoes are tender, about 4 hours.
4. Add sour cream. Mash with potato masher, adding up to a ½ cup warmed milk as needed for the consistency you want.
5. Taste for seasoning and add more salt and pepper if needed.

Tips:

If your cooker is very hot, it will take less than 4 hours. Potatoes may be kept in the cooker for about 2 hours before serving. Stir again before serving. This recipe is perfect for those big holiday dinners!

The Best Mashed Potatoes

Colleen Heatwole
Burton, MI

Makes 12 servings

Prep. Time: 30 minutes
Cooking Time: 5-6 hours
Ideal slow-cooker size: 5-7 qt.

5 lbs. potatoes, cooked, peeled, mashed, or riced
8-oz. pkg. reduced-fat cream cheese, room temperature
1½ cups reduced-fat sour cream, room temperature
1 Tbsp. garlic or onion salt
1½ tsp. salt
¼ tsp. pepper
2 Tbsp. butter, optional

1. Combine all ingredients in slow cooker.
2. Cover. Cook on Low 5-6 hours.

Tips:

We use this recipe every Thanksgiving, and since we serve up to 40 people, this recipe is tripled and put in 3 slow cookers. It is an all-time favorite and my cookbook opens to this page. I have always made my lower-fat version. My daughter and niece now take over the Thanksgiving preparation and borrow my slow cooker.

Variations:

Sometimes I leave the skins on the potatoes if they are new potatoes.

Instant Magic Mashed Potatoes

Beverly Hummel
Fleetwood, PA

Makes 12 servings

Prep. Time: 15 minutes
Cooking Time: 2-4 hours
Ideal slow-cooker size: 5 qt.

3½ cups water
2 cups milk
1 tsp. salt
4 cups instant mashed potato flakes
6 Tbsp. butter
½ cup sour cream

1. In saucepan, bring water and milk to a boil. Add salt and potato flakes.
2. Stir in sour cream and butter.
3. Transfer mixture to greased slow cooker and keep on Warm or Low for 2-4 hours.

Tips:

If there is no time to make homemade mashed potatoes, my family cannot tell the difference when I doctor these instant potato flakes up with sour cream and butter. The sour cream keeps them soft.

Variations:

I use leftover instant mashed potatoes to make potato cakes. Add an egg, flour, and milk and mix. Shape into cakes and place in greased frying pan and cook 3 minutes per side.

German Potato Salad

Bob Coffey
New Windsor, NY

Makes 15-20 servings

Prep. Time: 30 minutes
Cooking Time: 6-8 hours
Ideal slow-cooker size: 6.5 qt.

5 lbs. red potatoes
½ cup cider vinegar
⅓ cup sugar
1 tsp. dry mustard
1 Tbsp. kosher salt
5 strips bacon, cooked and chopped
1 large white onion, diced
fresh parsley, chopped finely

1. Peel potatoes about 80%, leaving some skin here and there. Cut into bite-sized pieces.
2. In slow cooker, whisk together vinegar, sugar, mustard, and salt.
3. Add potatoes, bacon, and onion. Stir.
4. Cover and cook on High for 2 hours and then Low for 4-6 hours, until potatoes are tender.
5. Stir parsley in approximately 20 minutes before end of cooking. Serve warm.

Tips:

This dish is best done the first time while you're home and can keep an eye on things, to see how long your cooker needs to get the potatoes done nicely.

Good go-alongs with this recipe:

This is great during the warmer months as a side to grilled meats, especially pork chops.

Autumn Sweet Potatoes

Melinda Wenger
Middleburg, PA

Makes 4 servings

Prep. Time: 20 minutes
Cooking Time: 2-3 hours
Ideal slow-cooker size: 4 qt.

4 medium sweet potatoes, peeled, sliced thinly
1 large Granny Smith apple, peeled and diced
½ cup raisins
2 Tbsp. maple syrup
zest and juice of ½ orange
toasted, chopped walnuts, for serving, optional

1. Place sweet potatoes in lightly greased slow cooker.
2. Top with apples, raisins, and orange zest. Drizzle with maple syrup and orange juice.
3. Cover and cook on High for 2-3 hours, until sweet potatoes are tender. Serve sprinkled with walnuts if you wish.

Sweet Potato Souffle

Lynn Higgins
Marion, OH

Makes 6-8 servings

Prep. Time: 20 minutes
Cooking Time: 2½ hours
Ideal slow-cooker size: 3 qt.

3 cups cooked, mashed sweet potatoes
⅔ cup sugar
½ tsp. salt
2 Tbsp. butter, melted
2 eggs
½ cup milk

Topping:
⅓ cup brown sugar
2 Tbsp. flour
2 Tbsp. butter
½ cup chopped pecans
½ cup grated coconut

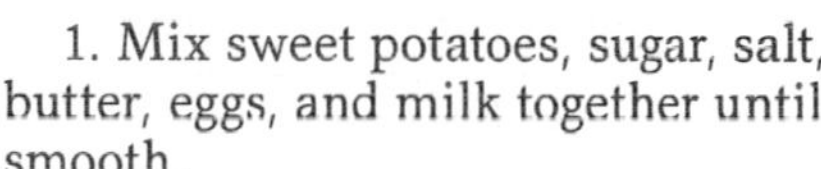

1. Mix sweet potatoes, sugar, salt, butter, eggs, and milk together until smooth.
2. Place in lightly greased slow cooker.
3. Cover and cook on High for 2 hours.
4. Separately, mix topping ingredients. Sprinkle over sweet potatoes.
5. Cook with the lid off for an additional 30 minutes on High.

Good go-alongs with this recipe:

Any Thanksgiving menu or a ham dinner.

Potato Herb Stuffing

Lewis J. Matt III
Holbrook, PA

Makes 8 servings

Prep. Time: 30 minutes
Cooking Time: 6-8 hours
Ideal slow-cooker size: 6 qt.

4 ribs celery with leaves, chopped
1 large onion, chopped
½ cup (1 stick) butter
4 large potatoes, cooked and diced
10 slices whole wheat bread, diced
5 eggs
½ cup chopped fresh parsley
1 tsp. dried basil
½ tsp. dried thyme
¼ tsp. dried rosemary
1 tsp. freshly ground pepper
1 tsp. salt
3-4 cups vegetable broth

1. In a skillet, sauté celery and onion in butter until softened. Transfer to slow cooker, being sure to get all the butter.
2. Add to slow cooker the potatoes, bread, eggs, parsley, basil, thyme, rosemary, pepper, and salt. Mix gently.
3. Add 3 cups broth and mix again. If Stuffing is not moist enough, add up to another cup broth.
4. Cover and cook on Low for 6-8 hours, until firm and browning around edges.

Good go-alongs with this recipe:

Serve with any gravy, or allow to cool and slice and serve cold. Excellent with currant or cranberry jelly, chutney, or relish.

Holiday Side-Dish Dressing

Jean Turner
Williams Lake, British Columbia

Makes 6-8 servings

Prep. Time: 20 minutes
Cooking Time: 8 hours, 45 minutes
Ideal slow-cooker size: 3 qt.

1 cup (2 sticks) butter
2 cups chopped onion
2 cups chopped celery
¼ cup fresh chopped parsley
2 4-oz. cans sliced mushrooms, drained
12-13 cups dry bread cubes
1 tsp. poultry seasoning
1½ tsp. salt
1½ tsp. sage
1 tsp. dried thyme
½ tsp. pepper
½ tsp. marjoram
2½ cups chicken broth
2 eggs, beaten

1. Melt butter in skillet. Sauté onions, celery, mushrooms, and parsley.
2. Transfer mixture, including butter, to slow cooker. Stir in bread cubes.
3. Separately, combine seasonings, broth, and eggs. Whisk well.
4. Stir broth mixture into bread and vegetables in slow cooker. Mix well.
5. Cover and cook on High for 1 hour. Turn to Low and cook for 6-8 hours, until Dressing is set and edges are turning brown.

Tips:

This dressing can be used as a side to the turkey dinner when you have a large gathering. Also goes well with chicken or pork chops as a side dish.

Extra Stuffing

Theresa Leppert
Schellsburg, PA

Makes 10 servings

Prep. Time: 20 minutes
Cooking Time: 4-6 hours
Ideal slow-cooker size: 4 qt.

1 cup diced onion
1 cup sliced celery
1 cup (2 sticks) butter
12 cups dried bread cubes
3 cups chicken or turkey broth
2 eggs, beaten
1 tsp. salt
¼ tsp. pepper

1. In a skillet, sauté onions and celery in butter until softened.
2. Transfer vegetables and butter to slow cooker.
3. Add rest of ingredients. Mix well.
4. Cover and cook on Low 4-6 hours, stirring a few times.

Tips:

This is a great recipe for big holiday dinners when the oven is full and I know people are going to want extra stuffing with their turkey or chicken.

Variations:

Add 1 cup diced fresh mushrooms in Step 1.

Good go-alongs with this recipe:

Turkey and gravy, of course!

Slow-Cooker Dressing

Shelia Heil
Lancaster, PA

Makes 8-10 servings

Prep. Time: 20 minutes
Cooking Time: 4-5 hours
Ideal slow-cooker size: 6 qt.

14-15 cups bread cubes
3 cups chopped celery
1½ cups chopped onion
1½ tsp. dried sage
1½ tsp. saffron
1 tsp. salt
1½ cups chicken broth, or more (enough to moisten the bread)
½ cup (1 stick) melted butter

1. In a mixing bowl, combine all ingredients except for butter. Mix well.
2. Add melted butter and mix again.
3. Transfer mixture to lightly greased slow cooker.
4. Cover and cook on Low for 4-5 hours.

Tips:

This is a very moist dressing, but the crusty edges of the dressing might well be your favorite part.

Good go-alongs with this recipe:

Roast turkey or chicken.

Carol's Best Baked Beans

Carol Eveleth
Hillsdale, WY

Makes 20 servings

Prep. Time: 20 minutes
Cooking Time: 7-14 hours
Ideal slow-cooker size: 6 qt.

2 lbs. dry pinto beans
24 oz. ketchup
2 Tbsp. Worcestershire sauce
3 tsp. salt
2 cups brown sugar
1 tsp. liquid smoke
1 large onion, diced
6 Polish sausages, sliced

1. Place beans in slow cooker and cover with water 2" above beans.
2. Cook on Low until beans are soft, about 4-6 hours depending on the age of the beans.
3. Drain off cooking liquid, reserving 1 cup.
4. Return 1 cup liquid to the cooker with the beans. Add rest of ingredients.
5. Cover and cook on High 3-4 hours or Low 6-8 hours.

Tips:

I like to cook the beans in the slow cooker overnight so they are soft in the morning, and then add the rest of the ingredients.

Variations:

You can use various meats . . . bacon, ham, sausage, hot dogs, or even leave out the meat for low-fat beans or vegetarian beans.

Easy Baked Butternut Squash

Janet Batdorf
Harrisburg, PA

Makes 10-15 servings

Prep. Time: 5 minutes
Cooking Time: 6-8 hours
Ideal slow-cooker size: 5 qt.

1 butternut squash, 2-3 lbs.
¼ cup water

1. Wash squash thoroughly.
2. Place whole squash in slow cooker with water.
3. Cook covered on Low for 6-8 hours, until squash is tender when pricked with a fork.
4. Carefully remove squash from cooker, cut in half, and scoop out seeds. Scoop flesh out of shell. Eat hot with butter and salt, or freeze in portions to use where cooked pumpkin is called for in a recipe.

Roasted Butternut Squash

Marilyn Mowry
Irving, TX

Makes 15-20 servings

Prep. Time: 1 hour
Cooking Time: 4 hours on High or 6 hours on Low
Ideal slow-cooker size: 6 qt.

¼ cup olive oil
2 tsp. ground cinnamon, divided
½ tsp. ground cumin
1¾ tsp. salt, divided
5-lb. butternut squash, split in quarters and seeds removed
2 carrots, diced
1 large white onion, diced
2 Granny Smith apples, peeled, cored, and quartered
1 can chipotle chile en adobo, seeds scraped out, chopped roughly
10 cups chicken stock

1. Mix olive oil, 1 tsp. cinnamon, and ¾ tsp. salt in mixing bowl. Brush over the flesh of the quartered squash.
2. Place squash cut side down on a rimmed baking sheet lined with foil.
3. Add carrots, onions, and apples to bowl with oil and toss. Spread on another foil-lined sheet.
4. Roast both trays 40-50 minutes at 425° until squash is soft and onion mix is golden brown. Scoop out the squash.
5. Put squash, veggie mix, chipotle, 1 tsp. salt, and 1 tsp. cinnamon in slow cooker. Add chicken broth.
6. Cover and cook on High 4 hours or Low for 6 hours. Mash with a potato masher or puree with immersion blender.

Tips:

Top with pumpkin seeds and a little crème fraîche. Or melt butter, add sugar and cinnamon, and toss in day-old cubed French bread for croutons. Then toast these in oven at 350° for 10-12 minutes.

Winter Squash with Herbs and Butter

Sharon Timpe
Jackson, WI

Makes 6-8 servings

Prep. Time: 30 minutes
Cooking Time: 3-8 hours
Ideal slow-cooker size: 3-4 qt.

3 lbs. whole winter squash, mixed kinds, ideally 1 small butternut, 1 small Golden Nugget, 1 small acorn squash
4 Tbsp. butter
4-5 Tbsp. honey
4-8 sprigs fresh herbs, such as tarragon, basil, thyme, and/or rosemary
salt, to taste

1. Peel and halve squash, removing seeds and strings. Cut squash in ¼" slices.
2. In lightly greased slow cooker, make layers of squash half-moons, butter, drizzle of honey, and herb sprigs.
3. Cover and cook on High for 3-4 hours or Low for 6-8 hours, until squash is tender.
4. Sprinkle lightly with salt to taste before serving.

Tips:

If transferring to a serving dish, garnish with a few additional fresh herb sprigs. A rectangular or oval cooker works best for this recipe.

A slow-cooker recipe is good for kids to start learning to cook. They don't have to stir food while it cooks in a hot pan on a hot stove. — Martha Deaton, Fulton, MS

Glazed Carrots

Beverly Hummel
Fleetwood, PA

Makes 4 servings

Prep. Time: 5 minutes
Cooking Time: 3 hours
Ideal slow-cooker size: 3 qt.

1-lb. bag baby carrots
¼ cup brown sugar
¼ cup water
½ tsp. salt
1 tsp. lemon juice
chopped fresh parsley, for garnish

1. Combine carrots, brown sugar, water, salt, and lemon juice in slow cooker.
2. Cook on High for 2 hours. Turn heat to Low for another hour, stirring occasionally.
3. Sprinkle with parsley before serving.

Horseradish Carrot Coins

Janet Batdorf
Harrisburg, PA

Makes 4 servings

Prep. Time: 15 minutes
Cooking Time: 3-4 hours
Ideal slow-cooker size: 4 qt.

12 carrots, cut in coins
¼ cup (½ stick) butter, cubed
⅓ cup honey
2 Tbsp. horseradish
1 tsp. vinegar
1 tsp. salt

1. Combine all ingredients in slow cooker. Mix well.
2. Cover and cook on Low for 3-4 hours, until carrots are done to your liking. Stir again before serving.

Harvard Beets

Marjorie Yoder Guengerich
Harrisonburg, VA

Makes 4-6 servings

Prep. Time: 20 minutes
Cooking Time: 2 hours
Ideal slow-cooker size: 3 qt.

⅓ cup sugar
2 Tbsp. flour
¼ cup beet juice
¼ cup vinegar
2 16-oz. cans sliced beets, ¼ cup juice reserved
salt and pepper, to taste

1. In a small bowl, mix sugar, flour, beet juice, and vinegar. Whisk well.
2. Combine sauce with beets in slow cooker.
3. Cover and cook on High for 2 hours, stirring once, until sauce thickens and everything is hot.
4. Season with salt and pepper to taste.

Beets with Capers

Mary Clair Wenger
Kimmswick, MO

Makes 6 servings

Prep. Time: 20 minutes
Cooking Time: 3-4 hours
Ideal slow-cooker size: 3 qt.

8 cups diced fresh beets, peeled or not
3 Tbsp. olive oil
4 garlic cloves, chopped
¼ tsp. fresh ground pepper
½ tsp. salt
1 tsp. dried rosemary
1-2 Tbsp. capers with brine

1. In slow cooker, mix together beets, olive oil, garlic, pepper, salt, and rosemary.
2. Cover and cook on High until beets are tender, 3-4 hours.
3. Stir in capers and brine. Taste for salt. Serve hot or room temperature.

German Red Cabbage

Annie C. Boshart
Lebanon, PA

Makes 12 servings

Prep. Time: 15 minutes
Cooking Time: 3-4 hours
Ideal slow-cooker size: 6 qt.

1 large red cabbage, shredded
3 apples, peeled and cored, sliced thinly
1 onion, thinly sliced
1 Tbsp. brown sugar
1 tsp. salt, or more to taste
⅛ tsp. pepper
2 bay leaves
7-10 whole cloves
½ lb. bacon, chopped
3 Tbsp. white vinegar

1. Mix cabbage, apples, onion, brown sugar, salt, pepper, bay leaves, and cloves in lightly greased slow cooker.
2. Fry bacon. Sprinkle bacon and drippings over top of cabbage. Sprinkle vinegar on top of all.
3. Cover and cook on Low for 3-4 hours. Remove bay leaves and cloves (or warn people!) before serving.

Tips:

Serve with mashed potatoes and sausages with brown mustard. Also great next to baked beans.

Cauliflower Cassoulet

Susie Shenk Wenger
Lancaster, PA

Makes 6 servings

Prep. Time: 30 minutes
Cooking Time: 4-6 hours
Ideal slow-cooker size: 6 qt.

1 cup uncooked brown rice
½ tsp. salt
2 cups water
1 cup sliced fresh mushrooms
1 large sweet onion, chopped
½ cup chopped red bell pepper
3 cloves garlic, chopped
1 Tbsp. butter
1 Tbsp. olive oil
1 large head cauliflower, chopped
½ cup diced Parmesan cheese
1 tsp. dried basil
½ tsp. dried oregano
salt and pepper, to taste
juice and zest of 1 lemon

1. Put rice and ½ tsp. salt in lightly greased slow cooker. Pour water over rice.
2. Sprinkle in mushrooms, onion, bell pepper, and garlic. Sprinkle lightly with salt and pepper. Dot with butter and drizzle with olive oil.
3. Sprinkle in cauliflower and diced Parmesan. Sprinkle with basil and oregano, adding salt and pepper to taste.
4. Cover and cook on Low for 4-6 hours, until rice is cooked and cauliflower is tender.
5. Drizzle with lemon juice and zest before serving.

Chinese Vegetables

Rebecca Leichty
Harrisonburg, VA

Makes 6 servings

Prep. Time: 20 minutes
Cooking Time: 3-4 hours
Ideal slow-cooker size: 5 qt.

4 ribs celery, sliced on the bias
6 green onions, sliced on the bias, divided
1 cup sliced fresh mushrooms
1 cup sliced green cabbage
16-oz. bag Asian stir-fry frozen vegetable mix
1 Tbsp. sugar
1 Tbsp. rice vinegar
3 Tbsp. soy sauce
¼ tsp. black pepper
2 Tbsp. water
1 Tbsp. cornstarch
2 cups fresh bean sprouts

1. Combine celery, 4 sliced onions, mushrooms, cabbage, and frozen vegetables in slow cooker.
2. Separately, whisk together sugar, vinegar, soy sauce, pepper, water, and cornstarch. Pour over vegetables, stirring gently to combine.
3. Cover and cook on Low for 2-3 hours, until vegetables are as tender as you like them and sauce is thickened.
4. Stir in sprouts and remaining 2 green onions. Cover and allow to rest for 15 minutes before serving.

Good go-alongs with this recipe:

Serve with hot rice for a main dish. Also nice with toasted sesame seeds on top.

Succotash

Andy Wagner
Quarryville, PA

Makes 6-8 servings

Prep. Time: 15 minutes
Cooking Time: 4 hours
Ideal slow-cooker size: 4 qt.

16-oz. pkg. frozen corn
16-oz. pkg. frozen lima beans
14.75-oz. can cream-style corn
¼ cup minced red bell pepper
¼ cup minced sweet onion
½ tsp. salt
pinch black pepper
½ cup whole milk, room temperature
2 Tbsp. flour

1. Combine corn, lima beans, cream-style corn, bell pepper, onion, salt, and pepper in slow cooker.
2. Cover and cook on Low for 3 hours.
3. Separately, whisk together milk and flour. Stir into corn mixture.
4. Cover and cook on Low for an additional hour, stirring occasionally, until thickened.

Variations:

Add ½ cup smoked cheddar cheese in Step 4.

Cheesy Creamed Corn

A. Catherine Boshart
Lebanon, PA

Makes 12 servings

Prep. Time: 5 minutes
Cooking Time: 4 hours
Ideal slow-cooker size: 2-4 qt.

3 16-oz. pkgs. frozen corn
8 oz. cream cheese, room temperature, cubed
¼ cup (½ stick) butter
¼ cup water
¼ cup milk
2 Tbsp. sugar
½ cup shredded sharp cheddar cheese

1. Combine all ingredients in lightly greased slow cooker.
2. Cover and cook on Low for 4 hours, stirring twice in the first hour.

Potluck Baked Corn

Velma Stauffer
Akron, PA

Makes 10-12 servings

Prep. Time: 15 minutes
Cooking Time: 3-4 hours
Ideal slow-cooker size: 6 qt.

2 quarts frozen corn, thawed and drained
4 eggs, beaten
2 tsp. salt
1¾ cups 2% or whole milk
2 Tbsp. melted butter
3 Tbsp. sugar
6 Tbsp. flour

1. Mix all ingredients in mixing bowl until well combined.
2. Pour into greased slow cooker.
3. Cover and cook on High 3-4 hours until set in the middle and lightly browned at edges.

Broccoli Corn Casserole

Gerry Bauman
Grimes, IA

Makes 6 servings

Prep. Time: 25 minutes
Cooking Time: 4 hours
Ideal slow-cooker size: 3 qt.

10-oz. pkg. frozen chopped broccoli
2 cups cream-style corn
1 cup cracker crumbs, divided
1 egg, beaten
½ tsp. salt
½ tsp. dried rosemary
½ tsp. dried thyme
2 green onions, diced
2 Tbsp. grated Parmesan cheese
2 Tbsp. butter, melted

1. Break broccoli apart if it has clumped, but keep it frozen.
2. In slow cooker, combine corn, ½ cup cracker crumbs, egg, salt, rosemary, and thyme. Stir well.
3. Add broccoli and stir gently.
4. Cover and cook on Low for 3 hours, until set.
5. Combine remaining ½ cup cracker crumbs, green onions, Parmesan, and melted butter. Sprinkle on top of casserole.
6. Remove lid, turn cooker to High, and cook an additional hour.

Scalloped Cabbage

Edwina Stoltzfus
Lebanon, PA

Makes 6-8 servings

Prep. Time: 25 minutes
Cooking Time: 3-5 hours
Ideal slow-cooker size: 4 qt.

1 Tbsp. butter
12 cups chopped cabbage
¼ cup chopped onion
¼ cup chopped fresh parsley
1 cup grated sharp cheese
¼ cup flour
12-oz. can evaporated milk
½ cup diced, cooked bacon, optional

1. Use butter to grease slow cooker.
2. Combine cabbage, onion, parsley, and cheese in slow cooker.
3. In a mixing bowl, whisk together flour and milk until lump free.
4. Pour milk mixture over cabbage mixture.
5. Cover and cook on Low for 3-5 hours, until cabbage is soft and sauce is thick.
6. Sprinkle with bacon if you wish before serving.

Variations:

If you're adding bacon to the top, use bacon grease instead of butter to grease the crock. Add 1 tsp. of your favorite dried herb.

Asparagus Bake

Leona M. Slabaugh
Apple Creek, OH

Makes 4-6 servings

Prep. Time: 20 minutes
Cooking Time: 3½-4½ hours
Ideal slow-cooker size: 4 qt.

5 medium potatoes, unpeeled, sliced
1 onion, sliced
1 cup sliced fresh mushrooms
1 bunch fresh asparagus
salt and pepper
3 Tbsp. butter
½-¾ cup grated smoked cheddar cheese

1. In greased slow cooker, layer potatoes and onion. Sprinkle with salt and pepper. Add mushrooms and asparagus. Sprinkle again with salt and pepper.
2. Dot with butter.
3. Cover and cook on Low for 3-4 hours, until potatoes are tender.
4. Uncover and turn to High. Sprinkle with cheese. Cook uncovered an additional 30 minutes as cheese melts and extra moisture evaporates.

Saucy Mushrooms

Donna Lantgen
Arvada, CO

Makes 4 servings

Prep. Time: 15 minutes
Cooking Time: 4-6 hours
Ideal slow-cooker size: 3 qt.

1 lb. small whole fresh mushrooms, cleaned
4 cloves garlic, minced
¼ cup chopped onion
1 Tbsp. olive oil
¾ cup red wine
½ tsp. salt
⅛ tsp. pepper
¼ tsp. dried thyme
¼ cup water
2 Tbsp. cornstarch

1. Combine mushrooms, garlic, onion, olive oil, red wine, salt, pepper, and thyme in slow cooker.
2. Cover and cook on Low 4-6 hours, until mushrooms are nicely done.
3. Whisk together water and cornstarch. Turn cooker to High and stir in cornstarch mixture. Cook on High, stirring occasionally, until thickened, 20-30 minutes.

Good go-alongs with this recipe:

Serve as a sauce over pasta, or as a side dish with steaks and baked potatoes.

Caramelized Onions in the Crock

Kelly Bailey
Dillsburg, PA

Makes 16 servings

Prep. Time: 15 minutes
Cooking Time: 11-13 hours
Ideal slow-cooker size: 5 qt.

8 large onions, about 5 lbs., thinly sliced to yield about 8 cups
3 Tbsp. butter
salt, optional

1. Place onions in slow cooker and dot with butter.
2. Cover and cook on High for an hour.
3. When the butter is melted, give the onions a good stir to coat with melted butter. Salt if you wish.
4. Cover and turn to Low. Cook for 10-12 hours or until onions are caramelized to a deep brown color.

Tips:

Use to make French onion soup or quiche, or as a topping for burgers or steaks. Delicious! I like to portion these out into freezer containers and freeze for future recipes.

Variations:

If I find that my onions are getting "tired" and wilted, I'll often make a batch of caramelized onions. I have used all types of onions and find that they all work.

Good go-alongs with this recipe:

We love having these for make-your-own burgers in the summer. I'll set out toppings and folks can just add what they want. The caramelized onions are usually the first things to go.

Mediterranean Onions

Barbara Warren
Folsom, PA

Makes 4-6 servings

Prep. Time: 25 minutes
Cooking Time: 4-8 hours
Ideal slow-cooker size: 3 qt.

4 large yellow onions, sliced in thin rings
½ tsp. freshly ground pepper
1 tsp. salt
¼ tsp. turmeric
1 tsp. dried thyme
½ tsp. dried basil
1 Tbsp. butter
1 Tbsp. olive oil
1 Tbsp. fresh lemon juice
⅓ cup chopped fresh parsley
⅓ cup crumbled feta cheese
oil-cured black olives, pitted, chopped, optional

1. Combine onions, pepper, salt, turmeric, thyme, basil, butter, and olive oil in slow cooker.
2. Cover and cook on Low for 4-8 hours, stirring once or twice, until onions are soft and getting brown.
3. Remove onions to serving dish. Gently stir in lemon juice and parsley. Sprinkle with feta and optional black olives. Serve hot or room temperature.

Variations:

Add more lemon juice or even some lemon zest if the onions need some brightening up.

Good go-alongs with this recipe:

We serve the onions hot on pasta or couscous the first night. Any leftovers are next served at room temperature with crusty bread, or tucked into a pita pocket with hummus and lettuce.

Armenian Eggplant

Donna Treloar
Muncie, IN

Makes 6 servings

Prep. Time: 30 minutes
Cooking Time: 3-4 hours
Ideal slow-cooker size: 6 qt.

1 large sweet onion, diced
4 garlic cloves, chopped
4 ribs celery, diced
2 cups fresh green beans in 2" pieces
3 Tbsp. olive oil
2 tsp. dried basil
¼ tsp. black pepper
1 tsp. salt
1 medium eggplant, cubed
28-oz. can tomatoes with juice
2 Tbsp. lemon juice
2 Tbsp. capers

1. In slow cooker, combine onion, garlic, celery, green beans, olive oil, basil, black pepper, and salt.
2. Layer in eggplant. Pour tomatoes and juice over all.
3. Cover and cook on Low 3-4 hours, until vegetables are tender.
4. Add lemon juice and capers. Stir gently. Serve hot or room temperature with good bread and olive oil for dipping.

Stewed Tomatoes

Michelle Showalter
Bridgewater, VA

Makes 8-10 servings

Prep. Time: 20 minutes
Cooking Time: 4 hours
Ideal slow-cooker size: 4 qt.

2 quarts canned tomatoes (or equivalent peeled, fresh tomatoes), with 2-3 Tbsp. juice reserved and set aside
½ cup diced onion
½ cup diced green bell pepper
3 Tbsp. sugar
1 tsp. salt
¼ tsp. black pepper
dash dried basil
1 Tbsp. cornstarch

1. Combine tomatoes (reserve 2-3 Tbsp. juice), onion, bell pepper, sugar, salt, pepper, and basil in cooker.
2. Cover and cook on High 3 hours.
3. Mix cornstarch with reserved tomato juice. Whisk into hot tomato mixture, whisking until well combined. Stir occasionally until thickened, 20-40 minutes.

Tips:

Serve hot over macaroni and cheese.

Variations:

Toast bread cubes in butter in skillet, and sprinkle on top before serving. Add hot peppers and more basil if you like a more intensely flavored dish.

Good go-alongs with this recipe:

Green beans and steamed fish; fried chicken, mashed potatoes, and coleslaw.

Baked Stuffed Tomatoes

Leslie Scott
Troy, NY

Makes 6 servings

Prep. Time: 30 minutes
Cooking Time: 3-4 hours
Ideal slow-cooker size: 5 qt.

6 medium-sized tomatoes
3 Tbsp. butter, melted
2 tsp. chopped fresh basil
2 tsp. chopped fresh oregano
2 tsp. chopped fresh parsley
2 garlic cloves, minced
1 cup grated Parmesan cheese
¾ cup fine bread crumbs
salt and pepper, to taste

1. Remove cores from tomatoes, and cut away an additional inch or so underneath to make a little cavity in each tomato.
2. Mix together butter, herbs, garlic, Parmesan, bread crumbs, and salt and pepper.
3. Gently stuff each tomato with mixture.
4. Set tomatoes in lightly greased slow cooker.
5. Cover and cook on Low for 3-4 hours, until tomatoes are soft and hot through.

Zucchini Pizza-Style

Marcella Roberts
Denver, PA

Makes 6 servings

Prep. Time: 20 minutes
Cooking Time: 2½ hours
Ideal slow-cooker size: 4 qt.

3 medium zucchini, mix of yellow and green, unpeeled and cut in discs
1 large tomato, diced
½ cup pizza sauce
1 cup grated mozzarella cheese
sliced black olives, optional

1. Layer zucchini in lightly greased slow cooker, alternating colors.
2. Mix tomato and pizza sauce together. Pour over zucchini.
3. Sprinkle with mozzarella and optional black olives.
4. Cover and cook on High for 2 hours, until bubbly. Remove lid and cook an additional 30 minutes on High to dry out some of the liquid.

Tips:

Add basil and oregano and chopped garlic if you want to really amp up the pizza flavor.

Good go-alongs with this recipe:

Serve with bread sticks or French bread.

Green Bean Casserole

Beverly Hummel
Fleetwood, PA

Makes 6 servings

Prep. Time: 20 minutes
Cooking Time: 2-3 hours
Ideal slow-cooker size: 3 qt.

2 Tbsp. butter, melted
2 Tbsp. flour
1 tsp. sugar
1 cup sour cream
2 lbs. frozen green beans, cooked and drained
½ cup shredded cheddar cheese
1 cup French fried onion rings

1. In a saucepan, melt butter. Whisk in flour until smooth. Add sugar and sour cream. Stir over low heat until thick and hot.

2. Combine green beans with sour cream sauce. Place in slow cooker.

3. Sprinkle green bean mixture with cheese and onion rings.

4. Cover and cook on Low 2-3 hours.

Good go-alongs with this recipe:

Beef roast and mashed potatoes.

Southern Green Beans

Pat Bishop
Bedminster, PA

Makes 4-6 servings

Prep. Time: 10 minutes
Cooking Time: 2-4 hours
Ideal slow-cooker size: 3-4 qt.

2 cups chicken broth
1 lb. fresh or frozen cut green beans
1 cup chopped onion
½ cup cooked, chopped bacon
1 Tbsp. white vinegar
1 Tbsp. soy sauce
¼ tsp. pepper
1 clove garlic, minced

1. Toss all ingredients together in slow cooker.

2. Cover and cook on Low for 4 hours or on High for 2 hours.

Green Beans Caesar

Carol Shirk
Leola, PA

Makes 6-8 servings

Prep. Time: 15 minutes
Cooking Time: 2-3½ hours
Ideal slow-cooker size: 3-4 qt.

1½ lbs. green beans, ends trimmed
2 Tbsp. olive oil
1 Tbsp. red wine vinegar
1 Tbsp. minced garlic
salt and pepper, to taste
½ tsp. dried basil
½ tsp. dried oregano
¼ cup plain bread crumbs
¼ cup grated Parmesan cheese
1 Tbsp. butter, melted

1. In slow cooker, combine green beans, olive oil, vinegar, garlic, salt and pepper, basil, and oregano.

2. Cover and cook on High for 2-3 hours, until green beans are as soft as you like them. Stir.

3. Combine bread crumbs, Parmesan, and butter. Sprinkle over green beans and cook an additional 30 minutes on High with lid off.

Hot Fruit

Michele Ruvola
Vestal, NY

Makes 10 servings

Prep. Time: 5 minutes
Cooking Time: 2-3 hours
Ideal slow-cooker size: 5-6.5 qt.

2 24-oz. jars unsweetened, chunky applesauce
2 15-oz. cans pears, cut into bite-sized pieces, drained
2 15-oz. cans peaches, cut into bite-sized pieces, drained
14-oz. can tart pitted cherries, drained
1 Tbsp. ground cinnamon
¼ cup (½ stick) butter, sliced into 6-8 pieces

1. Combine fruits in slow cooker. Stir in cinnamon.
2. Space pats of butter over top.
3. Cook on High for 2 hours, or until hot and butter is melted. Stir once more before serving.

Variations:

Can use cans of fruit cocktail if you prefer.

Good go-alongs with this recipe:

Great with a holiday ham dinner.

Pumpkin Chutney

Ginny Birky
Cortez, CO

Makes 12-16 servings

Prep. Time: 25 minutes
Cooking Time: 4-6 hours
Ideal slow-cooker size: 3 qt.

4 cups diced, peeled raw pumpkin or winter squash
2 cups diced, peeled apples
1 cup raisins
1 cup chopped dried apricots, dates, prunes, and/or pineapple (a mixture is fine)
1 small onion, diced finely
1" piece fresh ginger, diced finely
⅓ cup dark brown sugar
2 Tbsp. apple cider vinegar
1 tsp. curry powder
½ tsp. salt

1. Combine all ingredients in slow cooker.
2. Cover and cook on Low 4-6 hours, until pumpkin and apple are soft. Stir occasionally.

Tips:

Serve hot or cold with roast pork or turkey. Also good as an appetizer with crackers and cream cheese.

Pineapple Casserole

Eunice Kauffman
Alto, MI

Makes 6-8 servings

Prep. Time: 15 minutes
Cooking Time: 2½ hours
Ideal slow-cooker size: 3 qt.

2 20-oz. cans pineapple chunks with juice
5 Tbsp. flour
¼ cup sugar
1 cup shredded sharp cheese
1½ cups cracker crumbs
5 Tbsp. butter, melted

1. In lightly greased slow cooker, pour pineapple chunks and juice.
2. Separately, mix flour and sugar. Sprinkle over pineapple.
3. Sprinkle cheese over flour mixture.
4. Cover and cook on High for 2 hours, until bubbling.
5. Mix cracker crumbs and melted butter. Sprinkle on top of casserole.
6. With lid off, cook for an additional 15-30 minutes on High.

Good go-alongs with this recipe:

Excellent side dish for a holiday meal with ham.

Cranberry Applesauce

Margaret W. High
Lancaster, PA

Makes 6-8 servings

Prep. Time: 20 minutes
Cooking Time: 3-4 hours
Ideal slow-cooker size: 3 qt.

12-oz. bag fresh or frozen cranberries
4-6 apples, mixed varieties
⅓-½ cup sugar, depending how sweet your apples are and how tart you like your sauce

1. Cut apples into eighths, no need to core or peel.
2. Combine apple slices and cranberries in slow cooker.
3. Cover and cook on Low for 3-4 hours until apples are totally soft.
4. Put hot apples and cranberries through a food mill or applesauce sieve.
5. Add sugar to taste to the hot/warm sauce, depending how tart or sweet you like things.
6. Serve room temperature or chilled.

Tips:

Our favorite way to have cranberry sauce at Thanksgiving!

Variations:

Use only 4 apples for a really deep red sauce with strong cranberry flavor, or use 6 (or more) apples to get more applesauce flavor and a lighter red. If you don't have a food mill or strainer, simply peel and core the apples before cooking. When the cranberries and apples are soft, mash them with a potato masher for a chunky texture or puree them with an immersion blender for a silky texture.

Good go-alongs with this recipe:

Creamed chicken over cornbread; split pea soup and biscuits; Swedish meatballs and egg noodles.

One day I wanted to make applesauce for my children, but I didn't want to be tied to the kitchen and the stove all day. Put on my thinking cap, and voilà! Apples in the slow cooker on Low for 6 hours, then use the potato masher.
— Melanie Miller, Flemington, NJ

My daughter's birthday party had 6 slow cookers going. I had macaroni and cheese, Spanish rice, lasagna, mashed potatoes, apple spice cake, and peach cobbler. This way there was something for all the picky eaters. — Cindy Mishou, Kingsburg, CA

I am known for baking, decorating, and selling desserts from my home. Every occasion we're invited to, I make at least one dessert. Once I made a cake in the slow cooker. It was funny to see everyone looking around and asking why I didn't bring a dessert, but when they started smelling the cake, they knew! Of course, I was proud to take the empty slow cooker home. — Delilah Swinford, Anderson, IN

Sweets and Desserts

Triple-Chocolate Lava Cake

Carol Sherwood
Batavia, NY

Makes 12 servings

Prep. Time: 15 minutes
Cooking Time: 3 4 hours
Ideal slow-cooker size: 4 qt.

15-oz. pkg. devil's food cake mix
1⅔ cups water
3 eggs
½ cup canola oil
2 cups cold 2% milk
3-oz. pkg. instant chocolate pudding
2 cups semisweet chocolate chips

1. In a large bowl, combine cake mix, water, eggs, and oil. Beat on low speed for 30 seconds. Beat on medium speed for 2 minutes.
2. Transfer to greased slow cooker.
3. In another bowl, whisk milk and pudding mix for 2 minutes. Let stand for 2 minutes or until soft set.
4. Spoon pudding over cake batter in cooker. Sprinkle with chocolate chips.
5. Cover and cook on High for 3-4 hours or until a toothpick inserted in cake portion comes out with moist crumbs. Serve warm.

Good go-alongs with this recipe:

Scoop of vanilla ice cream.

My tricks for getting my slow cooker to do its best work:

Do not lift the lid until the time is up.

Hot Fudge Cake

Lucille Hollinger
Richland, PA

Makes 8 servings

Prep. Time: 20 minutes
Cooking Time: 2-3 hours
Ideal slow-cooker size: 3 qt.

1¾ cups brown sugar, divided
1 cup flour
6 Tbsp. unsweetened cocoa powder, divided
2 tsp. baking powder
½ tsp. salt
½ cup milk
2 Tbsp. melted butter
½ tsp. vanilla
1½ cups chocolate chips
1¾ cups boiling water

1. In a small bowl, combine 1 cup brown sugar, flour, 3 Tbsp. cocoa, baking powder, and salt.
2. In another bowl, combine milk, butter, and vanilla. Stir wet into dry ingredients just until combined.
3. Spread batter into greased slow cooker. Sprinkle with chocolate chips.
4. In another bowl, combine the remaining ¾ cup brown sugar and 3 Tbsp. cocoa.
5. Stir in boiling water. Pour over batter, and do not stir.
6. Cover and cook on High for 2-3 hours, or until a toothpick inserted near center of cake comes out clean.

Tips:

Serve warm with ice cream.

Variations:

Add 1 cup chopped nuts to Step 1. Omit chocolate chips.

—Juanita Weaver

Use 2 Tbsp. vegetable oil in place of butter.

—Sylvia High

Peanut Butter Fudge Pudding Cake

Beverly Hummel
Fleetwood, PA

Makes 6 servings

Prep. Time: 20 minutes
Cooking Time: 2-3 hours on High
Ideal slow-cooker size: 3 qt.

¼ cup brown sugar
½ cup flour
2 Tbsp. unsweetened cocoa powder
1 tsp. baking powder
½ tsp. salt
½ cup milk
2 Tbsp. melted butter
½ tsp. vanilla
¼ cup peanut butter, your choice of chunky or smooth

Topping:
2 Tbsp. unsweetened cocoa powder
½ cup sugar
1 cup boiling water

1. To make cake, combine brown sugar, flour, cocoa powder, salt, and baking powder in a good-sized bowl.
2. Add milk, melted butter, peanut butter, and vanilla and stir until smooth.
3. Pour into greased slow cooker.
4. To make Topping, mix cocoa powder, sugar, and boiling water together.
5. Pour over mixture in slow cooker. Do not stir.
6. Cover. Cook on High 1½-2 hours, or until toothpick inserted in center of cake comes out clean.
7. Serve warm. If you've refrigerated any leftovers, warm them in the microwave before eating.

Toffee Treasure Cake

Jeanne Allen
Los Alamos, NM

Makes 12-15 servings

Prep. Time: 30 minutes
Cooking Time: 2-4 hours
Ideal slow-cooker size: oval or round 6 or 7 qt.

¼ cup sugar
1 tsp. cinnamon
2 cups flour
1 cup sugar
1½ tsp. baking powder
1 tsp. baking soda
¼ tsp. salt
1 tsp. vanilla
8 oz. sour cream
1 stick (½ cup) butter, softened
2 eggs
¼ cup chopped nuts of your choice
6⅝-oz. chocolate-toffee candy bars, coarsely crushed
½ stick (¼ cup) butter
melted confectioners' sugar, optional

1. Combine ¼ cup sugar and 1 tsp. cinnamon. Set aside.
2. Grease interior of slow-cooker crock, or a 9x5 or 8x4 loaf pan, or a baking dish that fits into your slow cooker.
3. In a mixer bowl, combine flour, 1 cup sugar, baking powder, baking soda, salt, vanilla, sour cream, 1 stick softened butter, and eggs.
4. Blend at low speed until moistened. Beat 3 minutes at medium speed, scraping bowl occasionally.
5. Spoon half of batter into greased crock, loaf pan, or baking dish.
6. Sprinkle with cinnamon-sugar mixture, then with nuts and crushed candy bars.
7. Top with remaining batter.
8. Pour ½ stick of melted butter over top.
9. Either suspend loaf pan from edges of slow-cooker crock or place loaf pan or baking dish on jar rings or small trivet in bottom of crock.
10. Prop slow-cooker lid open at one end with a wooden spoon handle or chopstick to allow steam to escape.
11. Cook on High 2-4 hours, or until tester inserted in middle of cake comes out clean.
12. Remove pan or dish from cooker and allow to cool.
13. Cut into slices or squares with a plastic or silicone knife.
14. If you wish, dust with confectioners' sugar and serve.

Bay Pound Cake

Nancy J. Reppert
Mechanicsburg, PA

Makes 12 servings

Prep. Time: 30 minutes
Cooking Time: 3-4 hours
Ideal slow-cooker size: 6 qt.

4 bay leaves
½ cup milk
½ cup (1 stick) butter, softened
¾ cup sugar
2 eggs, room temperature
1 cup all-purpose flour
½ cup whole wheat flour
¼ tsp. salt
1 tsp. baking powder

1. Mix together bay leaves and milk in saucepan. Heat until milk is steaming hot, stirring occasionally. Set aside to cool to room temperature.
2. When milk is cooled, beat butter until fluffy.
3. Add sugar and beat again. Add eggs and beat again.
4. Separately, stir together flours, salt, and baking powder. Stir gently into butter mixture until just barely blended.
5. Strain bay leaves from milk. Add milk to batter, stirring until just mixed. Do not overmix.
6. Prepare an 8x4 loaf pan by greasing and flouring. It should fit into your slow cooker without touching the sides. Place a jar lid or ring or trivet on the floor of the crock so the loaf pan will not sit directly on the floor of the crock.
7. Pour batter into prepared pan. Place pan on jar lid/ring/trivet.
8. Cover slow cooker and prop the lid open at one end with a wooden chopstick or wooden spoon handle.
9. Cook on High for 3-4 hours, until tester inserted in middle of cake comes out clean.
10. Wearing oven gloves to protect your knuckles, remove hot pan from cooker. Allow to cool 10 minutes before running a knife around the edge and turning cake out onto a cooling rack. Serve warm or room temperature, plain or with saucy fruit.

Perfectly Peachy Cake

Ruthie Schiefer
Vassar, MI

Makes 4-6 servings

Prep. Time: 20 minutes
Cooking Time: 6-8 hours
Ideal slow-cooker size: 3 qt.

¾ cup biscuit baking mix
¼ cup brown sugar, packed
⅓ cup sugar
2 eggs, beaten
2 tsp. vanilla
¼ cup evaporated milk
2 Tbsp. butter, melted
3 peaches, peeled, pitted, and mashed
¾ tsp. ground cinnamon
vanilla ice cream or whipped cream, for serving

1. In large bowl, combine baking mix and sugars.
2. Stir in eggs and vanilla until blended. Mix in milk and butter.
3. Fold in peaches and cinnamon until well mixed.
4. Spoon mixture into lightly greased slow cooker. Lay a double layer of paper towels across the top of the cooker (to absorb condensation).
5. Cover and cook on Low 6-8 hours.
6. Serve warm with a scoop of ice cream or a dollop of whipped cream.

Banana Chocolate Chip Bars

Carol Huber
Austin, TX

Makes 12-15 servings

Prep. Time: 20 minutes
Cooking Time: 2-3 hours
Ideal slow-cooker size: oval 6 or 7 qt.

1½ sticks (¾ cup) butter, softened
⅔ cup granulated sugar
⅔ cup brown sugar
2 eggs
1 tsp. vanilla
3 ripe bananas, mashed
2 cups flour
2 tsp. baking powder
½ tsp. salt
12-oz. pkg. semisweet chocolate chips

1. Grease a 9x5 or 8x4 loaf pan that will either hang on the edges of your oval slow-cooker crock, or will sit down in the slow-cooker crock on metal jar rings or small trivet.
2. In a good-sized mixing bowl, cream together butter and sugars.
3. Add eggs and vanilla. Mix well.
4. Stir in mashed bananas and stir well.
5. In a medium bowl, sift together flour, baking powder, and salt.
6. Stir dry ingredients into creamed mixture.
7. Stir in chocolate chips.
8. Pour into greased loaf pan.
9. Suspend pan on edges of slow-cooker crock, or place on trivet or jar rings on bottom of crock.
10. Vent slow-cooker lid at one end by propping it open with a wooden spoon handle or chopstick.
11. Cook on High 2-3 hours, or until toothpick inserted in center comes out clean.
12. Uncover pan and remove from cooker. Let cool before slicing into bars.

Gooey Cookie Dessert

Sue Hamilton
Benson, AZ

Makes 8 servings

Prep. Time: 10 minutes
Cooking Time: 2 hours
Ideal slow-cooker size: 5 qt.

3½ cups full-fat vanilla ice cream (half of 1.75-quart container)
16.5-oz. roll refrigerator ready-to-bake chocolate chip cookie dough

1. Turn empty slow cooker to High to preheat.
2. Place ice cream in warmed crock, spreading and pushing it to make it a layer. Lumps are fine—they will melt.
3. Slice cookie dough into 12 slices.
4. Press the slices into the ice cream.
5. Cover and cook on High for 2 hours, until edges are browning and the center is cooked.

Tips:

Great served warm with whipped cream. It might be good cold but there is never any left. Instead of measuring the ice cream, I cut the container in half. It saves the mess of measuring.

Variations:

Use different ice creams and different cookies—there are many flavor options!

If you want your bar cookies to have clean edges, use a pizza cutter to cut them.

Cinnamon Bread Pudding

Orpha Herr
Andover, NY

Makes 6 servings

Prep. Time: 15 minutes
Cooking Time: 3 hours
Ideal slow-cooker size: 4 qt.

8 cups cubed, stale cinnamon rolls (scrape any frosting off), or cinnamon bread
1 cup raisins
2 cups milk
4 eggs
¼ cup sugar
¼ cup (½ stick) butter, melted
½ tsp. vanilla
¼ tsp. ground nutmeg
¼ tsp. salt

1. Place cubed rolls or bread in lightly greased slow cooker.
2. Stir raisins into cubed bread.
3. In mixing bowl, combine milk, eggs, sugar, butter, vanilla, nutmeg, and salt.
4. Pour milk mixture evenly over bread/raisins. Stir gently.
5. Cover and cook on Low for 3-4 hours, stirring edges into the middle after the first hour. Pudding is done when it is set in middle and lightly browned at edges.

My tricks for getting my slow cooker to do its best work:

If I'm cooking something that is collecting and keeping too much moisture, I prop the lid open with a toothpick or two.

Bread Pudding with Caramel Sauce

Frances Kruba
Baltimore, MD

Makes 6 servings

Prep. Time: 25 minutes
Cooking Time: 4 hours
Ideal slow-cooker size: 3 qt.

8 slices bread, cubed
4 eggs
2 cups milk
¼ cup sugar
¼ cup (½ stick) butter, melted
¼ cup raisins
½ tsp. ground cinnamon

Caramel Sauce:
2 Tbsp. butter
2 Tbsp. all-purpose flour
1 cup water
¾ cup brown sugar
¼ tsp. salt
1 tsp. vanilla

1. Place bread cubes in greased slow cooker.
2. In a bowl, whisk together eggs, milk, sugar, butter, raisins, and cinnamon.
3. Pour over bread cubes.
4. Cover and cook on High 1 hour. Stir edges into middle. Cover again and cook on Low 2-3 more hours until set in the middle. Remove lid and allow to cool a bit while you make Sauce.
5. Make Caramel Sauce just before serving. Melt butter in saucepan.
6. Stir in flour until smooth. Add water, sugar, and salt. Bring to boil and stir for 2 minutes or until thickened. Add vanilla.
7. Serve hot sauce with warm bread pudding.

Noodle Pudding

Jean Harris Robinson
Pemberton, NJ

Makes 12 servings

Prep. Time: 30 minutes
Cooking Time: 2 hours
Ideal slow-cooker size: 3-4 qt.

18 oz. wide egg noodles, uncooked
6 eggs
1½ cups ricotta cheese
1 cup sour cream
¾ cup sugar
2¼ cups whole milk
¾ cup golden raisins
6 Tbsp. butter, melted
1 Tbsp. vanilla
1 tsp. grated orange zest
1 tsp. lemon zest or 1 Tbsp. lemon juice
1 Tbsp. salt

1. Cook noodles in boiling water until just barely tender, very al dente. Drain and set aside.
2. In a mixing bowl, whisk eggs. Add ricotta, sour cream, and sugar. Whisk again.
3. Add milk, raisins, and melted butter. Whisk. Add vanilla, orange zest, lemon zest, and salt. Whisk.
4. Stir noodles into egg mixture. Pour in slow cooker.
5. Cover and cook on High for 2 hours or until set in the middle.

Tips:

Combine everything except for noodles the night before and refrigerate. When you're ready to make the Pudding, just cook the noodles and add the liquid.

Apple Cobbler

Kendra Dreps
Liberty, PA

Makes 8 servings

Prep. Time: 25 minutes
Cooking Time: 2-4 hours
Ideal slow-cooker size: 4-6 qt.

7-8 apples, peeled and sliced
2½ cups sugar, divided
¾ tsp. cinnamon, divided
2 cups flour
2 tsp. baking powder
¾ tsp. salt
2 eggs
⅔ cup butter, melted

1. Combine apples, ½ cup sugar, and ½ tsp. cinnamon. Place in greased slow cooker.
2. Combine ¼ tsp. cinnamon, flour, 2 tsp. baking powder, salt, and eggs. Pour evenly on top of apples.
3. Pour melted butter over all.
4. Cover and cook on Low for 2-4 hours, until apples are tender and top is baked.

Tips:

Serve warm with vanilla ice cream.

Apple Crisp

Judi Manos
West Islip, NY

Makes 12 servings

Prep. Time: 20 minutes
Cooking Time: 4 hours
Ideal slow-cooker size: 6 qt.

3.4-oz. pkg. vanilla instant pudding
½ cup sugar, divided
1 tsp. ground cinnamon
3 lbs. Granny Smith apples, about 10, peeled, sliced
1 cup dried cranberries
6 Tbsp. butter, melted, divided
12 vanilla wafers, coarsely chopped
¼ cup sliced almonds or pecans

1. Mix dry pudding mix, ¼ cup sugar, and cinnamon.
2. Toss apples and cranberries with 4 Tbsp. melted butter in large bowl. Add pudding mixture and mix lightly.
3. Spoon into slow cooker. Cover and cook on Low 4-6 hours or High 2-3 hours.
4. Meanwhile, combine chopped wafers, nuts, and remaining 2 Tbsp. melted butter and ¼ cup sugar in shallow microwaveable dish. Microwave on High 1 minute. Stir. Microwave 1½-2 minutes more or until golden brown, stirring every 30 seconds. Cool.
5. Sprinkle apple mixture with cooled nut mixture just before serving.

Tips:

Serve with vanilla ice cream. Add ½ tsp. ground nutmeg. I sometimes double the vanilla wafers to 24 and the nuts to ½ cup for the topping.

Variations:

Can use 1 cup fresh or frozen cranberries instead of dried cranberries.

My tricks for getting my slow cooker to do its best work:

If too much moisture forms on the lid, put paper towel over crockpot and then put the lid on. Too much moisture could make apples mushy.

Extra-Crisp Apple Crisp

Christina Gerber
Apple Creek, OH

Makes 4 servings

Prep. Time: 15 minutes
Cooking Time: 3-6 hours
Ideal slow-cooker size: 6 qt.

5-6 cups tart apples, sliced
¾ cup (1½ sticks) butter
1 cup rolled or quick oats
1½ cups flour
1 cup brown sugar, packed
3 tsp. ground cinnamon

1. Place apples in lightly greased slow cooker.
2. Separately, melt butter. Add rest of ingredients and mix well.
3. Crumble topping over apples.
4. Cover and cook on High for 3 hours or Low for 4-6 hours. Allow cooker to sit, turned off with lid removed, for about 30 minutes before serving, so Crisp is nicely warm for serving.

Tips:

This is the recipe for people who can never get enough crisp topping on their apple crisp!

Variations:

Add 1 tsp. salt to topping in Step 2.

Good go-alongs with this recipe:

Ice cream or whipped cream.

Apple Pandowdy

Ann Mather
Lansing, MI

Makes 8 servings

Prep. Time: 20-30 minutes
Cooking Time: 2-3 hours
Ideal slow-cooker size: 4 qt.

5 cups peeled, sliced apples
1 cup brown sugar
¼ cup flour
¼ tsp. salt
1 tsp. vinegar
1 cup water
¼ tsp. cinnamon
dash nutmeg
1 tsp. lemon juice
1 tsp. vanilla
¼ stick (2 Tbsp.) butter, melted
1 cup flour
2 tsp. baking powder
¾ tsp. salt
3 Tbsp. shortening
¾ cup milk

1. Grease interior of slow-cooker crock.
2. Arrange apples evenly over bottom of crock.
3. In a saucepan, mix together brown sugar, ¼ cup flour, and ¼ tsp. salt.
4. Stir in vinegar and water.
5. Cook, stirring constantly until thickened. Cool.
6. Stir in cinnamon, nutmeg, lemon juice, vanilla, and butter. Mix well.
7. Pour over apples.
8. In a bowl, sift together 1 cup flour, baking powder, and ¾ tsp. salt. Cut in shortening with 2 knives or pastry cutter until mixture is crumbly.
9. Add milk. Mix well.
10. Drop dough by spoonfuls over top of apples and sauce.
11. Prop slow-cooker lid open at one end with a wooden spoon handle or chopstick to allow steam to escape.
12. Cook on High 2-3 hours, or until toothpick inserted in dough comes out clean and dough begins to pull away from the sides of the cooker.
13. Serve warm from slow cooker.

I make jams, fruit butters, and sometimes chutneys in it, depending on the recipe. I hate standing by the stove, so this way is much easier, much faster, and the results taste great. I cherish my slow cooker—I can't imagine life without it! —Kathaleen Jones, Rancho Cordova, CA

Crockery Apple Pie

Ruthie Schiefer
Vassar, MI

Makes 10-12 servings

Prep. Time: 20 minutes
Cooking Time: 6-7 hours
Ideal slow-cooker size: 4 qt.

8 tart apples, peeled, cored, and sliced
2 tsp. ground cinnamon
¼ tsp. ground allspice
¼ tsp. ground nutmeg
¾ cup milk
2 Tbsp. butter, softened
¾ cup sugar
2 eggs, beaten
1 tsp. vanilla
1½ cups biscuit baking mix, divided
⅓ cup brown sugar, packed
3 Tbsp. cold butter

1. In large bowl, toss apples with spices. Spoon mixture into lightly greased slow cooker.
2. In separate bowl, combine milk, soft butter, sugar, eggs, vanilla, and ½ cup baking mix. Stir to mix well.
3. Spoon batter over apples.
4. Place remaining baking mix in small bowl. Cut cold butter into it with a pasty cutter until coarse crumbs form.
5. Sprinkle crumbs over batter in slow cooker.
6. Cover and cook on Low for 6-7 hours.

Variations:

I like to use my homemade biscuit mix instead of store bought: 5 cups all-purpose flour, ¼ cup baking powder, 1 Tbsp. sugar, 1 tsp. salt, ¾ cup vegetable oil. Mix well. Store in tight container.

—Kelly Bailey

Baked Apples

Karen Ceneviva
Seymour, CT

Makes 6-8 servings

Prep. Time: 20 minutes
Cooking Time: 2-7 hours
Ideal slow-cooker size: 5 qt.

2 Tbsp. raisins
¼ cup sugar
6-8 medium baking apples, washed and cored
1 tsp. ground cinnamon
2 Tbsp. butter

1. Mix raisins and sugar and fill center of apples.
2. Place apples in cooker. Sprinkle with cinnamon and dot with butter. Add ½ cup water.
3. Cover and cook on Low 6-7 hours or High 2-3 hours.

Tips:

Use as many apples as you can fit in your slow cooker.

Good go-alongs with this recipe:

Whipped cream.

My tips for converting oven and stove-top recipes into good slow cooker recipes:

Use less liquid, about half the recommended amount in the traditional recipe.

Slow-Cooker Peach Crisp

Amanda Gross
Souderton, PA

Makes 6 servings

Prep. Time: 15 minutes
Cooking Time: 4-5 hours
Ideal slow-cooker size: 6 qt.

¼ cup biscuit baking mix
⅔ cup quick or rolled oats
1½ tsp. ground cinnamon
¾ cup brown sugar
4 cups canned peaches, cut in quarters or slices, juice reserved
½ cup peach juice from jar

1. Mix together biscuit mix, oats, cinnamon, and brown sugar in a bowl.
2. Place peaches and juice in greased slow cooker.
3. Add oat mix. Stir gently once or twice so as not to break the peaches.
4. Cook on Low 4-5 hours. Remove lid for the last 30 minutes of cooking.

Variations:

Use canned pears instead of peaches.

Good go-alongs with this recipe:

Vanilla ice cream is a must to pair with this dish!

My tricks for getting my slow cooker to do its best work:

Grease your crockpot!

Sour Cherry Cobbler

Margaret W. High
Lancaster, PA

Makes 6-8 servings

Prep. Time: 20 minutes
Cooking Time: 2 hours
Ideal slow-cooker size: 6 qt.

½ cup whole wheat flour
¾ cup all-purpose flour, divided
1 Tbsp. sugar, plus ⅔ cup sugar, divided
1 tsp. baking powder
¼ tsp. salt
¼ tsp. ground cinnamon
¼ tsp. almond extract
1 egg
¼ cup milk
2 Tbsp. melted butter
4 cups pitted sour cherries, thawed and drained if frozen

1. In mixing bowl, combine whole wheat flour and ½ cup all-purpose flour. Mix in 1 Tbsp. sugar, baking powder, salt, and cinnamon.
2. Separately, combine almond extract, egg, milk, and butter. Stir into dry ingredients just until moistened.
3. Spread batter in bottom of greased slow cooker.
4. Separately, mix remaining ¼ cup flour with ⅔ cup sugar. Add cherries. Sprinkle cherry mixture evenly over batter in slow cooker.
5. Cover and cook on High 2 hours or until lightly browned at edges and juice is bubbling from cherries.

Tips:

Cobblers are wonderful served warm with vanilla ice cream, whipped cream, or custard sauce.

Variations:

Use blueberries instead of sour cherries. Reduce sugar to ½ cup and use vanilla extract instead of almond.

Chocolate Blueberry Dessert

Sharon Timpe
Jackson, WI

Makes 6-8 servings

Prep. Time: 5 minutes
Cooking Time: 3 hours on Low
Ideal slow-cooker size: 3 qt.

21-oz. can blueberry pie filling
15-oz. pkg. chocolate cake mix
½ cup (1 stick) butter, melted
1 tsp. ground cinnamon

1. Pour pie filling in lightly greased slow cooker.
2. Combine dry cake mix and cinnamon. Mix in melted butter.
3. Sprinkle over pie filling.
4. Cover and cook on Low for 3 hours. Allow to cool a bit before serving with ice cream or whipped cream.

Variations:

Use cherry pie filling and yellow cake mix; sprinkle with 1 cup white chocolate chips in Step 3.

—Michele Ruvola

Omit butter and cinnamon. Spread half the dry cake mix in crock, half the pie filling, and repeat layers.

—Marla Folkerts

Pumpkin Pie Pudding

Orpha Herr
Andover, NY

Makes 6-8 servings

Prep. Time: 10 minutes
Cooking Time: 5-7 hours
Ideal slow-cooker size: 3 qt.

15-oz. can solid-pack pumpkin
12-oz. can evaporated milk
¾ cup sugar
½ cup biscuit baking mix
2 eggs, beaten
2 Tbsp. melted butter
2½ tsp. pumpkin pie spice
2 tsp. vanilla
whipped cream or ice cream, for serving

1. In large bowl, combine all ingredients (except for whipped cream or ice cream).
2. Transfer to lightly greased slow cooker.
3. Cover and cook on Low for 5-7 hours or until set and a cooking thermometer reads 160°.
4. Serve in bowls with whipped cream or ice cream.

Pinescotch Pudding

Lorene Diener
Arthur, IL

Makes 10-12 servings

Prep. Time: 30 minutes
Cooking Time: 2-3 hours
Ideal slow-cooker size: 4 qt.

Pineapple Mixture:
1½ cups flour
½ tsp. salt
2 tsp. baking powder
4 eggs
2 cups sugar
2 tsp. vanilla
2 cups crushed pineapple, drained and juice reserved for Sauce below
1 cup broken nuts of your choice
whipped topping

Butterscotch Sauce:
1 stick (½ cup) butter
1⅓ Tbsp. cornstarch
2 cups brown sugar
½ cup pineapple juice, reserved from crushed pineapple
½ cup water
2 eggs, beaten
2 tsp. vanilla

1. Grease interior of slow-cooker crock.
2. In a medium bowl, sift together flour, salt, and baking powder.
3. In a large bowl, beat 4 eggs until well mixed. Gradually add sugar, beating until mixture is ivory colored. Stir in 2 tsp. vanilla and mix well.
4. Fold in drained pineapple and nuts.
5. Gently fold in dry ingredients.
6. Pour into slow-cooker crock.
7. Cover top of cooker with 3 paper towels before you put the lid on. The towels will absorb condensation and prevent it from dripping down on the Pudding.
8. Place cooker cover on top of paper towels. Cook on High 2-3 hours, or until tester inserted in middle of Pudding comes out clean.
9. While Pudding is cooking, make Butterscotch Sauce by melting butter in a saucepan.
10. Blend in cornstarch, stirring constantly.
11. Add brown sugar, pineapple juice, and water. Boil 3 minutes, stirring frequently.
12. Beat 2 eggs in small bowl. Add a bit of hot Sauce to eggs and stir.
13. Then stir eggs into hot Sauce and cook 1 minute.
14. Stir in 2 tsp. vanilla.
15. Cool slightly before serving.
16. Remove crock from cooker and let stand with the cake, uncovered, until nearly cool.
17. Slice with a plastic or silicone knife and serve with whipped topping or Butterscotch Sauce.

Grapenut Pudding

Florence Miller
Elizabethtown, PA

Makes 6-8 servings

Prep. Time: 20 minutes
Cooking Time: 4-6 hours
Ideal slow-cooker size: 3 qt.

5 cups whole milk
2 eggs, beaten
1 Tbsp. cornstarch
⅔ cup sugar
1 tsp. vanilla
¼ tsp. ground nutmeg
¼ tsp. salt
1 cup grapenuts
¾ cup raisins
1 Tbsp. butter

1. In a mixing bowl, whisk milk, eggs, cornstarch, sugar, vanilla, nutmeg, and salt.
2. Stir in grapenuts and raisins.
3. Grease crock with butter.
4. Pour milk mixture into crock.
5. Cover and cook on Low for 4-6 hours, stirring twice in the first hour, until pudding is thick.
6. Allow to cool to warm before serving, or chill and serve later.

Good go-alongs with this recipe:

Lovely topped with real whipped cream and some fresh berries or peaches.

Real Tapioca Pudding

Ruthie Schiefer
Vassar, MI

Makes 4-6 servings

Prep. Time: 10 minutes
Cooking Time: 2½ hours
Ideal slow-cooker size: 3 qt.

½ cup small pearl tapioca
4 cups 2% milk, room temperature
¾ cup sugar
½ tsp. vanilla
pinch salt
2 large eggs

1. Place tapioca, milk, sugar, vanilla, and salt in slow cooker. Stir.
2. Cover and cook on Low for 2 hours.
3. In mixing bowl, thoroughly whisk eggs.
4. Continue whisking and add a large spoonful of hot tapioca mixture. Once combined, add another hot spoonful and whisk well. This prevents eggs from curdling in the next step.
5. Thoroughly fold egg mixture into remaining tapioca mixture in slow cooker.
6. Cover. Turn to High and let cook 30 additional minutes, stirring every 10 minutes, or until tapioca pearls are plump and translucent and pudding is thick.
7. Serve warm or chilled.

Simple Egg Custard

Paula Winchester
Kansas City, MO

Makes 6 servings

Prep. Time: 25 minutes
Cooking Time: 2-3 hours
Ideal slow-cooker size: 6 qt.

1½ cups whole milk
1 cup half-and-half
3 eggs
⅓ cup sugar
½ tsp. vanilla extract
pinch salt

1. In mixing bowl, whisk ingredients well until smooth and totally combined.
2. Prepare slow cooker by finding a shallow oval baking dish that can fit inside. Place jar rings or lids or trivets on the floor of the crock so the baking dish is not touching the bottom or sides of the crock.
3. Pour custard liquid in baking dish. Set in crock.
4. Carefully pour water into the crock (not the baking dish!) to reach halfway up the side of the baking dish.
5. Cover slow cooker. Cook on High for 2-4 hours, or until custard is set in the middle.
6. Wearing oven gloves to protect your knuckles, remove baking dish from cooker. Allow to cool for at least 20 minutes before serving warm. May also serve chilled.

Tips:

There are different ways to flavor the Custard. Heat the milk and add 1 bay leaf. Allow to steep and cool. Remove bay leaf and proceed with Step 1. Alternatively, sprinkle top of Custard with ½ tsp. ground nutmeg or cinnamon in Step 3.

Variations:

May use 4-5 baking ramekins instead of 1 shallow baking dish.

Good go-alongs with this recipe:

Any fresh fruit, especially berries that have been lightly sugared. Lovely served chilled with sliced peaches and buttered toast for a summer breakfast.

Easy Rice Pudding

Michele Ruvola
Vestal, NY

Makes 6 servings

Prep. Time: 5 minutes
Cooking Time: 4 hours
Ideal slow-cooker size: 5 qt.

2 quarts whole milk
1 cup Arborio rice, uncooked
1 cup sugar
3 Tbsp. butter
1 tsp. vanilla
½ tsp. ground cinnamon
dash salt

1. Combine ingredients in slow cooker. Stir.
2. Cover and cook on Low for 4 hours, until creamy and thickened. Serve warm or chilled.

Variations:

Add raisins, nuts, or cranberries for different variations of pudding. Add ½ tsp. ground cardamom for another variation. For an adult version, add rum-soaked raisins to pudding and cook for 15 minutes more to heat through. Use vanilla soy milk in place of cow's milk, although the pudding will be less creamy.

Brown Rice Pudding

Colleen Heatwole
Burton, MI

Makes 6 servings

Prep. Time: 15 minutes
Cooking Time: 4-6 hours
Ideal slow-cooker size: 3 qt.

2½ cups cooked brown rice
1½ cups evaporated milk
3 eggs, beaten
½ cup raisins
½ cup brown sugar
2 Tbsp. butter, softened, plus a little more for the crock
½ tsp. ground cinnamon
½ tsp. salt
2 tsp. vanilla

1. Combine all ingredients thoroughly in mixing bowl.
2. Pour into buttered slow cooker.
3. Cover and cook on Low 4-6 hours, stirring once after the first hour. Allow to cool to warm before serving.

Tips:

Lovely with whipped cream and some more fruit on top.

Variations:

Can be doubled.

Strawberry Rhubarb Sauce

Tina Snyder
Manheim, PA

Makes 8 servings

Prep. Time: 15 minutes
Cooking Time: 4-6 hours
Ideal slow-cooker size: 3 qt.

6 cups chopped rhubarb
¾ cup sugar
1 cinnamon stick
½ cup white grape juice
pinch salt
2 cups chopped fresh strawberries

1. In slow cooker, stir together rhubarb, sugar, cinnamon stick, and grape juice.
2. Cover and cook on Low for 4-6 hours, until rhubarb is tender.
3. Stir in strawberries and cook 30 minutes longer.
4. Remove cinnamon stick. Chill.

Good go-alongs with this recipe:

Serve as a sauce over pudding, angel food cake, or ice cream.

Bold Butterscotch Sauce

Margaret W. High
Lancaster, PA

Makes 16 servings

Prep. Time: 10 minutes
Cooking Time: 2-3 hours
Ideal slow-cooker size: 3 qt.

½ cup (1 stick) salted butter
1 cup dark brown sugar, packed
1 cup heavy cream
½ tsp. salt, or more to taste
2 tsp. vanilla extract, or more to taste

1. Cut butter in slices. Add to heat-proof bowl that will fit in your slow cooker.
2. Add sugar, cream, and salt.
3. Add water to crock and place bowl with butter mixture in crock so that water comes halfway up its sides.
4. Cover and cook on High for 2-3 hours, until sauce is steaming hot.
5. Wearing oven mitts to protect your knuckles, remove hot bowl from cooker.
6. Add vanilla. Stir. Taste. Add more vanilla and/or salt to achieve a bold butterscotch flavor.

Tips:

Store Butterscotch in lidded jar in fridge for several weeks. Warm and stir before serving.

Good go-alongs with this recipe:

Fabulous poured over chocolate cake, gingerbread, angel food cake with berries, vanilla ice cream, sliced pears, and graham cracker pudding (and also eaten straight from the fridge, cold!).

Hot Fudge Sauce

Marlene Fonken
Upland, CA

Prep. Time: 10 minutes
Cooking Time: 2½ hours
Ideal slow-cooker size: 1-3 qt.

1 cup sugar
⅓ cup baking cocoa
2 Tbsp. flour
¼ tsp. salt
1 cup boiling water
1 Tbsp. butter, melted
1 tsp. vanilla

1. Grease interior of slow-cooker crock.
2. Place all ingredients in slow cooker and stir together.
3. Cover and cook on High 30 minutes.
4. Stir with a whisk to eliminate any lumps and to keep from sticking on the bottom.
5. Cover. Cook on Low 30 minutes.
6. Stir again with a whisk to remove lumps and prevent sticking.
7. Cover. Cook on Low 1½ hours.
8. Stir and serve warm over ice cream, pound cake, apple or strawberry slices, or banana chunks.

Dulce de Leche

Rebekah Zehr
Lowville, NY

Makes 8-10 servings

Prep. Time: 5 minutes
Cooking Time: 8-10 hours
Ideal slow-cooker size: 1 qt.

14-oz. can sweetened condensed milk

1. Pour sweetened condensed milk in a pint-sized canning jar. Loosely place lid on jar.
2. Fill slow cooker ¾ full of water and place jar in water, making sure water doesn't completely cover jar.
3. Cook on Low for 8-10 hours, until milk has turned a caramel color.

Tips:

This caramel-like topping is great with a variety of desserts including ice cream, cookies, mixed into frosting, or added to coffee. Also a pretty delicious spread on toast for breakfast!

Chocolate Fondue

Jessalyn Wantland
Paris, TX

Makes 6 servings

Prep. Time: 5 minutes
Cooking Time: 1 hour
Ideal slow-cooker size: 1-2 qt.

2 cups milk chocolate chips
⅔ cup half-and-half

1. Stir chocolate chips and half-and-half together in greased slow cooker.
2. Cover and cook on Low for 1 hour. Stir halfway through cooking time and again when Fondue is finished.

Tips:

Dip fresh strawberries or chunks of angel food cake, or anything, really, that you think needs a chocolate coat.

Chocolate Nut Clusters from the Crock

A. Catherine Boshart
Lebanon, PA

Makes 24 servings

Prep. Time: 15 minutes
Cooking Time: 2 hours
Chilling Time: 45 minutes
Ideal slow-cooker size: 4 qt.

1½-lb. pkg. almond bark
4-oz. pkg. sweet German chocolate bar
8 oz. dark chocolate chips
8 oz. peanut butter chips
1 lb. salted peanuts
1 lb. unsalted peanuts

1. Layer ingredients into slow cooker in order as listed.
2. Cover. Cook on Low for 2 hours. Do not stir or lift lid during cooking time.
3. At end of 2 hours, stir and mix well.
4. Drop by teaspoonfuls or tablespoonfuls on wax paper or parchment paper.
5. Refrigerate for 45 minutes until hard.
6. Store in tight container in cool place.

Dates in Cardamom Coffee Syrup

Margaret W. High
Lancaster, PA

Makes 12 servings

Prep. Time: 15 minutes
Cooking Time: 7-8 hours
Ideal slow-cooker size: 3 qt.

2 cups pitted, whole dried dates
2½ cups very strong, hot coffee
2 Tbsp. sugar
15 whole green cardamom pods
4" cinnamon stick
plain Greek yogurt, for serving

1. Combine dates, coffee, sugar, cardamom, and cinnamon in slow cooker.
2. Cover and cook on High for 1 hour. Remove lid and continue to cook on High for 6-7 hours until sauce has reduced.
3. Pour dates and sauce into container and chill in fridge.
4. To serve, put a scoop of Greek yogurt in a small dish and add a few dates on top. Drizzle with a little sauce.

Tips:

I make decaf coffee for this recipe, using a few extra scoops of ground coffee when I make it. The dates get tastier the longer they sit in the sauce, up to 2 weeks in the fridge.

Pears in Ginger Sauce

Sharon Timpe
Jackson, WI

Makes 6 servings

Prep. Time: 20 minutes
Cooking Time: 3-5 hours
Standing Time: 45 minutes
Ideal slow-cooker size: 6 qt.

6 fresh pears with stems
1 cup white wine
½ cup sugar
½ cup water
3 Tbsp. lemon juice
1 tsp. ground ginger
pinch nutmeg
pinch salt
¼ cup toasted coconut, for serving

1. Peel pears, leaving whole with stems intact.
2. Place pears in buttered slow cooker, upright, shaving bottoms slightly if necessary.
3. Combine wine, sugar, water, lemon juice, ginger, nutmeg, and salt. Pour evenly over pears.
4. Cover and cook on Low for 3-5 hours until pears are tender.
5. Allow pears and liquid to cool.
6. To serve, set a pear in a dessert dish, drizzle with sauce, and sprinkle with toasted coconut.

Festive Applesauce

Dawn Day
Westminster, CA

Makes 12 servings

Prep. Time: 25 minutes
Cooking Time: 6 hours
Ideal slow-cooker size: 5 qt.

8 medium apples, mixed varieties, peeled and cubed
5 pears, peeled and cubed
1 cup fresh or frozen cranberries
1" piece fresh ginger root, minced
3 Tbsp. dark brown sugar
½ cup apple cider
3 tsp. ground cinnamon
¼ tsp. ground nutmeg
¼ tsp. ground cloves
pinch salt
juice and zest of 1 lemon

1. Combine all ingredients in slow cooker except for lemon zest and juice.
2. Cover and cook on Low for 6 hours, until apples and pears are soft and falling apart.
3. Stir in lemon zest and juice. Serve hot, warm, or chilled.

Good go-alongs with this recipe:

Also makes a nice side dish with pork or chicken for a holiday.

Golden Compote

Judi Manos
West Islip, NY

Makes 8 servings

Prep. Time: 10 minutes
Cooking Time: 4-6 hours
Ideal slow-cooker size: 3 qt.

1-lb. 13-oz. can peach slices in juice, undrained
½ cup halved dried apricots
¼ cup golden raisins
¼ tsp. ground cinnamon
¼ tsp. ground nutmeg
¾ cup orange juice

1. Combine all ingredients in slow cooker, being sure fruit is covered with liquid.
2. Cover and cook on Low for 4-6 hours.
3. Serve warm or chilled as a sauce for sponge cake, vanilla tapioca, or ice cream.

Cranberry Apple Compote

Charlotte Shaffer
East Earl, PA

Makes 8 servings

Prep. Time: 15 minutes
Cooking Time: 4-6 hours
Ideal slow-cooker size: 3 qt.

6 apples, peeled and sliced
1 cup fresh cranberries
¾ cup sugar
zest and juice of ½ orange
2 Tbsp. red wine
pinch salt
pinch cinnamon
Greek yogurt, for serving

1. Combine all ingredients (except Greek yogurt) in slow cooker.
2. Cover and cook on Low 4-6 hours.
3. Serve warm in small dessert dishes with dollops of Greek yogurt.

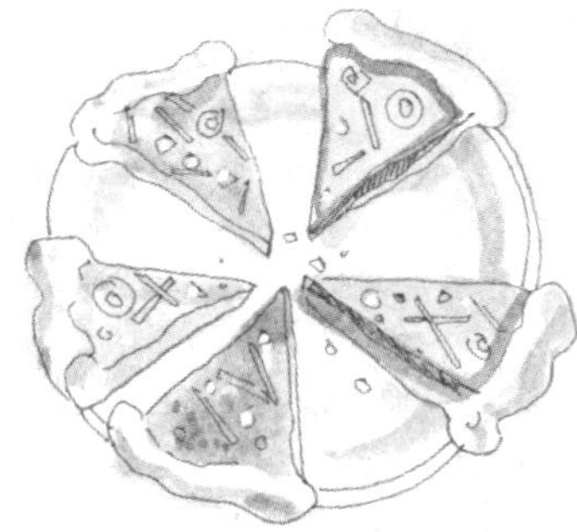

Chicken Stock

Shari Jensen
Fountain, CO

Makes 12 servings

Prep. Time: 5 minutes
Cooking Time: 8-10 hours
Ideal slow-cooker size: 5 qt.

1 carcass from roasted chicken or turkey, or about 2 lbs. chicken backs, necks, wing tips, etc., fresh or left over from dinners
3 quarts water
½ cup dry white wine
3 medium carrots, chopped in large chunks
2 medium onions, cut in quarters
3 ribs celery with leaves on, chopped in large chunks
2 tsp. salt
3 whole cloves
1 bay leaf
1 tsp. dried thyme
5 peppercorns
1 Tbsp. dried parsley
2 large sage leaves, optional
2 cloves garlic, peeled, optional

1. Place chicken, water, wine, carrots, celery, onions, and salt in slow cooker.
2. Tie cloves, bay leaf, thyme, sage leaves, garlic, peppercorns, and parsley in a square of cheesecloth. Place in slow cooker.
3. Simmer on Low 8-10 hours.
4. Cool. Remove cheesecloth packet. Strain Stock into a large bowl.
5. Cover and chill overnight. Skim solidified fat off before using Stock.

Tips:

I prefer to strain the Stock through another piece of cheesecloth to clarify it. However, when in a hurry, I will strain it through a wire sieve. I like to put this in the slow cooker before I go to bed and just let it simmer all night. I turn it off when I get up and by the time the kids go to school, the Stock is cool enough to sieve. Save some out for a pot of soup that day or the next and freeze the rest. Freeze the Stock in pint canning jars to use in recipes later. I also freeze some of this Stock in ice cube trays for small amounts to add to sauces later.

Variations:

For Fish Stock: omit the garlic, sage, and cloves. Substitute about 4 cups of shrimp shells, crab shells, and/or fresh fish bones (collect a mixture in a plastic bag in your freezer until you have enough).

Beef Stock

Margaret W. High
Lancaster, PA

Makes 20 servings

Prep. Time: 10 minutes
Cooking Time: 12-24 hours
Ideal slow-cooker size: 6 qt.

3 lbs. meaty beef bones, preferably with marrow
1 onion, unpeeled, cut in chunks
1 tsp. salt
5 peppercorns
1 Tbsp. vinegar
water

1. Place all ingredients in crock, adding water to within 1" of top.
2. Cover and cook on Low for 12-24 hours, however much time you have, adding more water as needed.
3. Allow Stock to cool for an hour or two before straining. Be sure to get the marrow out into the strainer and press on everything to get all the good stuff into the Stock.
4. De-fat the Stock by chilling it and lifting off the layer of solidified fat or by using a fat separator with the warm Stock.
5. Keep Stock in fridge for up to a week, or freeze in containers.

Tips:

We don't like the smell of Beef Stock cooking, especially not for hours on end, so I usually put the slow cooker in the basement (a garage would work, too). I write a note to myself in the kitchen so I remember to check on it. The vinegar helps to extract the calcium, gelatin, and minerals from the bones. It doesn't flavor the finished Stock.

Variations:

Add carrots, celery, garlic, and odds and ends of greens or parsley. Avoid brassicas such as broccoli and cabbage because their flavor is too strong.

Vegetable Broth

Rebekah Zehr
Lowville, NY

Makes 6-8 servings

Prep. Time: 5 minutes
Cooking Time: 6 hours
Ideal slow-cooker size: 3 qt.

4 cups frozen vegetable scraps
2-3 sprigs herbs such as rosemary and thyme
2-3 cloves garlic
1" piece ginger, optional
8 cups water

1. Combine ingredients in slow cooker. Water should just cover everything.
2. Cover and cook on Low for 6 hours.
3. Strain Broth, pressing on vegetables in strainer to get all the good stuff.
4. Store Broth in canning jars in fridge for up to 2 weeks, or freeze.

Tips:

I collect vegetable scraps in a gallon freezer bag in my freezer: odds and ends of peelings, tops, outer leaves, etc. When my bag is full, I make Broth. This Broth is great for using as a soup base. It can also be used to replace water when cooking rice. This method of saving vegetable scraps is a conscious way of cooking to get more vitamins and minerals in the body and reduce waste.

Plain Beans in the Slow-Cooker

Margaret W. High
Lancaster, PA

Makes 6 servings

Prep. Time: 5 minutes
Cooking Time: 3-6 hours
Ideal slow-cooker size: 4-5 qt.

2 cups dried beans such as navy, black, kidney, pinto, etc.
6-7 cups water

1. Rinse and pick over dried beans to remove any stones or debris.
2. Place beans and water in cooker.
3. Cover and cook on Low for 3-6 hours, depending on the age of the beans, how hot your cooker cooks, and how soft you want them. May need to add additional water to keep it just covering the beans.
4. Allow to cool. Portion beans and cooking liquid into containers (1- and 2-cup amounts are most convenient for me) and keep in fridge for up to a week or freeze.

Tips:

A healthy way to save money on canned beans, which usually have lots of sodium. This is the only way I cook dried beans now. It took a few times for me to feel confident with my slow cookers and how much water to use, but now this process is habitual and easy.

Variations:

Drain cooked beans, spread in a single layer on a tray or shallow container, and freeze. When they're frozen, bag them up and return them to the freezer. Now you can scoop out any amount you want for recipes. Chickpeas (garbanzo beans) are harder and take more time to cook; soak them in the water overnight before cooking. They will probably take closer to 6 hours than 3 to get soft.

Delicious Shredded Chicken

Donna Treloar
Muncie, IN

Makes 10-12 servings

Prep. Time: 5 minutes
Cooking Time: 4-6 hours
Ideal slow-cooker size: 6 qt.

3 lbs. boneless/skinless chicken breasts or thighs, or both
1 cup low-sodium chicken broth
1-oz. pkg. ranch salad dressing, optional

1. Place chicken pieces in slow cooker. Add broth and optional powdered ranch.
2. Cover and cook on Low 4-6 hours, checking at 4 hours to see if chicken shreds easily. Use 2 forks to shred chicken.
3. Serve in buns as sandwiches, or cool and roll up in wraps. Also great for casseroles and salads.

Tips:

Freezes well. May add barbecue sauce after chicken is cooked and shredded.

Hot Bacon Dressing

Margaret W. High
Lancaster, PA

Makes 8-12 servings

Prep. Time: 15 minutes
Cooking Time: 2-4 hours
Ideal slow-cooker size: 2 qt.

4 slices bacon, chopped
1½ cups water
1 cup milk
1 egg, well beaten
4 Tbsp. apple cider vinegar
4 Tbsp. sugar
4 Tbsp. flour
1 Tbsp. prepared mustard
½ tsp. salt

1. Fry bacon until crisp. Scrape bacon and drippings from skillet into slow cooker.
2. Whisk together remaining ingredients until smooth. Whisk into bacon in cooker.
3. Cover and cook on High for 2-4 hours, whisking twice, until dressing is thickened and bubbly.
4. Serve warm over lettuce, spinach, or early spring dandelion greens.

Variations:

Mix 4 cups chopped Swiss chard leaves or spinach directly into hot dressing when it's done cooking. Greens should wilt and soften a bit. Serve over biscuits or fried potatoes.

Good go-alongs with this recipe:

Boiled potatoes or fried potatoes.

Cheese Sauce

Carol Eveleth
Hillsdale, WY

Makes 6 servings

Prep. Time: 10 minutes
Cooking Time: 2-3 hours
Ideal slow-cooker size: 3 qt.

3 Tbsp. flour
1½ cups milk
3 Tbsp. butter, diced
1½ cups grated sharp cheddar cheese
1 tsp. salt
¼ tsp. paprika
1 tsp. ketchup
pepper, to taste, optional

1. In slow cooker, mix flour and milk together until smooth.
2. Add butter, cheese, salt, paprika, and ketchup.
3. Cook in slow cooker for 2-3 hours on Low, stirring occasionally, until thickened.

Tips:

Put on Warm setting to serve this cheese sauce. Serve with baked potatoes, taco salad, haystacks, or soft pretzels—anywhere you want some warm, gooey cheese!

Applesauce

Beverly Hummel
Fleetwood, PA

Makes 6 servings

Prep. Time: 30 minutes
Cooking Time: 8-10 hours
Ideal slow-cooker size: 6 qt.

5 lbs. apples, preferably mixed varieties
½ cup water
sugar, to taste
cinnamon, to taste, optional

1. Peel, seed, and chop apples. Place in slow cooker with water.
2. Cook until soft, 8-12 hours on Low, stirring occasionally.
3. Puree with blender if you want a smooth texture or just mash with potato masher for chunky texture.
4. Add sugar and cinnamon to taste. Serve warm or cold.

Tips:

Great way to use leftover apples. Delicious aromas during the cooking process.

Variations:

Different varieties of apples mixed together create a very flavorful applesauce.

Do-It-Yourself Velveeta Cheese

Phyllis Good
Lancaster, PA

Makes 14 ounces

Prep. Time: 25 minutes
Cooking Time: 0 minutes

¾ cup whole milk
2 tsp. unflavored gelatin
12 oz. shredded cheddar or Colby cheese
¾ tsp. salt

1. Prepare a 9x4 loaf pan by lining it with plastic wrap OR use a glass loaf pan.
2. Pour milk in small saucepan and sprinkle gelatin on milk. Set aside for 5 minutes to soften.
3. Combine cheese and salt in food processor and pulse several times to combine.
4. Over low heat, warm milk and gelatin until just steaming, stirring several times. Do not boil.
5. With the food processor on, slowly pour the hot milk/gelatin into the cheese and process until cheese is completely melted and smooth.
6. Immediately scrape mixture into prepared pan and cover. Refrigerate for at least 3 hours to set completely before using. Store in the fridge for up to 2 weeks.

Homemade Frozen Hash Browns

Phyllis Good
Lancaster, PA

Makes 8 servings

Prep. Time: 30 minutes
Cooking Time: 3-6 hours
Standing Time: 2 hours
Ideal slow-cooker size: 3 qt.

2 lbs. potatoes, scrubbed well

1. Prick each potato with fork.
2. Place in lightly greased slow cooker.
3. Cover and cook on Low for 3-6 hours, until potatoes are tender but firm. Start checking at 3 hours. The time really varies with the size and variety of the potatoes you are using.
4. When potatoes are cooked but firm, remove them from cooker and allow to cool to room temperature, about 2 hours.
5. Grate potatoes. Portion into containers, label, and freeze.

Tips:

Use these Hash Browns in any recipe calling for frozen hash browns. Follow recipe directions for whether or not to thaw. To serve Hash Browns by themselves, heat some oil in a skillet. Place frozen Hash Browns directly in hot skillet and fry over high heat, breaking them up as the potatoes thaw and brown. Fry until hot and browned. Serve with eggs and toast for breakfast.

Smooth Salsa

Jo Zimmerman
Lebanon, PA

Makes 6-8 servings

Prep. Time: 20 minutes
Cooking Time: 2½-3 hours
Ideal slow-cooker size: 3 qt.

10 plum tomatoes, stem spot removed
2 garlic cloves
1 small onion, cut in wedges
2 jalepeño peppers, stems removed
½ tsp. salt
¼ cup chopped cilantro

1. Insert garlic cloves in 2 tomatoes by cutting small slits and pushing clove into slit.
2. Place tomatoes, onions, peppers, and salt in slow cooker.
3. Cover and cook on High for 2½-3 hours or until vegetables are soft.
4. Allow to cool.
5. Add cilantro. Blend with an immersion blender or transfer to a stand blender to process until smooth.

Metric Equivalent Measurements

If you're accustomed to using metric measurements, I don't want you to be inconvenienced by the imperial measurements I use in this book.

Use this handy chart, too, to figure out the size of the slow cooker you'll need for each recipe.

Weight *(Dry Ingredients)*

1 oz		*30 g*
4 oz	*¼ lb*	*120 g*
8 oz	*½ lb*	*240 g*
12 oz	*¾ lb*	*360 g*
16 oz	*1 lb*	*480 g*
32 oz	*2 lb*	*960 g*

Slow-Cooker Sizes

1-quart	*0.96 l*
2-quart	*1.92 l*
3-quart	*2.88 l*
4-quart	*3.84 l*
5-quart	*4.80 l*
6-quart	*5.76 l*
7-quart	*6.72 l*
8-quart	*7.68 l*

Volume *(Liquid Ingredients)*

½ tsp.		*2 ml*
1 tsp.		*5 ml*
1 Tbsp.	*½ fl oz*	*15 ml*
2 Tbsp.	*1 fl oz*	*30 ml*
¼ cup	*2 fl oz*	*60 ml*
⅓ cup	*3 fl oz*	*80 ml*
½ cup	*4 fl oz*	*120 ml*
⅔ cup	*5 fl oz*	*160 ml*
¾ cup	*6 fl oz*	*180 ml*
1 cup	*8 fl oz*	*240 ml*
1 pt	*16 fl oz*	*480 ml*
1 qt	*32 fl oz*	*960 ml*

Length

¼ in	*6 mm*
½ in	*13 mm*
¾ in	*19 mm*
1 in	*25 mm*
6 in	*15 cm*
12 in	*30 cm*

Substitute Ingredients for When You're in a Pinch

For 1 cup **buttermilk**—use 1 cup plain yogurt; or pour 1⅓ Tbsp. lemon juice or vinegar into a 1-cup measure. Fill the cup with milk. Stir and let stand for 5 minutes. Stir again before using.

For 1 oz. **unsweetened baking chocolate**—stir together 3 Tbsp. unsweetened cocoa powder and 1 Tbsp. butter, softened.

For 1 Tbsp. **cornstarch**—use 2 Tbsp. all-purpose flour; or 4 tsp. minute tapioca.

For 1 **garlic clove**—use ¼ tsp. garlic salt (reduce salt in recipe by ⅛ tsp.); or ⅛ tsp. garlic powder.

For 1 Tbsp. **fresh herbs**—use 1 tsp. dried herbs.

For ½ lb. **fresh mushrooms**—use 1 6-oz. can mushrooms, drained.

For 1 Tbsp. **prepared mustard**—use 1 tsp. dry or ground mustard.

For 1 **medium-sized fresh onion**—use 2 Tbsp. minced dried onion; or 2 tsp. onion salt (reduce salt in recipe by 1 tsp.); or 1 tsp. onion powder. ***Note:** These substitutions will work for meatballs and meat loaf, but not for sautéing.*

For 1 cup **sour milk**—use 1 cup plain yogurt; or pour 1 Tbsp. lemon juice or vinegar into a 1-cup measure. Fill with milk. Stir and then let stand for 5 minutes. Stir again before using.

For 2 Tbsp. **tapioca**—use 3 Tbsp. all-purpose flour.

For 1 cup canned **tomatoes**—use 1⅓ cups diced fresh tomatoes, cooked gently for 10 minutes.

For 1 Tbsp. **tomato paste**—use 1 Tbsp. ketchup.

For 1 Tbsp. **vinegar**—use 1 Tbsp. lemon juice.

For 1 cup **heavy cream**—add ⅓ cup melted butter to ¾ cup milk. ***Note:** This will work for baking and cooking, but not for whipping.*

For 1 cup **whipping cream**—chill thoroughly ⅔ cup evaporated milk, plus the bowl and beaters, then whip; or use 2 cups bought whipped topping.

For ½ cup **wine**—pour 2 Tbsp. wine vinegar into a ½-cup measure. Fill with broth (chicken, beef, or vegetable). Stir and then let stand for 5 minutes. Stir again before using.

"Quick and Easy" Recipe Index

APPETIZERS, SNACKS, SPREADS, AND BEVERAGES

BEEF MAIN DISHES

BREAKFASTS AND BREADS

CHICKEN AND TURKEY MAIN DISHES

EVERYDAY FROM-SCRATCH BASICS

PORK MAIN DISHES

SOUPS, STEWS, AND CHILIS

SWEETS AND DESERTS

VEGETABLES AND SIDE DISHES

Recipe and Ingredient Index

C

About the Author

Phyllis Good is a *New York Times* bestselling author whose books have sold more than 12 million copies.

She authored *Fix-It and Forget-It Cookbook, Revised and Updated*, which appeared on *The New York Times* bestseller list, as well as the bestseller lists of *USA Today*, *Publishers Weekly*, and *Book Sense*. In addition, she authored *Fix-It and Forget-It Lightly* (which also appeared on *The New York Times* bestseller list); as well as *Fix-It and Forget-It Christmas Cookbook; Fix-It and Forget-It 5-Ingredient Favorites; Fix-It and Forget-It Vegetarian Cookbook; Fix-It and Forget-It Cooking Light, Revised and Updated; Fix-It and Forget-It Slow Cooker Diabetic Cookbook, Revised and Updated* (with the American Diabetes Association); *Fix-It and Forget-It BIG Cookbook; Fix-It and Forget-It Kids' Cookbook*, and *Fix-It and Forget-It New Cookbook*.

Her commitment is to make it possible for everyone to cook who would like to, even if they have too little time or too little confidence.

Good has authored many other cookbooks. Among them are *Fix-It and Enjoy-It Healthy Cookbook* (with nutritional expertise from Mayo Clinic), *The Best of Amish Cooking*, and *The Lancaster Central Market Cookbook.*

Good spends her time writing, editing books, and cooking new recipes.